THE OFFICIAL® PRICE GUIDE TO

COLLECTING BOOKS

SIXTH EDITION

By Marie Tedford and Pat Goudey

House of Collectibles
New York Toronto London Sydney Auckland

House of Collectibles and colophon are registered trademarks of Random House, Inc.

RANDOM HOUSE is a registered trademark of Random House, Inc.

This book is available for special discounts for bulk purchases for sales promotions or premiums. Special editions, including personalized covers, excerpts of existing books, and corporate imprints, can be created in large quantities for special needs. For more information, write to Random House, Inc., Special Markets/Premium Sales, 1745 Broadway, MD 6–2, New York, NY 10019 or e-mail specialmarkets@randomhouse.com.

Please address inquiries about electronic licensing of any products for use on a network, in software, or on CD-ROM to the Subsidiary Rights Department, Random House Information Group, fax 212–572–6003.

Visit the House of Collectibles Web site: www.houseofcollectibles.com

Printed in the United States of America

10 9 8 7 6 5 4 3 2 1

ISBN: 978–0–375–72293–6

ISSN: 1542–0329

Sixth Edition

To Jenny, who could not read but would have loved the fact of this book.

CONTENTS

ACKNOWLEDGMENTS

We owe a debt of gratitude to the many booksellers and collectors who spoke with us to provide information and guidance for an industry that has come into a new age and gone through many changes in recent years.

We are ever grateful to the Vermont Antiquarian Booksellers who have been Marie's professional home association since she helped found the organization some 30 years ago.

Thank you to Kathleen Roberts of K Roberts Fine Books who spoke so eloquently of children's books, decorated bindings, and the experience of entering the antiquarian book world in this new age. Thank you also to George Webb of Tennessee Books and Autographs; Ray Giordano, of The Antiquarian Scientist in Southampton, Massachusetts; Michael Ginsberg of Michael Ginsberg Books in Sharon, Massachusetts; Anne and Maynard Hill of F. M. Hill Books in Tennessee; Danielle Hargis of Books Never-Ending in Ringold, Georgia; Kathryn Smiley, editor of *Firsts, The Book Collector's Magazine;* Kenneth Anderson of Kenneth Anderson Books in Middlebury, Vermont; Robert Rulon-Miller of Rulon-Miller Books in St. Paul, Minnesota; John Jeffcoat of The Great Site Bibles; Donna Howard of The Eloquent Page in Saint Albans, Vermont.

And our heartfelt thanks to Jonathan Draudt, the digital photographer at Tamarac Arts in Warren, Vermont, who so carefully and faithfully photographed some of our treasures.

We are also grateful for the dedication and integrity of the serious book lovers the world over who are continually striving to maintain our industry's long-held and valued reputation for scholarship and ethics in our dealings with each other and with the public. We are pleased to share our love of books with you.

INTRODUCTION

This book is written as a companion to accompany both established book lovers and those new to this field as they step away from their computers and go out to visit the world of antiquarian books in the real world. It is intended to be read casually, and we hope with enjoyment and relish, during quiet moments, but also to be carried along on the hunt for "books in the wild," as an aid, a guide, and a reference.

The general public has developed a far greater awareness of books as valuable and collectible items since we came into the trade more than thirty years ago. To promote this interest, we offer information and discussion with an eye toward encouraging the quality of education and scholarship that book lovers need to successfully navigate the terrain.

This book is designed to help in the search for books and for information about books. No one volume can contain all the information an antiquarian book dealer or collector will need. The print literature available and the new Internet sites include an enormous body of reference material for bibliographic and pricing data. Cross-checking information from book to book and site to site will help to ensure that you have accurate publication data and a realistic price for your item.

For this edition, we have updated listings and prices and have interviewed and quoted numerous dealers and collectors on the changes that have now settled in to our industry, as well as to the enduring nature of our mutual enterprise.

We planned this book to do more than tell you the going rate for a particular title in the marketplace. Books are more than a commodity with a price tag. As always, our intention is to inform, pique your interest, and perhaps to entertain you as you learn about our calling.

We hope you enjoy our book and the time you spend among all books.

HOW TO USE THIS BOOK

The books in our listings are arranged alphabetically by author's last name, or if no author, then by title. They are not categorized by genre or subject in the general listings. We believe this is a simple and "user-friendly" system.

We discuss genre in our chapter on Collecting in Genres, and explain terms in the Glossary. Some titles and authors are listed by genre in the Selected Index of Collectible Genres.

Careful readers will soon be able to categorize books by genre for themselves.

In most listings, the name of the author is followed by the title, place of publication, publisher, and/or date of publication. Dates have been taken from the title pages or copyright pages. In preferred bibliographic format, which we endorse and use in our own business, dates taken from the copyright page are in parentheses. We have endeavored to adhere to this style as closely as possible, whenever this information is available to us.

We have not limited ourselves to listing first editions, but we have identified first editions in the majority of cases. Where a question remains as to whether or not you have a first edition in hand, further research in reference bibliographies is called for. Several excellent research sources are listed in the appendices of this book.

In most cases, the number of pages in a volume is not given, but where we considered it helpful or where identification of a work requires it, we have included page counts.

Similarly, where illustrations include colored or engraved plates, we have included the number of plates in many cases, especially when identification of a book might be dependent on that information. (Note: When examining any volume, check the table of contents or list of illustrations against the plates present to be sure they are all accounted for, since some people remove plates from an old book to frame and sell them separately. The process of checking for the presence of all pages, plates, illustrations, maps, etc., is called "collating.")

Readers will notice that many books listed are not first editions. This is because some titles are rare or sought after in whatever editions they can be found. Later editions, too, may contain signatures, provenance, or other attributes of note or may be illustrated by artists of great renown, making those editions more valuable than the first.

Unless otherwise stated, the prices given are for books in their original bindings, except for those dating to the 17th century or earlier, in which case a good period binding is assumed.

Our prices reflect fair retail value based on a consensus of asking prices and prices realized for books on the open market over the past three years.

Dealers typically offer a 10–20 percent discount to other bookmen. A dealer may pay as much as 50 percent of retail for a book bought from a private individual if a customer is waiting in the wings for that book. For stock books, a dealer will more often offer from 10 percent to 30 percent of a book's retail value.

When presented with an extremely rare and sought-after book, the client or dealer may suggest a consignment arrangement. The dealer will then act as an agent to market the book and take only a commission on the sale.

This happened to us recently when we discovered Professor Albert Einstein's signature on a dinner menu and program from a 1930s transatlantic ocean liner. Prof. Einstein was on the program to entertain that evening playing his violin. We informed the owner of the menu, who was not aware of the signature, and with her permission sent the document to a New York auction house. We were thrilled to be the agents in this case, and discovering this signature was great fun.

And, for an extensive library of modern first editions, primarily American authors of the 20th century, but including some Kipling items—many of which were signed and limited editions—we recently accepted a consignment arrangement to bring the books to market. Many of these books were marketed to dealers and collectors alike online, while others were sold through direct contact with buyers. Some details of those transactions are included in the current Market Review chapter. Prices realized for these items reflected the books' rarity and condition, and the current level of demand for authors like Virginia Woolf, e. e. cummings, Thornton Wilder, John Steinbeck, and Willa Cather.

At times, the variations in our price listings reflect the slight differences in the condition of books offered by different dealers. At times, it reflects the vicissitudes of the market where a book may fetch a smart price in the mountains of New England but go far more cheaply in the deserts of Arizona. Or a dealer may offer a book at one price in a shop while patrons at an auction house pay a far different price.

At times, we have listed the same title in varying conditions, or in more than one edition, to illustrate the collectibility and variability of these items.

On the Internet, or reading dealers' catalogues, you will likely find an even wider range of prices. We have not shied away from listing these ranges so the reader can see the idiosyncrasies of the antiquarian book trade.

In all cases, books are assumed to be in at least very good condition unless stated otherwise. Where modern first editions are concerned, excellent condition is assumed. To realize their best price, modern first editions must be in original dust jackets, intact. Some listings do not cite dust jackets, and these books have been offered or sold at lower prices than they would have fetched if jackets had been present. Many modern firsts without jackets are worth more than the fifty cents charged at library sales—indeed we had several in the library sold on consignment mentioned above—and we've included some here.

At all times, remember that this is a guide and not a guarantee of prices. The marketplace, forever in flux, determines the real value of a used or collectible book. We have endeavored to verify statistics for each listing, but no book of this type can guarantee freedom from error. The serious bibliophile will not depend on any one source, but will use multiple research tools to verify data on important books.

– 1 –
MARKET REVIEW

The antiquarian and collectible book trade has settled into its niche in the electronic age, and booksellers and collectors alike are looking around to see how the environment will influence their industry over the long haul. While these new markets are here to stay, the book world is still in the process of recreating itself to accommodate them, striving to hold onto past strengths while adapting to modern technology.

In most genres, the most dramatic changes affect the mid-level price ranges (approximately $75–$750) where a supply of secondary source books and shelf stock—works written about Charles Darwin or Albert Einstein rather than written by Darwin or Einstein, or tales about Civil War heroes rather than books by General Sherman or a survivor with first-hand experience in the fray—often outstrip demand, driving prices down on these long-time staples of the trade.

New booksellers report a continuing brisk business in lower-end books and reader's copies of fiction and nonfiction alike. The $5–$40 used book in good condition continues to find a market online, though these books may have to compete with a new phenomenon—the proliferation of books listed at less than a dollar. Still, a bookseller who sells books in good readable condition can put a rational price on a used book and experienced buyers will pass over the 98-cent volumes to purchase a clean, sound book with all pages and illustrations present.

As they have down through the decades, high-end markets continue to attract dedicated collectors to bookstores, national and international fairs, and major auction houses. The great bulk of these venues that handle books valued in the thousands of dollars to tens of thousands and more now include a Web presence with opportunities to view detailed images of books online, shopping carts for immediate purchase, and systems permitting electronic or fax/phone bidding in auctions.

Even those who resisted moving into the computer age generally agree now that book-selling cannot return to the small, collegial world of familiar names and faces that it once was. Yet hopeful signs point to the resurgence of central values of the industry from years gone by. While an influx of dilettantes and newcomers interested in a quick sale remains in the picture, a focus on scholarship, meticulous care in describing and representing books, and a high level of integrity and customer service are resurging among many of those who've decided to make a career of their new bookselling enterprise.

Michael Ginsberg of Michael Ginsberg Books in Sharon, Massachusetts, has been associated with the Colorado Antiquarian Book Seminar almost since the inception of the professional program some thirty years ago. The seminars are a weeklong series of intensive lectures and workshops—dubbed "Boot Camp for Booksellers" by participants—on all aspects of schol-arship and business practices, designed to impart the skills needed to succeed in the anti-quarian and rare book trade (see www.bookseminars.com). Taught by some of the most successful dealers and experts in the field, the annual seminars attract students with a seri-ous interest in entering the industry.

Ginsberg said that during the early years of the program, attendance reached as many as one hundred students per weeklong session in August, and some years students had to be turned away. Registration had been declining for several years leading into the new millen-nium, he said, with a low of about thirty students three or four years ago, but that trend seems to have reversed itself. In 2007, approximately sixty students were registered, up from fifty-five the year before, and approximately forty in 2005. Ginsberg said an informal poll of students indicated that many were planning to open stores in addition to maintaining a presence on the Internet. While not ready to declare it a trend, he said he is encouraged that people coming into the industry are again thinking about participating in face-to-face com-merce as well as online sales.

A relative newcomer to the trade, Kathleen Roberts of K Roberts Fine Books in Burling-ton, Vermont, may be typical of this new professional who entered the industry during the Internet age. Roberts came to the antiquarian and rare book world about ten years ago as a literary scholar and casual collector of children's books after a career as a librarian and post-graduate educator in the field of children's literature. With a longtime interest in the con-tent of these books—and a growing library of her favorite titles—Roberts eventually realized she would enjoy learning about the books themselves and decided to begin selling rare, collectible, and antiquarian children's literature. Since that time, she's added an eso-teric specialty that is beginning to attract attention—decorative cloth bindings, and artist-signed bindings, dating to the era between 1830 and about 1910.

Gingerly dipping her toes into the market like many newcomers, Roberts first began listing children's titles at modest prices, starting out selling copies of popular books on sites like Amazon, Barnes & Noble, and Alibris. As her knowledge and stock progressed to more col-lectible and rare titles, she established a home page and posted a list on AbeBooks, and con-ducted auctions on eBay, all venues she continues to use.

Children's books on display at the booth of Roy and Jean Kulp of Hatfield, Pennsylvania, show the quality of condition expected of these beloved volumes.
Photo by Ilan Fisher.

In the spring of 2007, Roberts discussed her experience launching and developing her business at the beginning of the Internet age.

Kathleen V. Roberts, Burlington, Vermont:

KR: I started out selling on the Internet. Selling on Amazon has been very good for me. For several years, I did well there and had excellent sales. Volume was good. I priced my books fairly; I wasn't trying to be the top-dollar seller, and yet I wasn't trying to be the lowest either.

Q: You weren't competing with 98-cent wonders?

KR: We didn't have those 98-cent wonders at first. That's a relatively new phenomenon. In the beginning, people were listing antiquarian books on Advanced Book Exchange (ABE, now AbeBooks), and at that point Amazon wasn't dealing with older books. They were selling books published from 1970 and on—books with ISBNs (International Standard Book Numbers, unique identifiers that can be assigned to individual editions of any title), which began in 1970. Those listings were primarily used books, but not antiquarian and rare.

That's no longer true of Amazon. You can list any book there now regardless of what year it was published. I am still doing quite well on Amazon listing my older bindings today.

A comfortable place to sit and read among the used and collectible books at Danielle Hargis' Books Never-Ending bookstore in Ringold, Georgia.

Q: Do you see the industry continuing to evolve and change?

KR: Absolutely. It's very volatile. Over the years, booksellers from the Midwest, for instance, would traditionally stop at my place to buy books and pick up inventory on their way to the Boston book shows. Many have been mid- to high-end dealers, which is a world I feel very comfortable in, and I've built up a clientele of those dealers. Many of them will no longer buy anything published after 1970. That market is just glutted.

There is a key here. In the past [ten years ago], when you researched a book to list it on ABE, you might find ten or fifteen copies of that same title for sale. Today, if you research the exact same volume, you may find eighty books listed.

The difference is due to technological advances, especially the ability to digitally scan ISBN numbers now. New technology allows researching those books on the spot. Designed to be used with a cell phone, a number of very inexpensive programs are available that are associated with various online databases, primarily Amazon. Book buyers can use their scanner program to determine the average selling price online for a book with a particular ISBN in very good to fine condition. So you check book prices before you purchase stock. Thus, you have people with very little knowledge of books—or even interest in books—going to library sales or bookshops, anywhere they have used books for sale, turning over a book, hitting the scanner, and immediately learning the average price of that book on Amazon or some other venue. They take the book or reject it based on the price that comes up.

The result is, a great many people now sell books on that basis. When they list them online, they don't necessarily describe the condition. They'll say "Typical used condition. May have dust jacket. May have remainder mark."

If Marie or I were listing a book, we'd include information like "Red cloth covered boards, edge tears, price-clipped dust jacket, some foxing to endpapers, contents tight and clean." We describe the entire book.

Danielle Hargis, bookseller and owner of Books Never-Ending, tends stock in her store in Ringold, Georgia.

With this change in the way people are buying and selling comes the advent of the seventeen-cent book, the ninety-eight-cent book, the dollar-and-ten-cent book.

Q: So, used and reader's copies of most books published in the past thirty-five to forty years are now easy to find online, and you need a volume with true collectible qualities for it to demand more than a few dollars or cents?

KR: Yes. When you think in terms of how the market in used books has changed—in the area of children's books, or I would say any book published after 1970—academic press books still do well, and some textbooks do well. University press books don't usually stay in print very long, so the markets are less saturated. They're the exceptions. But certainly for any book published after 1970 from a mainstream publisher like Harper or Knopf or Random House, that book's monetary value is dramatically reduced.

For books from that era, you have to have signed copies, and true first editions from collectible authors and illustrators. In the area of children's books, you look for Caldecott Medal winners like Jerry Pinkney (illustrator, *The Ugly Duckling*, 2000) and Mary Azarian (illustrator, *Snowflake Bentley*, 1999). People will always be collecting very good first editions of that quality of book—first edition, first printing.

For other books, post-1970, to have value they have to be signed, and they have to be something special.

Going back to a publishing date of 1959 is another story—more of them will hold their value—but you're still going to see many more offered for sale because there are so many more people selling online now.

I constantly monitor and adjust the inventory and price of books I sell online. I consistently sell on Amazon, and high-end books do quite well for me there. There will always be a market for a high-end, quality book. But there may not be as large a number of people buying those today as there once was.

Virginia Woolf, *Kew Gardens*. The Hogarth Press. 1927. Third edition (and first illustrated edition), ltd 500 cc, signed by Woolf and her sister, artist Vanessa Bell. $4,000.00

An illustration by Vanessa Bell in *Kew Gardens*, by Virginia Woolf, published by Hogarth Press, 1927.

Q: How do you decide where you will list your various titles?

KR: I list the exact same books on AbeBooks.com that I put on Amazon; I don't segregate books on different sites. I do, however, take my very high-end books to an auction house. It's an intuitive choice to decide which ones will be auctioned.

I've been selling with PBA Galleries in San Francisco (originally Pacific Book Auction Galleries, dealing in rare books and paper, now at www.pbagalleries.com). I like their auctions in that they make the process fairly easy for the seller. And I've had good results.

If I think something will sit among my listings on AbeBooks for many years—which does happen—and I think it might go more quickly at auction, I'll often send it out. Every auction house will do things differently, but at PBA, they estimate what a book may realize, offering a low-end and high-end figure. They do not sell for less than half the lower estimate. It's the bookseller's call to take that risk.

When I have a good piece of Americana, selling at auction is a good option for me because people don't think of me as an Americana dealer. That item will reach a wider audience through PBA.

Now, I am more likely to keep some of my high-end children's books and market them myself, those that may sell for perhaps $400 to $1,500 or more.

Q: Do you list those items on Amazon as well as AbeBooks.com?

KR: Sure. They go on Alibris, AbeBooks, Amazon, and they come up at Barnes & Noble.com, which is associated with Alibris, though I rarely sell an antiquarian book at B & N.

Q: People who use book search engines like Bookfinder, AddAll, or viaLibri will see your listings reported multiple times, then (Note: see discussion of search engines in chapter three).

KR: Yes. That is true. But I think many people don't use the book search engines. A young man called me recently about a four-hundred-dollar book. It was a first edition of *The Lorax* by Dr. Seuss (*The Lorax*. NY. Random House, 1971. $400.00–$1,000.00). He was collecting first editions of Dr. Seuss and asked about the condition of the book and wanted to know if I could send him a scan of it.

I asked him out of curiosity where he had been buying books and he said, "Oh, eBay." Here was a man spending four hundred dollars on a book, and he is buying on eBay.

I asked how he had found his way to me, and he said, "Google." He had entered the search words "Lorax for sale" and my book came up. What that says to me is, there aren't many good first editions of *The Lorax* available, so mine floated to the top of the list for him.

There's an important message here. This is the young new buyer of the future. We assume as booksellers that people are familiar with the book search sites like Bookfinder and AddAll and viaLibri because book people use them all the time.

But my friends and relatives and people in their thirties don't know those sites.

They know Amazon. To them, Amazon equals books. They've branded that term. And this generation is so comfortable doing a standard keyword search—they do it for someone's phone number, for someone's resume. For whatever information they need in their lives, they do a Google search.

That's their Internet. The search engine is key.

The young man looking for *The Lorax* didn't tell me which listing site came up. It had to be AbeBooks or Alibris where I listed that book, but the listing site was irrelevant to him.

So, technology has changed how we sell, but it has also dramatically changed how people buy books. It's a two-way street.

Michael Ginsberg, too, spoke of the antiquarian book markets online as a double-edged sword. When people first began to use the Internet to reach the millions of buyers in a worldwide market, relatively few people were selling books online and those people were reaching buyers and earning a living. As time has passed, more and more people, many of them casual sellers, began listing books and, with increased competition and numerous copies of so many titles now offered, the market may have peaked. He suspects that sellers who closed the doors of their shops, or who stopped selling at regional and national book fairs like those sponsored by ABAA each year, may be finding their way back to face-to-face sales to supplement their dwindling revenues. Participation in the larger fairs is growing again, he said.

Michael Ginsberg, Sharon, Massachusetts:

Q: How successful are the regional and national fairs now?

MG: There are still large crowds that come to the ABAA fairs. Some of the local fairs seemed to be drawing less and also having difficulty in filling up exhibit space. Some people apparently felt that if they were selling on the Internet, they didn't need book fairs. But that trend is beginning to change.

When I first came onto the Internet, there were only a few people selling books there. Then a few more came. Then more. Then a lot.

The more booksellers that came on, the less each one sold. It has peaked somewhat in the last few years and people who were earning a good living suddenly aren't because of all the competitive copies that are showing up. Some people's inventories decreased in value by as much as a third.

Some of those people are going back to the book shows now as a supplement. What they're making on the Internet isn't as high as it was before.

The fairs tend to be more filled than they were five years ago.

Q: Do you think that face-to-face traffic will pick up again?

MG: That is difficult to say. But there are still people who don't use computers, who don't care about the Internet. They like to go to fairs and feel a book in their hands. They like to look at catalogues.

And then, there will always be people who will only buy on the Internet because that's the medium they were brought up with; that's what they understand. It does make a significant difference to be able to handle a book, but it doesn't make all the difference.

Another thing to be said for the Internet is that as much as it has hurt the dealer's ability to buy and sell books because so many more copies of a title are available and people can find out what is offered instantly, the helpful part is that you're able to reach millions of people that you could never possibly reach any other way except through an electronic medium. We are now able to reach buyers in places I didn't know existed.

Longtime specialists like George Webb of Rogersville, Tennessee, and Ray Giordano of Southampton, Massachusetts, say they hold to their practice of issuing print catalogues that

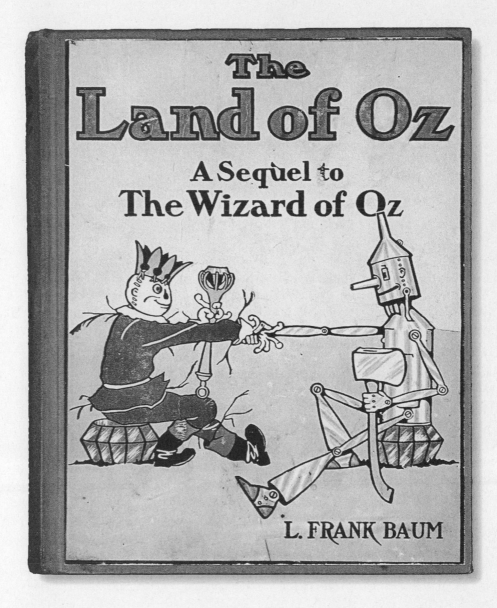

The Land of Oz, a sequel to *The Wizard of Oz*, Rand
McNally, 1939, color and black-and-white boards.
*Digital photography by Jonathan Draudt, Tamarac
Arts.*

Miniature and micro-books on display in the Isaiah Thomas Booksellers of Massachusetts booth at the Vermont Antiquarian Booksellers Fair, Pomfret, Vermont.

are mailed to carefully compiled lists of past customers. But neither of these experienced bookmen is a stranger to the Internet these days. Webb uses venues like eBay and Giordano has a select number of books on AbeBooks.com. While electronic sales have become important to the continuation of their businesses, both booksellers emphasize the importance they still place on finding their markets by traditional means.

A specialist in Tennesseeana, Webb says he believes he has dealt with or heard of just about every serious collector in his genre from the state of Tennessee and most from around the South. His primary customers remain academics and universities, who depend on him to find research materials, historic and important items for special collections. And he has "treaty agreements" with dedicated collectors, keeping their preferences in mind when reviewing books at auctions and estate sales.

Ray Giordano, of the Antiquarian Scientist in Massachusetts, now posts a select list of books on AbeBooks, but he maintains only a few hundred books on the site. He holds out his best books for listing in his catalogue first. If an item doesn't find a buyer through a network of collectors to whom he sends his catalogue, he may list the book online where customers materialize from all over the world. He said buyers from overseas have recently outnumbered U.S. customers for books listed online. "But they don't necessarily buy from me a second time," he said. "They respond to something they find online, a book they've been searching for, and they buy it. Few of them respond a second time to something in a catalogue that's sent to them."

Booksellers in all genres have noted that segments of inventory in their specialties—not the least of them secondary source books in science and medicine, and children's series books— have lost significant value with the introduction of worldwide markets that replaced the older regional system. With the influx of sellers to the World Wide Web, resource books once hard to find, and series books that once languished on basement shelves, are now offered at bargain prices, easily filling the demand and bringing prices down.

Though someone seeking a book in a particular genre can search online for a title rather than get in touch with someone like George Webb to find a book in his area, a dealer or collector in regional material or genre books would still do well to visit live markets from time to time. In an age of worldwide reach, an on-site visit can still unearth great books at estate sales, auctions, flea markets, and among the myriad of shops from Maine to Arizona— items that might never find their way into electronic markets, as dealers like Webb, Giordano, and Roberts attest.

For specialists who hope to bring new and rare books to market—who want to offer something everyone else on the Internet doesn't already have—mining electronic markets won't be enough. They'll have to get up and go on a trip from time to time to find the books that elicit the level of response from bibliophiles needed to support bookselling as a business. And taking the time to look for books somewhere besides the Internet just might be fun.

In the spring of 2007, Marie was contacted by a husband and wife, collectors of modern first editions, who were ready to sell many of the books in their library. Some of these were signed limited editions, some in slipcases, many with first edition dust jackets. Many were in near fine to fine condition, but others had faded or damaged covers, and torn or soiled jackets. The books were marketed online, offered at auction on eBay, and sold through private communication with collectors of modern first editions.

The prices realized by these items reflect the appeal of these writers to collectors of modern first editions on today's markets, as well as the rarity and condition of the specific titles in this collection.

Below are some of the prices realized for sales of these books in both online and private transactions:

Willa Cather. *Lucy Gayheart*. NY. Knopf. 1935. limited. sgn.	$179.50
_____. *Sapphira and the Slave Girl*. limited. sgn. dj.	$227.00
Robert Graves. *Poems*. Seizin Press. Lon. 1929.	$150.00
Rudyard Kipling. *The Jungle Book* and *The Second Jungle Book*. 1894 and 1895. 1st ed. sgn.	$2,000.00
Thomas Mann. *Nocturnes*. sgn.	$145.00.
Eugene O'Neill. *The Hairy Ape*. NY. Liveright. 1929. ltd 750 cc. sgn. [Pictured on page 33 are the patterned boards and black cloth spine.]	$250.00.
John Steinbeck. *Of Mice and Men*. 1st ed. fine condition. soiled and damaged. dj.	$2,000.00
_____. *The Grapes of Wrath*. NY. Viking. 1939. illustrated cover. no dj. soiled.	$169.00
_____. *To a God Unknown*. 1st ed. fine condition. dj.	$3,239.00.
Virginia Woolf. *Kew Gardens*. Hogarth Press. 1927. First ed. thus (first illustrated ed.), ltd 500 cc. signed by Woolf and her sister, artist Vanessa Bell.	$4,000.00
_____. *A Room of One's Own*. 1st ed. sgn.	$3,589.00.

_____. *Monday or Tuesday*. 1st ed. no dj. $788.00.

_____ *On Being Ill*. Hogarth Press. limited. sgn. dj. slipcase. $1,500.00

_____. *Street Haunting*. San Francisco. Grabhorn Press. 1930. limited. sgn. stained cover. cocked spine. $750.00

_____. *Three Guineas*. Harcourt, 1938. dj. $75.00

_____. *To The Lighthouse*. Hogarth Press. London. limited. sgn. dust jacket soiled and damaged. $4,500.00

– 2 –
A CLOSER LOOK AT THE BOOK TRADE

Books are the legacies that a great genius leaves to mankind, which are delivered down from generation to generation, as presents to the posterity of those who are yet unborn.

The Spectator, 1711

The Internet as a venue for commerce is well established the world over and has taken a place at the center of the antiquarian book trade for the foreseeable future.

In the last decade of the 20th century, business in general struggled to adapt to the online marketplace, creating new procedures and learning new tactics amid concern over the ability of "brick-and-mortar" stores to survive the onslaught of long-distance Web commerce. Many book shops eventually moved to Internet-only status, some closed their doors entirely, and others kept their physical stores open but coped with decreases in traffic by adding Internet sales to the mix.

An accommodation to technology is now in place and many businesses that don't actively accept online orders and payments will nonetheless maintain a Web presence to facilitate communication with shop owners, offer research materials and information about products, and provide customer service that smoothes the way for direct sales.

By its nature, antiquarian book collecting was destined to be transformed by this new commercial paradigm.

Historically, the antiquarian and collectible book trade was a face-to-face endeavor that put great store by reputation, a world in which personal relationships tended to endure for many years. The world of devoted collectors and professional bookmen was not so large, and many small booksellers and scouts established close ties to major antiquarian collectors, scholars, auction houses, and dealers.

These relationships created a collegial network of known collectors, scouts, and traders for whom integrity and trust were paramount—all in the service of communicating information and locating and circulating the rare and collectible books that the industry reveres.

Networks of dealers and collectors maintained these relationships across regions and around the world. Information was disseminated unofficially by dealers, scouts, and collectors who annually traveled the rounds of shops, auctions, and sales, comparing books and sharing their research. Professional association and auction newsletters, as well as publications like the now-defunct print magazine *AB Bookman's Weekly,* contained timely articles on issues pertinent to the trade, bibliographic information on specific books, lists of books for sale, and "want lists," or lists of books that dealers and collectors were seeking.

In this way, collectible books were moved from region to region and country to country in the hands of dedicated book lovers.

It was a small, well-contained world.

Enter the Internet, and in the course of little more than a decade, the small networks grew as large as the World Wide Web, in the process losing much of the face-to-face intimacy that had been so central. Books that once were considered scarce when buyers sought them regionally are now easily and instantly discovered in large numbers on the Web. Buyers who once gave want lists to dealers to search the professional networks can now go online and often find the book they seek directly, skipping the middle man.

There was a time not so long ago when, if you wanted a book on Flatbush, you would depend on a bookseller in New York to find it for you. He was there, on-site. He could search for books in his region, and people would come to him because he had developed channels for buying and selling regional books. Now you can do your own search on the Internet and you'll find books listed all over the world on every subject you can imagine. If the Flatbush title is being offered, chances are you will come across it, perhaps more than one.

By the same token, you can now market your regional and specialty books directly to millions of dealers and collectors all over the world. However, by bypassing a bookseller who is a specialist in the field, you lose valuable counsel and you risk under-pricing a book for sale or paying for an inferior book you might not want in your collection, simply because you did not have the opportunity to talk it over with an experienced professional. This can apply to any specialty genre.

Progress of Internet Trading

We asked collectors and sellers if they thought the industry might progress past the upheavals of the last decade and settle into a new pattern that incorporates both old and new practices—re-energizing personal relationships and trust while expanding the reach and scope of markets from coast to coast and beyond.

Some grew wistful for times past and some looked forward with hope. And some had entered the trade in the age of the Internet and have little experience with any other mode of business.

Most took a pragmatic view, saying they hope for an element of personal and long-lasting relationships with clientele, and a renewed interest in educating buyers and sellers. All desire a high level of trust and a renewed expectation of integrity in dealings, though they recognize the risks attendant to dealing anonymously or at a great distance with all comers online. The Internet is available to the honest and dishonest alike, and even during the era of personal relationships, the antiquarian book industry has never been completely immune from exploitation by forgers and other unsavory types.

Discussing recent experiences in his association with the Colorado Antiquarian Book Seminars (www.bookseminars.com), bookseller Michael Ginsberg, a past president of ABAA and owner of Michael Ginsberg Books in Sharon, Massachusetts, said that in the early years of the bookseller training seminars, which are going into their thirtieth year in 2008, as many as one hundred people or more attended the weeklong program that was designed to teach skills needed by antiquarian and rare book dealers and enthusiasts.

Ginsberg said participation in the seminars had dropped to about thirty registrants several years ago, but interest and participation are growing again.

Ginsberg said he asked how many of those attending in 2006 were planning to open brick-and-mortar shops in their areas of specialty or featuring books they believed would allow them to earn a living. At least thirty people raised their hands. "That's sixty percent of a small sampling," he said, "but the level of interest has been strong throughout." In addition, he noted that seminar attendees ranged in age from people in their twenties to some over seventy. In an esoteric industry like antiquarian bookselling that is concerned about attracting new blood, any such trends in this area are worthy of notice and encouragement.

Kathryn Smiley, editor, *Firsts, A Book Collector's Magazine*:

Q: As someone who has straddled old-time antiquarian collecting and the modern Internet age, what is your take on the changes taking place?

KS: The Internet is a tool. As with any tool, for instance if you have a hammer, you can build a house with it or you can tear one down. It depends on how you use it. The Internet has certainly changed the book world hugely.

As a collector, you can find a bargain on the Internet. Also, as a collector, you can have your pockets picked. If you know what you're doing, and you buy intelligently, you can do OK. It certainly makes it easier to find books you're looking for. However, I can't tell you how many would-be collectors have called and described problems they've had with purchases online.

For instance, one individual bought a book by Gene Stratton Porter and found that the illustrations were colored in. (Note: Stratton Porter is a celebrated naturalist, novelist,

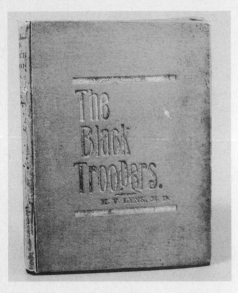

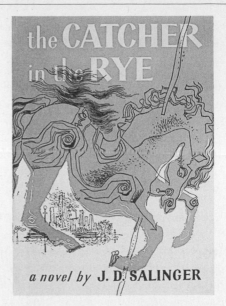

A rare copy of *The Black Troopers,* written by African-American physician M. L. Lynck in 1898. It contains biographies of Black American soldiers in the Spanish-American War.
Digital photography by Jonathan Draudt, Tamarac Arts.

J. D. Salinger's *The Catcher in the Rye,* first edition. Boston, 1951. The book was published in black cloth with pictorial dust jacket. A photograph of the author appears on the back cover of the first edition dj.
Digital photography by Jonathan Draudt, Tamarac Arts.

and photographer. Her book, *A Girl of the Limberlost* (NY. Doubleday Page. 1909. 1st ed. dj.) in good to fine condition, is offered online at $250–$450; if inscribed, $800–$1,000.) The bookseller said the customer must have colored them because the book didn't leave the store that way. Obviously, that's a difficult problem to resolve.

Also, book scouting, once prominent, has become a "gone thing" now because so many people put their own books online. But there's so much unfiltered information. The Internet is the world's hugest unedited book.

For safer sites, the ABAA is a good place to start. They have a code of ethics for members, an ethics committee, and standards for listing. I would tend to go toward them before anybody else.

Q: What other changes has the industry gone through?

KS: Bookselling has always been a relationship thing. It has always been done long distance with a handshake, with a letter, with a phone call. The people who are serious booksellers tended to be very reputable as a community. I would always brag when we got into the field that it was the last bastion of the honorable American businessperson. I'd call you up and you'd send me a very expensive book for approval. If it was what I wanted, I'd send you a check; if it wasn't, I'd send the book back.

Q: Is regionalism a thing of the past because of availability of world listings on the Internet?

KS: I don't know if it's just a human characteristic to pigeonhole things or if it's a marketing thing, but regional writers do tend to stay regional in appeal.

Consider author Marjorie Rawlings—she's a tremendous writer, a wonderful writer, but she gets pigeonholed as a children's writer for *The Yearling* (NY. Scribner's Sons. 1938. 1st ed. dj. $400–$1,000; inscrb. $1,500–$2,000; 1939 ltd. illus. by Wyeth. sgn by author and illustrator. $2,500–$4,500) or as a regional writer for Florida. She's not much known. People sort of know her for *The Yearling*, but not much about her other books, and I think regionalism has a lot to do with that.

I think there is still a trend to regionalism that limits where books will be in demand to an extent.

Stocking a Bookseller's Shelves

Supplying a bookshop has changed, as well. Where once dealers frequented flea markets and estate sales to discover good books and offer a means to bring them to market, the general public now has access to online auctions and book sites where amateur sellers and collectors can complete a sale without recourse to a professional dealer.

Kenneth Andersen, Sporting and General Antiquarian Books, Middlebury, Vermont:

Q: Have you changed the way you obtain stock for your business, and is there still a market for your special expertise?

KA: Numerous dealers used to sell to me as an outlet and I had a network of collectors interested in various subjects. What has happened is many of those dealers go directly to the Internet now, as do many collectors.

Through book fairs and the ABAA, I developed very rewarding relationships with a number of America's premier old-line booksellers: George Goodspeed of Boston, who started working in his father's book shop in 1924 on the afternoon he graduated from Harvard; Charles Vincent, who ran a shop in Old Mystic, Connecticut. He earlier studied with Robert Goddard, the father of American rocketry.

I rubbed elbows with fascinating people through their interest in books, but there is less of that today.

General booksellers are leapfrogging over the specialist and going directly to the Internet to sell their wares. The problem is that a specialist basically spent many years learning his subject. I myself was a literature teacher and loved teaching and the scholarship that went along with it. I brought that to bookselling.

Specialists were once guardians of the gate. A person went to them and they gave you information—they told you what was good and what was not. Now, all that knowledge and expertise and affection you have for the business, all that you learned that is in your brain now, you can't always charge a price for it. The customers don't come to you first, they go to the Internet.

Many of my [continuing] customers are professional people who don't have the time to check into each book on their own. But they can call me at night and say, "Ken, you know what I like. Suggest some books for me," or "You've seen this book, right? Do you think I'd like it?"

As a specialist, you have to read everything in your field and provide a service to your customers, and they in turn will trust you implicitly.

It was a Goodspeed mantra that the bookseller would provide good books to their clientele who would then sell those books back to them at some later date—or their family would, through their estate.

This way, they kept good books in circulation.

Rob Rulon-Miller, Rulon-Miller Books, St. Paul, Minnesota:

Q: How has your business changed in recent years?

RR-M: There was a time when books moved up the food chain, dealer to dealer; now, it seems, many books make quantum leaps, from the small dealer right into the hands of the last or final customer.

I've always been very fortunate in being able to buy privately—not a book at a time, not even a box of books at a time, but a truckload of books at a time—from prominent collectors who are looking to sell their libraries.

In the old days, many of these books would have ended up at auction, but I think in order to get material now, dealers have to be competitive with auction houses. These libraries cost a lot of money; you end up finding more and more partnerships among booksellers. I can't tell you the number of books I own with one other person, or two or three, in order to afford the purchase price of a collection. Buying privately is absolutely the best way to buy books in large quantities.

Donna Howard, The Eloquent Page, in St. Albans, Vermont:

Q: Has the Internet affected the way you choose stock for your store?

DH: It has changed the way I can buy books for resale and still make a profit.

Occasionally we get some particularly unusual children's books. But the problem is, for the usual series book, say, people who stop in at the store used to look at them. But now, if you go online, you find literally hundreds of copies of series books available. There's no incentive for a dealer to list the three hundred and first copy of any book.

We had a homeopathic book from the 1800s—they used to be pretty scarce here. The book was well worth having because there were people interested in the subject. But online, there are 150 of them. You now see inventory from all over the world.

In the past, there were a number of dealers and collectors who made the rounds of bookshops. You'd see them on a semi-regular basis. And there were groups of them, so

Three-quarter leather cover with marbled boards; *The Europeans,* by Henry James, published by Houghton Osgood and Co., Boston. 1878.

Decorated leather with gilt lettering; *The Europeans,* by Henry James, 1878.

Endpapers for *The Europeans,* by Henry James, 1878.

every couple of months or so, you'd see them coming through, buying stock for their own shops.

That doesn't happen so much anymore.

As dealers and collectors alike have pointed out, with the proliferation of books online from around the globe, many books once thought rare, hard to find, or scarce are easily found in distant locales and so have lost their special status and much of their value. Leif Laudamus of New England Book Auctions in Northhampton, Massachusetts and Ray Giordano of The Antiquarian Scientist in Southampton, Massachusetts, said this phenomenon occurs especially in the field of secondary source books for science and medicine, which once enjoyed strong sales. Prices for these items have dropped as copies proliferate on the Internet and individual booksellers' sales fall off.

These dealers stress that the first work in a specialized field and books by the giants of science, medicine, and technology like Newton, Darwin, or Einstein are still highly prized items. But secondary books on a subject—those that draw on the scholarship of the giants and explain these disciplines, for instance—are now more easily found in quantity and so less in demand from an individual bookseller.

This affects price and changes the appeal of a particular book for buyer and seller alike. When a previously rare title comes up in a search, buyers may find that the treasure they were looking for is common and they can buy that book at a lower price, which is a good deal for collectors who want to round out a reading library on a subject as well as acquire high spots in the subject.

On the other hand, if they want to sell a once-thought-rare title, they may find the competition on the Internet a little discouraging. Readjusting expectations and buying books at the right price is important if they don't want to lose their shirt when they turn to selling.

Remember the adage "You can't teach an old dog new tricks"? Well, as time goes on, those dogs young and old who manage to stay in business are the ones who learn new tricks.

Marie's Web site with AbeBooks.com has certainly "brought the world to her doorstep" here in rural Vermont. Over the past several years since she has been selling online, she has made the acquaintance of many bibliophiles in the far corners of the globe, including a professor in Australia, a World War II enthusiast from the Netherlands, and several Virginia Woolf fans in California whose correspondence over the subject of sought-after books often brightens her day.

And yet, personal visits from her longtime clientele of dealers and collectors are still the highlight of doing business at Mountain Reverie Books. Visits are fewer and further between these days, but Marie still maintains a stock of books and ephemera that she does not feature online and offers exclusively to her established network of genre enthusiasts and dealers.

When Is an Old Book Collectible?

A reasonable question. Instead of thinking in terms of "old," consider your books as used, out-of-print, or rare. These descriptions apply to books of any age. Rather than how old they are, think about content and quality: What is the book about, or who wrote it, or who published it?

If you have an eye toward investment and you must choose between two books, one printed in London in 1632 by an obscure British poet, and the other a 19th-century tome on the American Indian published in New York, choose the one on the American Indian.

There remains an ongoing market for Native Americana and the book will likely find a customer in the collectible book market. If you love poetry and are building a collection in the genre, by all means take the poetry. It's fun to have on the shelf, but it isn't automatically a collector's item. Don't buy it with the hope of reselling at a profit.

We don't think anybody can provide a cut-off date for what qualifies as an "antiquarian" book. Is it the 19th century? Early 20th?

Unless you are a rare-book dealer focusing on the earliest printed material—incunabula or the first printed books in the New World—put actual age out of your mind and learn which books are sought by dealers and other collectors. You'll discover a busy trade in books from past centuries and even some from last year, from antiquarian volumes to modern first editions.

Where Will I Find Books for My Collection?

The answer to that question is changing with the times, but not so much that some old habits don't still serve.

While most people today will jump online to see what is available, we still think first of the antiquarian and collectible book dealer. Though we prefer a personal conversation or phone call to "virtual" communication, the fact is many professionals maintain a presence on the Internet where their wares can be reviewed and they can be contacted for additional information.

And information is key.

For many genres, used bookstores and professional Web sites will yield exactly what you're after, often at a wide range of prices, so learning the finer points of edition and condition will hold you in good stead. If you're dealing with a professional, you can throw in a little conversation or a few e-mails back and forth with the bookseller, and you've added to your education as well as to your collection.

We cannot stress enough that a book bought from a reputable dealer has been prescreened for you, and you will have more confidence in the authenticity of your find.

Away from the computer for a while, all manner of used books are still commonly available at library sales, flea markets, secondhand stores and antique shops, and even at the typical garage sale. Armed with some knowledge, a scout can still spend an enjoyable day on the hunt and come away with a good book or two. The inveterate bibliophile should not lose sight of these sources merely because the Internet is so close and so easy. Many is the treasure still languishing on roadside tables, waiting for a discerning eye to discover it and take it home.

For example, Marie was looking through some books left over from a local library sale. When the sale was completed, the librarian still had about twenty boxes of used books on the tables. The "free" sign went up and the public was invited to take whatever they liked.

Marie's eye fell on one book—a copy of *Home Run Feud*, #22 in the Chip Hilton series, by Claire Bee (Grosset & Dunlap. 1964. first edition). It was in fine to very fine condition, surprising for a children's book published in 1964. The binding was the original design and the list of books in the series printed on the copyright page ended with that particular title, indicating that it was probably a true first edition.

Several years ago, the book in fine to like-new condition listed online from $50 to $350. Copies offered on eBay in scuffed and bumped condition sold for $35–$40. Last year [2007], first edition copies in fine condition had gone down in value but were still being offered at prices ranging from $20 to $40. Not a princely sum, but worth the time it took to check those "free" boxes.

We still attend auctions and haunt out-of-the-way shops on our travels from state to state, but we too find it more difficult to restock our shelves these days. If we do find an item of interest, it is less often bought on speculation and more often chosen because we have a buyer in mind for it back home. On occasion, we accept items for sale on consignment, which is another way to be associated with libraries of fine books and bring them to market.

Estate sales remain viable at present for acquiring books in larger numbers, individually or in partnership with other dealers. As an option for acquiring stock, boxes of books from an estate may well contain both wheat and chaff, but when the purchase price for a library is right, a few good books for resale can make the endeavor worthwhile.

As primarily wholesale booksellers, we rarely buy from online dealers but we occasionally take a look at the offerings on auction Web sites, though admittedly with a cautious eye.

For the book enthusiast intent on mining the Internet, he's now advised to bone up on his subject before he starts his quest. He will have far more volumes at his fingertips, but unless they're listed on a professional site, they are unvetted. Many sites are open to listings by casual sellers who don't yet have a bookseller's wealth of information gathered through years of experience. The online collector must place his faith in information offered by someone he has never seen. Not to say that many, many reputable booksellers cannot be found on the Internet. But how to discern who knows his business and who is a novice? There's the rub.

The Bauman Rare Books site at *www.baumanrarebooks.com* is among many professional sites that include reference information and guidance for the book lover. A quote in

E. G. Martin and John Irving, *Cruising and Ocean Racing,* a copiously illustrated book on sport sailing from the Londale Library.
Digital photography by Jonathan Draudt, Tamarac Arts.

Bauman's essay on "Books About Books and Book Collecting" states: "While the Internet serves its purpose, the book lover who is interested in becoming a collector will eventually be drawn to the source of his passion: a book."

If you love the printed volume, you may want to turn off the computer for a while and sit down with a good book about books. We've listed many staples of the trade for you in our Reference section, and many more are available, if you seek them out.

How Do I Navigate Internet Book Sites?

Book search sites make it easy for the novice to find book listings by scouring the Internet for authors, titles, and topics, and presenting them in an orderly list, sorted by date of publication, length of time on sale, or price. Several large Web sites have moved to the forefront of this industry for both listing and search services, including listing sites like AbeBooks (originally Advanced Book Exchange) at *www.abebooks.com* and Alibris at *www.alibris.com,* or global search sites dedicated to books and ephemera like BookFinder at *www.bookfinder.com,* AddAll Book Search and Price Comparison at *www.addall.com,* or viaLibris at *www.vialibris.com.*

Commerce sites like Barnes & Noble include antiquarian titles among their offerings at *www.barnesandnoble.com,* as does the Internet bookselling giant Amazon.com. And don't forget the general merchandise auction and retail mega site, eBay (*www.ebay.com*), where both beginner and experienced booksellers market titles ranging from new or used reading copies to more high-priced collectibles. Additional dealer and specialty sites are too numerous to mention.

We're told the younger crowd who have grown up with the Internet are going straight to search engines like Google and Froogle, using titles or authors' names as search terms. If this works for them, we cannot criticize, but the dedicated sites for listing and searching for books are, to our mind, better organized and presented for anyone seriously interested in finding the best books offered.

To find their way into these book searches and see their stock featured, independent booksellers can subscribe to one of many listing sites where they can set up a Web page and post their own books for sale, advertise wants, and perform searches for clients, all for monthly fees usually based on the number of books posted or the amount of activity their books generate for the book site.

For newcomers to the Internet, technical support for managing these pages is usually available. After ten years with the Internet as an integral part of bookselling, most established dealers now have at least a working knowledge of how to navigate the territory. Thousands of booksellers have availed themselves of these services or set up their own sites, including experienced specialists and brand-new entrepreneurs.

Technology is progressing at amazing speeds, but at present, most smaller private Web sites maintained by antiquarian dealers (and there are many wonderful such sites!) are not searched by the dedicated book search engines, though there's a chance they'll show up high enough on Google or Froogle to be noticed. Such independent dealer listings will appear on Bookfinder and AddAll searches, however, if they're also featured on association sites like ABAA or ILAB-LILA. Who knows what the future holds for these options? The serious bibliophile is well advised to seek out these independent sites, however, to mine them for excellent information and to see what treasures they offer for sale.

Currently popular and growing ever more central to the industry are group listing sites like AbeBooks.com and Alibris, with additional choices like Biblio.com, TomFolio.com, and the widely popular European site, Antiqbook.com, among the many such choices online.

For the discerning buyer who prefers dealing with vetted professionals, a first stop might be the Antiquarian Booksellers' Association of American (ABAA, *www.abaa.org*) or the International League of Antiquarian Booksellers (ILAB-LILA, *www.ilab-lila.com*). Each offers a search of books listed on the site by members who are professional dealers. The member listings often lead a buyer to the members' own independent Web sites, where additional information is offered.

These professional sites are not open to the casual seller and demand a level of scholarship and professionalism from dealers who list there. As with anything on the Internet, the circle of options expands exponentially as you follow the links from site to site. A buyer can log on and search the dealer lists for specific books, or just browse among the many titles offered.

Our best advice for you, as a buyer, is to know your books well and learn something about the dealer you're working with before committing your money to a sale. Check to see if the dealer has a return policy.

For dealers, if you're new to the field, learn about books, how to evaluate their rarity and condition, and how to properly describe them to a potential buyer before putting a price on them and posting them for sale to the world. This was good advice when listings were primarily found in magazines and print catalogues (which many dedicated dealers continue to issue!), and it holds as well for the world of electronic bookselling.

We have included terms for describing books and condition in the glossary in Appendix A at the back of this book.

When looking online for books, you'll find that if you are looking for a particular Hopalong Cassidy title, the number of items that may come up in a search will amaze you. A keyword may call up hundreds of volumes of a single title, from books in pristine collectible condition to dog-eared reading copies. And the prices will range from "I can afford that" to "You've gotta be kidding!"

For most online sites, you can refine your quest by limiting the search to a certain price range, asking to see only first editions, signed copies, or hardcover books with dust jackets.

Booksellers themselves have long considered other dealers a prime source of good stock bought directly through bookstores, dealer catalogues, advertisements, industry periodicals, and at book fairs. These practices haven't completely fallen out of favor but they don't produce the numbers and quality of volumes they did in the past.

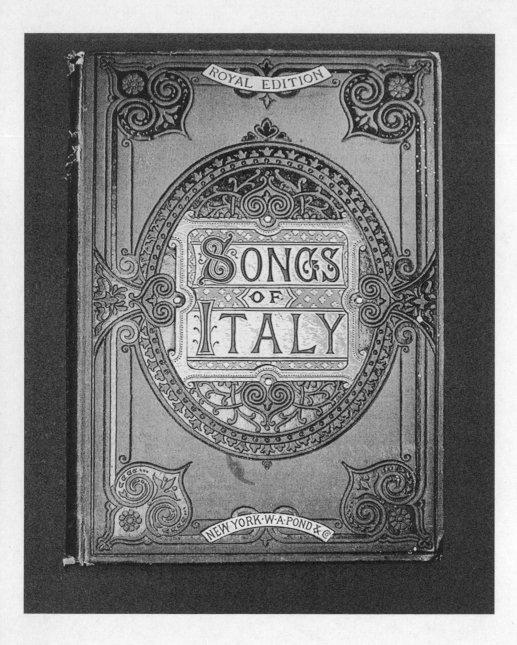

Songs of Italy, NY: W. A. Pond & Co. Royal Edition.
This is an example of decorative cloth binding from
the late 19th century.
*Digital photography by Jonathan Draudt, Tamarac
Arts.*

What Can I Find at Book Fairs?

Small book fairs report they're feeling the pinch of Internet incursion into their customer base, but the largest fairs, those sponsored by the major professional organizations, are reportedly attracting crowds of collectors who still enjoy spending time in the atmosphere of a room full of bibliophiles.

A review of the ABAA 36th California International Antiquarian Bookfair in February 2003 said it well, and it remains true:

"The Internet may be increasingly popular with some collectors, but when a book fair happens, there is still no substitute for seeing and handling books in person, and there is a happy serendipity which brings a collector together with a book he never knew he wanted until he saw it, but at that instant knew he simply had to have it."

(Note: Massachusetts author Nicholas Basbanes attended this fair and signed copies of his book, *Among the Gently Mad: Perspectives and Strategies for the Book-Hunter of the 21st Century*, published in 2002 by Henry Holt & Co. Basbanes has written a number of books on book collecting from an experiential perspective, rather than from the point of view of a dealer or investor. His other titles include *A Gentle Madness* [Holt. 1995] and *A Splendor of Letters* [Harper Collins. 2003].)

The pros and cons of the Internet for booksellers can be legitimately argued. A plus for sellers is that they are now able to reach a broader audience with information about their wares, increasing the pool of buyers for truly scarce books in excellent condition. We are eager to see, in the coming years, how the industry adjusts to the changes while providing a measure of confidence to buyer and seller alike that online transactions will be mutually satisfactory.

Nonetheless, the Internet is just one venue for buying and selling books. The true enthusiast can still attend regional fairs and national shows. They're great fun as pure recreation for book lovers, a good way to expand a personal network, and excellent for learning about books. Many fairs remain popular around the country, not the least the three major events sponsored annually by ABAA in New York, Boston, and either San Francisco or Los Angeles.

Kenneth Andersen, Sporting and General Antiquarian Books, Middlebury, Vermont:

Q: Has membership in ABAA proven a benefit to your business?

KA: I appreciate participation in ABAA especially for the access it provides to the organization's book fairs. They're held three times a year in New York, Boston, and alternately Los Angeles or San Francisco, and they are the country's major antiquarian book shows.

The nice thing about being a member of ABAA is I felt that if I bought something significant during the year, I would be able to find a buyer for it through ABAA.

For instance, before one of these fairs, I had gone into an attic here in Vermont. The owner had some wonderful Vermontiana but, in the end, I wasn't offered any books. Still, there were many automobile catalogues and paper items, and I took some of those.

27

It was exceedingly hot up there and I thought, "Well at least I got something from this day spent in an incredibly hot attic." When I brought the catalogues to an ABAA show, I hoped someone would appreciate them after all the work I went through to get them.

A gentleman at the fair approached me and said, "I'll take this and this and this."

He totaled up $400 or $500 worth of paper and said, "Here's my check."

I didn't know him, so I asked for identification.

He mentioned Mike Ginsberg, a past president of ABAA and a dealer at the fair. "Mike knows me," he said. "Ask him."

Mike told me that at a recent Sotheby's auction, the gentleman had purchased over $1 million worth of botanicals. "He's definitely good for it."

The gentleman came back to my booth and he had that look in his eye. "Did you check me out?" He actually was appreciative of what I had done.

He gave me his check and his card and now I have him as a regular customer. When I run across items in his field, I know he has a virtually unlimited budget for things he's looking for.

Q: What are some other typical ABAA experiences?

KA: There's the story of a copy of *Huck Finn* I brought to a fair on consignment in the early 1990s. It was in shabby condition; if you picked it up, it would fall apart. But it was a first printing, and the book was signed by Twain.

Signed first printings of *Huck Finn* are rare. Twain's books have many points, as pages were pulled off the presses and elements were changed and fixed during printing and binding. (Note: See more on this in Kathryn Smiley's discussion on 19th century book production methods that resulted in numerous states and points of issue within the first printing of a first edition in chapter 3.)

I took a chance and brought it to the Boston Book Fair. I decided to ask $10,000 for it.

Bauman Rare Books of Philadelphia, another well-known member of ABAA, looked at the book and bought it for $10,000, less their dealer's discount. (Note: Booksellers regularly offer a discount on retail prices to other dealers.)

I saw the book offered several years later at auction. It went up for sale at Swann Galleries in New York and it sold for a price in the mid-teens. (Note: Several unsigned copies published in New York by Charles Webster, 1885, with numerous first edition points—though not necessarily all points—were offered at prices ranging from $9,000 to $18,000 in the summer of 2007.)

ABAA gives me access to a range of collectors that I wouldn't have had otherwise. You know, you can always shop for a bargain, but there are people who look for the best material, and they like the security and convenience of shopping at Shreve Crump & Lowe or Tiffany's. That's the type of person who follows ABAA fairs.

Q: Doesn't the change in attitudes toward small fairs lose sight of the enjoyment many book lovers derive from the serendipity of finding something unexpected?

KA: What used to happen is, people would come to a fair and they would find something that they never knew existed. And that's how they would broaden their knowledge.

And that would interest them in the next show. Attending fairs became an exercise in finding books, holding them, looking through them, as well as being in that environment. It's the company of kindred souls, basically.

People today are living online and on the phone, 24/7, and they don't take a whole day away from the family to pursue an interest that isn't shared with their spouse or their children. But they miss those great browsing opportunities.

By all accounts, book shows and fairs continue to draw dedicated bibliophiles who enjoy the opportunity to see and examine a multitude of books and who appreciate the opportunity to talk to knowledgeable dealers, but other dealers agree that smaller local shows saw a drop during the early part of the new millennium.

Casual buyers and investment-oriented collectors are increasingly attracted to the ease of cyber-commerce, and dwindling attendance at regional shows at the turn of the century reflected this. It may be too early to know whether this trend has turned yet, but dealers are cautiously hopeful that recent years are seeing a return of booksellers willing to participate in fairs and collectors returning to these events.

Fairs remain an excellent education unto themselves, nonetheless. Nothing is more satisfying than to hold a book in your hand and take the time to examine it for yourself. If you have a question, dealers can give you an answer right then and there.

Where Else Should a Collector Look for Books?

Other continuing sources are the long-popular flea markets, estate sales, auctions, the Salvation Army, antique stores, Friends of the Library sales, and garage sales. These are the places where professionals continue to find books, though the rare valuable collectible turns up here less and less frequently these days.

To be sure, some of us are involved with collectible books for reasons other than merely earning a living. Traditional bibliophiles enjoy the hunt through the stacks, scouring the countryside for books long out of circulation, leafing through private collections to find the one or two treasures among them, holding history in their hands even if only for a moment. They enjoy the heft and feel of a book almost as much as the words and images on a page. They enjoy the people they meet and the opportunities for invigorating conversation on topics of shared interest. These are among the esoteric pleasures of antiquarian bookselling and collecting that the Internet cannot replace.

Catalogue advertising and dealer-to-dealer selling have evolved along with the new technology, as well. Many dealers no longer spend as much time and resources to create and mail comprehensive print catalogues when so many serious collectors have access to the Internet, though prodigious numbers of professionals have begun placing catalogue-quality scholarship in their listings on the better book Web sites (for instance, ABAA, ILAB, and individual seller sites). A collector can glean an excellent education from these sources.

Others, however, continue to offer limited edition catalogues to their mailing-list customers, and the utility of targeted print catalogues, too, may be rebounding.

Can a Collector Avoid Scams?

Given the nature of arm's-length commerce online, most buyers no longer have personal knowledge of a seller's expertise and reputation. On open-market sites like eBay and AbeBooks, highly qualified booksellers are joined by newcomers with little background or knowledge, and the occasional unscrupulous seller. Buyer education is critical to avoid costly mistakes.

"Caveat emptor" has been good advice for millennia, and no one can guarantee that you won't make a mistake. The best protection is to seek some information about the person you're buying from, and to learn about the books themselves. The more you understand about antiquarian and collectible books, the better equipped you will be to judge an offering at a distance, though nothing can substitute for first-hand knowledge of a book before buying.

The ABAA and ILAB-LILA, national and international professional booksellers' organizations, require a level of knowledge and include a stringent code of ethics for their members, many of whom publish book listings with extensive scholarship, photographs, and documentation as a matter of course. Their Internet sites (ABAA at *www.abaa.org*; ILAB-LILA at *www.ilab-lila.com*) provide prodigious information for the professional development of member booksellers and to educate visiting collectors.

And the Independent Online Booksellers Association (IOBA) Web site includes a code of ethics that requires bookseller members to guarantee the authenticity of their wares, with a return policy that seeks to protect the buyer's interests as well as the seller's (IOBA at *www.ioba.org*).

Computer technology has facilitated long-distance commerce, but with it, we lose the ability to closely examine a book to determine if it is in fact what has been represented to us before we decide to buy. The Summer 2003 edition of the ABAA Newsletter included a detailed article by Jennifer Larson on forgeries in which she described several notorious events, some of which predate the Internet age and so are not all attributable to online commerce. But with the increasing popularity of Internet buying and ease of creating copies, the issue becomes even more important and complex.

Larson pointed out that, historically, book dealers have placed their professional reputations behind the authentication of a book's provenance and of handwritten inscriptions or signatures, and those reputations carried great weight. With the proliferation of long-distance commerce between strangers, authentication needs to be based on more. A buyer needs to ask for detailed description, points of issue, and for evidence of provenance to authenticate items. In real estate circles, they say that three things are important to a sale—location, location, and location. In the antiquarian book world, we suggest the three elements critical to success are education, education, and education.

Bibliophile and author Nicholas Basbanes (*A Gentle Madness*, 1995; *Among the Gently Mad*, 2003) offers some gentle advice: "If you're going to take on a project that involves the nuances of intellectual expression, then it makes sense that you do your homework."

As bookselling over the Internet continues to evolve, educated and experienced buyers and sellers are looking for the best ways to find each other. Book dealers, independently and in association with their peers, are finding their way to technologically savvy site designers and marketing specialists to increase the likelihood that quality online listings will show up on the public's favorite search engines.

An educated public is well advised to visit these better book sites, as well, where a search will turn up fewer 99-cent copies of a title or questionable editions, and more legitimate offers of quality antiquarian and collectible stock.

Over time, the proliferation of online book markets may settle into their niches with lower-end used books and reader's copies finding a ready outlet on the open sites. Sales of more expensive and rare items may shift to the professional organizations and bookseller sites that are developing procedures to function with a level of assurance that replicates the industry's hallmark of ethical dealing during the face-to-face era.

How Good Are Auctions for Buying and Selling Books?

Books at local auctions are still plentiful and a good source of collectibles. A dealer with a client waiting for a book can find saleable wares, but auctions are less the wholesale venues they were in years past, becoming of more use to the collector today, as you can't be sure of picking up a bargain any longer unless the crowd is dull about books.

In too many cases, except perhaps at the larger, more exclusive rare book and collectible houses, the popularity of auctions has brought with it a kind of recreational bidder. In the heat of competition for an item, prices may be driven much higher than a dealer would be willing to pay. Even a collector can sometimes do better in a bookstore or in a private transaction. There's a skill to buying at auction and those with the skill do well there.

Great books can still be had for excellent prices if buyers exercise caution, know how much they are willing to pay ahead of time, and sit on their hands when the bidding gets rowdy.

If you're selling books, live auctions and dealers are on a par, each having their strong and weak points. On a particular day, if an auction attracts a spirited audience, you could do well. On an off day, you risk having your books sell for less than you'd hoped unless you're able to place a floor (reserve) on the amount you'll accept for them. Some auctions allow reserves, others don't. Sellers are advised to ask before consigning a book.

Selling through dealers requires more of your time and effort, but dealers have pipelines to collectors who may be looking for just the book you're selling. Then again, those collectors may follow auctions and be in the audience when your book comes up at a location that publicizes upcoming events.

For the high-end collector, the better auction houses offer an excellent opportunity to discover truly rare treasures in your genre. Houses like PBA Galleries (Pacific Book Auction Galleries at *www.pbagalleries.com*) and Swann Auction Galleries (*www .swanngalleries.com*), longtime quality organizations, provide arrangements for registered clientele to conduct online bidding for items coming up for auction at their brick-and-mortar auction houses. They're not sites where absentee sellers can list books for weeks or months at a time, however.

Information about upcoming auctions held twice-monthly at Leif Laudamus' New England Book Auctions in Massachusetts is available online at *www.nebookauctions.com*. Laudamus makes catalogues for his twice-monthly auctions available to his mailing list subscribers. The catalogues include a form for absentee bidding.

The largest online auction site, eBay, has a lively book community, but the scholarship is sketchy. Buyers can acquire wonderful finds there, but great care is needed to avoid spending time and money only to find that the item is not as it was represented. Auctions typically run anywhere from three days to a week, so there's time to check on the bona fides of the seller—Marie herself occasionally places items there—and to ask questions about the book on the block before tendering a bid.

In the final analysis, we can only tell you where books can be found. You must choose the venue that is right for you and learn the skills and techniques that make for rewarding experiences.

What Books Should I Pick Up?

There's no single answer to this question. Before you ask it, you have some decisions to make, and then the question will begin to answer itself. Are you buying books for investment or fun? Are you a collector? A dealer? Will you specialize or be a generalist?

Kathryn Smiley, editor, *Firsts* magazine:

Q: What advice do you have for someone just starting a collection?

KS: Our advice to someone just starting out is, first and foremost, collect what you love. That is always our first advice. Because otherwise, what's the point?

Eugene O'Neill's *The Hairy Ape,* **NY:** Liveright, 1929. ltd 750 cc. signed. Pictured are the patterned boards and black cloth spine.

An illustration from Eugene O'Neill's *The Hairy Ape,* 1929.

Original slipcase and patterned cover of Eugene O'Neill's *The Hairy Ape,* 1929.

Book collecting for investment is not a great idea. We never advise anyone to get into book collecting with an eye to making a gazillion dollars, particularly modern books, because it's difficult to predict which ones will be popular down the line.

For instance, you can pick up a popular book from the 1940s and look at the back cover where the publisher lists upcoming hot titles. Chances are you will have heard of very few of them.

So, our first advice is always collect what you love. If down the line your books also appreciate in value, that's icing on the cake. But at least you're surrounded by books that mean something to you, that you value, that enrich your life.

Bibliophiles agree that carefully bought collectible books hold their value well and grow in value at a steady rate of up to 10 percent per year. They're generally a safe investment, but with rare exceptions, they're not speculative and won't make you a killing.

As an example of the quality of investment, we refer to the sale of the Raymond Epstein collection, placed on the block at Swann Auction Galleries in April 1992.

Mr. Epstein had carefully recorded the purchase prices of his books, which were maintained in excellent condition, providing an unusual opportunity to compare market prices over an approximately thirty-year period, even longer with prices updated to 2004.

A copy of *Dracula* bought in 1965 for $46 was maintained in a specially made case costing $38. The book realized $11,000 at auction in 1992. First editions in 2004, some later issue, were listed from $10,000 to $17,000. In 2007, a signed first edition was offered at $20,000, and a presentation copy inscribed by Bram Stoker to a prominent newspaperman on the day the book was published was offered at an asking price of $75,000.

A copy of *Ulysses* bought for $400 in 1965 and maintained in a $350 case sold for $19,800 in 1992. In 2004, dealers were asking $25,000 to $35,000 for limited first editions printed in London from the Bodley Head. By 2007, dealers were listing signed first editions from the Bodley Head (100 copies out of a limited edition of 1,000) for as much as $48,000.

Mr. Epstein acquired *Tom Sawyer* in 1966 for $1,250 and it sold for $9,350 in 1992. *Tom Sawyer*, in a later issue first edition, was offered for $6,750 in 2004. A true first edition from Chatto & Windus in London was offered in 2007 for $40,000. Second and later printings of the first American edition were at the $4,000 to $6,000 level in 2007.

This is clear evidence that careful collecting can be a solid investment over time, with some occasional fluctuation. Still, as often as not, even those who collect for investment wind up excited by the hunt and end up collecting for fun, too.

If you decide to specialize, whether bookseller or collector, learn all you can about your subject. Don't neglect allied subjects that broaden your knowledge. Visit bookstores, talk to dealers, read dealer descriptions to see what's being offered and what someone else wants. Visit libraries.

Michael Ginsberg told us he likes to read the bibliographies in the back of books related to his specialty to discover other books to read and some he might want to collect or resell.

What are Categories or Ana?

When you get more involved as a dealer or collector, you'll become familiar with references to the common genres and specialties, sometimes called "ana" (see Glossary). These will include topics like the settling of the Americas, native peoples, Black studies, maritime trades, foreign countries, children's books, medicine, science, sporting books, zoology, anthropology, magic, antiques, the military, cooking, poetry, railroads, billiards, the radical labor movement, and on and on. Add to that limited editions, fine presses, fine bindings, illustrated books—the list doesn't end. And each genre has subgenres, ad infinitum.

These categories help dealers and collectors to communicate. Dealers use them to describe their specialties and collectors use them to define their area of interest. But genres are not mutually exclusive; there's enormous overlapping, and they are just one tool for evaluating books. We go into greater detail in our chapter on Popular Genres.

We have also included a list of collectible titles and authors, by genre, at the end of this book.

What Does "Americana" Refer To?

A very popular specialty is Americana, but what do bookmen mean by the term? Do they refer to books on the discovery, exploration, political and cultural development of the United States? Or do they adopt the broader and truer meaning of the term and include all the Americas from Canada to Argentina?

In modern vernacular, the meaning of "Americana" has narrowed to refer to the United States and its territories, though some dealers use it in the more inclusive form. To be technically correct when referring to the United States, the term "U.S.iana" was coined by bibliographer Wright Howes, author of *U.S.iana,* issued in 1954, but the term is less widely used.

How Important Is Condition?

This is probably the most important judgment you will make about a book you're buying or selling. Depending on its condition, a book can be a collector's item or just a nice book to read. We often see the same look of perplexity on the faces of people not in the trade when we reject the old book in their hand. "But it's old!" No matter.

Unless the book is an Eliot Bible, or another great rarity, it must be in good condition— bindings attached, pages all there, illustrations accounted for, no underlining, no tears, and clean covers. If the book was issued with a dust jacket, the jacket must be present and in good condition, especially for modern first editions. The absence of the jacket radically reduces the value of a collectible book that was issued in a jacket.

Sounds cranky, doesn't it? But we can't stress enough the importance of condition in collectible books.

Christine von der Linn, a book specialist at Swann Galleries, wrote: "Condition is to antiquarian and collectibles what location is to real estate. A book collector seeks a volume in its original binding and the best condition possible. Other desirable attributes include provenance, association, special and limited editions, and fine bindings." (Note: Quoted from *A Book Has Many Covers*, Swann Auction Galleries, www.swanngalleries.com. Founder Benjamin Swann established Swann Auction Galleries as a fine book auction house in New York City in 1941. It has since expanded its offering to other "works of art on paper," including maps, posters, autographs, and photography. The Swann Auction Galleries Web site is a treasure trove of information for the bibliophile.)

The relevance of a book's binding to the description of a book and a determination of its condition is paramount. Collectors enjoy holding history in their hands, and so a book in its original binding has special appeal.

At times, as we discuss in our chapter on the Care and Repair of Books, an old, rare, and valuable book in serious disrepair will warrant repair or rebinding. An accomplished bookbinder can evaluate the volume and decide whether to incorporate elements of the original binding into the rebound version. At times this is accomplished by salvaging leather as part of the new book, or binding in an original spine with new boards and endpapers.

Maintaining as much of the original volume as possible enhances the book's continued value to collectors who appreciate their treasures for their historical continuity as well as for the information contained in their pages.

Still, don't throw away that interesting book if it's in less than good condition. Scholars, researchers, and recreational readers are another market for inexpensive reading copies of important books.

How Important Is the First Edition of a Book?

Rare book collectors want first editions because they reflect the first time these particular thoughts of an author appeared in print. They are perceived to be closest to the author's true intent. As further editions are issued, the supply of books is increased, thereby diminishing the value of succeeding editions. But the relative scarcity of firsts remains constant. At least, this was true of books published before the latter half of the 20th century, when a common print run might have been fewer than 5,000 books. Volumes produced in much larger quantities for national markets today tend to flood the markets, and their first editions don't achieve sufficient scarcity to command collectible prices.

As often as not, collectors who specialize in firsts don't read their prizes but buy them to enjoy the possession of something rare and special, something others don't have. Scholars and readers will pay a price for later editions they want to read, but it will be a mere shadow of the price paid for a first edition.

Now, after having said that, let us confuse you further. Popular titles are often reissued in limited editions. Printed on high quality papers, with fine bindings and slipcases, these commonly include illustrations by noted artists. Limited editions may command higher prices than first editions, since most are numbered and signed by the author, the artist, or both.

And then you have modern first editions, published in the past year or two and already commanding a collectible price, which nullifies the idea that age determines price. See more on this subject in our discussion on collecting popular genres.

How Do I Price a Book?

The plain truth is, there is no one right price for a used book. It's all subjective. The law of supply and demand is in play.

With a book in your hand, you'll do the research and then settle on a number. In the end, the value of a book is only what you or your customers are willing to pay. You will notice for some books we've listed, the price range is narrow. According to our sources, including dealers' pricing and auction records, folks agree on the current value of those books. For others, the range is hundreds or even thousands of dollars. These are actual prices people have asked for and paid. They reflect differing opinions from one dealer to another or from one part of the country to another. Such disparities are common, though broad access to the Internet is beginning to even out some of these prices.

We've listed some titles more than once in this volume to show the difference in price between, for instance, trade and limited editions, the first edition and a later edition, a first edition with dust jacket and one without, or a signed copy and an unsigned one. We've assigned our prices assuming very good to fine condition, with the rare exceptions noted.

Where you don't find the actual title you're after, but we list other titles by the same author, you've verified the author as important if not collectible. You have more research to do, however, before you can price the book in your hand. Some authors have many titles to their credit, not all prized. The whole subject is fraught with cautions.

Talk to people in the business; consult price guides and dealer catalogues; visit antiquarian bookstores and Web sites. Learn as much as you can and then learn some more. Pricing stock for a shop begins when you buy the books. Will your initial investment be tied up for months or a year, or do you have a ready customer for the book? Do you have a shop with overhead costs or do you mail order or sell on the Web?

As dealers, when we know exactly what book we're looking for, in the past we'd find it through our network of dealers and professionals, and determine a value. Today, we consult our network and the Internet.

Dealers have historically purchased books from each other for sale to their own list of customers. The practice is less common today, but Marie is still a wholesaler, selling largely to a select clientele of other professionals, pricing her books for that market.

You must make your own price judgments based upon your growing knowledge of the business. In the end, you're bound to make some mistakes. It's that kind of business.

Are New Dealers and Collectors Entering the Trade?

Dealers and collectors alike speak of a need to attract new people to the field, not a simple matter in a world dominated by electronic media. As people become more isolated online, finding personal connections is key.

Kenneth Andersen, Sporting and General Antiquarian Books, Middlebury, Vermont:

Q: Where do you find collectors who don't frequent the ABAA shows?

KA: When I first started out in the seventies, I used to do quite a few sportsmen's shows in the greater Boston area and I still do some. Again, this might sound elitist, but these aren't shows for book people. These are attended by people interested in fishing and field sports who come to the shows to visit a variety of items related to the sport they enjoy. So it's a pretty good test of their level of interest.

When I started out, the nice man who runs the show said he had many requests for a limited number of booths, but I was bringing books and that was interesting to him, so he let me in.

And people would buy these books—admittedly inexpensive ones—at $10, $15, $25. They would push each other to get at them because they knew about them. They'd say, "My grandfather put me on his knee and told me about this book." They had the tradition and knew the authors.

One woman found a book she wanted; she literally jumped straight up and shouted, "Wow!"

Now, I do the same kind of show twenty-five or thirty years later. People walk by and look at the books and say, "That's work. Reading is what we do in school. I'm not interested."

People have no experience of reading the books now. If they're interested in fly tying, they prefer to learn from a video. They don't want to read a book about it anymore. In twenty or thirty years, the whole nature of the discourse has changed.

Q: Are new book lovers coming into the industry, then, along with the online traders?

KA: Many people are moving away from the standard industry. Many longtime dealers are not buying newer books any longer. They buy very early travel, very rare and esoteric items that weren't printed in numbers that would allow them to show up on the Internet in numerous iterations.

Often dealers have moved toward original art, etchings, and ephemera to round out their stock, selling material that lends itself to one-of-a-kind items or more rare items that don't show up in great numbers online.

When I started years ago, I used to visit a number of book dealers regularly. Many were in the Back Bay section of Boston. That aspect, visiting bookshops, is one way that people became interested in books and learned about books.

Visiting shops, they could find a $2 book, pick it up, hold it, read it. They might think, "I'd like to see some more from this author." They would find another for $5, and another, and over a period of time, they would be collecting books or authors they liked and buying $200 or $300 books.

This is how book lovers get into it. You get into it by holding books in your hand, by looking at them, examining them, by the treasure hunt of finally finding the book you want on a bookstore shelf. And unfortunately, in this country, that is going by the way.

Marie believes that attracting new collectors and creating new bibliophiles to carry on the traditions should be high on the agenda of today's antiquarian book world. As with so many esoteric interests of the past, the population is aging and new blood is not entering the field in as large numbers as in the past. She believes creating book events designed for children, with new and old books featured, can bring the experience of books to young people and help raise the next generation of bibliophiles.

Go into the schools and libraries, she advises the bookseller, and bring the experience and excitement of books to the kids. She's done it in the past, and the response was exactly what she hoped it would be: interest and awe.

Collectors have historically been drawn to books they have experience with or books that represent high points in their profession. As modern culture moves away from a focus on books, perhaps the emphasis needs to shift from the familiar to the historic—from books that were revered in youth to books that helped to shape the world.

Perhaps the new generation of antiquarian bibliophiles will be drawn in large part from the legion of online booksellers who are now in their apprenticeship in this changing industry.

– 3 –
COLLECTING IN GENRES

All the world knows me in my book and my book in me.

—Michele de Montaigne

The collector learns about collecting by collecting. So advises John Winterich in his enter-taining book, *A Primer of Book Collecting,* published in 1926. We think his sage words ring as true today as they did when he wrote them.

There is much to learn and it is best learned through hands-on experience.

"But what will I collect?" so many ask. That depends on what attracts your attention. Why do you find yourself buying books in the first place?

You may be interested in picking up items for your own collection or you may be on the hunt for books to sell. You may look for titles based on your favorite authors, on fine bind-ings, or on topics of special interest to you. These are some of the ways we define the myr-iad genres among collectible books—genres like medicine, mysteries, science fiction, modern first editions, and the like. Many collectors limit their attention to a specific genre. In this chapter, we will provide an introduction to some of the more commonly known genres.

Earlier books on collecting emphasized literature and specific writers, along with books of incunabula, which is the term for books printed before the year 1501. We don't want to go into a sociological analysis here, but suffice it to say that tastes have changed since writers like Henry James were in demand. Certainly there are still collectors of Mr. James, but today's collector is more apt to go for the late 20th century writers—Larry McMurtry, Joyce Carol Oates, Henry Miller, Tobias Wolff, and a host of other commendable writers. We do not want to leave the impression that many of the earlier writers are not collectible, but let's say the audience for them has slimmed down.

While some once-popular authors have been abandoned by today's markets, still others continue to interest the collector down through the decades. Any title by Hemingway, Faulkner, Fitzgerald, Steinbeck, Crane, Harte, or Virginia Woolf will certainly attract collectors. Along with these old venerables have been added the masters of mystery, science fiction, children's literature, science, exploration, and others, many of which we will address in this chapter.

The number of titles and authors that cross over genres are legion. Arthur C. Clarke, August Derleth, Theodore Sturgeon, Jules Verne, Ray Bradbury—these are only a few of the top science fiction writers who also swell the list of today's collectible literary authors and modern first editions.

Clearly, the topic of collectible genres can fill a book of its own. In these pages, we provide an introduction to the subject, some discussion provided by specialists in the fields, and list some of the most collectible authors and titles, those the fledgling book enthusiast is likely to find. If collecting in specific genres is your primary interest, we urge further research and study, and provide some suggested reading.

Modern First Editions

Today, one of the top genres for collecting is modern first editions. If any area of book collecting is in danger of falling victim to fads, this is it. Modern first editions prove the fact that a book can be published in the past year or two and already have a collectible price affixed.

Sue Grafton's crime novels, for example, have been popular with collectors of modern first editions over the past two decades. Her first book, *"A" is for Alibi*, published in 1982 (NY. Holt Rinehart &Winston), can be found at prices ranging from $75 to $100 for later printings of the first edition, to as much as $800 for a true first edition, and $1,500 or more for signed or presentation copies.

But interest in her books waxes and wanes, especially those titles further down the alphabet. *"F" is for Fugitive* (NY. Holt. 1989) is listed at $30–$50 for a first edition, $150–$350 if signed. *"Q" is for Quarry* (NY. Putnam. 2002) can be had for $12 to $25 for a good early copy, $100 for a signed first edition. Whether Grafton will remain collectible fifty years from now remains to be seen.

Kathryn Smiley, editor, *Firsts* magazine:

Q: What advice do you have for someone just starting out looking for first editions?

KS: We advise someone just starting out, first and foremost, to collect what you love. Book collecting for investment is not a great idea, particularly modern books because it's difficult to predict which ones will be popular down the line.

For instance, you can pick up a popular book from the 1940s and look at the back cover where the publisher lists upcoming hot titles. Chances are you will have heard of very

Clair Bee, *Home Run Feud* (Chip Hilton series #22), Grosset & Dunlap, 1964, in original binding with pictorial cover. This title is the last one listed inside, indicating a first edition.

few of them. As with every other pursuit, book collecting has currents. Right now, hot titles, not authors, are drawing premium prices in first editions.

Q: You mean some modern first editions are collectible but other titles by the same author are not particularly valued?

KS: Yes. For example, a Marjorie Rawlings. She wrote *The Yearling* and that book is highly prized. (NY. Scribner's Sons. 1938. 1st ed. dj. $400–$1,000. Signed and special editions go into the thousands.) Several other titles of hers are also prized. But others, it wouldn't matter a darn if you had them, no one would want them. So, it's not merely the name of the author; it's the particular book.

Q: Collecting all of one author's work, or a particular type of book, is not necessarily a good investment, then? Is there ever a reason to do that?

KS: There are areas where a complete collection is important because there are different philosophies of collecting. There are those we call "completists" and there are those who collect "high spots"—important works in literature or in a subject. It's difficult to predict down the line what will affect the value of your collection, but hopefully you're not just in it for the money.

Let me say offhand that all collectors are aware of the value of their collection. That's not something that we turn up our nose at, but hopefully it's not the primary reason for creating a collection.

Q: Do some people purchase several copies of books by new and popular authors, hoping the name and title will rise to collectible status?

KS: Yes, but it's a risk. There's a funny sideline to that. It means that very recent books by major publishers are unlikely to become collectible over time because people take very good care of them and there are many more found in very good condition, which affects the market!

The true first editions (underline and exclamation point!) of the Harry Potter books are highly prized, especially the first book, which was released before the series became well known. (Note: J. K. Rowling. *Harry Potter and the Sorcerer's Stone*. Scholastic Press. 1998. First U.S. Edition. Copies were offered at prices ranging from $300–$400 for book club editions with jackets in 2007. From $900–$1,200 for an as-new first printing. Signed copies were offered from $1,700–$2,500. There is no telling how these prices will hold ten or twenty years down the line. They may increase, or enthusiasts may have moved on by then to the next new thing.)

Book collecting, like every other collectibles market, is driven by supply and demand.

If you have a large number of copies of a collectible title in beautiful condition, you'd release one every couple of years.

(Note: Many dealers and collectors mentioned that television programs like *The Antiques Road Show*, and online sites like eBay have encouraged people to think they have treasures languishing in an attic or basement. Some people do, but more often what they have is important to them but to few others. Or people may tend to inflate the value of their property and are disappointed when they find their item has sentimental significance, but not dollar value.)

Q: How do you know if you have a true first edition?

KS: One of the biggest misconceptions people coming into the first editions market bring with them, either from a selling or buying point of view, is that identifying a first edition from any era is an automatic thing, that it's easy, or that it is consistent.

Publishers have never been consistent in the way that they identify first editions. The reason for that is, it's an accounting procedure for them, and first edition identification itself is not of primary importance and it never has been.

Different publishers will identify first editions in different ways in different eras. There are even publishers who have put out editions in different months with different ways of identifying first editions. It isn't an automatic thing, and it isn't an easy thing. It's something you have to learn.

There are guide books, but there is not one guide book that covers all the ins and outs. It's that esoteric, particularly for books from the earlier part of the last century.

(Note: Information on guides to identifying first editions is included in the References and Resources appendix.)

With very modern books it's a little easier, but for books published in the earlier part of the 20th century, there are some you have to take on a title-by-title case. Besides the fact that the publishers were inconsistent, there are what are called "points of issue"—a typo or piece of broken type, or the publisher ran out of manufacturing materials midway through the press run and used a different color or quality of paper or cloth.

This shouldn't put anybody off. It's lots of fun to learn how to identify first editions. But it also means you have to be twice as careful when you're buying books from a bookseller you don't know, particularly on the Internet, because lots and lots of instant booksellers have climbed onto the bandwagon and some of them don't know—I'll give them that—they just don't know what they're doing. And some of them don't care.

Someone unfamiliar with books may see a premium price online and think, "Well, I've got that book and it looks really nice. I'll put the same price on it." But they don't know if their copy is a first or not.

We just received a book—not an expensive one—it was a book club edition with a later impression dust wrapper. It said "Book Club" on the book and the dust wrapper said "second impression," but it was mistakenly sold as a first edition in dust jacket on the Internet. And yet all the seller had to do was look at it; there are red flags all over it.

Q: Do publishers design different dust jackets for different editions?

KS: Yes. In some cases, differences in the dust jacket are included in the points that determine edition, and switching jackets from one copy to another can cloud that issue. At times, people will "marry" a dust jacket from one volume to another of the same title.

Marrying a copy means taking a dust wrapper off one book and putting it on another—which is perfectly OK within your own collection. If I buy a collectible book and I find a copy later that has a much nicer dust jacket but is a lesser quality book, I'll marry the copy. I'm not a bookseller, except to weed out a personal book collection, and then I only sell to booksellers to avoid a conflict of interest with the magazine, but if I intend to sell a book with a dust jacket and it's a married copy, I'll say so.

In many cases, it doesn't matter to the buyer as long as the jacket and book are within the same edition and issue, but I feel that I should be very forthright about that. That's how I want to buy books, so that's how I want to sell books.

Q: Why is identifying firsts from the 19th century so different from the 20th century? You said manufacturing had changed. How?

KS: Some of the manufacturing process unwittingly created the "points of issue" for many books.

If you think about books today, the publisher orders from the printer, and the printer has huge presses and huge stocks of material. They manufacture books in line. They're by and large done in one place, printed and sent to the bindery department, and then the dust jackets are put on.

In the 19th century, they didn't have that sort of manufacturing facility. Also selling books was a different process. For instance, the Mark Twain books were sold by subscription. They would announce a title and people would write in and order the book.

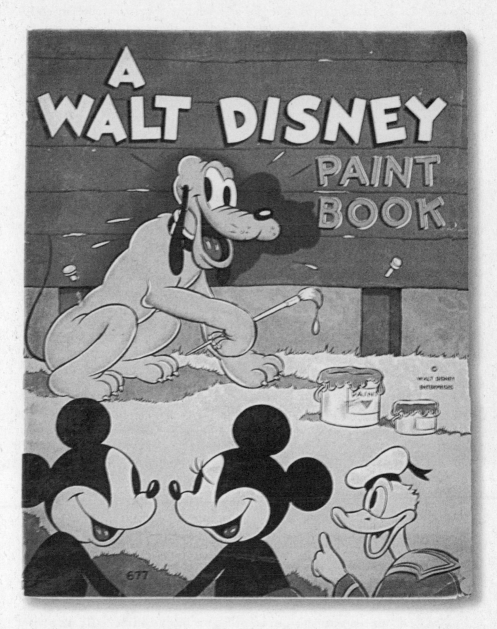

A Walt Disney Paint Book, folio, circa 1940s–50s.
Collectible coloring books like this are more valuable
if the pages have not been colored in. Many Disney
items were published by Whitman of Racine,
Wisconsin.
*Digital photography by Jonathan Draudt, Tamarac
Arts.*

They'd say, "OK, we have orders for 468 copies," so they might print enough sheets for 500 books, or if they were feeling optimistic, they'd do a thousand sets [of pages]. But they'd bind up 468 copies.

If they got another lot of 200 orders, they'd bind up some more and some more. Well, somewhere in there, they might run out of printing materials, or binding cloth, and the next lot would be a little different.

Or the publisher might say, "Hey, before you bind up any more of those, I have a new set of ads to go in the back." So they'd print up the new set of ads and insert them. Things were done on a much more bit-by-bit basis.

Each change created what are called different "states." And sometimes you get what is called a "mixed state." For instance the publisher might have some new ads but he still had some of the old binding cloth.

For instance, there's *Huckleberry Finn,* bound in blue cloth and green cloth. People who had the *Tom Sawyer* in blue wanted their *Huck Finn* in the same color as their *Tom*. The two colors are considered the same edition—they were issued simultaneously—but the blue cloth was specially ordered and there were fewer of them bound, so it's scarcer.

People think there was some sort of mystique to these things, but by and large it had to do with the manufacturing process. Today as before, that is a factor. Multiple covers of a first edition are a new marketing idea for modern books. At times, there are preferences for one cover over another, but that changes from book to book.

Q: There is a great deal of esoteric information to learn, isn't there? Can you talk about some other examples?

KS: In one of Laurie R. King's books (Note: King has written several series mysteries, including her second book *The Beekeeper's Apprentice*, St. Martin's, 1994, based on the character of Sherlock Holmes in retirement. In 2007, $150–$200 for first edition; $300–$450 signed.) There is a dedication written in Hebrew and you can tell the genuine first edition, first state of that book because the dedication was printed backwards. So the second state is the exact same book except they corrected that page. Unless you know what Hebrew is supposed to look like, you wouldn't know to look for it.

Snow Falling on Cedars is a recent collectible book, not that expensive. I believe on the dust jacket it had the character's name misspelled the first time around. That's a point of issue. (David Guterson, *Snow Falling on Cedars,* 1994; this author's first novel, about the World War II Japanese internment in the United States, was a literary sensation. Signed first editions list at $200–$450.)

When you go out to buy a first edition, you wouldn't think to check something like that unless the seller told you about it. You're as likely to pick up a second state. It's not a difference of a lot of money, but you could wind up with a book that's not a true first.

Q: How long have you been involved with first editions and publishing your magazine?

KS: For about twenty years, and we've been publishing for seventeen years.

Q: What sort of information do you offer your readers?

KS: We always do a feature on a collectible author. Last month it was Faulkner.

But we don't always do the giants—what we call the Fitz-herni-faulk-steins—Fitzgerald, Hemingway, Faulkner, and Steinbeck, all of whom we love. But we don't necessarily focus on writers of that caliber, although we certainly mention them a lot. But there are so many other wonderful writers, many of whom are in danger of being forgotten. So we have tended to cover a lot more of those than the giants.

Our features are generally a mixture of biography, writing history, and commentary. We talk about their lives and how they produced their books. And there's always a checklist that includes the primary book-length works, the first edition identifiers for those works, and a price range for collectible copies.

Q: Do you write more about collectible titles, or do you concentrate more on authors?

KS: Our magazine includes more than just a featured author. We always run a couple more features, perhaps on a genre or a subgenre, or additional writers. For instance in May, the collected author was William Faulkner, and the second author was his brother, John (Note: novelist, John Faulkner, most famous for his nonfiction written about his brother).

Or we'll have something about book collecting in general. Our most popular column is called "Points" where people can write in with questions about points and other book collecting issues. And then there's "Books Into Film"; that's Robin's column about collectible books and the films that were made from them.

(Note: The magazine also features a Q&A column to which readers can submit questions about a book in hand. Robin Smiley, Kathryn's husband and partner, provides answers and additional resources for continued research.)

Q: Do you and your husband enjoy collecting, as well?

KS: We are collectors, too. There are different types of collectors. Some have a very tightly focused collection. A good anecdote about that is one that a bookseller told us about the Los Angeles ABAA Fair.

A man was going from booth to booth and asking, "Pigeons? Do you have any books about pigeons?" He came to one booth and asked about pigeons and the bookseller said, "No, I don't have any pigeons, but I have some books about chickens." The customer said, "Well, I'll look at them, but my heart won't be in it."

Robin and I are on the other end of the collecting spectrum. We have a lot of American literature, but we also have a lot—boy, do we have a lot—of classic mysteries, Western

The Jungle Book and *The Second Jungle Book*, by **Rudyard Kipling.** London: Macmillan and Co., 1894 and 1895. Books are in dark blue decorated cloth covers with gold gilt images and lettering.

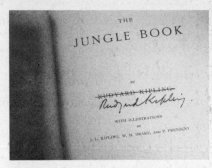

Rudyard Kipling signed this copy of *The Jungle Book* (1894) by crossing out his printed name on the title page and signing his name beneath it.

fiction, and Western Americana. If you look at any issue of our magazine, that's what we're crazed about most recently. We have a core collection and most of it is classic American literature or classic mysteries.

Our peripheral collection, books that come and go, is subject to change. Right now, we're very focused on the ancient world.

Q: As a collector, do you occasionally review your books, cull out items to clear the decks?

KS: We do, but we don't cull out nearly as much as we should. When we moved into our house, we thought, "Ah, shelf space." Now we say, "Where are we going to put everything?"

We have seven storage units, mostly full of books, and some of back issues of the magazine. Our position is that a collection is a living thing. It's an evolving thing. And so, we have what we call our core collection, which are books that will only leave here after we're dead.

They will never, ever leave us, no how. The cats and dogs can starve, the nieces and nephews can drop out of college, but these books will never be sold.

Q: What sort of books reach that status?

KS: My copy of *To Kill a Mockingbird* with a note from Harper Lee in it (Lippincott, 1960, inscribed and rebound, $10,000–$12,000. Near fine in dj, $20,000–$28,000); some Twain. I have a copy of *Invisible Man* with a note from Ralph Ellison (Random House, [1952]. First edition, inscribed, $6,000–$16,000). And various other things. And then a lot of things that are not personalized but that we value personally.

And the next step down are books that will likely stay for some time. And then there are a whole cast of characters that come and go. I'll fall in love with a writer and buy all the books, read them all, and then a few years later there's another writer I need space for. That's when the books will be—carefully—moved to another shelf, if there's room, or—carefully—boxed up and put into storage.

Carefully means in dust jacket protectors and placed in double-sided, double-topped storage boxes, placed in there so they won't shift, and then placed into temperature-controlled storage. I still love them, but I don't love them as much as I once did. But I can't bear to part with them, either. Most collectors have books that they love, and then other books that come and go—their peripheral or secondary collection.

When we got into book collecting a while back, the Harper Lee was the book I wanted. It was $600 at the time. And that was a lot back then. I couldn't get $600 and didn't see how I could spend it on a book.

So, I bought one about five years later for $2,400; that was an outstanding buy at the time. It was a great price made to me by a dear friend. Now, three years ago, I was offered $12,000 cash for it. On some level, I find that obscene, but I wouldn't sell it for any price.

Writers like John Galsworthy, once a popularly collected author, now get scant attention from collectors. The prolific writer Stephen King's first novel, *Carrie*, in first edition with dust jacket, is offered for $900–$2,200 as universities now offer courses on his works, (Note: Stephen King. *Carrie*. Doubleday. 1974. dj. $900–$2,200) and signed copies are offered at $2,500–$7,500. Whether books by Grafton and other popular writers of today like King, Tom Clancy, John Grisham, Ann Tyler, and Anne Rice will have staying power as collectibles remains to be seen.

(Note: Those authors who move into the literature category have the best chance of remaining collectible. Collectors often buy literary modern firsts and put them aside, hoping the authors will be studied, thus sealing their value. Smiley said later books by authors like Stephen King, however, may never be particularly collectible, even though his work is becoming the subject of college courses. His books are issued in such huge press runs, she said, that they will never become scarce enough to gain value on the collectible market.)

Kathryn Smiley, editor, *Firsts* magazine:

Q: Are there authors in the past ten years whose first editions seem to retain collectible interest?

KS: Ten years is way too short a time to know if someone is going to remain in demand. There will be some really wonderful writers working in those ten years. Does that mean they'll endure? Who knows? I wish I had a crystal ball. I wish I had picked up on remainder some of the books that will be collectible in the future.

Here's a great example. Who was the best-selling author of the 19th century, hands down, bar none? You'll never guess it. Her name was Marie Corelli. She wrote many novels. And actually, I've never read a word she wrote.

(Note: Corelli is the nom-de-plume—pseudonym, or pen name—of Mary Mackay, a colorful 19th century figure in cultural and literary circles. She wrote fanciful and highly plotted stories, often with occult themes. She was lionized by the public in her era and then faded from view. Born in Scotland, 1855, she died in 1924. Some of her titles, especially the early ones, are still collected; for example, *The Secret Power*, London, Methuen, 1921, $50–$145.)

Her name disappeared from the public scene and she's not well known any longer. You see her books listed, but I've never really dipped into one. There is an example of trying to predict who will be collectible.

There are wonderful writers producing work today. There's a guy named Chris Offutt who is just terrific. I don't know if he's got a publisher currently. There's the other problem: the publishing industry. Between bottom-lining and mergers, large publishers lack literary vision. Although to be fair, Maxwell Perkins used to complain in his time. He would say that if someone brought in the Old Testament, publishers would cut it by half.

Perkins was a preeminent editor of the 20th century. Working for Scribner's in the early and mid-century, he introduced writers like F. Scott Fitzgerald and Ernest Hemingway to the literary scene. Notably, he brought the works of Thomas Wolfe to light. He became a close friend of Wolfe's and was the executor of his estate. He edited and published Wolfe's final two books, *The Web and the Rock* and *You Can't Go Home Again,* after Wolfe's death.

In addition to noted titles mentioned by Smiley, there are cases like the first edition of Raymond Chandler's 1939 mystery, *The Big Sleep*, introducing the character of detective Philip Marlowe. In a near perfect dust jacket, the book sold for $7,150 in 1992, more than twice what experts had estimated it would bring. By 1996, experts were setting the price closer to $5,000. In the year 2004, the book with its dust jacket was offered for $9,000–$17,000 on the Internet. The difference in price is due to the book's condition. Considered a classic in the genre for its era, *The Big Sleep* was dramatized in a movie starring Humphrey Bogart as detective Philip Marlowe.

Was it exposure that brought the price of that book up? What really sets the pace for what a book is worth? We suspect that whimsy has a lot to do with it. On the other hand, *The Big Sleep* is considered by many to be a literary classic, having crossed over from the mystery genre.

This is the way it is with modern first editions. Books may become classics—part of the popular culture, most notably through movies these days—or they are recognized as literature and are studied in the classroom, and thus their value climbs. Or they pass into oblivion and are relegated to the penny box.

Percy Muir had a wonderful discussion on the subject in his delightful commentary *Book Collecting as a Hobby*, published first in 1945. He says when a contemporary author is "hot," the demand for first editions will drive up the price. When the demand is satisfied, prices decline. If the author's work has lasting substance, collectors will rediscover him and prices will rise again.

Muir cautions, "Never, never collect an author when he is in the height of fashion." He advises anticipating who will be the next to rise, if you can, or waiting until authors have weathered the test of time. We believe this advice remains relevant today.

Kathryn Smiley, editor, *Firsts* magazine:

Q: Do you have some comments on collectible books from independent and small publishing houses? Fine presses? Short run books?

KS: Happily, the situation in large publishing houses, where the bottom line affects the quality of what is produced, has encouraged the rise of some smaller independent publishers who are trying to take up the slack. The whole issue for them now is distribution and advertising. But they are publishing some wonderful writers.

The problem is getting some of these wonderful writers noticed.

I'm glad they exist. Then there are people who collect nothing but fine bindings—books with superior paper and manufacturing qualities. These are collected sometimes by the title and sometimes by which press produces the book.

These enter into the collectible realm as fine press books, but not as first editions. And they must be really special to command higher values, based on a different set of criteria.

(Note: Some fine binding houses include Nonesuch, Clarenden, Stinehour, and Arion.)

Kenneth Andersen, Sporting and General Antiquarian Books, Middlebury, Vermont:

Q: What advice do you have for collectors? What kind of books should they look for?

KA: First of all, collect according to your interest, not according to investment.

Things like that are chancy with books. *The Antiques Road Show* is interesting, but it can give people false expectations. If books don't give you pleasure in and of themselves, I would not suggest that you even bother.

So many people, when you show them something you think is nice, they ask, "What's it worth?" I feel that is a degradation of the product. I think they should turn it around and say, "What is money worth relative to this priceless thing in my hands?"

Literature and books are the way we have transmitted our culture over thousands of years. Even Plato was a collector. He kept tablets of the ancients in a library that he maintained for them. The monks in the Middle Ages transmitted classical knowledge through their writing. They wrote it out in their beautiful books of ink and drawings and kept the traditions going.

The book is a sacred thing. It is our way of transferring what we know from the past to the future. As Winston Churchill said, "If you don't know where you've been you have no idea where you're going." The book tells us where we've been.

Q: Are there some general references for learning about the history of books?

KA: For the collector who wants to focus on the high spots of printing, there's a book called *Printing and the Mind of Man* (Note: John Carter and Percy H. Muir, eds. *Printing and the Mind of Man: A Descriptive Catalogue Illustrating the Impact of Print on the Evolution of Western Civilization during Five Centuries*. 2nd ed. revised and enlarged. London, 1983. $150–$250).

The authors put together a descriptive catalogue related to a museum exhibit of the same name at a British museum held in 1963.

(Note: similarly titled, *Printing and the Mind of Man, Catalogue of an Exhibition Assembled at the British Museum and at Earls Court*. London. F. W. Bridges & Sons, 1963. wraps. $50–$100.)

This work by Carter and Muir is one of the most important books ever published in terms of its effect on culture. There are not too many of them available anymore. Many can be found in university and college libraries these days.

(Note: Carter and Muir have each published numerous reference works highly valued in the world of book collecting. See especially John Carter, *ABC for Book Collectors*, and Percy Muir, *Book Collecting as a Hobby: A Series of Letters to Everyman*.)

Q: Can you explain the attraction of the collectible book to the collector?

KA: You can buy books about the Civil War by Bruce Catton, a product of this generation. There have been many such general summary books and they're very nice and provide good information.

But if you really want to get what Walter Cronkite used to call the "You Are There" experience, you buy Civil War regimentals. Those are written by the individuals in the units. They speak directly to what they did. They're eyewitness accounts of battle.

And so Civil War regimentals are extremely attractive to collectors and they tend to hold their money very well, because they give you this immediacy about the subject.

Now, what is happening is they're being reprinted. I talked to a Civil War dealer recently and he told me he could always get very, very good money for regimentals, but now that they're being reprinted, demand is down.

Which is OK, too, for disseminating that information. It's good for those who are interested in genealogy and history. It brings some of that information to a wider audience who don't need a first edition.

Children's Books

If you are thinking into the future or you're making a list for your children to collect, keep these authors in mind: Brian Jacques, James Marshall, Daniel Pinkwater, Madeline L'Engle, Betsy Byars, Maurice Sendak, and the inimitable Chris Van Allsburg, to mention just a few.

The children's book market is a very active sector in the out-of-print book world, and shows no sign of declining. The Frank Baum *Oz* books, *Uncle Wiggily*, *Mary Frances*, *Palmer Cox's Brownies*, the *Teenie Weenies*, *Arthur Ransom*, and Volland Publishing still have special appeal for collectors and nostalgia buffs. Long-established collectors will gravitate to these books now seen as the classics. Younger collectors will seek out books they grew up with—some of the new names mentioned above—classics of the future.

The world of children's books is wide and varied and contains many subdivisions—picture books, series, chapter, pop-up, toy, fiction, nonfiction, illustrated, and more.

One of the best ways to educate yourself is to read listings offered by dealers who specialize in children's literature. We have space only to skim the surface of this delightful collecting category. So, if your interest in collecting or selling leans toward the whimsical, but you find yourself in a tangled forest with lurking goblins and roads to nowhere, look for a knowledgeable bookseller who can set you on the right path.

Kathleen Roberts, K Roberts Fine Books, Burlington, Vermont:

Kathy Roberts holds a master's degree in library science from the State University of New York at Albany. She was children's librarian at the Fletcher Free Library in Burlington, Vermont, for eight years, and she taught graduate courses in children's, young adult, and multicultural children's literature at Saint Michael's College in Colchester, Vermont, for six years. She has been a bookseller for eight years, specializing in children's literature and decorative cloth bindings.

Q: What got you started down the road to working with antiquarian books?

KR: I began buying children's books at antique shops, books sales, and flea markets as a personal interest in the mid to late 1990s. After a while, I had amassed a fairly large collection of my favorite titles and I realized the books were starting to pile up. When my husband asked what I planned to do with them, I had an epiphany—I was going to sell them. That was in 1998.

I hadn't previously thought in terms of collectible quality or resale, but had been buying books for about five years according to their literary value and my interest in particular titles. I knew the subject matter really well. When I found a book that was in good condition and the subject matter interested me, I bought it.

Having some specialized knowledge based on my library experience, I knew which books were popular and which were out of print, so I would just buy them. Then, of

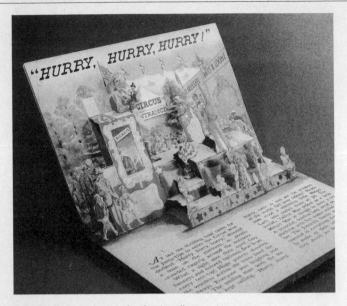

A lovely children's pop-up book. *The Jolly Jump-Ups See the Circus,* from McLoughlin Bros. Inc., Springfield, Mass., 1944. Cardboard construction with six pop-ups, including an image of the famous gorilla "Gargantua." *Digital photography by Jonathan Draudt, Tamarac Arts.*

course, my buying changed because I was now buying for resale. And it has been changing every day ever since.

Q: Describe some of that change?

KR: When I started selling and researching the books, I realized that books that were to me near and dear had almost no resale value because there were thousands of them out there. They were very common. For example, *Julie of the Wolves,* a Newbery Medal winner by Jean Craighead George. The Newbery Medal is the Pulitzer of the children's world. When a book like this wins the award, they print many thousands of copies. It never goes out of print. (Jean Craighead George. *Julie of the Wolves.* NY. Harper & Row. 1972. Used later printings and editions, $5.00–$10.00. First edition with dj, $100.00–$150.00. First edition, dj, sgn, $200.00–$300.00).

In the beginning, I was not looking at whether something was fourteenth printing, twenty-second printing—I wasn't paying attention to that. But when I went to sell used books, I realized they had little monetary value. Anyone could go to Barnes & Noble and buy a brand new one. The market for used copies in pristine condition was almost nil. Most copies of such popular books were only going to gain value in the used market if the title went out of print, and then copies were going to be valued at a very small amount because they'd been published so widely.

It was at that point that I really started learning the antiquarian book business. I realized that I had the content knowledge in children's books—I knew the Greenaways and the Caldecotts—but I knew nothing about selling and buying for the antiquarian market. I had been a librarian all of my life. As a librarian your goal is to stamp it, put a cover on it, and put it out there. If it comes back dirty, clean it off and keep it going for a few more circulations.

Whereas in the antiquarian market, you want the condition of that book to be as if no one ever touched it, like it just came out of the box and has been wrapped in tissue paper ever since. So, I learned very quickly about condition. And I learned about scarcity. I educated myself as much as I could, reading books on the subject. I wasn't looking at just children's books in terms of learning about rare book selling. I wanted to know about first editions, and to learn about book identification, research tools, bibliographies.

Q: You were changing your view of these books, going from reader and fan to appreciating them on a whole new level.

KR: In terms of the children's book market, I started as a collector. Traditionally, children's book collectors have loved the Caldecotts, the Greenaways, Rackhams, Neilsen, and other illustrators. Illustrators are the stars of the children's book world. Books like those by turn-of-the-century British and American writers—Beatrix Potter, for example. When you study antiquarian children's books—selling them—that's where the emphasis lies, on classical children's literature.

But my experience has been that, in the children's book world, people tend to collect what they have an emotional attachment to—either something that was read to them as a child, or something that was passed down to them that a grandparent loved and they grew to love. Or a book that they read to their own children. Somehow, there's that emotional attachment.

But those people who had the Caldecotts and the Rackhams passed down to them are no longer with us. So with each new generation, the demand changes. I don't have a great deal of success selling Greenaways and Caldecotts. I have them in good condition, but that is certainly not the bulk of what I sell.

A perfect example is a young man who called me to ask about a copy of *The Lorax* that I'd listed. He's collecting Dr. Seuss because he grew up with Dr. Seuss. I hear from a great many people who want books from the 1950s, 1960s, and 1970s. When you go back before that, the market doesn't necessarily go down in the value of the book, but the number of people who are looking for the book declines.

What you have then, in terms of the chapbooks, the nineteenth century chromolithographs, and Victorian children's books—they're stunning and I've listed many online, but I don't know when I'm going to sell those books. Very few copies are available, but the market comes down to a very specialized collector.

A copy of an early printing of Rudyard Kipling's *Just So Stories* (1902) showing red cloth boards decorated with black-and-white illustrations by Kipling.

The same is true of African American children's literature—Black literature. There will always be a market for this genre, but it is becoming highly specialized. I remember when I first started out, I could always sell a *Little Black Sambo,* but now it will take longer to find a buyer. Dealers in Black literature are well supplied with such stock now and don't snap them up the way they once did. The collectors of Black children's literature have become better educated in the market and are more selective about what they buy now.

Q: What titles and authors do you see now becoming popular?

KR: Tasha Tudor at the moment is almost cultlike. There is a mystique about Tudor and you know if you pick one up, it will sell. That will most likely continue. If one of her titles is out of print, any copy in good condition is going to sell. The first editions are especially high.

Q: How do you determine the edition and whether or not a Tasha Tudor title is out of print?

KR: The Hares' bibliography will tell you (William John Hare and Pricilla Hare. *Tasha Tudor: The Direction of Her Dreams: The Bibliography and Collector's Guide.* Oak Knoll Press). You need a bibliography to really determine what you have, although many are stated first editions.

Q: What do collectors in this genre look for most now?

KR: In the children's book world, I have found that the illustrators and the illustrations are primarily sought after, rather than books by a particular author. This specialty is a visual medium. I can step back from that and say that *Oz* books, Baum books, are excellent sellers. There is always a high-end interest in the *Wizard of Oz* books.

But, in my experience, I don't necessarily exhibit at a lot of book shows. I believe that the children's booksellers who sell on the show circuit are selling older books, more of the classical children's literature than is sold in the online world. I think those are two very different selling venues. The collector is going to a book show hoping to find that unique book. That person is going to be interested in the tactile experience, is going to be knowledgeable, and more demanding.

Q: Do you sell more in a certain area of children's literature? For instance, young adult, chapter books, Read-to-Me books?

KR: I do them all. I find that the illustrated books are the best sellers. Picture books are now being published for young adults—it's a wide range.

I do sell a fair amount of children's fiction. Here's a case in point, Roald Dahl—*Charlie and the Chocolate Factory, James and the Giant Peach, Fantastic Mr. Fox.* Roald Dahl is always very desirable. But they've all been reissued in new dust jackets, and collectors want the dust jacket they're familiar with from the 1970s, so I sell a fair amount of Dahl in the original dust jacket. (Roald Dahl. *James and the Giant Peach.* London. George Allen & Unwin. 1967. First UK edition. dj. $350–$400; NY. Alfred A. Knopf. 1961. First edition. dj. $750–$1,500. Later editions are numerous in used book listings from $5.00–$40.00.)

The same is true of Madeleine L'Engle's *A Wrinkle in Time* (1962). For the books in Laura Ingalls Wilder's *Little House on the Prairie* series, we all think of the illustrations by Garth Williams. But few people know that Helen Sewell and Mildred Boyle did illustrations when the books were first published. Those jackets are very, very rare. That would be a classical collector's book—high end. (Note: Books in the Little House series are often listed with illustrator Helen Sewell preceding author Laura Ingalls Wilder's name. *Little House in the Big Woods*. NY. Harper Bros. 1932. First edition in very good condition. Illustrated by Sewell. $3,000. Typical later editions sell for $15.00–$50.00.)

Whereas for *Little House on the Prairie* with the Garth Williams illustrations—there is much more of a demand for those because those people are Boomers like me who read them all in those jackets from the 1950s and 1960s, though the prices for them are not as steep. (*Little House on the Prairie*. NY. Harper & Row. 1953. illustrated by Garth Williams. $20.00.) Garth Williams also did illustrations for E. B. White's *Charlotte's Web* and *Stuart Little*.

Q: You've been in the field for ten years. How have the various areas of children's books held up over that time?

KR: Children's series books once had a strong market, but that has been influenced by eBay and online selling. As the numbers of volumes listed has increased, the prices have dropped. This is an area in which buyers aren't necessarily looking for the original dust jackets that accompanied the first editions. There's now a market in the $15 to $40 range for series books with later dust jackets or covers, and a smaller market for prized early printings in original jackets at the $50 to $100 range.

I still do well with *Uncle Wiggily* books. Tasha Tudor titles and illustrations are wildly popular and can sell at several price points from modest to high.

Q: Can you name some other authors, illustrators, or titles that are currently collectible?

KR: Edward Gorey stories and illustrations are popular in children's and adult books. Dr. Seuss books (Note: Dr. Seuss is the pen name of Theodore Seuss Geisel. See the illustrated resource to Dr. Seuss's bibliography: Helen and Marc Younger and Dan Hirsch. *First Editions of Dr. Seuss Books: A Guide to Identification*. Saco, Me. Custom Communications, 2002. ltd 1000 cc. sgn. $150–$200).

Pop-up books and movable books sell well, but they must be in *pristine* condition. A society sprang up during the 1990s around these books, founded by Ann Montanaro, the head librarian at Rutgers University, who put together an exhibit of these titles. (Note: For information on pop-up and movable titles, see Peter Haining. *Movable Books: An Illustrated History*. London. New English Library Limited. 1979. $125–$150; and Ann R. Montanaro. *Pop-up and Movable Books: A Bibliography*. Metuchen, N.J. Scarecrow Press. 1993. $90–$200).

Maurice Sendak is very, very popular and collectible—his own books and those he's associated with, for instance books for which he has written forewords or has done the illustration for other writers. His collectors want his work in all its forms.

(Note: The first book illustrated by Sendak was by Maxwell Leigh Eidinoff. *Atomics for the Millions*. NY. McGraw Hill. 1947. 1st edition. $700–$1,200. His most famous illustrated children's book, *Where the Wild Things Are*. NY. Harper & Row. 1963. First printing in first issue dj. $10,000–$18,000)

The Nancy Drew series—many in the original printing with the "digger endpapers" are popular (Note: Illustration shows Nancy hiding behind a tree while a man digs a hole in the ground). Price points for the titles are similar in all bindings, except for first editions, which are higher. Some collectors seek titles in all variant bindings. (Note: New series titles, reprints, and updates of old titles have continued in publication from 1930 to the present. Careful bibliographic research is necessary to determine edition and value. The first Nancy Drew title written for the Stratemeyer Syndicate by Mildred W. Benson, under the series pseudonym Carolyn Keene, was *The Secret of the Old Clock*. NY. Grossett and Dunlap.1930. Later editions are listing for $12–$40. First editions ask $40–$50).

I now include scans of my books with the listings so collectors can compare the books to others offered online.

With numerous copies of children's series books like the Nancy Drews, Chip Hiltons, and Dana Girls in circulation, learning the finer points of the genre becomes a necessity in order to distinguish between a clean early copy or first edition and a later printing. Typical of series books, the earliest titles were re-released each time a new title came out, meaning numerous editions of these books were printed. Titles that appeared later in the series saw fewer reprints and consequently, fewer copies are now available. To determine whether you have a first edition of a series book, look inside where a list of all the titles in the series is featured. If the book you have in hand is last on that list, then you probably have one of the first or earliest printings of that title. If it had been reprinted along with the next installment in the series, it wouldn't be last on the list inside.

Children's book specialist Donna Howard of St. Albans, Vermont, described her experience selling to a buyer who was accustomed to picking up titles on eBay: "We sold a science fiction first edition recently. It was a collectible, but the person had been buying on eBay. He bought a first edition from us, but he'd picked up a number of book club editions online and wanted ours to be similarly priced. There's a lot of that happening now."

Howard noted that identifying a book club edition is not usually difficult. Book club dust jackets are not printed with a price on them, for a start. And they often don't have composition covers. It's not that hard to work out which are the book club editions and which ones aren't. Most book club editions don't have prices in them. Most don't have composition covers (illustrated, high quality), which are more expensive to produce.

Children's, History, Science Fiction, Reader's Digest, Doubleday—such book clubs typi-cally release books in dust jackets that do not carry prices. Some book clubs issue books with a blindstamp somewhere on the cover, and often the quality of paper or workmanship in a book club edition doesn't rise to the level of the trade editions.

Howard recommended *A Pocket Guide to Identification of First Editions,* by Bill McBride, which includes various methods for identifying book club volumes. She said no consistent patterns exist for identifying first editions of children's books, and publishers have their own conventions. Often Random House, for example, puts publication information at the back of a book instead of on the title or copyright page, letting readers get right into the story when they open the covers.

Separate bibliographies are available for various series books—girls series, boys series, Nancy Drew. And some author bibliographies are available—for Tasha Tudor, see Gary J. Overmann, *Bibliography and Price Guide to Books Illustrated by Tasha Tudor.* Ohio: Books of the Ages. 1998. ltd 90 cc, sgn by Tudor and Overman.

E. Lee Baumgarten compiled the *Price Guide and Bibliographic Check List for Children's and Illustrated Books 1880–1970*, West Virginia: Baumgarten Books, 2004. See also, Mattson and David. *A Collector's Guide to Hardcover Boys' Series Books 1872–1993.* Newark, Del. Mad Book Co.

For Golden Books, see *Tomart's Guide to Golden Books.*

Science Fiction, Horror, Fantasy

Science fiction and fantasy are often grouped together under the rubric of fantastic litera-ture, though the genre admits to numerous subgenres.

Occasionally, books that fall within these genres may also be included in mystery and even modern first edition genres. Some have even achieved the status of literary classics—witness the likes of Robert Heinlein's *Stranger in a Strange Land* (Putnam, 1961. First edition points. $2,500–$6,000), Arthur C. Clarke's *2001* (New American Library. 1968. $500–$700; signed or presentation, $900–$2,000), and works by Theodore Sturgeon, Ray Bradbury, Jules Verne, Edgar Rice Burroughs, H. P. Lovecraft, August Derleth, Edgar Allan Poe, Ambrose Bierce, Isaac Asimov, and Kurt Vonnegut.

Frank Herbert's books about the planet Dune enjoy a mystique that lures fans and book collectors alike. And horror master Stephen King is said to be the most collected living au-thor, especially his early books, including *Carrie,* which was his first novel and the first among many to become a major motion picture.

First editions in excellent condition with dust jackets of his other early books, *Salem's Lot, The Shining, Night Shift* and *The Stand,* are also sought by collectors of his work.

By way of comparison, though incredibly popular with movie fans, Star Wars books have been issued in such great numbers that they have not yet achieved status on the collectible

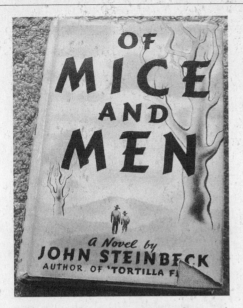

First edition copy of John Steinbeck's *Of Mice and Men*, Covici Fried, 1937, in dust-faded and torn dust jacket. This book realized $2,000.00 at auction in 2007.

A copy of a first edition of John Steinbeck's *Of Mice and Men*, 1937, in fine condition. This volume with the original dust jacket was sold in 2007 for $2,000.00.

market. The same can be said for most Star Trek titles, except for a few of those published as Bantam paperbacks in the 1970s, written by established science fiction writers.

Lloyd Currey, L. W. Currey, Inc., Elizabethtown, New York; online at www.lwcurrey.com:

LWC: This genre includes anything that falls into the category of being fantastic in one way or another. My particular specialty—what I most like to deal in—is early material, pre-1940.

The modern material is of less interest to me after nearly fifty years in the business. So, as best I can, I am handling the material that I like and that sophisticated customers are interested in buying.

Q: What titles should sellers and collectors be aware of, and how can new people begin to navigate this genre?

LWC: The best way to learn which titles are of interest is to consult bibliographies. First, identify which period you're interested in and then go from the very general to the more specific. The very general would start out with something like Reginald's *Science Fiction and Fantasy Literature*, published by Gale Research Company, 1979, in two volumes. Additional supplements have been added since 1979.

The first series covers books from 1700 to 1974. A supplement, also published by Gale in 1992, covers books published from 1975 through 1991 and adds missed items from the earlier period. The combined volumes list more than 37,500 fiction and non-fiction books.

Another is Bleiler's *Checklist of Fantastic Literature* that originally came out in 1948, with a revised edition that came out in 1978 (Note: Everett F. Bleiler, *The Checklist of Fantastic Literature*, Shasta Pub., 1948. Bleiler also published numerous anthologies of science fiction and fantastic literature as well as other guides to the genre).

Those two books comprise the entry-level checklists and comprehensive book bibliographies, by no means complete, but they are the listings that one would start out with. After that you get more specific.

Your next step depends on what you're trying to do. My bibliography, for instance, identifies first editions. (Lloyd W. Currey. *Science Fiction and Fantasy Authors: A Bibliography of First Printings of Their Fiction and Nonfiction.* 1979; revised CD-ROM edition, 2001.)

As far as bibliographies are concerned, Reginald and Bleiler are the most comprehensive. Beyond that, if someone wanted to study science fiction and learn more about its background, the best book would be a specialized encyclopedia. There's an encyclopedia of science fiction edited by John Clute and Peter Nicholls, published by St. Martin's Press and Orbit in England. It's also available on CD-ROM. (John Clute and Peter Nicholls, editors. *The Encyclopedia of Science Fiction.* New York. St. Martin's Press. 1993. second edition, revised and expanded.)

The revised edition is an update and considerable expansion of the 1979 edition. It contains over 4,300 entries, 1,500 more than the original. Clute produced a companion volume along with a guy by the name of Grant. (John Clute and John Grant. *The Encyclopedia of Fantasy.* New York. St. Martin's Press. 1996; published by Orbit in 1997.) These two books—each one of them is huge—have entries for authors, for subjects, and for motifs like "lost race." Or "Hungarian science fiction." If you want to look up Hungarian science fiction, there's an article on that.

Michael Burgess wrote the *Reference Guide to Science Fiction, Fantasy, and Horror* (Englewood, Colo. Libraries Unlimited. 1992). This is a comprehensive guide to secondary sources for the study of these genres.

Burgess's work covers individually published monographs, excluding magazines or dissertations. In twenty-eight sections, he provides extensive analysis of a large body of reference material from descriptive bibliographies to short pamphlets and leaflets. It is an essential guide to monographic reference material on fantastic literature. Plus it's a general bibliography of scholarship and research in the field. You can go to an entry, for example, and find all of the best bibliographic and critical studies that exist in the field you're working on.

For instance, mystery fiction is one of the areas of literature that has been literally studied to death. There are more books on science fiction and fantasy probably than on any other genre except English literature as a whole, and mystery comes along as the second most studied genre in literature.

There is also an international guide that covers basically European material. The authors include articles about the various bibliographies available and information about all sorts of other source material. For example, you can look me up in Clute and Nicholls' *Encyclopedia of Science Fiction* and there's a listing of the things that I've done.

For foreign-language works, see Pierre Versins' *Encyclopedie de l'Utopie,des Voyages Extraordinaires, at de la Science Fiction.* (Lausanne: L'Age d'Homme [1972].) It's the only non-English-language encyclopedia of science fiction and fantasy literature containing entries on people in the field, as well as historical and critical essays on themes, film, magazines, comics, music, and other topics. It is especially valuable for its strong coverage of fantastic literature published prior to 1900, including critical evaluations of many European works that have not been translated into English.

Q: So this is not a field that is easily accessed by a generalist?

LWC: There's a lot of interest and an incredible amount of material out there that someone would have to digest as a collector. You break it into science fiction and fantasy, and certainly mystery fiction, and those break down into what they call "motifs" or subgenres. Within my field, there are areas like specialty press books such as those published by Arkham House, Gnome Press. They're collected by the book number. Someone buying Arkham House books wants all the books released by that publisher, no matter who the author was.

Q: How far back does the genre of science fiction reach? Are there any titles before the 1800s?

LWC: In science fiction, you get into things like Lost Race, Utopian literature, etc. So when you ask how far back does this work go, it goes as far back as people have been writing things down.

I can't think of anything that could really be called science fiction, at least in the English language, prior to the 1630s. But Lucian wrote *A True History*—there are English translations—several hundred years B.C.

A tale of an interplanetary journey, it's the first one known in the genre. (Note: Lucian of Samosata's *Verae Historiae*, "True Histories," parody adventure stories of his era. The work is a fantastic journey narrative and is widely seen as the earliest example of science fiction in the Western tradition. Modern commentaries on the work are widely available.)

In any event, science fiction goes back a long way. Fantasy goes back to tales in the Bible, because there are stories there. There are things like talking about the end of the world in Revelation, told in fantastic language.

All fantasy goes back to telling stories around the fire, literally. These were ghost stories, stories of strange happenings, imaginary voyages. You can call them tall tales. Someone says, "Boy, have I got a story. You know on the other side of the hill there's a big huge pit and if you walk over the hill, you'll fall into the pit and be consumed by a devil."

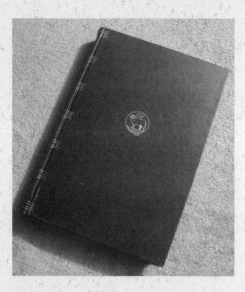

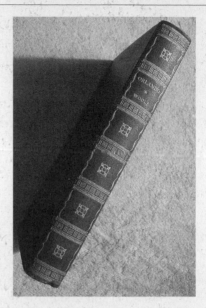

A volume of the first edition of *Orlando* by Virginia Woolf, published by Crosby Gaige, 1928; limited to 861 copies, signed by Woolf.

Spine of first edition of *Orlando* by Virginia Woolf, showing gilt lettering and bands. The book was published by Crosby Gaige, limited to 861 copies, signed by Woolf.

The guy who told the story was the shaman or witch doctor. He wanted people to believe in these supernatural stories as a way of maintaining control over them. This goes back to very ancient cultures. This type of thinking was carried forward into what we now know as modern supernatural horror. The ideas of vampires, ghouls, the undead and all that, go back to these ancient myths.

You can look back at writers like Herman Melville. Most people don't think of him as a fantasy writer, but all of his books are allegorical, and one of them, *Mardi*, is a utopian allegory. After writing two unsuccessful books, he wrote *Mardi*, the forerunner to *Moby Dick*. It's the story of two men who jump ship in the South Seas and have an adventure when they're captured by aborigines. They end up in a Shangri-La, basically (Herman Melville, *Mardi*, NY. Harper.1849. 2 vols. cloth. $2,000–$4,500; London. Bentley. 1849. 3 vols. precedes U.S. edition, author's third book $6,500–$8,000).

Q: Can people new to the field find good books at entry level rates?

LWC: As with most genres, if you know what to look for or where to look, you can find just about anything within reason. Scouts can find a tremendous amount of good books in a bookstore because they're using their knowledge and the seller may not be a specialist.

The only advice that I can give to a new bookseller or collector just starting out is: Do your homework. You have to learn as much about your topic as possible so you can converse knowledgeably with the bookseller. You have a list of books that you're interested in—a "want list." You've done enough of your homework so that you have a grasp of the subject matter. This is a problem for scouts going out to rummage sales to look for good used books. If they don't know what they're looking for, then they'll make a lot of mistakes, buy the wrong thing or miss the right books.

And if they're doing it for a profit motive, they aren't going to succeed.

Collectors should collect what they can afford and they should look for books that interest them, not what is valuable. That is the mistake a lot of new people make. They say, "Oh, well, let's go out and buy some first editions. Let's buy a *Scarlet Letter*. That's a well-known book." When they're in that territory, they're playing with the big boys and they've just got to know what they're doing. (Nathaniel Hawthorne. *The Scarlet Letter.* Boston. Ticknor, Reed, and Fields. 1850. blindstamped brown cloth, rebound. $5,000; original cloth, $12,000.)

I recently had an e-mail from someone who received a gift of a signed copy of Heinlein's *Friday* and they wanted it appraised. (Robert A. Heinlein. *Friday.* NY. Holt Rinehart and Winston [1982]. 1st edition. limited to 500 copies. numbered and signed. slipcase. $300–$650. L. W. Currey also lists a limited edition lettered copy "A"—the only one he has seen.)

They sent me a JPEG picture. It turned out to be a later printing, not the first edition. So, I sent them a note saying the bad news is, it's a later printing; the good news is, it's signed. For an appraisal, I charge a fee.

Q: So you're saying you can't boil it down to a few good books or a few good authors?

LWC: When you set out to tell people what they should look for in collectible books, well, the list is endless. Some of the specifics that you might mention—is the book for everybody, is it a children's book, travel, or any other genre? They should know about Pat and Allen Ahearn's guides to collecting books.

(Among many titles, see Allen and Patricia Ahearn. *Collected Books, the Guide to Values.* Putnam, 2001.)

They can also see Robert Wilson's *Modern Book Collecting* (first edition, 1980, Knopf, dust jacket, $25 used). Reprints are available from 1992. He deals primarily with firsts and talks about what to collect and how to find the books, a pre-Internet guide.

Nicholas Basbanes' *A Gentle Madness* is good reading and educational. What this amounts to is you need some background information to interpret any price, whether it's at auction, or through a bookseller. If you went onto the ABAA Web site and saw who's listing three or four books there, I would be willing to bet the prices would cluster. If I'm pricing an item, I look for a cluster. If you do find ten copies and they're all the same edition and in similar condition, you'll have a cluster of prices at the center that gives you a good idea where the book is actually selling.

Full-time book dealers need to price at a level that will sell. You pretty much can count on it that their prices are somewhere within the realm of reality.

You have to remember, though, that many book dealers have their own regular customers. If I price a book at $1,000, I have placed that book at a level I expect to get for it—perhaps less 10 percent if I sell to a dealer.

Q: Can you talk about how you go about listing a book for sale?

LWC: I can tell you the story of an obscure nonfiction book on the Russo-Japanese War. Two other dealers were listing it. One called it a yellow-peril novel, which it isn't. He was asking about $250 for his copy.

The other dealer ran a military bookstore in England. He was asking $114. His copy was graded "good plus," and I had a better one.

Since it wasn't a book I was interested in keeping until I die, I priced mine at $125, since it was in somewhat better condition than the military specialist's book. I also went to the British Library and found the name of the author—the book was written pseudonymously under the letter "O." Other dealers listed it under the pseudonym.

In any event, I found out who wrote it and found out he was a war correspondent for the London Times. Armed with information, I was able to write a better description than either of the other two dealers, explaining what it was the potential buyer would get.

I highly recommend my ABAA colleagues who work within a strict code of ethics and guidelines, and there are many non-ABAA booksellers who are extremely professional and honorable.

I also recommend that people new to the field read books like John Carter's standard *ABC for Book Collectors*. This book is especially informative because, in addition to a glossary of terms, it physically identifies parts of the book. On the title page, at the bottom, it says "title page." The endpapers are so identified, etc. People interested in books should learn words like "calf" and "vellum" and "octavo."

Our genre has the obvious high spots—first editions of Huxley's *Brave New World*, or Orwell's *1984* and *Animal Farm*. Something that has affected book dealers in recent years has been the reprinting of these high spots of some early writers—Theodore Sturgeon, for instance. This has affected the sale of their work, not the original editions, but the later, mid-level material that was sold to readers in the past.

Q: How does reprinting great works affect the world of collectors?

LWC: When you're dealing in genres, collectors are interested in the work itself, not just in collecting valuable books. You're also dealing with the information that's inside the book. You're buying it because you want to read it.

Without Sorcery—among Theodore Sturgeon's first books—used to go for between $100 and $150 with dust jacket. Many fans might want to read that book but they couldn't or didn't want to spend that kind of money, so they'd have to take a pass. Others would buy it.

Now they don't have to pay that price. They can get a volume of Sturgeon's short stories for $30. For $150, they can get his collected works. Some collectors want the complete works in their library, and they'll buy whatever they can afford to buy. This affects demand, and prices on his firsts are not rising like they might have at one time.

Books by the classic "proto-fantastic" writers like Voltaire, Thomas More's *Utopia*—originals of these books are virtually unobtainable today. (Note: Thomas More's *Utopia*. London. Kelmscott Press. 1893. $2,500–$15,000.) Take, for example, the earliest modern science fiction or modern gothic novel—there's an ongoing quarrel over whether it's gothic or science fiction—consider *Frankenstein*. (Mary Shelley. *Frankenstein or the Modern Prometheus*. London. Colburn and Bentley. 1831. illustrated edition. $10,000–$13,000; 2-vol. Whitaker 2nd edition. 1823, offered for $40,000. Various movie editions of the book are retailing for $200-$500.)

Modern science fiction as we think of it today started in 1871 with several books, one of them *The Battle of Dorking,* a "future war" item. (Sir George Chesney. London. Blackwood. 1st UK edition. wraps. $75–150. The book is the story of a fictitious invasion of England as seen from a time more than fifty years in the future.)

During that period, the Victorian, you start seeing a cluster of recognizable titles. Another was Bulwer Lytton's *The Coming Race* (NY. 1871. utopian fiction. $75–$150). A later obvious Victorian high spot is *Dracula* (Bram Stoker. London: Constable and Company, 1897. 1st edition, points, $8,000–$10,000; inscrb by Stoker, $30,000–$35,000). *Dracula* and *Frankenstein* are probably the two best-known titles; the man on the street recognizes them. They are the 19th-century high spots right on top of the heap. Then it goes on from there.

There are reader's guides for science fiction/fantasy, as well. One of those is Neil Barron's *Anatomy of Wonder* (NY. Bowker. 1976. 1st ed with dust jacket. $35–$60; NY: R. R. Bowker. 1981. 2nd ed. $25–$50; 3rd ed. 1987; 4th ed. 1995). If someone were looking for a list of high spots, that's where you'd find the really important books.

Books like the *Survey of Modern Fantasy Literature* and *Survey of Science Fiction Literature* are of value because they offer useful short critical essays on many books considered key genre works by academics, many of which are classics and collectible.

These types of books, originally published by Bowker or by Salem Press (Frank N. Magill, ed. *Survey of Modern Fantasy Literature*. N.J. Salem Press. 1983. 5 vols, $150; Frank N. Magill and Willis E. McNelly, eds. *Survey of Science Fiction Literature*. N.J. Salem Press. 1979. 5 vols. $200–$375), were aimed at libraries. Basically what they contain are summaries and discussion of content.

Collectors and dealers should understand: Research is the key to genres.

Civil War and Military

Some people categorize wars and subjects relating to the military as *militaria*, but the major conflicts of the United States such as the Revolution, Civil War, and World Wars I and II are also collected as individual genres, the most popular being the Civil War.

Diaries, memoirs, biographies of noted officers, and battles are all grist for the collector's mill. Anything pertaining to the Confederacy is highly sought after and commands good prices.

Two references that include lengthy bibliographies of Civil War collectible books as well as information about the genre are by Tom Broadfoot and Ronald Seagrave. (*Civil War Books, Confederate and Union,* Ronald R. Seagrave, Fredericksburg, Va. Also, *Civil War Books,* Tom Broadfoot, Wilmington, N.C.)

Western Americana

Stories about the winning of the west, from the arduous journeys of pioneering families to the lawlessness of men like Jesse James and his gang have always interested the American public. Memoirs of early gold miners are important research items that show the development of California.

Anything on cowboys, homesteading, Native Americans, the Rocky Mountains, relations with Mexico in border state conflicts, explorations and discoveries—these and many more subjects whet the appetite for collectors of Western Americana.

Some collectible topics, titles, and authors in this genre are listed in the Index of Authors and Titles by Popular Genre.

Fine Bindings

Fine bindings—that is, leather-bound books with gold-tooled cover decorations, gilt lettering, high quality paper, color plates, and wood engravings—all have an audience who prize them not only as decorative pieces but also as investments. Fine press books from publishers such as Albion, Golden Cockerel, Clarendon, Stinehour, Nonesuch, and others are sought after for their unique treatment and superior quality, and they are generally sold at the high end of the price scale, often in the thousands of dollars.

Illustration

Here is one genre that collectors snap up, especially books with color plates. Of course those most prized are famous illustrators, the likes of Arthur Rackham, who brought a finely detailed and whimsical style to children's books, and Edmund Dulac, another artist who decorated books with enchanting illustrations. See Kathleen Roberts's discussion of children's book illustrators on pages 58–59 for further information. The field is so large we could not do justice here to the collectible artists who make this genre so much fun.

An early copy of Rudyard Kipling's *Captains Courageous,* in decorated cloth boards, published by Macmillan & Co., London, 1897, with illustrations by J. W. Taber.

To name just a few, W. W. Denslow drew the characters for the Oz books, and N. C. Wyeth, Howard Pyle, and Maxfield Parrish brought the Scribner's Classics to life. Then you have books on horticulture, natural history, and medicine, illustrated by John Gould, Audubon, and others, not to mention engravings and chromolithographs by a host of anonymous artists whose works are prized in their own right. When you come across one of these books, you have a prize item.

Some illustrations, such as color plates from an early Audubon book, can be framed and sold individually, and some people will break a book with that in mind. We disagree with the practice unless the illustration has been salvaged from an already damaged book.

Decorated Cloth Bindings

Kathleen Roberts discussed this new area of scholarship and collecting, a genre some are calling "publishers' trade bindings."

Q: So this is a new area of interest to come along for bibliophiles in the past few years?

KR: Yes, the market is just awakening. An interesting time.

Booksellers haven't paid that much attention to this genre in the past, but it is coming into consideration now, due to the work of Sue Allen, the leading historian and scholar in the field of publishers' cloth bindings from the period when they were used to replace leather beginning around 1830, until the eye-catching decorated bindings were replaced by paper dust jackets at the beginning of the 20th century.

Decorated cloth bindings can be arranged according to their decade, and seen in terms of the history of book binding and the changeover from leather to cloth. These bindings came about as a product of several factors, including the Industrial Revolution, the American slave economy, and the nature of 19th century cotton markets between England and America.

The United States was growing cotton within the context of a slave economy, but the industrial revolution hit Europe before it reached our shores, and England was further along in weaving cloth than the United States. Trade, therefore, included shipments of bulk cotton to England with finished cloth coming back to the New World.

While the industrial revolution happened faster in England, education and social change was accelerated on this side of the ocean. With the advance of universal public education in the United States, the demand for books increased with an increasingly literate populace who were now able to read for pleasure as well as necessity. As Americans pushed west, laying track from coast to coast, people began to pick up reading material at train stations to help them pass the time on their long journey. The country needed a means to produce books faster and in larger numbers to serve a growing market.

Circumstances like these, coupled with the emergence of the new role of publisher, an entity that would now buy the rights to print, bind, market, and distribute books for authors, sparked manufacturers to develop new and more efficient methods for book production. Cloth, being easier to manage and more plentiful, came into favor as a substitute for leather, which was previously the preferred book covering. By the 1830s, books were being produced with cloth covers—a new turn of events.

Toward the end of the 19th century, book publishers became more astute about the market aspects of their business. They realized that the cover of a book could sell the book, and they began hiring artists and designers to create elaborate and colorful designs to be applied to the cloth covers to attract the attention of more readers. This then was the 1890s, the era of artist-signed bindings, which have now become extremely sought-after items.

There's a very active collectible market in these books currently, with a demand for artists like Margaret Armstrong, who designed lavish lavender covers for the Victorian romance writer Myrtle Reed. New scholarship is active in the field and reference books are being produced now that speak to the body of these individual artists' work.

But the phenomenon of the artist-signed binding was short-lived. By 1910, the paper dust jacket arrived on the scene and put an end to the heyday of decorated cloth. Artist-signed bindings had enjoyed about a fifteen- to twenty-year run.

Several samples of decorated cloth bindings are pictured in the pages of this book. More information about them can be found online at www.handsomebooks.com.

Science and Medicine

Science and medicine is a highly specialized genre and some of the most exciting antiquarian books can be found in this field—though rare and hard to find, especially those with handsome woodcut illustrations of scientific discoveries and medical wonders.

Nineteenth-century books on medicine during the Civil War have a ready audience and cross-over from the science and medicine to the Civil War genres. Books by men such as Sir William Osler and William Harvey are valued in any collection. Early discoveries, inventions, and biographies of inventors and scientists round out a collection.

Raymond V. Giordano, The Antiquarian Scientist, Southampton, Massachusetts:

Raymond Giordano is a specialist in scientific and medical books as well as instrumentation and memorabilia.

Giordano has been reluctant to enter into online trading by placing his catalogues of books for sale on the Internet, though his business has been listed in the rosters of several online organizations where the wider book-buying public could locate him and get in touch directly. In recent years, he has begun to list selected inventory on AbeBooks.com.

Q: What has been the nature of your experience since adding Internet sales?

RG: I do have a home page that spells out the details of my business and allows the public to browse my books. I don't have many books up, but it's been OK. I don't think there's been a month in the past year that I don't sell something, and as my books typically begin at around $75 and go to as much as a few thousand dollars, it's worked out over that time. What I've decided to list so far is material that I've otherwise offered in catalogues. So anything that sells on ABE is a sale that is outside of my normal mailing list, since I've already tried It with my regular customers. So far.

I may decide to begin to list some new material that I have, but I remain interested in issuing print catalogues—a little bit more irregularly than I had in the past, but I want the print catalogue to contain material that hasn't been exposed on the Internet first.

Q: How well do you see your books holding their value now that buyers have the world in which to shop?

There's no question that I'm aware of changes, and my colleagues who have handled secondary source books in their field, or even lesser books that are antiquarian, have seen some losses. Clearly, when you look online, you can see several copies, or even lesser copies, and that has influenced price. The books that one might put into the middle ground or better in dollar value [Author Note: many dealers put this range at books approaching the $100 value and greater], especially in my field of science and medicine, as well.

Those books are distributed to a smaller number of booksellers, logically, than the millions of people online generally.

Q: How are prices holding?

RG: For these specialty dealers, if a book doesn't sell, their first inclination is not to drop the price. A portion of their inventory just doesn't find a buyer even in the best of times. It's possible that, if the economy becomes very difficult, antiquarian bookselling could become a casualty as well, but in my time in this industry we've had a couple of recessions and I haven't seen prices for good books dropping.

As I've been selling online now, for these past months I've probably sent more of the books I've sold out of the country than in. That is one of the characteristics now—you end up finding quite a lot of customers that you never had before. They don't necessarily repeat with you. That I've found as well. One or two of those I've sent books to overseas have responded to offers of future sales or catalogues that I sent out. I think that they're persuaded by what they see on ABE to buy a particular copy of a book, but they're not typically buying widely in my field.

It's fun, but I'm not an over-endorser of it. It's definitely affecting our business, but I had a copy of a book that was a fair book, but it was a special copy because some notable 19th century doctors had owned it. I got a call from a person who wanted to buy it, a person who was a descendant of one of those doctors and had been researching her past.

There's no way that we would have found each other any other way. And for her to have found this copy, especially an association copy, would not have happened before the Internet.

I'm one of the reluctant old-timers who have been slow to go this Internet route. I still prefer, and enjoy, issuing catalogues. I have a strong mailing list that I continue to use and maintain. But I'm taking steps now to increase my use of the Internet to reach a clientele.

(Note: A large part of Giordano's business over the course of his career has included dealing with institutions as well as individuals, though the personal collector is the mainstay of his business, he said. In the past, he handled scientific instruments as well as books on science and medicine, though he no longer carries the instrument line. He said he has found fewer younger clients coming along in the past two years or so. This is a comment he hears from colleagues oversees, as well. And yet, he cautioned that such transitions shouldn't be judged too quickly.)

Q: Over the years, then, who has been your primary customer?

RG: Certainly academics, and those in commercial sciences who work in one of the fields. The really serious collectors often have something serious going in their background related to the subject, so in recent years for example, as the computer became really prominent, there's a whole collecting base with an interest in the history of calculating and the computer. That brought some of those people—from Silicon Valley or similar locations—to be interested in the underpinnings of the subject, mathematics and physics. They started with an interest in the computer or calculator or slide rule, and they expanded to a serious interest in the foundations of those sciences. They started with some of the leading books and that brought them to the early rare books.

Q: How can people on the hunt recognize a good book in science and medicine?

RG: For medicine, they can read Garrison and Morton, abbreviated G-M in many dealer catalogues. It's not a price guide but a comprehensive index oriented toward topics in the history of medicine. It contains 7,000 entries of collectible items. Collectors have looked at it as a guide to significant works in medicine. There's nothing comparable in other science areas, but there are some good guides.

100 Books Famous in Science by the Grolier Club was published in 1964. It contains details of high spots in science publication. Also *100 Books Famous in Medicine* published by Grolier Club in 1995.

Other high spots are included in *Printing and the Mind of Man*, referred to by many as PMM.

Dr. Haskell Norman formed a great library in science and medicine, which was catalogued in detail by his son and his bibliographer, Jeremy Norman. The catalogue is known as the *Norman Library of Science and Medicine* and is often referred to because of the wealth of data and for the illustrations. In many cases, Dr. Norman had special copies of books and those are well described. Each item is numbered and it's often referred to when used in dealer catalogues by the specific library number.

The Norman Library collection also was sold and three large catalogues were created at Christie's for that sale. The information included in Jeremy Norman's bibliography was reproduced with additional information by Christie's. That sale took place in 1998. The library realized in the area of $19,000,000.

Prices have been going up since then even though people said at the time that these were rather remarkable results in many cases. There have been sales in the last couple of years of very comparable and good material, and the sales have been even higher than those of the Norman Library.

If you were to acquire a set of these catalogues, you would almost certainly get a set of prices realized laid in. So they can be a reference to what the values were approximately a decade ago. (Note: Catalogues were offered for $200 with prices realized laid in through ABE Books in the summer of 2004.)

Q: So, it's your experience that the genre of science and medicine maintains value?

RG: In all the years I've been in this business I've not seen any downward prices. We're talking about primary source books that are above the Internet level.

The secondary source books in our field, and I think in any field, have actually gone down in value. People had thought when we did business the old way that certain books were much more uncommon than they really are. Our ability to collect and buy books was much more of a punctuated experience. Now it's a continuous flow of information. The Internet certainly has changed that part of the field. People who specialized in good scholarly secondary source books have had to reappraise their position because values were tempered by Internet availability.

For example, we're talking about monographs referring to the history of chemistry or physics. Or that refer to important figures like Galileo or Newton or Robert Boyle or others like that. Books about these figures would all be scholarly secondary source books. Some of them are even more general; they tell the history of science in a broader sweep.

All of those books have come under this umbrella of secondary source books whose values have been adjusted downward by what's been happening on the Internet.

Books that have maintained their values are the earlier books and the rare books. They are also available on the Internet, but often many of those offered aren't the valuable collectible editions. If you go back into older catalogues and compare descriptions and prices, you can see whether you have a comparable copy.

Q: Are you seeing a different type of collector today than in the past?

RG: I think that there are many people whose main experience in book collecting has been Internet source material. They have not had the experience of interacting with professional booksellers generally. They have not had the benefit of visiting antiquarian bookshops or reading antiquarian book catalogues where, just by those experiences alone, they can gain a sophistication in the nature of books and the field they're interested in.

That interaction has always been a benefit—mutually in fact—between the seller and the collector. Collectors know specialized information because they get intensely interested in a subject area over a long period of time. In fact, they often impart their special knowledge to the bookseller rather than the other way around.

But in any case, booksellers have a perspective on their field that, by telephone conversation or meeting with their clients, they provide at no additional cost as a benefit. We took that benefit for granted some years ago and it's slowly disappearing today.

Also, one has to realize that people who have been professionals in the field—the dealers—some of these people are struggling a bit today, in part perhaps because they haven't adapted to technology as well as they need to. As those people withdraw from the trade by attrition, there are fewer professional booksellers who can impart the kind of experience that in the past we took for granted.

That's why one hopes that some of the young blood coming into the antiquarian book trade in the future will continue to develop along the lines that a long tradition has fostered—providing scholarship and information about the books, with subject matter at the forefront.

Q: What books remain highly collectible?

RG: The classics, which have been doing very, very well. Prices for Darwin's *Origin of Species*, Newton's *Principia*, Galileo's *Dialogo*—they range up into six figures now. (Note: Charles Darwin. *The Origin of Species*. London. 1859. 1st edition, 1st issue. $50,000.00–$95,000.00; Isaac Newton. *Principia Mathematica*. Cambridge. 1713. 2nd ed. $25,000.00–$30,000.00.)

You can list a book for $125,000 and it's not unrealistic that somebody might call up and buy it. That reflects changes in the real world, and people are willing and capable of participating in that market. Those types of books are well collected right now.

In general, early mathematics has become quite "hot"—certainly the leading figures in early mathematics are important—people like Gauss, Euler, LaGrange. Even earlier mathematics going back into the 16th and some 17th century books—they might seem obscure when they come up for sale at auctions, but they're collectible.

The German mathematician Bernhard Riemann's work is quite valuable. A number of 19th century mathematicians are important—for instance, Hamilton, Boole, Bolyai. The market starts to change as time goes on, and they have to be associated with a major achievement for the book to be of particularly high value.

Q: What other subjects are popular?

RG: Other areas are physics and astronomy. Early works are very much in demand. In physics especially, works that relate to optics and scientific instruments are sought. They're usually illustrated with interesting plates, and these can be very desirable. There are quite a number of people forming collections in the field.

The kinds of books I'm speaking of are not that often found at the grassroots level anymore. At one time, if you ran around to the bookstores, you'd find a major book at a reasonable price. Now, if you want the kind of book I'm describing, you'll have to pay a commensurate price, not a discovery price where you buy something for $10 or $20 and find it's worth ten or a hundred times that.

In our experience, collectors in science and medicine can also look for books on early rockets, communications, medical cures, technological firsts, anything vintage on airships, planes, the atom bomb, parachutes, windmills, and other scientific pursuits.

Sporting and Spelunking

A highly specialized field, sporting books are based in the English tradition of field sports such as riding, angling, hunting, and mountaineering. Cave exploration is also a popular subject. If you tread onto the baseball diamond or a basketball court, you're in another genre. Sporting collections are currently enjoying considerable popularity, and trade in books on these topics is brisk.

Kenneth Andersen, Sporting and General Antiquarian Books, Middlebury, Vermont:

Q: Who are some important authors for sporting collectors to know about?

KA: Consider Robert Traver, who wrote the mystery novel *Anatomy of a Murder*. He's a popular writer of books about fly fishing. His book, *Trout Madness,* is a great testament to the spiritual aspects of fishing. This is a book that sporting people should have. It's one of the classic books, but you can only tell the first edition by the dust jacket price. Now there are about a hundred copies online starting at $40 and going up to $150. How is a new collector to learn what's what? (*Trout Madness.* St. Martin's Press. 1960. Traver also wrote *Trout Magic*, NY. Crown. 1974; and *Anatomy of a Fisherman,* NY. McGraw-Hill. 1964. Robert Traver is the pseudonym of attorney and Michigan Supreme Court Justice John Voelker, who also wrote the novel *Anatomy of a Murder*, NY. St. Martin's Press, 1958. The book was made into a successful movie in the mid-20th century.)

Q: Are there some basic references sporting and angling collectors should know about?

KA: Collectors can get in touch with dealers and specialists to find out if catalogues are available. Study the books that are listed. Visit their sites online, if they catalogue books and information there. Subscribe to a good magazine in the sport and notice books being advertised, and the authors who write the articles.

For angling, *Fly Fisherman* is a good magazine to see.

Many collectible books in these genres are books that are not that old and people are still able to get them. Hold onto them for a while. Study the market. Think in those terms if you are buying for value as well as interest in the subject.

Q: Can you point out some book or authors that have appreciated in value and describe their history?

KA: Dana Lamb is a 1960s-era writer on angling, a writer of essays on trout and salmon fishing. He was a member of the Angler's Club, a very exclusive and preeminent club in New York that published a number of books, as well.

Lamb, too, stressed the experience of angling, the spiritual aspect of the sport. His first book, *On Trout Streams and Salmon Rivers* (Barre, Mass. Barre Publishers, 1963. ltd 1500 cc. slipcase) sold for $25.

Books by Lamb were printed in limited editions, about 1,500 copies. Deluxe editions included perhaps 50 to 300 copies. Over the years, there has been such a demand for his work that his books have escalated in price.

Q: What do you think attracts the sporting enthusiast to this subject?

KA: When anglers go fishing, they spend $10,000–$12,000 to travel to, say, Russia. And they throw the fish back. They're not interested in keeping the fish; as I mentioned before, they're interested in the experience, the spiritual aspect of the sport.

Do you remember Hemingway's *The Old Man and the Sea*? (NY. Scribner's. 1952. dj. True first edition includes "A" on copyright page.) It didn't matter if the old man didn't bring the fish in. It was the experience of being out there that was transformative—the connection to an elemental force of nature. Collectors are looking for well-written books that remind them of this experience. And they're looking for high spots that make a contribution to our knowledge and enjoyment of these subjects.

Q: What are some other books and references a collector would be interested in?

KA: They can look for George LaBranche, *The Dry Fly in Fast Water*, a great book. It's one of the earliest books on American dry fly fishing. LaBranche also did a book on salmon and the dry fly. He's credited with being first in America to talk about dry fly fishing for salmon.

Also, Theodore Gordon's books, or periodicals in which his articles appear.

Q: Can you suggest some additional sporting high spots?

KA: Look for Bethune who took Isaac Walton's most famous work, *The Compleat Angler*, and Americanized it and made it approachable for the U.S. audience. (Note: *The Compleat Angler* is credited with more than 600 editions since it was written in 1653. The Rev. George Washington Bethune's edition was published in the United States in 1847, the first to be published outside of England.)

Bethune's is a very significant book because it takes a classic work, one that has been published more often than anything other than Shakespeare and the Bible, and makes it palatable to American readers and tries to accommodate it to American streams and fishing.

Also, consider books by or about women in American fishing. Charles Orvis created a famous fishing store in Manchester, Vermont, in the 1850s. It is still one of the most prominent angling stores in the United States, featuring clothing, fishing gear, and paraphernalia. Orvis's daughter, Mary Orvis Marberry, wrote a book on angling, *Favorite Flies and Their Histories*, a big thick book for which she corresponded with a number of people around the country, and she included glorious chromolithograph plates of fishing flies. (Mary Orvis Marberry, *Favorite Flies and Their Histories*. Boston/NY. Houghton Mifflin. 1892. illus.; reprinted by Wellfleet Press, 1988.)

I was selling that book to people who weren't in the fishing area until I found out what they were doing with those books—taking the plates out, framing them, and selling them for $50, $75, $100 each and throwing the book away. So, I stopped selling to them.

Q: What books are good in other sporting fields?

KA: Some of the sports fields are also actively collected. For instance, golf. Golf books were published mostly for the country club set, and there weren't that many golfers so they didn't print that many books.

There are more golfers now since men like Arnold Palmer got involved, and Tiger Woods. Collectors look for the early books but you really can't find them.

(Golfing collectibles include such titles as Miles Bantock, *On Many Greens: A Book of Golf and Golfers*. NY. Grosset & Dunlap. 1901; Kenneth Brown, *Putter Perkins*. NY. Houghton Mifflin. 1923; and Bob Jones, *Rights and Wrongs in Golf*. A.G. Spalding Bros., 1935.)

On mountaineering, see for instance, Guido Rey, *The Matterhorn*. Lon: Fisher Unwin, 1907, a scarce first edition.

Big game hunting: Look for books on early explorations into Africa and Asia, and discovering North America, particularly Alaska when it was still wilderness.

Q: Do you have any additional advice for people coming into these fields?

KA: A lot of people are branching out into related fields, like ephemera, or paper items. When you come on these perishable items, save them—hold on to information and preserve it for future collectors or donate it to a museum.

These resources are recommended by Andersen:

American Fishing Books. Charles M. Wetzel, 1950, reprinted 1997. Contains more than 2,000 titles.

Catalogue of the Collection of Books on Angling. Dean Sage, 1886 first edition, reprinted 1995. More than 2,000 titles with annotations.

Bibliotheca Piscatoria: A Catalogue of Books on Angling, Fisheries and Fish-Culture. T. Westwood and T. Satchell. Originally printed 1883 and 1901.

Hunting, Hawking, Shooting. C. F. G. R. Schwerdt. Four volumes, illustrated and comprehensively annotated.

– 4 –
BIBLES

Although the Bible has been on the bestseller list since Gutenberg put it on his printing press, more recently printed Bibles are generally not collectible.

Even so, collectors remain interested in notable Bibles, and they continue to seek out the more ornate, well-illustrated, and well-produced newer volumes, as well.

To separate the wheat from the chaff in this area of interest, a few caveats for the novice are in order.

European Bibles published before 1700 are often collectible. American Bibles dated 1800 or later are unlikely to have collectible value unless they are associated with an important event or family, are the first to be published in a particular language (perhaps a Native American tongue), or are illustrated and signed by a noteworthy individual.

For instance, a Bible that chronicles family births, marriages, and deaths written in Mary Todd Lincoln's hand would certainly qualify as one that derives value from the association.

And yet, for a Bible published after 1800, don't merely assume a lack of collectible status. Ask for counsel from a credible bookseller on whether or not you have a prize. Some later editions have association or special publication value based on where they were designed or printed, so don't discard a fine old Bible indiscriminately based on date alone.

Throughout our discussions of the book world, we cannot stress enough the value of consulting with knowledgeable collectors and dealers, and the value of holding a book in one's hand to examine it directly.

What else besides age makes a Bible valuable? Well, you might one day run across the first Bible printed in a particular place, country, state, or city. Or the first Bible printed in a particular language, such as the "Eliot" or Natick Bible printed for the Natick colony of "praying Indians" west of Boston, completed in 1663. (Few copies of the original printing of this work, believed to be approximately 2,000 copies, survive today. Many were destroyed during King Philip's War, 1675. A second revised edition was printed in 1685. The 1661–63 editions are now valued on the order of $500,000 or more. Single leaves are reported to sell in the thousands of dollars. The Boston Public Library includes an Eliot Bible in its special collections.)

John J. Jeffcoat, Jr., owner and editor of The Great Site (*www.greatsite.com*):

Jeffcoat specializes in new, antiquarian, and facsimile reproductions of collectible Bibles and related material.

JJ, from *The Great Site:* Although the first Bible printed in America was done in the native Algonquin Indian language by John Eliot in 1663, the first English-language Bible to be printed in America, done by Robert Aitken in 1782, was a King James Version. This Bible was also the only Bible ever authorized by the United States Congress. In 1808, Robert's daughter, Jane Aitken, would become the first woman to ever print a Bible. In 1791, Isaac Collins vastly improved upon the quality and size of the typesetting of American Bibles and produced the first "family Bible" printed in America, also a King James Version. Also in 1791, Isaiah Thomas published the first illustrated Bible printed in America, a King James Version.

While Noah Webster, just a few years after producing his famous *Dictionary of the English Language,* would produce his own modern translation of the English Bible in 1833, the public remained too loyal to the King James Version for Webster's version to have much impact. It was not really until the 1880s that England's own planned replacement for their King James Bible, the English Revised Version (E.R.V.) would become the first English language Bible to gain popular acceptance as a post–King James Version modern–English Bible. The widespread popularity of this modern–English translation brought with it another curious characteristic: the absence of the fourteen Apocryphal books.

Up until the 1880s every Protestant Bible (not just Catholic Bibles) had 80 books, not 66. The inter-testamental books written hundreds of years before Christ, called the "Apocrypha," were part of virtually every printing of the Tyndale-Matthews Bible, the Great Bible, the Bishops Bible, the Protestant Geneva Bible, and the King James Bible until their removal in the 1880s.

The original 1611 King James contained the Apocrypha, and King James threatened anyone who dared to print the Bible without the Apocrypha with heavy fines and a year in jail.

Only for the last 120 years have the Protestant churches rejected these books, and removed them from their Bibles.

Another early printing in the New World, the Saur Bible, was printed in the United States in 1743 in the German language by Christoph Saur.

This was the first European-language Bible printed in America, arriving after the Eliot Bible. A later 1776 version of Saur's is referred to as the Revolution Bible or the Gun Wad Bible, because British soldiers reportedly used unbound pages to wrap gunpowder. Very few copies from the 1743 edition have survived. Only a handful of copies of the Gun Wad Bible are believed to have survived.

The first Bible printed, translated or edited by a woman would be a prime example of a significant printing. Also, Bibles owned by famous people, miniature Bibles called "thumb–Bibles," hieroglyphic Bibles, or other unusual volumes in fine bindings, or those printed for children, are sought after.

John Jeffcoat offers some rule of thumb measures for judging collectibility of Bibles:

JJ, from *The Great Site*: The value (the price) of antiquarian and rare Bibles is determined by a variety of factors, including:

Rarity: How many of this printing exist?

Historical Significance: Is it an historically important printing?

Market Demand: Do collectors want to buy this type of material?

First Edition Status: Is it a first (or early) printing of its type?

Age: How old is this printing?

Condition: Are the pages in good condition?

Collation: Are any pages missing? Which ones and how many?

Binding: Is it nice? Original? Is restoration or rebinding needed?

Provenance: Did someone famous own it? Did they sign it?

All of these factors are fairly simple and self-explanatory, but we do need to elaborate on one of them: condition. It is important to understand that the condition of the binding, and whether or not the binding is original, is not a major factor in the value of most ancient Bibles. . . . The condition and completeness (collation, or presence of all pages) of the "text block" (the pages) is very important to the value of an ancient Bible. Concern-

MAMUSSE
WUNNEETUPANATAMWE
UP-BIBLUM GOD
NANEESWE
NUKKONE TESTAMENT
KAH WONK
WUSKU TESTAMENT.

Ne quoſhkinnumuk naſhpe Wuttinneumoh *CHRIST*
noh aſoowesit

JOHN ELIOT·

CAMBRIDGE:
Printeuoop naſhpe *Samuel Green* kah *Marmaduke Johnſon.*
1 6 6 3.

**The earliest example in history of an entire Bible published in
a language of the New World,** translated by John Eliot. Known
as the "Eliot Bible" or "Natick Bible" it was prepared for a
community of Praying Indians in Natick, Massachusetts, west
of Boston. Old and New Testaments were completed in 1663.
Image used courtesy of the Trustees of the Boston Public Library.
Photographed by Marilyn Green.

ing the condition and completeness of the pages, it is important to understand that price increases exponentially as you approach "perfection."

Jeffcoat states that Bibles printed in the 1900s, with rare exceptions, are worth no more than $100, and more likely weigh in at about $20.

Some Bibles printed in the 1800s may bring up to $300, but more likely $30. Those printed in the 1700s in America, or printed in Europe in the English language, are worth taking a second look and consulting a dealer. Those printed in the 1700s in Europe, and not in English, are more often not collectible.

Bibles printed from the 1600s and earlier deserve a closer look, especially if the pages are in good condition and the entire Bible is present (no lost pages or covers).

Most people think of the family Bible—old, leather-worn, and bearing the ancient script of a long-deceased ancestor—as surely a valuable treasure. Indeed, it is a treasure, not in dollars, but in the pleasure and fortune of having a precious family heirloom tucked away safely or prominently spotlighted in your home.

Listed below are some collectible Bibles and Bible-related volumes:

American Bible. The "Eliot" or "Natick Bible." Cambridge, Mass. 1663. Indian language translation. Scarce. We were able to examine and photograph a copy of the Natick Bible at the Boston Public Library a decade ago. $400,000–$500,000.

American Bible. Phila. 1790. 2 vols. 1st American ed of the Douai or Roman Catholic Bible.
                    $10,000–$12,500.

American Bible. Phil. 1794. pocket size. $200–$300.

A Selection from the Book of Psalms, for School and Family Use. Cincinnati: Hebrew Sabbath-School Union of America. 1888. shelfworn. $70.00–$90.00

Bible in English. Oxford. Baskett. 1717. 2 vols. large folio. Contains many errors and is called the "Vinegar Bible" for a proofreading error in Luke XX, where the word "vinegar" is substituted for "vineyard." $3,500–$5,000.

Holy Bible: Old and New Testaments, translated from the Original Tongues, with Apocrypha, Concordance and Psalms. Philadelphia. William W. Harding. 1868. shelfworn.
                    $90.00–$110.00

The text of the New Testament of Jesus Christ. . . . Rheims-Bishops' version. 1601.
                    $5,000.00–$6,000.00

Bible. New York. 1846. Old Testament, New Testament, and Apocrypha. illuminated.
                    $200.00–$275.00

New Testament. Cambridge. 1881. American Committee of Revision, full morocco, aeg, 606 pp. $130.00–$180.00

"Nonesuch Bible." Lon. Nonesuch Press. 1924–27. 5 vols. $500–$750.

"Nonesuch Bible." Lon. Nonesuch Press. 1963. reprinted with Apocrypha. 3 vols.
$200.00–$250.

The Book of Ruth. Lon. Reed Pale Press. 1934. ltd. 250 cc. numbered. quarter vellum and paper boards, handmade paper, slipcase. $150.00–$190.00

A collectible reference book containing additional information on Bibles is:

Dibden, Rev. Thomas Frognall. *An Introduction to the Knowledge of Rare and Valuable Editions of the Greek and Latin Classics.* Lon. 1827. 2 vols. 4th ed.

– 5 –
CARE AND REPAIR OF BOOKS

Books created from quality papers are surprisingly durable when treated well and maintained under favorable conditions. Consider the number of incunabula (books created before 1501) that have survived in sturdy enough shape to delight collectors and to serve as reference materials for serious scholars to this day.

Our own examination of a 300-year-old copy of Eliot's Natick Indian Bible at the Boston Public Library during the 1990s revealed a book with pages solid enough to withstand the careful attentions of readers and researchers for many more years.

Even ignored and uncared for, an ancient volume left undisturbed, without excessive humidity, may survive without damage for centuries. Leather bindings will certainly dry out and crack without occasional dressing, but the pages of old books are stubbornly durable.

Avoiding Damage

Unfortunately, 20th-century books may not last so long, though the quality of materials used at the close of the millennium had begun to improve over those used for the better part of the 1900s.

Common manufacturing practices during the last century made it possible to produce a lot of paper quickly, but the quality of material used in books was often of inferior quality, high in acid content, which hastens the degradation of paper. Consequently, many mass-produced books from that era will have a far shorter lifespan.

The high acid content of the standard paper used in book manufacture causes the paper's fibers to degrade, discolor, and the pages to become brittle and fall apart after only a few

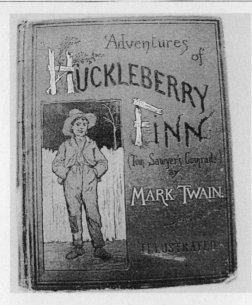

Mark Twain's *Adventures of Huckleberry Finn.* NY.
Charles L. Webster. 1885. The book shows the green-
variant decorated cloth cover binding. A second
binding, less common, is in blue decorated cloth.

decades. Pulp paper used in newspapers and cheap magazines shows this defect in the ex-
treme, as newspapers may yellow and become brittle in a mere few days.

Toward the end of the 20th century, however, authors and publishers who recognized the
problem banded together to encourage the use of acid-free papers in the publication of important books, especially the first editions of books.

A "Commitment Day" ceremony was held in 1989 during which authors and publishers
pledged to use acid-free paper for first printings of hardcover trade books.

Over the next decade, most University Presses reported switching to acid-free paper for the
bulk of their hard-bound first editions. The federal government, too, has been encouraged
to print important documents and publications on quality paper that stands a better chance
of being preserved for posterity. And many mainstream publishing houses were signatories
to the pledge, as well.

Acid-free paper for the manufacture of paperback volumes has been longer in coming, but
the industry and public are now aware of the problem and of the need to make the necessary changes.

In fact, the general public, insofar as it is aware of paper at all, has now come to recognize
the value of acid-free papers and mats used in many areas of printing and the arts. Those
books from the 20th century that were printed on acidic paper are still in danger of

Spine of a volume in fine condition of Virginia Woolf's *A Room of One's Own.* The book was published by The Fountain Press in New York and The Hogarth Press in London. This is one of an edition printed by Josephy in October 1929, limited to 450 copies signed by Woolf.

Virginia Woolf's signature on the half-title page of *A Room of One's Own,* limited edition, printed by Josephy, October, 1929.

degrading at an accelerated rate, but if the industry continues to remedy the problem—and the public continues to recognize and ask for the use of acid-free materials—then copies of books printed now will be available to collectors well into future centuries.

Some Additional Enemies of Books and Paper

Fire. Fire has totally or partially destroyed many important libraries, often during war (for example, the burning of the Alexandrian Library by Caesar's troops, and the destruction of the Library of Congress in Washington by the British in the War of 1812), and sometimes by accident. The Jenkins Company of Austin, Texas, lost an extensive inventory to fire in December 1985. Fortunately, some of the more valuable items—many acquired from other collection dispersal sales through the years—were stored in a large walk-in vault and survived that blaze.

Light or moderate fire damage to a book may be repairable to a degree, but a reduction in the book's value as a collectible item remains probable. An important and difficult-to-replace volume can be salvaged, however, for the value of its content and its connection to history.

Bindings can be replaced and page ends, if scorched, may be trimmed. If a badly scorched book is still worth the effort, the leaves may be unbound and mounted to new paper by a professional bookbinder.

Some precautions can be taken to minimize the threat of fire damage to a collection. A book room where valuable volumes are stored should have fire retardant carpets; draperies and curtains should be kept to a minimum; upholstered and overstuffed furniture should be avoided. Glass-enclosed bookshelves are safer than open shelves where fires are a risk. A fire extinguisher should be kept handy and the door kept shut when the room is not in use.

Water. Books can be water-damaged by floods, fire-fighting efforts, plumbing problems, storms, or any occasion when water comes into contact with covers and leaves.

Whether or not a soaked book can be salvaged depends on the paper quality. Vellum can often take a soaking and respond to reconditioning. A good rag paper has the best chance, but the book must be dismantled and each leaf dried separately.

Modern books on coated paper, such as art books, are a loss. The coating disintegrates with moisture and you're left with incomplete images on pages that often stick together. Newspapers, too, cannot take moisture; they absorb water and return to the pulp they started from.

Properly drying out a book is a delicate process and should be done by a professional. Restoration is an expensive procedure, so a book should be evaluated carefully to determine whether it is worth the cost.

Some steps to take to guard against water damage include avoiding rooms with overhead water pipes for book rooms. Be aware of kitchens and bathrooms on the floor above. In many buildings, those pipes are not always visible, but they can still leak down onto your books if they burst. Avoid basement rooms that may leak or be damp at best. Cover books carefully when transporting them outdoors.

Excessive Humidity or Excessive Dryness. Dry air damages leather bindings. Humid air breeds mold and mildew, curls paper, and loosens bindings. The ideal humidity for books is around 50 percent, give or take ten points.

In a humid environment, without a dehumidifier, it's best to store books on open shelves rather than in glass cases where moisture will build up inside.

To help leather remain supple in all environments, but especially in dry air, treat it regularly with a leather dressing. This will be taken up at greater length when we discuss leather care.

Rough Handling. Be gentle when handling all of your books, not just those that appear fragile. Even big, brawny folios can be easily damaged—sometimes by the weight of their own pages pulling on their spine—if they're not handled well.

Don't open any book too wide or press it flat on a table to copy from it; this cracks the hinges. Many an older volume can be found described as "shaken," or "spine separating from pages" caused by such handling.

Older books with metal clasps require special handling. If the clasps are tight, don't tug or pry at them to open them. Instead, gently squeeze the outer edges of the book until the

Chapbooks were popular fare during the 19th century, often sold door to door by traveling salesmen commonly called chapmen. These books are in Special Collections at the Bailey-Howe Library at the University of Vermont. Pictured: (top row) *The Farm House,* Mahlon Day, early 1800s; *The Red Squirrel,* A. Phelps, 1846; *Cinderella of the Glass Slipper,* H. & E. Phinney, 1834; (bottom row) *Stories for Children About Whales,* Rufus Merrill, 1843; *Cock Robin's Courtship and Marriage,* Sidney's Press, 1824; *The Young Sailor, or the Sea Life of Tom Bowline,* Kiggins & Kellog, 1840s.

clasps loosen and pop open easily. To close them, squeeze again and gently fit the clasps back in place. If they won't close, don't force them. Over time, these books, especially vellum, may have swelled to the point where the clasps no longer fit. Leave them open or risk damaging the binding with too much squeezing.

Improper Storage. A book can be damaged by improper shelving, though the harm is often done almost imperceptibly over time, so you may not notice it's happening until it's too late. Common mistakes include wedging books too tightly on a shelf or letting books flop about on unfilled shelves, stacking books flat on their sides, one atop another, or shelving books on the fore-edge.

Most spine problems of folio books and larger volumes are the result of shelving on the fore-edge, causing the books to develop loose sections or covers, bent edges and corners, and possibly damaged pages. While it's tempting to place a book that's too large for the shelf on its edge, you should resist the impulse. The weight of the pages will pull them away from the spine and you'll end up with a broken book.

If you can, rather stand large books on top of the bookcase, supported by bookends to avoid cocking the spines. If you can't do this, place them flat on the shelf, but don't put other books on top of them.

Light. The ultraviolet component of direct sunlight degrades many kinds of paper and fades the color—or "mellows" the bindings—of books that stand for long periods in the

Lilian Garis, *Gloria at Boarding School* and *Gloria: A Girl and Her Dad,* Grosset & Dunlap, 1923. Two children's series books, clothbound, in dust jackets. $5.00–$25.00
Digital photography by Jonathan Draudt, Tamarac Arts

sun. Nothing is more discouraging to a bibliophile than to see a table full of books at a flea market warping and wilting unprotected from a hot summer sun.

Bookcases shouldn't receive direct sunlight if it can be avoided, though indirect sunlight to brighten a room is OK. Interior lighting should be incandescent. Fluorescent light also damages books.

Insects and pests. A particularly nasty enemy of books is the bookworm. Not the bookish person devoted to reading, but insect larvae that feast on the binding and paste of books. Bugs, too, can wreak havoc on books. Some bugs, like silverfish, love a meal of sizing and starches used in the manufacture of paper. Some like the dyes and materials used in bindings like buckram.

The best recourse, if worms or insects are attacking your collection, is to call in a professional and have the entire house treated, but don't spray insecticide directly onto your volumes. You may cause more damage than the bugs.

Displaying Your Books

Bookshelves. You'd think it would be simple to figure out how to store and display your books. Put them on a bookshelf, of course. But, it's not so simple as it sounds. Many book enthusiasts think that old books belong in old bookcases and they will go out to an antique shop or an auction and buy the first old bookcase they see. Wrong.

It's important to look past the brass trimming and the darling carved gargoyles to see how the bookcase is constructed. Are the shelves adjustable in height? Are they sagging, cracked, or splintered? Are all the shelf supports present? Are they sturdy enough to carry the weight of heavy books, tall enough to stand your folios upright?

Whether or not your bookcase should have glass doors depends on several factors. Do you want the books handled? Are there children in the house too young to appreciate the delicacy of your treasures? Will the books be stored in a dry environment, or humid? Do you have pets who like to sit on top of a shelf of books? (Cats do.)

Glass doors are a great protection from dust and they cut down on the work you must do, as well as on wear and tear on your books, by keeping the collection clean. But they are bulky and stand between you and your books in a way that open shelves don't.

Bookends. Many bookends are collectible, intricately carved or stunning in brass, copper, and bronze such as those from the Art Nouveau and the Arts and Crafts movements. But do they do the job?

Bookends should keep your books from tumbling around and should support heavy volumes upright. If you find you're constantly repositioning and straightening or tightening them up, they aren't working and should be replaced. For the best service, and at a fraction of the cost of the fancy bookend, we recommend the L-shaped or T-shaped models in which the lower portion slides beneath the first several books. Be sure they're tall enough to support your books and that the edges are smooth and won't scuff the covers and pages.

Book Repair

We cannot emphasize too strongly leaving repair of a rare and valuable book to a competent bookbinder who understands how to effect a repair without causing further damage to those aspects of a book that make it collectible. For the more common or moderately priced books, learning a few pointers on how to repair them yourself is worthwhile.

Professional Bookbinding. A good bookbinder is a valuable resource, and anyone interested in used and old books should get to know one. He provides first aid for books, rescuing broken and defective volumes from oblivion, making suggestions and offering alternatives for repair that you might not have realized were possible.

Do not order a complete new binding if the old, loose one is in fairly sound condition. Rather, a loose cover can be rehinged, and missing leather can be replaced. New bindings can be created in which usable portions of the old leather are inlaid into a leather of similar grain and color. The old spine—or what's left of it—can be reset into a new spine.

These procedures are expensive and probably not worth the cost unless your book has some special appeal or is particularly ancient or rare. In that case, incorporation of original parts of the book help to preserve its appeal to collectors.

When pages or gatherings are loose, the book may need resewing. If the paper is too fragile to permit this, the book can be dismantled and the inner edges of the leaves can be attached to guards—paper extensions—which are then sewn together. When guards are used, it is generally not possible to recase the volume—that is, return it to its original binding—because the page ends will now protrude from the fore-edge. A new binding is necessary.

Paul Laurence Dunbar, *When Maundy Sings,*
Chicago, 1903. Decorated cloth binding by Margaret
Armstrong.
Digital photography by Jonathan Draudt, Tamarac
Arts

Home Repair. You may try some home repair on mildly damaged books that are not so rare or expensive that a mistake would be a disaster. Some of the more common repairs are:

- Loose Bindings. Loose cloth bindings can usually be repaired by opening the book midway through the pages, laying it face downward, and brushing glue along the inner side of the spine. Do not use cement-type glues; polyvinyl acetate, such as Elmer's Glue, does the job best. Use it sparingly. When completed, hold the book tight with large rubber bands and allow it to dry for several hours.

- Cracked Inner Hinges. Inner hinges can be strengthened by folding a narrow strip of paper and pasting it along the hinge. The paper should be about as heavy as an index card for best results. Make sure it is trimmed to the same height as the pages of the book, neither too long nor too short.

- Torn Spines. Spines are best treated by simply brushing a small quantity of glue on the torn sections, pressing them firmly into place, and allowing them to dry under the pressure of a rubber band. Be certain that the fore-edges of the binding are protected from creasing by the rubber band itself.

- Notations or Underlinings. Markings done in pencil are easily—but gently!—erased. When the marks are in ink, nothing removes them satisfactorily, and it is probably wise not to make the effort. The paper could be damaged by using strong cleansers or by scraping. At times, the notations might be of interest and could even provide evidence of the book's previous ownership—called provenance. If the markings are not extensive, they may not detract much from the book's value.

- Moisture stains. Treat the book before the pages dry. Once stains are set by drying, they won't come out. Now, the treatment we recommend may seem a little strange but, if the book doesn't warrant professional attention, try this anyway.

First mop up any surface water by patting gently with soft paper towels. Place an oversized sheet of wax paper between all leaves that have gotten wet. In a wooden box about twice the size of the book, place an inch-thick layer of dry pipe tobacco and lay the book in it. Sprinkle a few more tobacco leaves over the book and seal the box tightly. Store the box in a dry place for several weeks. Some stains will probably remain, but they'll be less visible than if treatment had not been tried.

Care of Leather Bookbindings

Leather bindings, though more attractive than cloth, require more upkeep. Leather, an animal substance, has natural oils when new. As it grows old, the oils dry out and the leather becomes brittle. Red dust on your bookshelves is a sure sign that your bindings are dry and shedding. At that point, emergency treatment is necessary. It won't cure damage that has already occurred, but it will halt further deterioration.

Leather bindings must be dressed. This may not be the most pleasant chore, but it can be rewarding. Be sure to get a good leather care preparation, and use it intelligently. Too much will leave the binding sticky.

For best results, use a dressing made expressly for book bindings, such as the British Museum Leather Dressing. This old standby was once hard to get in America, and collectors sent to London for it and paid the price. Now, it can generally be purchased in the United States. Abide by the directions and don't be disappointed if the leather doesn't look polished. The aim in dressing leather is to give it a drink, not a shine.

Most old leathers will not polish and should not be expected to.

Give your leather-bound books a dressing about every six months. With regular care, any leather binding bought in good condition should remain so. But don't buy a shabby binding in the belief that it can easily be refurbished, as this is impossible.

– 6 –
COLLECTIBLE BOOK LISTING

Abbreviations

All edges gilt	.aeg	Ex libris, ex library	.xlib
Association Copy	.asso copy	Facsimile	.facs
Backed	.bkd	First Edition	.1st ed
Baltimore	.Balt	Folding	.fldg
Boards	.bds	Government Printing Office	.GPO
Boston	.Bos	Illinois	.Ill
California	.CA	Illustrated	.illus
Cambridge	.Camb	Inscribed	.inscrb
Catalogue	.cat	Leather	.lea
Chicago	.Chi	Limited Edition	.ltd
Chromolithographs	.chromo	Marbled	.mrbl
Cincinnatti	.Cinc	Pages	.pp
Cleveland	.Cleve	Philadelphia	.Phil
Connecticut	.CT	Pittsburgh	.Pitt
Copies	.cc	Signed	.sgn
Dublin	.Dub	Top Edge Gilt	.teg
Dust Jacket	.dj	Toronto	.Tor
Edinburgh	.Edin	United Kingdom	.UK
Edition	.ed	United States	.US
Editor	.(ed.)	University	.Univ
English	.Eng	Volume	.vol
Engravings	.engr	Wrappers	.wraps

1936, the Spanish Revolution. AK Press. Amsterdam and Berkeley. 1997. illus.
$15.00–$20.00

100 Greatest All Time Country Hits: Arranged for Voice, Piano and Guitar. NY. Tele House. wraps. $20.00–$30.00

2nd Urban Technology Conference and Technical Display: A Collection of Technical Papers. SF. American Institute of Aeronautics and Astronautics. 1972. 1st ed. $40.00–$50.00

A Brief Sketch of the town of Vinal Haven from Its Earliest Known Settlement . . . On the Occasion of Its One Hundredth Anniversary. Press of the Star Job Print. 1900. 1st ed. wraps.
$60.00–$75.00

A Memorial of Joseph Henry. D.C. GPO. 1880, 1st ed. $35.00–$40.00

A History of Windsor, New Hampshire. NH. Windsor History Committee. (1978). illus. fold-out map. blue cloth. $25.00–$40.00

A Negro Nurse in Republican Spain. Palo Alto. Vet. of the Abraham Lincoln Brigade. 1977. reprint of 1938 ed. wraps. $25.00–$30.00

A Trip through the Lakes of North America: Embracing a full Description of the St. Lawrence River. . . . J. Disturnell. 1857. 1st ed. illus. frontis, pull-out map. $700.00–$900.00

Aaron, Daniel. *Men of Good Hope: A Story of American Progressives.* NY. Oxford Univ Press. 1951. dj. $5.00–$10.00

Aaron, Daniel. *Writers on the Left.* NY. 1961. 1st ed. dj. 448 pp. very good cond.
$30.00–$50.00

Aaron, Henry, with Lonnie Wheeler. *I Had a Hammer: the Hank Aaron Story.* NY. Harper-Collins. 1991. 1st ed. photos. dj. $18.00–$22.00

Aaron, Henry, with Lonnie Wheeler. *I Had a Hammer: the Hank Aaron Story.* NY. Harper-Collins. 1991. 1st ed. photos. signed. dj. $100.00–$300.00

Abagnale, Frank. *Catch Me If You Can.* NY. Grosset and Dunlap. (1980). 1st ed. movie was based on book. sgn. dj. $375.00–$600.00

Abbatt, William. *Battle of Pell's Point.* NY. 1901. illus. map ports. 500 cc. $75.00–$145.00

Abbey, Edward. *Appalachian Wilderness.* NY. Dutton. 1970. 1st ed. dj. $100.00–$150.00

Abbey, Edward. *Appalachian Wilderness.* NY. 1970. 1st ed. illus. full color plates, dj.
$95.00–$115.00

Abbey, Edward. *Black Sun.* NY. Simon & Schuster. (1971). 1st ed. dj. $175.00–$200.00

Abbey, Edward. *Fire on the Mountain.* NY. Dial. 1962. 1st ed. dj. $600.00–$800.00

Abbot, Charles Greeley. *The radiation of the planet Earth to space.* Smithsonian Institution. 1929. wraps. $15.00–$22.00

Abbott, Dan. *Stairway to the Stars: Colorado's Argentine Central Railway.* Ft. Collins, Co. (1977). 1st ed. ltd. sgn. $140.00–$160.00

Abbott, Edwin A. *("A Square")*. *Flatland. A Romance of Many Dimensions*. Lon. Seeley. 1884. wraps. 2nd ed. new and rev. $400.00–$500.00

Abbott, Edwin A. *("A Square")*. *Flatland. A Romance of Many Dimensions*. Bos. Roberts. 1885. 1st Amer ed. $600.00–$1,450.00

Abbott, John S. C. *History of Hernando Cortez*. NY. Harper. 1855. 1st ed. illus. lea. marbled bds. $130.00–$160.00

Abbott, Lee K. *Love is the Crooked Thing*. Algonquin. 1986. 1st ed. sgn. dj. $25.00–$35.00

Abdill, George B. *Rail West*. NY. Bonanza. 1960. illus. dj. $5.00–$10.00

Abott, Morris W. *Cog Railway to Pike's Peak*. San Marino, CA. Golden West Books. (1918). later printing. illus. wraps. $5.00–$10.00

Abe, Kobo. *Woman in the Dunes*. NY. Knopf. 1964. 1st Amer ed. dj. $100.00–$200.00

Abel, Annie Heloise and Frank J. Klingberg (eds.). *Side-light on Anglo-American relations, 1839–1858. . . .* British and Foreign Anti-Slavery Society. Association for the Study of Negro Life and History. 1927. inscr. $80.00–$130.00

Abell, Sir Wescott. *Shipwright's Trade, The*. Cambridge. 1948. 1st ed. illus. $60.00–$100.00

Abercrombie, John. *Pathological & Practical Researches on Diseases of the Brain*. Phil. Carey & Lea. 1831. 1st US ed. $600.00–$800.00

Abercrombie, John. *Pathological & Practical Researches on Diseases of the Brain*. Phil. Lea & Blanchard. 1843. $300.00–$500.00

Abernethy, John. *Surgical Observations on Tumours and on Lumbar Abscesses*. Lon. 1811. 1st ed. $250.00–$300.00

Abraham, Pearl. *Giving Up America*. 1998. 1st ed. sgn. dj. $25.00–$35.00

Abraham, Pearl. *Romance Reader, The*. 1995. 1st ed. sgn. dj. $30.00–$40.00

Abrahams, Peter. *Path of Thunder, The*. NY. Harper. 1948. 1st ed. dj. $30.00–$90.00

Abrahams, Roger. *Singing the Master: the Emergence of African American Culture in the Plantation South*. NY. Pantheon. 1992. 1st ed. dj. $15.00–$22.00

Abrams, Albert. *Transactions of the Antiseptic Club*. NY. Treat. 1895. 1st ed. illus. pictorial blue cloth. frontis. $60.00–$90.00

Abrams, Bill. *The Traditions of Christmas*. NY: Avon Products (1989). $10.00–$12.00

Account of the Coal Bank Disaster at Blue Rock, Ohio, in Which Four Men were Buried beneath the Hill for Two Weeks & . Ohio. Ballou. 1856. wraps. woodcut. $150.00–$200.00

Achatenere, Romulo. *Oh, Mio Yemeya*. Cuba. Editorial Ed Arte. 1938. wraps. graphic by Hernandez Cardenas. $75.00–$100.00

Ackley, Edith. *Doll Shop of Your Own*. NY & Tor. Frederick A. Stokes. (1941). 1st ed. sgn. dj $50.00–$90.00

Ackroyd, Peter. *Chatterton*. Lon. Hamish Hamilton. (1987). 1st ed. bds. dj. $30.00–$50.00

Ackroyd, Peter. *Chatterton.* Lon. Hamish Hamilton. 1987. 1st ed. sgn. dj. $50.00–$80.00

Ackroyd, Peter. *Chatterton.* Grove Press. 1987. 1st Amer ed. dj. $30.00–$60.00

Ackroyd, Peter. *Chatterton.* Lon. London Limited Editions. (1987). 1st ed. ltd 150 cc. sgn. unprinted wrapper. $150.00–$180.00

Ackroyd, Peter. *Country Life.* Ferry Press. 1978. 1st ed. wraps. ltd 350 cc. sgn.
   $85.00–$100.00

Ackroyd, Peter. *English Music.* Franklin Library. 1992. ltd. lea. sgn. $40.00–$50.00

Ackroyd, Peter. *English Music.* Knopf. 1992. 1st US printing. uncorrected proof. wraps.
   $20.00–$30.00

Ackroyd, Peter. *English Music.* Hamish Hamilton. 1992. 1st ed. sgn. dj. $30.00–$40.00

Ackroyd, Peter. *First Light.* Lon. Hamish Hamilton. (1989). 1st ed. bds. dj. $15.00–$35.00

Ackroyd, Peter. *London Lickpenny.* Ferry Press. 1973. 1st ed. wraps. author's first book. inscrb. $100.00–$125.00

Across Africa. New York. Harper & Brothers. 1877. illus. red pictorial cloth, gilt border on cover and gilt lettering on spine, map in front pocket. $85.00–$125.00

Act for the Making of Bread. Lon. 1758. $50.00–$75.00

Activities of Ku Klux Klan Organizations in the United States. DC. GPO. 1966. wraps. 5 vols.
   $100.00–$250.00

Adams, A. L. *Field and Forest Rambles.* Lon. King & Co. 1873. 1st ed. illus. maps. woodcuts. gilt decoration. $125.00–$250.00

Adams, Ansel. *Born Free and Equal.* NY. US Camera. 1944. 1st ed. wraps. illus. rare.
   $850.00–$1,200.00

Adams, Ansel. *My Camera in the National Parks.* Bos. Virginia Adams/Yosemite National Park/Houghton Mifflin. 1950. illus. 97 pp. spiral bound. sg. dj. $500.00–$1,500.00

Adams, Ansel. *My Camera in the National Parks.* Yosemite. Virginia Adams. 1950. illus. 97 pp. spiral bound boards. sgn. no dj. $275.00–$450.00

Adams, Ansel. *Polaroid Land Photography.* Bos. New York Graphic Society. (1978). rev. ed. illus. dj. $90.00–150.00

Adams, Ansel. *Polaroid Land Photography.* Bos. New York Graphic Society. (1978). rev. ed. illus. sgn. dj. $170.00–$190.00

Adams, Ansel. *Polaroid Land Photography Manual.* NY. Morgan & Morgan. (1963). 1st ed. illus. sgn. cloth. dj. $100.00–$150.00

Adams, Ansel. *Polaroid Land Photography Manual.* NY. Morgan & Morgan. (1963). 1st ed. illus. cloth. dj. $60.00–$100.00

Adams, Ansel. *Yosemite Valley.* San Francisco. 1959. 1st ed. pictorial wraps.
   $45.00–$100.00

Adams, Ansel and Nancy Newhall. *This is the American Earth*. SF. Sierra Club. 1960. 1st ed. illus. 89 pp. dj. $50.00–$100.00

Adams, Charles. *Boontling: an American Lingo*. Austin. Univ of Texas Press. (1971). 1st ed. illus. photos. cloth. dj. $60.00–$70.00

Adams, Charles. *Lee at Appomattox and Other Papers*. Bos. Houghton Mifflin. 1902. 1st ed. $30.00–$60.00

Adams, Charles Francis. *Confederacy and the Transvaal*. Bos. Houghton Mifflin. 1901 wraps. $25.00–$50.00

Adams, Charles Francis, Jr. *Notes on Railroad Accidents*. NY. Putnam. 1879. 1st ed. decorated cloth. $150.00–$200.00

Adams, Douglas. *Dirk Gentley's Holistic Detective Agency*. NY. Simon & Schuster. (1987). 1st Amer ed. dj. $15.00–$20.00

Adams, Douglas. *Dirk Gentley's Holistic Detective Agency*. NY. Simon & Schuster. (1987). 1st Amer ed. sgn. dj. $100.00–$120.00

Adams, Douglas. *Hitchhiker's Guide to the Galaxy*. NY. 1979. 1st ed. sgn. dj. $300.00–$500.00

Adams, Douglas. *Hitchhiker's Guide to the Galaxy*. Lon. Barker. 1979. 1st ed. dj. $900.00–$1,200.00

Adams, Douglas. *Long Dark Tea-time of the Soul, The*. Lon. Heinemann. (1988). 1st ed. sgn. dj. $80.00–$150.00

Adams, Douglas. *Mostly Harmless*. NY. Harmony. 1992. 1st ed. dj. $10.00–$30.00

Adams, Elizabeth Laura. *Dark Symphony*. NY. Sheed & Ward. 1942. 1st ed. dj. $65.00–$100.00

Adams, George. *Treatise Describing the Construction, and Explaining the Use, of New Celestial and Terrestrial Globes*. Lon. pub by author. 1769. 2nd ed. plates. $600.00–$800.00

Adams, George Elbert. *Backs of Buttons*. Rhode Island. G.E. Adams. 1946. 1st ed. wraps. illus. light green wrps with lettering on cover. 42pp. $10.00–$15.00

Adams, Hannah. *Analysis of the Controversy between the Rev.* Jedidiah Morse, D. D. and the Author. Bos. 1814. wraps. $115.00–$250.00

Adams, Henry. *Democracy: an American Novel*. Lon. Macmillan. 1882. wraps. 1st UK ed. $200.00–$300.00

Adams, Henry. *Letters*. Bos. Houghton Mifflin. 1930. ltd ed. frontis. slipcase. $60.00–$85.00

Adams, Henry. *Letter to American Teachers of History, A*. Washington. 1910. 1st ed. cloth. sgn. $1,500.00–$1,850.00

Adams, John. *Message from the President of the United States*. Phila. Fenno. 1799. 1st ed. 42 pp. scarce. $250.00–$400.00

Adams, John D. *Arts-Crafts Lamps: How to Make Them*. Chi. 1911. illus. $250.00–$600.00

Adams, Joseph. *Salmon and Trout Angling*. Lon. Hutchinson. 1923. 1st ed. $30.00–$65.00

Adams, Richard. *Tales from Watership Down*. NY. Knopf. 1996. 1st US ed. dj.
$50.00–$60.00

Adams, Richard. *Traveller*. NY. Knopf. 1988. 1st ed. dj. $30.00–$50.00

Adams, Richard. *Watership Down*. NY. Macmillan. (1972). 1st ed. author's first novel. sgn. dj. $750.00–$900.00

Adams, Sara Swain. *How to Set the Table for Every Occasion*. NY. Derryvale Linen Co. 1918. pictorial boards. illus. $30.00–$35.00

Adams, Thomas. *Typographia: A Brief Sketch of the Origin, Rise, and Progress of the Typographic Art*. Phil. Thomas. 1837. 1st ed. illus. tables. rebacked. $900.00–$1,000.00

Adcock, Thomas. *Sea of Green*. NY. Mysterious Press. 1989. 1st ed. First Printing. sgn. dj.
$40.00–$90.00

Addams, Charles. *Favorite Haunts*. NY. Simon & Schuster. (1976). 1st ed. dj. $25.00–$40.00

Addams, Charles. *Homebodies*. NY. Simon & Schuster. 1954. 1st ed. dj. $25.00–$40.00

Addington, L. *Digest of the Revenue Laws of the United States, A*. Phila. Graves. 1804. 1st ed. calf. $200.00–$300.00

Adney, Edwin Tappan. *Klondike Stampede*. WA. 1968. reprint. ltd 750 cc. $50.00–$70.00

Adney, Edwin Tappan. *Klondike Stampede*. NY & Lon. Harper. 1900. 1st ed. illus. sketches.
$225.00–$275.00

Adventures of Sinbad the Sailor. Lon. Bancroft. 1960. 1st ed. illus. Pop-up Book.
$125.00–$200.00

Aesop's Fables for Children. Rand McNally. 1919. 1st ed. wraps. illus. by Milo Winter, oversize ills. cover. $18.00–$25.00

Agassiz, Louis. *Journal in Brazil*. Bos. Ticknor & Fields. 1868. 1st ed. illus. green cl.
$130.00–$600.00

Agassiz, Louis. *Journal in Brazil*. Bos. Ticknor & Fields. 1868. illus. 2nd ed. $90.00–$150.00

Agassiz, Louis. *Journal in Brazil*. Bos. Ticknor & Fields. 1868. illus. 5th ed. $35.00–$60.00

Agassiz, Louis. *Lake Superior*. Bos. Ticknor & Fields. 1850. 1st ed. illus. 15 plates. map.
$400.00–$675.00

Agassiz, Louis. *Structure of Animal Life: Six Lectures*. Scribner, Armstrong. 1866. 1st ed.
$80.00–$100.00

Agatha, Sister M. *Texas Prose Writings*. Dallas. Banks Upshaw. (1936). 1st ed. dj.
$40.00–$70.00

Agee, James. *Death in the Family*. McDowell Obolensky. (1956). 1st ed. 1st issue. "walking" for "waking" on p. 80. dj. $200.00–$700.00

Agricultural Implements and Machines. Bos. Ames Plow Co. 1901. illus. $30.00–$50.00

Aguilar, Grace. *Days of Bruce, The.* NY. Appleton. 1852. $70.00–$200.00

Aguilar, Grace. *Mother's Recompense, The.* NY. Appleton. 1851. $50.00–$70.00

Aickman, Robert. *Wine Dark Sea.* NY. Arbor House. (1968). 1st ed. dj. $30.00–$50.00

Aiken, Conrad. *Blue Voyage.* NY. Scribners. 1927. 1st ed. blue cloth. dj. $200.00–$250.00

Aiken, Conrad. *Jig of Forslin, The.* Bos. Four Seas. 1916. 1st ed. "r" missing from "warm" on p. 117. dj. $75.00–$200.00

Aiken, Conrad. *Jig of Forslin, The.* Bos. Four Seas. 1916. 1st ed. "r" missing from "warm" on p. 117. sgn. dj. $200.00–$400.00

Aiken, Henry. *Scraps from a Sketch Book.* Lon. 1823. illus. hand clr plates. folio. $500.00–$750.00

Ainsworth, Ed. *Cowboy Art.* NY. World Pub. (1968). 1st ed. illus. ltd 1,000 cc. aeg. sgn. slipcase. $50.00–$200.00

Akers, Floyd. *Boy Fortune Hunters in Alaska.* Chi. Reilly & Britton. (1908). 1st ed. later state (5 titles listed). $125.00–$175.00

Albee, Edward. *American Dream, The.* NY. Coward McCann. 1961. wraps. 1st paperback ed. $30.00–$40.00

Albee, Edward. *American Dream, The.* NY. Coward McCann. 1961. 1st ed. bds. sgn. dj. $75.00–$200.00

Albee, Edward. *Delicate Balance, A.* NY. Atheneum. 1966. 1st ed. sgn. dj. $250.00–$350.00

Albee, Edward. *Delicate Balance, A.* NY. Atheneum. 1966. 1st ed. dj. $125.00–$200.00

Albee, Edward. *Everything in the Garden.* NY. Atheneum. 1968. 1st ed. sgn.dj. $100.00–$150.00

Albert, Lillian. *Complete Button Book.* NY. Doubleday. 1949. 1st ed. dj. $50.00–$150.00

Albom, Mitch. *Five People You Meet in Heaven, The.* Hyperion. 2003. 1st ed. sgn. dj. $50.00–$60.00

Alcoholics Anonymous. NY. World Services. 1939. 1st ed. red cl. dj. $3,500.00–$8,000.00

Alcoholics Anonymous. NY. World Services. 1951. 14th printing. dj. $1,000.00–$1,200.00

Alcott, Louisa May. *An Old Fashioned Girl.* Bos. Roberts Bros. 1870. 1st ed. $150.00–$300.00

Alcott, Louisa May. *Aunt Jo's Scrap Bag.* Bos. Roberts. 1872. 1st ed. blue cloth. $50.00–$200.00

Alcott, Louisa May. *Jo's Boys.* Tor. Bryce. (1887). wraps. 2nd Canadian ed. $60.00–$70.00

Alcott, Louisa May. *Little Men.* Bos. Roberts Bros. 1871. 1st ed. $200.00–$300.00

Aldiss, Brian. *New Arrivals, Old Encounters.* NY. Harper. 1979. 1st US ed. dj. $10.00–$18.00

Aldiss, Brian W. and Harry Harrison. *Hell's Cartographers.* NY. Harper & Row. 1975. 1st US ed. dj. $30.00–$45.00

Aldrich, Herbert L. *Arctic Alaska and Siberia.* Chi/NY. Rand McNally. 1889. 1st ed. illus. photos. maps. $175.00–$200.00

Aldrin, Buzz and John Barnes. *Return, The.* NY. Forge. 2000. 1st ed. sgn by Aldrin. dj.
$200.00–$300.00

Alexander, Dave. *Star Trek Creator: The Authorized Biography of Gene Roddenberry.* NY. ROC. 1994. 1st ed. dj. $30.00–$50.00

Alexander, Dave. *Star Trek Creator: The Authorized Biography of Gene Roddenberry.* NY. ROC. 1994. 1st ed. sgn. dj. $80.00–$130.00

Alexander, David. *Most Men Don't Kill.* NY. Random House. 1951. 1st ed. author's first novel. dj. $20.00–$50.00

Alexander, E. P. *Military Memoirs of a Confederate.* NY. Scribner's. 1907. 1st ed.
$200.00–$350.00

Alexander, William. *History of Women.* Lon. Strahan and Cadell. 1779. 1st ed.
$1,000.00–$2,500.00

Alexander, William. *History of Women.* Lon. Dilly & Christopher. 1782. 3rd ed.
$600.00–$1,000.00

Alexie, Sherman. *Business of Fancydancing, The.* Hanging Loose Press. 1992. 1st ed. wraps. author's first book. sgn. $200.00–$900.00

Alexie, Sherman. *Indian Killer.* Atlantic. 1996. 1st ed. ltd 100 cc. sgn. dj. $30.00–$40.00

Alexie, Sherman. *Lone Ranger and Tonto Fistfight in Heaven, The.* Atlantic. 1993. 1st ed. sgn. dj. $50.00–$90.00

Alexie, Sherman. *Lone Ranger and Tonto Fistfight in Heaven, The.* NY. Atlantic Monthly. 1993. 1st Amer ed. wraps. $12.00–$20.00

Alexie, Sherman. *Lone Ranger and Tonto Fistfight in Heaven, The.* NY. Atlantic Monthly Pub. 1993. 1st Amer ed. wraps. sgn. $25.00–$30.00

Alger, Horatio. *Adrift in the City.* Phila. John Winston. 1895. $18.00–$30.00

Alger, Horatio. *Brave and Bold.* NY. Hurst. 1907. $12.00–$15.00

Alger, Horatio, Jr. *Luke Walton or the Chicago Newsboy.* Phila. Coates. nd. $60.00–$75.00

Alger, William Rounseville. *Life of Edwin Forrest.* Phila. Lippincott. 1877. 2 vols. pict cl. plates. $100.00–$200.00

Algren, Nelson. *Man With the Golden Arm, The.* Doubleday. 1949. 1st ed. tan cloth.
$100.00–$125.00

Algren, Nelson. *Man With the Golden Arm, The.* Garden City. Doubleday. 1949. 1st ed. sgn.
$500.00–$750.00

Algren, Nelson. *Somebody in Boots*. Vanguard Press. 1935. 1st ed. tan cloth. sgn. dj.
$900.00–$2,500.00

Algren, Nelson. *Walk on the Wild Side*. NY. Farrar, Straus & Cudahy. (1956). 1st ed. dj.
$75.00–$200.00

Algren, Nelson. *Walk on the Wild Side*. NY. Farrar, Straus & Cudahy. (1956). 1st ed. in-scrb. dj.
$200.00–$4,700.00

Ali Baba and the Forty Thieves. Houghton Mifflin. 1950. peep show book. 6 pop-ups.
$40.00–$200.00

Allan, William. *Army of Northern Virginia in 1862*. 1st ed. maps. $350.00–$600.00

Alldredge, Charles. *Some Quick and Some Dead: Poems*. NY. Cooper Square. 1964. 1st ed.
$100.00–$125.00

Allen, Charles Dexter. *American Book-Plates*. Lon. George Bell. 1895. 1st trade ed.
$30.00–$125.00

Allen, Grant. *Cruise of the Albatross, The*. Bos. Lothrop. (1898). $50.00–$75.00

Allen, Henry T. *Report of an Expedition of the Copper, Tana, and Koyakuk Rivers, in the Territory of Alaska in the year 1885*. DC. GPO. 1887. 1st ed. wraps. illus. 5 fldg maps. plates.
$200.00–$400.00

Allen, Hervey. *New Legends*. NY. Farrar & Rinehart. 1929. 1st trade ed. dj. $55.00–$70.00

Allen, Jean. *Jean Allen's Budget Cook Book*. NY. Arco. 1955. 1st ed. illus. dj. $15.00–$25.00

Allen, Miss A. J. *Ten Years in Oregon*. Ithaca. 1848. 1st ed. 1st issue. $200.00–$600.00

Allen, Miss A. J. *Ten Years in Oregon*. Ithaca. 1848. 1st ed. 2nd issue. $100.00–$200.00

Allen, Ralph B. *The Saga of Gisli Son of Sour*. New York. Harcourt Brace. 1936. 1st ed. illus. by Rockwell Kent. tan hc. $20.00–$100.00

Allen, Steve. *Funny Men*. NY. Simon & Schuster. 1956. 1st ed. dj. $10.00–$20.00

Allen, Steve. *Funny Men*. NY. Simon & Schuster. 1956. 1st ed. inscrb. $45.00–$60.00

Allison, Willie (ed.). *First Golf Review, The*. Lon. Bonar. (1950). 1st ed. $15.00–$25.00

Alliss, Percy. *Better Golf*. Lon. Black. 1926. 1st ed. $50.00–$100.00

Alphabetical List of Additions Made to the War Department Library May 1884 to June 1891. DC. GPO. (1991). reprint. $40.00–$50.00

Alsaker, Anna Lana. *The Sun-Diet Cook Book*. East Aurora. Sun-Diet Health. 1935. black leatherette boards, gold lettering. early macro-diet cookbook. very good. $15.00–$25.00

Alvarez, Julia. *How the Garcia Girls Lost Their Accents*. Algonquin. 1991. 1st ed. author's first novel. dj. $30.00–$50.00

Alvarez, Julia. *How the Garcia Girls Lost Their Accents*. Algonquin. 1991. 1st ed. author's first novel. sgn. dj. $30.00–$90.00

Alvarez, Julia. *How the Garcia Girls Lost Their Accents*. Chapel Hill. Algonquin. 1991. 1st ed. wraps. signed advance reading copy. $90.00–$150.00

Alvarez, Julia. *Yo!*. Algonquin. 1997. 1st ed. sgn. dj. $20.00–$35.00

Ambler, Charles Henry. *History of Transportation in the Ohio Valley*. CA. 1932. 1st ed. illus. $100.00–$150.00

Ambler, Eric. *Night-Comers*. Lon. Heinemann. 1956. 1st ed. dj. $25.00–$40.00

Ambler, Louis. *Old Halls & Manor Houses of Yorkshire*. Lon. Batsford. nd. preface dated 1913. $200.00–$350.00

American Boy's Book of Sports and Games. NY. Dick & Fitzgerald. 1864. $450.00–$750.00

American Bureau of Shipping. *1878 Record of American and Foreign Shipping*. NY. 1878. illus. $250.00–$350.00

American Car and Foundry Company. *Khaki; Its Production Achievements in the Great War*. NY. 1919. $90.00–$200.00

American Game Fishes. Chicago. Rand McNally Co. 1892. 1st ed. illus. blue illus. cover. col. plates. $100.00–$250.00

American Home Missionary Society. *Our Country: Its Capabilities, Its Perils, Its Hope*. NY. American Home Missionary Society. 1842. wraps. $100.00–$250.00

American Jack Stock Stud Book. Nashville. American Breeders Association of Jacks and Jennets. 1891. Vol. I. $125.00–$150.00

American Jack Stock Stud Book. Nashville. American Breeders Association of Jacks and Jennets. 1891. Vol. III. $125.00–$150.00

American Line Type Faces. Brooklyn. American Type Founder. nd. $150.00–$200.00

American Tract Society. *Elspeth Sutherland: Or the Effects of Faith*. NY. American Tract Society. nd. wraps. frontis. illus. sewn. $25.00–$40.00

American Type Founders Company, Specimen Book and Catalogue. Jersey City. 1923. $250.00–$300.00

Ames, Nathaniel. *An Astronomical Diary of an Almanac for the Year of Our Lord 1764*. Bos. 1763. $130.00–$400.00

Amherst, Alicia. *History of Gardening in England*. Lon. Bernard Quaritch. 1895. 1st ed. $250.00–$500.00

Amherst, Alicia. *History of Gardening in England*. Lon. Bernard Quaritch. 1896. 2nd ed. $175.00–$225.00

Amis, Martin. *Dead Babies*. Lon. Jonathan Cape. 1975. 1st UK ed. inscrb. dj. $400.00–$1,000.00

Amis, Martin. *Dead Babies*. NY. Knopf. 1975. 1st Amer ed. dj. $100.00–$150.00

Amis, Martin. *London Fields*. NY. 1989. 1st Amer ed. dj. $15.00–$18.00

Facsimile title page from the 1828 edition of **Fanshawe,** first book by Nathaniel Hawthorne, Boston.
Digital photography by Jonathan Draudt, Tamarac Arts.

Facsimile title page from *Tamerlane and Other Poems,* by "A Bostonian," 1827. The book was written by Edgar Allan Poe.
Digital photography by Jonathan Draudt, Tamarac Arts.

Amis, Martin. *London Fields.* Tor. (1989). wraps. uncorrected proof. $65.00–$85.00

Amis, Martin. *London Fields.* Tor. Lester & Orpen Denny. (1989). 1st Canadian ed. sgn. dj.
$50.00–$70.00

Amis, Martin. *Money: A Suicide Note.* Lon. Jonathan Cape. 1984. 1st ed. dj.
$100.00–$200.00

Amis, Martin. *Money: A Suicide Note.* Lon. Jonathan Cape. 1984. 1st ed. sgn. dj.
$220.00–$400.00

Amis, Martin. *Night Train.* Lon. Jonathan Cape. 1997. 1st ed. sgn. dj. $45.00–$60.00

Among the Pimas or The Mission to the Pima and Maricopa Indians. Albany. Ladies Union Mission School. 1893. 1st ed. green cl. black lettering on cover. near fine. $50.00–$200.00

Amsden, Charles Avery. *Navaho Weaving, Its Technic and History.* Santa Ana. Fine Arts Press. 1934. 1st ed. illus. $350.00–$800.00

Amundsen, Roald. *First Crossing of the Polar Sea.* NY. Doran. 1927. 1st ed. sgn. dj.
$400.00–$700.00

Amundsen, Roald. *South Pole.* Lon. John Murray. 1912. 1st ed. 2 vols. maps.
$2,000.00–$4,000.00

Andersen, Hans Christian. *Fairy Tales.* NY. Doran. (1924). illus. by Kay Neilsen. marbled endpapers. tipped in clr plates. $300.00–$900.00

Andersen, Hans Christian. *Ice Maiden and the Story of My Life.* Lon. 1863. 1st UK ed. illus. aeg. $200.00–$400.00

Andersen, Hans Christian. *Nightingale and Other Stories.* NY/Lon. Hodder & Stoughton. nd. 1st ed. illus. by Edmund Dulac. tip-in clr plates. $200.00–$250.00

Andersen, Hans Christian. *Picture Book Without Pictures.* NY. 1848. 1st Amer ed.
                                                                                       $150.00–$250.00

Andersen, Hans Christian. *Tumble Bug and Other Tales.* NY. Harcourt, Brace. 1940. 1st ed.
                                                                                       $40.00–$80.00

Anderson, Charles. *Fighting by Southern Federals.* NY. Neale. 1912. 1st ed.
                                                                                       $250.00–$300.00

Anderson, Christopher. *Annals of the English Bible.* Lon. Hamilton Adams. 1842. 1st ed.
                                                                                       $350.00–$425.00

Anderson, Edward. *Hungry Men.* 1935. 1st ed. cloth. $100.00–$250.00

Anderson, Eva Greenslit. *Chief Seattle.* Caldwell, ID. Caxton. 1943. 1st ed. sgn. dj.
                                                                                       $40.00–$80.00

Anderson, Galush. *Story of a Border City During the Civil War, The.* Bos. 1908. 1st ed. illus. plates. illustrated binding. $70.00–$90.00

Anderson, James. *Essays Relating to Agriculture and Rural Affairs.* Lon. Robinson and Cumming. 1800. 5th ed. 3 vols. folding plates. blue boards. $900.00–$1,000.00

Anderson, John. *American Theatre & Motion Picture.* NY. Dial. 1938. 1st ed. dj.
                                                                                       $40.00–$75.00

Anderson, Kenneth. *Nine Man-eaters and One Rogue.* NY. Dutton. 1955. 1st ed. dj.
                                                                                       $80.00–$125.00

Anderson, Kent. *Sympathy for the Devil.* Garden City. Doubleday. 1987. 1st ed. author's first novel. sgn.dj. $175.00–$250.00

Anderson, Lawrence. *Art of the Silversmiths in Mexico, 1519–1937.* NY. Oxford Univ Press. 1941. 1st ed. illus. 2 vols. $500.00–$750.00

Anderson, Lawrence. *Art of the Silversmiths in Mexico, 1519–1937.* reprint. $40.00–$75.00

Anderson, Martha Jane. *Social Life and Vegetarianism.* Mt. Lebanon. 1893. $60.00–$100.00

Anderson, Mary E. *Scenes in the Hawaiian Islands and California.* Bos. 1865. 1st ed. illus. clr frontis. $150.00–$200.00

Anderson, Nels. *The Hobo, the Sociology of the Homeless Man.* Chi. Univ Chicago Press. 1923. 1st ed. illus. photos. cl. scarce. $70.00–$100.00

Anderson, Poul. *Flandry of Terra.* Phil. Chilton. 1965. 1st ed. dj. $15.00–$30.00

Anderson, Poul. *Guardians of Time.* Lon. Gollancz. 1961. 1st ed. dj. $50.00–$110.00

Anderson, Poul. *Guardians of Time.* Lon. Gollancz. 1961. 1st ed. dj. $80.00–$125.00

Anderson, Poul. *Orion Shall Rise.* Phantasia Press. 1983. 1st ed. ltd 600 cc. numbered. sgn. slipcase. $50.00–$75.00

Anderson, Poul. *Perish By the Sword.* NY. Macmillan. 1959. 1st ed. sgn. dj. $150.00–$250.00

Anderson, Poul. *Perish By the Sword.* NY. Macmillan. 1959. 1st ed. dj. $90.00–$100.00

Anderson, R. B. *America Not Discovered by Columbus: A Historical Sketch of the Discovery of America by the Norsemen in the Tenth Century.* Chi. Griggs. 1874. 1st ed. $50.00–$90.00

Anderson, R. C. *Rigging of the Ships in the Days of the Spritsail Topmast. . . .* Marine Research Society. 1927. 1st ed. illus. dj. $100.00–$150.00

Anderson, Robert. *I Never Sang For My Father.* NY. Random House. (1968). 1st ed. play. inscrb. dj. $600.00–$7,500.00

Anderson, Robert. *Tea and Sympathy.* NY. Random House. (1953). 1st ed. inscrb. dj. $300.00–$400.00

Anderson, Rufus. *Hawaiian Islands.* Bos. Gould & Lincoln. 1864. 1st ed. illus. maps. $150.00–$375.00

Anderson, Sherwood. *Beyond Desire.* NY. Liveright. 1932. 1st ed. ltd 165 cc. sgn. numbered. $200.00–$300.00

Anderson, Sherwood. *Death in the Woods.* NY. Liveright. 1933. 1st ed. dj. $2,000.00–$4,000.00

Anderson, Sherwood. *Death in the Woods.* NY. Liveright. 1933. 1st ed. inscrb. dj. $5,500.00–$6,000.00

Anderson, Sherwood. *Perhaps Women.* NY. Liveright. 1931. 1st ed. dj. $100.00–$200.00

Anderson, Sherwood. *Poor White.* NY. Huebsch. 1920. 1st ed. dj missing. $40.00–$60.00

Anderson, Sherwood. *Poor White.* NY. Huebsch. 1920. 1st ed. 1st issue. dj. $400.00–$600.00

Anderson, Sherwood. *Poor White.* NY. Huebsch. 1920. 1st ed. 1st issue. sgn. dj. $500.00–$700.00

Anderson, Sherwood. *A Story Teller's Story.* NY. Huebsch. 1923. 1st ed. orange cloth. $20.00–$30.00

Anderson, Sherwood. *Tar, A Midwest Childhood.* NY. Boni & Liveright. 1926. 1st ed. dj missing. $35.00–$50.00

Anderson, Sherwood. *Tar, A Midwest Childhood.* NY. Boni & Liveright. 1926. 1st ed. dj. $75.00–$100.00

Anderson, Sherwood. *Tar, A Midwest Childhood.* NY. Boni & Liveright. 1926. 1st ed. ltd 500 cc. numbered and sgn. $150.00–$300.00

Anderson, Sherwood. *Winesburg, Ohio.* NY. Huebsch. 1919. 1st ed. later issue. $125.00–$200.00

Anderson, Sherwood. *Winesburg, Ohio.* NY. Huebsch. 1919. 1st ed. 1st state with points; lay on line 5, p 86; broken type the on line 3, p 251. $850.00–$2,500.00

Anderson, Sherwood. *Winesburg, Ohio.* NY. Heubsch. 1919. 1st ed. first issue. points. sgn. $6,500.00–$8,000.00

Anderson, Sherwood. *Winesburg, Ohio.* NY. Modern Library Edition. (1921). sgn. $1,000.00–$2,000.00

Anderson, William. *Japanese Wood Engravings.* Lon. Seely. 1895. 1st ed. illus. cloth. $35.00–$75.00

Andrade, Manuel J. *Quileute Texts.* NY. Columbia Univ Press. 1931. 1st ed. $40.00–$75.00

Andreev, Leonid. *Anathema: A Tragedy in Seven Scenes....* NY. Macmillan. 1910. 1st English ed. blue cloth. blindstamped. $40.00–$50.00

Andrews, Eliza Frances. *War-Time Journal of a Georgia Girl 1864–1865.* NY. 1908. 1st ed. $80.00–$125.00

Andrews, Mary Raymond Shipman. *Passing the Torch.* NY. 1924. 1st ed. dj. $35.00–$40.00

Andrews, Roy Chapman. *On the Trail of Ancient Man.* NY. Putnam. 1926. 1st ed. dj. $75.00–$100.00

Anfuso, Linda. *Stolen Daughter.* Wilton. Interset Press. (1996). sgn. wraps. $40.00–$45.00

Angelou, Maya. *Gather Together In My Name.* NY. Random House. 1974. 1st ed. sgn. dj. $100.00–$150.00

Angelou, Maya. *Just Give Me A Cool Drink of Water 'Fore I Die.* NY. Random House. 1971. 1st ed. sgn. dj. $80.00–$120.00

Angelou, Maya. *Just Give Me A Cool Drink of Water 'Fore I Die.* NY. Random House. 1971. 1st ed. dj. $65.00–$75.00

Angelou, Maya. *Now Sheba Sings the Song.* NY. Dutton. 1987. 1st ed. dj. $25.00–$125.00

Angelou, Maya. *Now Sheba Sings the Song.* NY. Dutton. 1987. 1st ed. inscrb. dj. $100.00–$120.00

Angelou, Maya. *Now Sheba Sings the Song.* Lon. Virago. 1987. 1 UK ed. cloth. dj. $50.00–$125.00

Angelou, Maya. *On the Pulse of Morning.* NY. Random House. 1993. ltd 400 cc. sgn. slipcase. $70.00–$150.00

Angelou, Maya. *On the Pulse of Morning.* NY. Random House. 1993. wraps. 1st softcover ed. $25.00–$70.00

Angione, Genevieve. *All-Bisque and Half-Bisque Dolls.* NJ. Nelson. 1969. 1st ed. sgn. dj. $40.00–$55.00

Angione, Genevieve. *All-Bisque and Half-Bisque Dolls.* NJ. Nelson. 1969. 1st ed. dj. $25.00–$50.00

Angle, Paul M. *Bloody Williamson; a Chapter in American Lawlessness.* NY. Knopf. 1952. 1st ed. sgn. dj. Ku Klux Klan. $25.00–$40.00

Animated Picture Book of Alice in Wonderland. NY. Grosset & Dunlap. 1945. 1st ed. illus. by Wehr. spiral bound. $200.00–$400.00

Anjou, Gustave. *Ulster County, NY: Probate Records.* 1906. illus. from 1665.$200.00–$225.00

Annesley, George. *Voyages and Travels to India, Ceylon, the Red Sea, Abyssnia and Egypt.* Lon. Rivington. 1811. 2nd ed. 3 vols. engr plates. maps. charts. $500.00–$1,000.00

Annesley, George. *Voyages and Travels to India, Ceylon, the Red Sea, Abyssnia and Egypt.* Lon. William Miller. 1809. 1st ed. 3 vols. engr plates. maps. charts. $2,500.00–$3,500.00

Anno, Mitsumasa. *Anno's Italy.* NY. Collins. 1980. illus. 1st Amer ed. pictures with no words. dj. $30.00–$70.00

Annual Report of the Adjutant-General of the Commonwealth of Massachusetts Dec. 31, 1865. Bos. Wright & Potter. 1866. brown blind-stamped cloth. binding worn, corners bumped. contents clean. $50.00–$100.00

Annual Report of the Board of Regents of the Smithsonian Institution & Year Ending June 30, 1901. DC. GPO. 1903. 1st ed. illus. $65.00–$130.00

Annual Report of the Board of Regents of the Smithsonian Institution & Year Ending June 30, 1902. DC. GPO. 1903. 1st ed. illus. $45.00–$100.00

Annual Report of the Board of Regents of the Smithsonian Institution & Year Ending June 30, 1903. DC. GPO. 1904. 1st ed. illus. $45.00–$70.00

Annual Report of the State Mineralogist of the State of Nevada for 1866. Carson City. Eckley. 1867. wraps. folding table. $800.00–$850.00

Anonymous (Samuel Ornitz). *Haunch, Paunch and Jowl.* NY. Boni and Liveright. 1923. 1st ed. $25.00–$45.00

Anson, Margaret. *Merry Order of St. Bridget: Personal Recollections of the Use of the Rod.* NY. privately printed. 1857. 1st ed. teg. $75.00–$100.00

Anson, Margaret. *Merry Order of St. Bridget: Personal Recollections of the Use of the Rod.* NY. 1891. reprint. $45.00–$55.00

Anstey, F. *Mr. Punch's Pocket Ibsen.* London: Heinemann, 1893.1st ed. illus. cloth.
                                                                 $235.00–$260.00

Anthon, Charles. *Classical Dictionary.* NY. 1841. 1st ed. $100.00–$125.00

Anthony, Gordon. *Russian Ballet.* Lon. Bles. 1939. 1st ed. illus. dark blue morocco.
                                                                 $700.00–$800.00

Anthony, Gordon. *Russian Ballet.* Lon. Bles. 1939. 1st trade ed. illus. photographs. cloth.
                                                                 $100.00–$250.00

Anthony, Piers. *Kirlian Quest.* Lon. Millington. 1979. 1st ed. in hardcover. dj.
                                                                 $50.00–$75.00

Anthony, Piers. *Out of Phaze.* NY. Ace/Putnam. 1987. 1st ed. dj. $20.00–$30.00

Anthony, Piers. *Vicinity Cluster.* Lon. Millington. 1979. 1st ed. in hardcover. dj.
                                                                 $50.00–$75.00

Apes, William. *Son of the Forest.* NY. William Apes. 1831. 2nd ed. revised. first autobiography of a Native American. frontis. $325.00–$500.00

Apes, William. *Son of the Forest.* NY. William Apes. 1829. 1st ed. first autobiography of a Native American. $750.00–$800.00

Apperley, C. J. *Life of John Mytton, Esq....* Lon. Routledge. 1837. 2nd ed. $800.00–$1,000.00

Apperley, C. J. *The Horse and the Hound, Their Various Uses and Treatment Including Practical Instructions in Horsemanship and a Treatise on Horse Dealing.* Edinburgh. 1863. frontis. plates. $75.00–$120.00

Applegate, Frank G. *Indian Stories from Pueblos.* Phila. 1929. 1st ed. $35.00–$45.00

Appleton, L. H. *Indian Art of the Americas.* NY. (1950). color plates. $100.00–$150.00

Appleton, Victor. *Moving Picture Boys, The.* NY. Grosset & Dunlap. 1913. #1. dj. $25.00–$50.00

Appleton, Victor. *Tom Swift Among the Firefighters.* NY. Grosset & Dunlap. 1921. 1st ed. #24. $25.00–$30.00

Appleton, Victor. *Tom Swift and His Airship.* NY. Grosset & Dunlap. 1910. tan cloth. pictorial cover. $10.00–$30.00

Appleton, Victor. *Tom Swift and His Electric Runabout.* NY. Grosset & Dunlap. 1910. #5. $15.00–$30.00

Appleton, Victor. *Tom Swift and His Ocean Airport.* Whitman. 1934. 1st ed. #37. dj. $500.00–$800.00

Appleton, Victor. *Tom Swift and His Ocean Airport.* Whitman. 1934. #37. later edition. dj. $40.00–$60.00

Aptheker, Herbert (ed.). *And Why Not Every Man?.* Berlin. Seven Seas. 1961. 1st ed. wraps. $15.00–$20.00

Aptheker, Herbert. *Negro Slave Revolts in the United States, 1526–1860.* NY. International. 1939. 1st ed. wraps. $15.00–$25.00

Archer, William. *Three Plays.* Lon. Constable and Co. 1927. 1st. edition. $50.00–100.00

Arizona Highways. 1987. wraps. illus. vol. 63, #11, very good. $5.00–$8.00

Arizona Highways. 1987. wraps. illus. vol. 63, #11, very good. $5.00–$8.00

Armstrong, Arnold B. *Parched Earth.* NY. Macmillan. 1934. 1st ed. dj. $100.00–$140.00

Armstrong, Benjamin G. *Early Life Among the Indians.* Ashland, WI. 1892. 1st ed. illus. plates. $100.00–$125.00

Armstrong, Harry G. *Principles and Practice of Aviation Medicine.* Balt. Williams & Wilkins. 1939. 1st ed. later printing. charts. dj. $75.00–$125.00

Armstrong, John M.D. *Young Woman's Guide to Virtue, Economy and Happiness....* Newcastle. nd. illus. $100.00–$150.00

Armstrong, John M.D. *Art of Preserving Health, A Poem*. Lon. 1774. $75.00–$100.00

Armstrong, John M.D. *Art of Preserving Health, A Poem*. Lon. 1757. $200.00–$275.00

Armstrong, John M.D. *Art of Preserving Health, A Poem*. Lon. 1744. 1st ed.
$400.00–$650.00

Armstrong, Margaret. *Blue Santo Murder Mystery*. NY. Random House. (1941). 1st ed. author's last mystery. dj. $40.00–$85.00

Armstrong, Martin. *Puppet Show, The*. Berkshire. Golden Cockerel Press. 1922. 1st ed. wraps. $40.00–$120.00

Army Regulations Adopted for the Use of the Army of the Confederate States. New Orleans. 1861. 98 pp. $500.00–$750.00

Arnaud de Ronsil, Georges. *Dissertation on Hernias or Ruptures*. Lon. Millar. 1748.
$200.00–$500.00

Arnold, Isaac N. *History of the Life of Abraham Lincoln and the Overthrow of Slavery*. Chi. 1866. 1st ed. illus. $100.00–$250.00

Arnold, Isaac N. *Sketch of the Life of Abraham Lincoln. . . .* NY. 1869. 1st ed. illus. lea. aeg.
$150.00–$250.00

Arnold, Matthew. *Essays in Criticism*. Lon. 1865. 1st ed. $150.00–$165.00

Arnold, Sir Edwin. *Light of Asia, The*. Lon. Bodley Head. 1926. new ed. ltd 3000 cc. teg.
$125.00–$250.00

Art Work of the State of Oregon. Portland. Harney. 1909. Edition Deluxe. folio. 107 leaves of images. 80 photogravures. $700.00–$800.00

Arthur, Sir George. *Life of Lord Kitchener: a Great British Life in the Middle East. . . .* Lon. 1920. 1st ed. $50.00–$85.00

Artistic Guide to Chicago and the World's Columbian Exposition, The. Columbian Art Co. 1892. illus. $25.00–100.00

Artists and Writers Golf Association 1935. NY. sgn by Rube Goldberg. $250.00–$300.00

Artwork of the Mohawk River and Valley, Its Cities and Towns. Chi. 1902. 1st ed. 9 vols.
$100.00–$120.00

Artzybasheff, Boris. *Poor Shaydullah*. NY. Macmillan. 1931. 1st ed. sgn. dj.
$100.00–$200.00

Artzybasheff, Boris. *Poor Shaydullah*. NY. Macmillan. 1931. 1st ed. dj. $80.00–$150.00

Asbury, Herbert. *Ye Olde Fire Laddies*. NY. Knopf. 1930. 1st ed. illus. pict bds. dj.
$100.00–$220.00

Ashburner, Charles A. *Bradford Oil District of Pennsylvania, The*. Phila. Transcript of Amer. Inst. of Mining Eng. 1879. fldg map. $30.00–$45.00

Ashby, Thomas. *Valley Campaigns, The*. NY. Neale. 1914. 1st ed. $350.00–$500.00

Ashley, Clifford. *Ashley Book of Knots*. NY. Doubleday. (1914). 1st ed. illus. oversized blue cl. pict dj. pict endpapers. $40.00–$55.00

Ashley, Frederick W. *Vollbehr Incunabula and the Book of Books. . . .* DC. GPO. 1932. 1st ed. wraps. illus. ltd 420 cc. slipcase. printed on hand. $85.00–$100.00

Ashton, John. *Chap-Books of the Eighteenth Century.* Lon. Chatto & Windus. 1882. ltd. 4to. $200.00–$250.00

Ashton, John. *Chap-Books of the Eighteenth Century.* Lon. Chatto & Windus. 1882. 1st ed. 8vo. $60.00–$150.00

Ashton, John. *Curious Creatures of Zoology.* Lon. John C. Nimmo. 1890. 1st ed. illus. re-bound. $100.00–$150.00

Ashton, John. *Curious Creatures of Zoology.* Lon. John C. Nimmo. 1890. 1st ed. illus. ltd 210 cc. ¼ lea. $200.00–$300.00

Asimov, Isaac. *Asimov's Biographical Encyclopedia of Science & Technology.* Doubleday. 1964. dj. $80.00–$100.00

Asimov, Isaac. *Asimov's Biographical Encyclopedia of Science & Technology.* Doubleday. 1964. rev. ed. no dj. $20.00–$65.00

Asimov, Isaac. *Asimov's Guide to Science.* NY. Basic. 1972. 3rd ed. inscrb. dj. $800.00–$1,000.00

Asimov, Isaac. *Currents of Space.* NY. Doubleday. 1952. 1st ed. sgn. dj. $300.00–$350.00

Asimov, Isaac. *Currents of Space.* NY. Doubleday. 1952. 1st ed. dj. $100.00–$300.00

Asimov, Isaac. *Death Dealers.* NY. Avon. 1958. 1st ed. wraps. original. author's first mystery. sgn. $35.00–$75.00

Asimov, Isaac. *End of Eternity.* Garden City. Doubleday. 1955. 1st ed. dj. $125.00–$195.00

Asimov, Isaac. *Foundation's Edge.* Garden City. Doubleday. 1982. 1st ed. dj. $15.00–$18.00

Asimov, Isaac. *How Did We Find Out About Atoms?* NY. Walker. (1976). wraps. 1st trade ed. inscrb. dj. $350.00–$500.00

Asimov, Isaac. *How Did We Find Out About Electricity?* NY. Walker. 1973. 1st ed. inscrb. dj. $350.00–$500.00

Asimov, Isaac. *How Did We Find Out About Robots?* NY. Walker. (1984). 1st ed. inscrb. dj. $350.00–$500.00

Asimov, Isaac. *I, Robot.* NY. Gnome Press. 1950. 1st ed. fine in fine dj. $1,200.00–$2,000.00

Asimov, Isaac. *I, Robot.* NY. Gnome Press. 1950. 1st ed. fine in fine dj. sgn. $3,000.00–$4,500.00

Asimov, Isaac. *Only a Trillion.* Lon/NY. Abelard. (1957). 1st ed. author's first science essays in book form. inscrb. dj. $500.00–$650.00

Asimov, Isaac. *Realm of Numbers.* Bos. Houghton Mifflin. (1959). 1st ed. inscrb. dj. $500.00–$600.00

Asimov, Isaac. *Short History of Biology, A.* Garden City. Natural History Press. (1964). 1st ed. inscrb. dj. $400.00–$600.00

Asimov, Isaac. *Tales of the Black Widowers.* Doubleday. 1974. 1st ed. dj. $100.00–$125.00

Asimov, Isaac. *Ugly Little Boy, The.* NY. Doubleday. 1992. uncorrected proof. sgn by Robert Silverberg. $50.00–$90.00

Asimov, Isaac. *Wellsprings of Life, The.* NY. Abelard-Schuman. 1960. 1st ed. sgn. dj.
     $500.00–$600.00

Askins, Charles. *Game Bird Shooting.* NY. Macmillan. 1931. 1st ed. illus. dj. $50.00–$100.00

Asquith, Cynthia (ed.). *Book of Modern Ghosts, A (Second Ghost Book).* NY. Scribner's. 1953. 1st Amer ed. dj. $15.00–$30.00

Asquith, Cynthia (ed.). *Ghost Book.* Lon. Hutchinson. 1st UK ed. nd. 1926.
     $100.00–$200.00

Asquith, Cynthia (ed.). *Ghost Book.* NY. Scribner's. 1927. 1st Amer ed. 1st printing. teal cloth. $75.00–$100.00

Asquith, Cynthia (ed.). *Second Ghost Book, The.* Lon. Barrie. 1952. 1st UK ed. dj.
     $30.00–$50.00

Association of Edison Illuminating Companies. *Edisonia. A Brief History of the Early Edison Electric Lighting System.* NY. 1904. 1st ed. illus. errata slip tipped in. $300.00–$400.00

Astaire, Fred. *Steps in Time.* NY. Harper & Bros. (1959). 1st ed. dj. $100.00–$150.00

Astaire, Fred. *Steps in Time.* NY. Harper & Bros. (1959). 1st ed. sgn. dj. $200.00–$600.00

Aston, F. W. *Isotopes.* Lon. Arnold. 1922. 1st ed. illus. plates. cloth. Nobel Prize–winning author. $400.00–$450.00

Atil, Esin. *Art of the Arab World.* DC. Smithsonian. 1975. stiff wraps. illus. $20.00–$45.00

Atkinson, Joseph. *History of Newark, NJ.* Newark. Guild. 1878. 1st ed. illus. by Moran. 334 pp. plates. $50.00–$90.00

Atkinson, Thomas Witlam. *Travels in the Regions of the Upper and Lower Amoor and the Russian Acquisitions on the Confines of India and China.* Lon. Hurst and Blackett. 1860. 1st UK ed. rebound. $260.00–$600.00

Atkinson, Thomas Witlam. *Travels in the Regions of the Upper and Lower Amoor and the Russian Acquisitions on the Confines of India and China.* NY. Harper. 1860. 1st Amer ed. re-bound. $200.00–$500.00

Atlas of Cuyahoga County, Ohio. Phila. Titus Simmons & Titus. 1874. folio. cloth. bds & lea. plates. maps. $1,500.00–$2,500.00

Atomic Energy Commission; Los Alamos Scientific Laboratory. *Effects of Atomic Weapons.* DC. GPO. 1950. 1st ed. original printed wraps. $15.00–$30.00

Atomic Energy Commission; Los Alamos Scientific Laboratory. *Effects of Atomic Weapons.* NY. McGraw Hill. 1950. 1st ed. in boards. $30.00–$50.00

Atomic Energy Commission; Los Alamos Scientific Laboratory. *Effects of Atomic Weapons.* DC. GPO. 1950. wraps. rev. $10.00–$25.00

Attaway, William. *Let Me Breathe Thunder.* NY. Doubleday, Doran. 1939. 1st ed. author's first book. dj. $90.00–$150.00

Atwater, Caleb. *History of the State of Ohio.* Cinc. (1838). 2nd ed. $200.00–$250.00

Atwater, Caleb. *Remarks Made on a Tour to Prairie Du Chien.* Columbus. Jenkins and Glover. 1831. 1st ed. $650.00–$900.00

Atwater, Mary Meigs. *Shuttle-Craft Book of American Hand Weaving.* NY. Macmillan. 1928. 1st ed. $75.00–$110.00

Atwood, E. Bagby. *Regional Vocabulary of Texas, The.* Austin. Univ of Texas Press. (1962). 1st ed. dj. $50.00–$70.00

Atwood, Margaret. *Bodily Harm.* NY. Simon & Schuster. (1982). 1st Amer ed. sgn. dj. $55.00–$75.00

Atwood, Margaret. *Bodily Harm.* Tor. McClelland & Steward. (1981). 1st Canadian ed. 1st printing. sgn. dj. $90.00–$125.00

Auchincloss, Louis. *Injustice Collectors.* Bos. Houghton Mifflin. 1950. 1st ed. dj. $50.00–$150.00

Auden, W. H. *City Without Walls and Other Poems.* Lon. Faber. (1969). 1st UK ed. dj. $50.00–$150.00

Auden, W. H. *City Without Walls and Other Poems.* NY. Random House. (1969). 1st Amer ed. dj. $40.00–$100.00

Auden, W. H. *Collected Poems. Franklin Center.* Franklin Library. 1976. 1st ed. ed by Edward Mendelson. lea. $50.00–$75.00

Auden, W. H. *Collected Poetry of W. H. Auden.* NY. Random House. (1945). 1st ed. dj. $90.00–$250.00

Auden, W. H. *Dance of Death.* Lon. Faber & Faber. (1933). 1st ed. dj. $150.00–$300.00

Auden, W. H. *Dance of Death.* Lon. Faber & Faber. (1933). 1st ed. sgn. dj. $500.00–$1,000.00

Auden, W. H. *Dance of Death.* Lon. Faber & Faber. (1933). 1st ed. ltd 1,200 cc. good dj. sgn. $500.00–$1,000.00

Auden, W. H. *Dance of Death.* Lon. Faber & Faber. (1933). 1st ed. slightly damaged or missing dj. $50.00–$150.00

Auden, W. H. *Poems.* Lon. Faber & Faber. 1933. 2nd ed. first in boards. dj. $150.00–$300.00

Auden, W. H. *Poems.* Lon. Faber & Faber. (1930). 1st ed. wraps. ltd 1,000 cc. $500.00–$2,000.00

Auden, W. H. *Secondary Worlds: Essays.* NY. Random House. 1968. 1st US ed. dj. $20.00–$75.00

Auden, W. H. *Secondary Worlds: Essays.* Lon. Faber & Faber. (1968). 1st ed. ltd 3000 cc. dj.
$75.00–$100.00

Audsley, George A. *Artistic & Decorative Stencilling.* Lon. 1911. $100.00–$150.00

Audsley, W. and G. Audsley. *Polychromatic Decoration as applied to Buildings in the Medieval Styles.* Lon. Sotheran. 1882. 1st ed. illus. folio. plates in gold and color. $400.00–$1,000.00

Audubon, John J. *Audubon's Western Journal.* Cleve. Arthur H. Clark Co. 1906. 1st ed. fldg map. reprint. $125.00–$250.00

Audubon, John J. *Birds of America.* NY. Macmillan. 1937. illus. folio. 500 clr plates. 2500 cc. no dj. $150.00–$200.00

Audubon, John J. *Quadrupeds of North America.* NY. V. G. Audubon. 1849. illus. 1st 8vo ed. 155 hand-clr plates. 3 vols. $10,000.00–$16,000.00

Audubon, Maria. *Audubon and His Journals.* Lon. Nimmo. 1898. 1st UK ed. illus. 2 vols.
$200.00–$325.00

Auel, Jean. *Clan of the Cave Bear, The.* NY. Crown. 1980. 1st ed. dj. $40.00–$150.00

Auel, Jean. *Clan of the Cave Bear, The.* NY. Crown. 1980. 1st ed. author's first book. cloth. sgn. dj. $200.00–$500.00

Auel, Jean. *Mammoth Hunters, The.* NY. Crown. 1985. 1st ed. dj. $10.00–$12.00

Aurthur, R. A. *Third Maritime Division.* DC. 1948. 1st ed. illus. $50.00–$175.00

Austen, Jane. *Pride and Prejudice.* Lon. T. Egerton. 1813. 2nd ed. 3 vols.
$13,000.00–$30,000.00

Austen, Jane. *Pride and Prejudice.* Lon. T. Egerton. 1813. 1st ed. 3 vols.
$40,000.00–$50,000.00

Austen, Jane. *Sense and Sensibility.* Lon. 1811. 1st ed. 3 vols. ltd 1000 cc.
$45,000.00–$50,000.00

Auster, Paul. *Ghosts.* LA. Sun and Moon Press. 1986. 1st ed. dj. $30.00–$100.00

Auster, Paul. *Ghosts.* LA. Sun and Moon Press. 1986. 1st ed. sgn. dj. $200.00–$225.00

Austin, Gregory, et al (eds.). *Drugs and Minorities.* MD. National Institute on Drug Abuse. 1977. wraps. $15.00–$25.00

Austin, Mary. *American Rhythm.* NY. Harcourt Brace. (1923). 1st ed. dj. $100.00–$225.00

Austin, Mary. *Arrow Maker.* NY. Duffield & Co. 1911. 1st ed. $65.00–$130.00

Austin, Mary. *Land of Little Rain, The.* Bos/NY. Houghton Mifflin. (1903). 1st ed. 1st issue. author's first book. $300.00–$400.00

Austin, Mary. *Land of Little Rain, The.* Bos/NY. Houghton Mifflin. 1903. 1st ed. 4th impression. author's first book. $50.00–$80.00

Austin, Mary. *Land of Little Rain, The.* Bos/NY. Houghton Mifflin. (1903). 1st ed. 1st issue. sgn. author's first book. $500.00–$750.00

Avary, Myrta Lockett. *Dixie After the War.* NY. Houghton Mifflin. 1906. 1st ed.
$50.00–$100.00

Avedon, Richard and Truman Capote. *Observations.* NY. Simon & Schuster. 1959. 1st ed. dj. slipcase. presentation copy by Capote.
$1,500.00–$2,000.00

Avedon, Richard and Truman Capote. *Observations.* NY. Simon & Schuster. 1959. 1st ed. dj. slipcase.
$400.00–$500.00

Averill, Charles. *Short Treatise on Operative Surgery, describing the principal operations as they are practised in England and France.* Phil. 1823. 1st US ed.
$95.00–$120.00

Avery, Al. *Yankee Flyer with the RAF.* NY. 1941. Air Combat Series #8.
$15.00–$20.00

Avey, Elijah. *Capture and Execution of John Brown.* Chi. Brethren. 1906.
$40.00–$50.00

Axelrod, George. *Seven Year Itch, The.* NY. Random House. (1953). 1st ed. play. sgn. dj.
$225.00–$275.00

Ayling, Augustus D. *Revised Register of the Soldiers and Sailors of New Hampshire in the War of the Rebellion 1861–1866.* Concord. 1895. rev. ed.
$125.00–$300.00

Ayton, Lawrence, et al. *Success at Golf.* Bos. Little Brown. 1914.
$100.00–$150.00

Babault, Guy. *Chasses et Recherches Zoologiques en Afrique.* Paris. Libraire Plon. 1917. 1st ed. illus. photos.
$80.00–$100.00

Babbitt, Bruce. *Grand Canyon.* Flagstaff. Northland. (1978). 1st ed. sgn. dj.
$50.00–$125.00

Babcock, Philip H. *Falling Leaves.* NY. Derrydale. (1937). 1st ed. ltd 950 cc. sgn.
$100.00–$150.00

Bachmann, Alberto. *An Encyclopedia of the Violin.* New York. D. Appleton. 1925. 1st ed. illus. green cloth, gold lettering.
$45.00–$60.00

Back, Captain. *Narrative of the Arctic Land Expedition to the Mouth of the Great Fish River& 1833, 1834, and 1835.* Phila. Carey & Hart. 1836. 1st Amer ed. fldg map.
$350.00–$600.00

Bacon, Benjamin C. *Statistics of the Colored People of Philadelphia. . . .* Phil. Chapman. 1856. 1st ed. wraps. 16 pp.
$600.00–$800.00

Bacon, Edgar Mayhew. *Narraganset Bay, Its Historic and Romantic Associations and Romantic Setting.* Putnam. 1904. 1st ed. illus.
$100.00–$150.00

Bacon, George W. (ed.). *New Large Scale Atlas of the British Isles.* From Ordnance Survey. . . . nd.
$900.00–$1,000.00

Bacon, George W. (ed.). *New Large Scale Atlas of the British Isles.* From Ordnance Survey. . . . 1884.
$500.00–$600.00

Bacon, Lee. *Our Houseboat on the Nile.* Bos. 1902. 1st ed. clr frontis.
$40.00–$50.00

Baden-Powell, Capt. R. S. *Pigsticking or Hog-Hunting.* Lon. Harrison & Sons. 1889. illus.
$200.00–$750.00

Baden-Powell, Lord. *Handbook for Brownies or Bluebirds.* Lon. Pearson. (1920). wraps.
$50.00–$90.00

Baedeker, Karl. *Belgium and Holland, including the Grand Duchy of Luxembourg.* Leipzig. 1897. 12th ed. $25.00–$40.00

Baedeker, Karl. *Belgium and Holland, including . . . Luxembourg.* Leipzig. 1901. 13th ed. $20.00–$30.00

Baedeker, Karl. *Berlin and Its Environs.* Leipzig. 1905. 2nd ed. $100.00–$120.00

Baedeker, Karl. *Berlin and Its Environs.* Leipzig. 1910. 4th ed. $50.00–$75.00

Baedeker, Karl. *Dominion of Canada.* Leipzig. 1894. 2nd ed. $100.00–$160.00

Baedeker, Karl. *Italy. First Part.* Leipzig. 1899. 11th ed. $35.00–$50.00

Baedeker, Karl. *Italy. Second Part.* Leipzig. 1928. 3rd ed. $60.00–$70.00

Baedeker, Karl. *Italy. Third Part.* Leipzig. 1890. 10th ed. $55.00–$90.00

Baedeker, Karl. *Northern Germany.* Lon. Dulau. 9th ed. $40.00–$65.00

Baedeker, Karl. *United States with Excursions into Mexico, Cuba, Puerto Rico, and Alaska.* Leipzig. 1909. wraps. 4th ed. $75.00–$150.00

Bagg, Aaron and Samuel Eliot. *Birds of the Connecticut Valley in Massachusetts.* MA. 1937. illus. clr frontis. b/w plates. $150.00–$225.00

Bagg, Aaron and Samuel Eliot. *Birds of the Connecticut Valley in Massachusetts.* MA. 1937. 1st ed. illus. clr frontis. b/w plates. sgn. $500.00–$600.00

Bailey, Carolyn Sherwin. *Little Reader Series No.* 3. Springfield. (1934). illus. by Ruth Hallock. original box. scarce. $60.00–$75.00

Bailey, C. W. *Brain and Golf, The: Some Hints.* Lon. Mills & Boon. (1924). 1st ed. $200.00–$300.00

Bailey, C. W. *Professor on the Golf Links.* Lon. Silas Birch. (1925). 1st ed. $450.00–$550.00

Bailey, Dana R. *History of Minnehaha County, South Dakota.* Sioux Falls. Brown & Sanger. 1899. 1st ed. illus. photos. $250.00–$600.00

Bailey, Florence M. *Birds of New Mexico.* DC. New Mexico Department of Game and Fish. 1928. 1st ed. ltd 350. lea. sgn. $350.00–$500.00

Bailey, Florence M. *Birds of New Mexico.* DC. New Mexico Department of Game and Fish. 1928. 1st trade ed. $95.00–$200.00

Bailey, L. H. *Cyclopedia of American Horticulture.* NY. 1900. 1st ed. illus. 4 vols. $150.00–$400.00

Bailey, L. H. *Cyclopedia of American Horticulture.* NY. 1902. 2nd ed. illus. 4 vols. $100.00–$350.00

Bailey, L. H. *Cyclopedia of American Horticulture.* NY. 1906. 6th ed. illus. 4 vols. $75.00–$150.00

Bailey, L. H. *Standard Cyclopedia of Horticulture.* NY. Macmillan. 1935. 3 vols. illus. $80.00–$100.00

Bailey, Lynn R. *Tale of the Unkilled. The Life, Times and Writing of Wells W. Spicer.* Tucson. Westmore Press. 1999. 1st ed. wraps. ltd 500 cc. sgn. $10.00–$15.00

Bailey, Major Theodore. *Military Courtesy.* NY. Review. (1919). illus. inscrb. $30.00–$40.00

Baines, Anthony. *European and American Musical Instruments.* NY. Viking. 1966. 1st ed. illus. $50.00–$75.00

Baird, Bil. *Art of the Puppet, The.* NY. Macmillan. 1965. 1st ed. illus. dj. $40.00–$65.00

Baker, Gen. L. C. *History of the U.S. Secret Service.* Phila. private printing. 1867. 1st ed.
$75.00–$125.00

Baker, J. H. L. *History of Geography, The.* Oxford. Blackwell. 1963. 1st ed. dj.
$45.00–$65.00

Baker, Marcus. *Geographic Dictionary of Alaska.* DC. GPO. 1906. wraps. 2nd ed.
$100.00–$130.00

Baker, Samuel W. *Ismailia: A Narrative of the Expedition to Central Africa for the Suppression of the Slave Trade.* NY. Harper. 1875. illus. 1st US ed. $150.00–$275.00

Baker, Samuel W. *Ismailia: A Narrative of the Expedition to Central Africa for the Suppression of the Slave Trade.* London. 1874. 1st ed. $200.00–$300.00

Baker, Samuel W. *Nile Tributaries of Abyssinia.* Lon. Macmillan. 1867. 1st ed. illus. ½ lea.
$500.00–$900.00

Baker, Samuel W. *Nile Tributaries of Abyssinia.* Lon. Macmillan. 1874. illus.
$100.00–$250.00

Baker, W. S. *The Origin and Antiquity of Engraving.* Phil. George Gebbie. 1871. 1st ed. rust color pebbly cloth gold lettering on cover and spine. 62pp. $35.00–$100.00

Bakst, Leon. *Designs of Leon Bakst for The Sleeping Princess.* Benn Bros. 1923. 1st ed. illus. ltd 1,000 cc. teg. sgn. $1,600.00–$2,200.00

Baldwin, James. *Blues for Mister Charlie.* NY. Dial. 1964. 1st ed. sgn. dj. $175.00–$350.00

Baldwin, James. *Blues for Mister Charlie.* Lon. Michael Joseph. (1965). 1st UK ed. dj.
$75.00–$100.00

Baldwin, James. *Fire Next Time, The.* NY. Dial. 1963. 1st ed. sgn. dj. $200.00–$300.00

Baldwin, James. *Fire Next Time, The.* NY. Dial. 1963. 1st ed. dj. $30.00–$50.00

Baldwin, James. *Going to Meet the Man.* NY. Dial. 1965. 1st ed. sgn. dj. $750.00–$800.00

Baldwin, James. *Going to Meet the Man.* NY. Dial. 1965. 1st ed. dj. $95.00–$200.00

Baldwin, James. *Go Tell It On the Mountain.* NY. Knopf. 1953. 1st ed. sgn. inscribed. dj.
$2,000.00–$5,000.00

Baldwin, James. *Go Tell It On the Mountain.* NY. Knopf. 1953. 1st ed. wraps. author's first novel. original dj. $500.00–$1,000.00

Baldwin, James. *Go Tell It On the Mountain.* Franklin Center. Franklin Library. 1979. 1st ed. ltd ed. author's first novel. red lea. sgn. $200.00–$300.00

Baldwin, James. *Go Tell It On the Mountain.* Lon. Michael Joseph. (1954). 1st UK ed. author's first novel. dj. $250.00–$800.00

Baldwin, James. *Tell Me How Long the Train's Been Gone.* NY. 1968. 1st ed. inscrb. white cloth. dj. $5,000.00–$6,000.00

Baldwin Locomotives. Phil. Baldwin Locomotive Works. 1931. wraps. Vol 9, number 4, April 1931. 84 pp. photos. diagrams. $60.00–$90.00

Balfour, William. *Illustrations of the Power of Emetic Tartar . . . in Preventing Consumption and Apoplexy.* Lexington. Palmer. 1823. $200.00–$250.00

Ball, Sir Robert. *Story of the Heavens, 1910.* Lon. Cassell. 1910. illus. folio. blue cloth with gilt decoration. color plates. photos. 568 pp. $200.00–$300.00

Ballard, J. G. *Passport to Eternity.* NY. Berkley. 1963. 1st ed. wraps. $30.00–$45.00

Balzac, Honore. *Hidden Treasures, The.* Kenfield Allen. 1953. lts 160 cc. 55 pp. illus. dj. $300.00–$350.00

Bancroft, Frederic, & William Dunning. *The Reminiscences of Carl Schurz.* NY. McClure. 1908. illus. binding worn, vol. 3, 1863–1869. $35.00–$50.00

Bancroft, Laura (L. Frank Baum*). Mr. Woodchuck.* Chi. Reilly & Britton. 1906.
$150.00–$175.00

Bangs, John Kendrick. *A House-Boat on the Styx.* NY. Harper. 1896. 1st ed. illus.
$35.00–$75.00

Bangs, John Kendrick. *Foothills of Parnassus.* NY. 1914. review copy. dj. $60.00–$90.00

Bangs, John Kendrick. *Ghosts I Have Met.* NY. Harper. 1898. 1st ed. illus. $50.00–$125.00

Bangs, John Kendrick. *Mr. Munchausen.* Bos. Noyes, Platt. 1901. 1st ed. illus. by Peter Newell. $90.00–$140.00

Bangs, John Kendrick. *Mrs. Raffles.* NY. Harper. 1905. 1st ed. illus. $75.00–$150.00

Bangs, John Kendrick. *Peeps at People.* NY. Harper. 1899. 1st ed. illus. by Penfield. presentation copy. $150.00–$170.00

Banks, Lynne Reid. *L-Shaped Room, The.* Lon. Chatto & Windus. 1960. 1st ed. author's first novel. movie made from book. sgn. dj. $120.00–$200.00

Banks, Russell. *Rule of the Bone.* NY. HarperCollins. 1995. 1st ed. sgn. dj. $25.00–$40.00

Bannerman, Helen. *Histoire du Petit Negre Sambo.* NY. Stokes. (1921). 1st ed. in French. dj.
$200.00–$275.00

Bannerman, Helen. *Little Black Sambo.* Racine. Whitman. illus. by Cobb and Shinn. 64 pp. dark brown cloth boards. $80.00–$120.00

Bannerman, Helen. *Little Black Sambo.* Akron. 1933. illus. by Peat. $50.00–$130.00

Bannerman, Helen. *Little Black Sambo.* Garden City. 1933. 27 color illus. by Wiese.
$200.00–$270.00

Bannerman, Helen. *Little Black Sambo.* wraps. illus. by Florence White Williams. good only. $55.00–$75.00

Bannerman, Helen. *Sambo and the Twins.* Phil. 1946. illus. by Bannerman. $50.00–$80.00

Baraka, Amiri (Jones, LeRoi). *Home: Social Essays by LeRoi Jones.* NY. William Morrow. 1966. 1st ed. dj. $60.00–$90.00

Baraka, Imamu Amiri (Jones, LeRoi). *Selected Poetry.* NY. Morrow. 1979. 1st ed. dj.
$50.00–$75.00

Baraka, Imamu Amiri (Jones, LeRoi). *Spirit Reach.* NY. Jihad. 1972. 1st ed. wraps.
$30.00–$35.00

Barbeau, Marius. *Indian Days in the Canadian Rockies.* Tor. Macmillan. 1923. 1st ed. illus. dj.
$40.00–$80.00

Barbeau, Marius. *Totem Poles.* Ottawa. National Museum of Canada. 1950. 1st ed. wraps. illus. 2 vols. $100.00–$200.00

Barbeau, Marius. *Totem Poles of the Gitksan, Upper Skeena River, British Columbia.* Ottawa. National Museum of Canada. 1929. wraps. 275 pp. $50.00–$150.00

Barbeau, Marius and Grace Melvin. *Indian Speaks, The.* ID. Caxton. 1943. 1st ed. illus. woodcuts. $15.00–$80.00

Barchilon, Jacques. *Perrault's Tales of Mother Goose.* NY. Pierpont Morgan Library. 1956. 1st ed. illus. 2 vols. tan cloth. slipcase. Stinehour Press. $200.00–$400.00

Bard, Samuel. *Compendium of the Theory and Practice of Midwifery. . . .* NY. Collins and Perkins. 1807. $2,500.00–$3,500.00

Barker, Clive. *Damnation Game, The.* Lon. Weidenfeld & Nicolson. 1985. 1st ed. sgn. dj.
$45.00–$100.00

Barker, Clive. *Everville: The Second Book of the Ark.* Lon. Harper Collins. 1994. 3rd ed. dj.
$15.00–$20.00

Barker, Clive. *Great and Secret Snow, The.* NY. Harper & Row. 1989. 1st ed. quarter cl. sgn. dj. $35.00–$60.00

Barker, Clive. *In the Flesh.* NY. Poseidon. 1986. 1st ed. inscrb. dj. $20.00–$30.00

Barker, Clive. *Weaveworld.* NY. Poseidon. 1987. 1st ed. sgn. dj. $35.00–$40.00

Barker, Clive. *Weaveworld.* NY. Poseidon. 1987. 1st ed. 1st printing. dj. $25.00–$35.00

Barkun, Michael. *Religion and the Racist Right: the Origins of the Christian Identity Movement.* Chapel Hill. Univ of North Carolina Press. 1994. wraps. $10.00–$12.00

Barnard, Edward Emerson. *Photographic Atlas of Selected Regions of the Milky Way.* DC. Carnegie Institute. 1927. illus. 2 vols. Vol 1, photographs and descriptions. Vol 2, charts and tables. $15,000.00–$20,000.00

Barnard, Edward Emerson. *Publications of the Lick Observatory & Vol. XI: Photographs of the Milky Way and Comets. . . .* Sacramento. Univ of California. 1913. illus. 46 pp.
$100.00–$1,500.00

Barnouw, Victor. *Acculturation and Personality Among the Wisconsin Chippewa*. American Anthropologist. 1950. wraps. $10.00–$35.00

Barnum, P. T. *Struggles and Triumphs*. Buffalo. Johnson & Co. 1873. illus. author's edition. $40.00–$55.00

Barrett, Charles. *Australian Wild Life*. Melbourne. Georgian House. 1943. 1st ed. illus. tan and green cloth, dj. $8.00–$24.00

Barrett, Edwin. *What I Saw at Bull Run*. Bos. Beacon Press. 1886. frontis. 48 pp. $200.00–$225.00

Barrie, J. M. *Peter and Wendy*. Lon. 1911. 1st ed. dj. $5,000.00–$5,200.00

Barrie, J. M. *Peter Pan*. NY. Scribner's. (1980). illus. by Trina Hyman. sgn by illustrator. $200.00–$220.00

Barrie, J. M. *Peter Pan in Kensington*. Lon. Hodder & Stoughton. 1906. 1st ed. illus. by Rackham. $2,000.00–$3,000.00

Bart, Sir John Lubbock. *The Origin of Civilisation and the Primitive Condition of Man*. New York. D. Appleton. 1895. illus. green cloth, gold lettering and decoration on spine. pull-outs. $75.00–$100.00

Barth, John. *Lost in the Funhouse*. NY. Doubleday. 1968. 1st ed. dj. $30.00–$80.00

Barth, John. *Lost in the Funhouse*. NY. Doubleday. 1968. 1st ed. ltd 250 cc. sgn. slipcase. $80.00–$125.00

Barth, John. *Sabbatical*. NY. Putnam's. 1982. ltd 750 cc. sgn. slipcase. $70.00–$150.00

Bartley, James Avis. *Lays of Ancient Virginia, and Other Poems*. Richmond. Randolph. 1855. 1st ed. ads. cloth. $200.00–$250.00

Baskin, Leonard. *Caprices and Grotesques*. Northampton. Gehenna Press. 1965. 1st ed. illus. $50.00–$60.00

Bass, Rick. *Platte River*. Bos. Houghton Mifflin. 1994. 1st ed. dj. $25.00–$30.00

Bass, Rick. *Sky, the Stars, the Wilderness, The*. Bos. Houghton Mifflin. 1997. 1st ed. dj. $12.00–$22.00

Bass, Rick. *Watch, The*. NY. Norton. 1989. 1st ed. dj. $40.00–$50.00

Battey, Thomas C. *Life and Adventures of a Quaker Among the Indians*. MA. Corner House. 1972. illus. reprint. dj. $14.00–$25.00

Battles and Leaders of the Civil War, The. New York. Century. 1888. illus. hinges cracked, fair cond. vol.1 only. $25.00–$40.00

Bau, Ming Chien J. *China and World Peace*. NY. Revell. 1928. very good. blue cloth. $20.00–$30.00

Baum, L. Frank. *Dorothy and the Wizard in Oz*. Chi. Reilly & Britton. 1908. 1st ed. 2nd state. illus by John R. Neill. blue cloth. $60.00–$80.00

Baum, L. Frank. *Dorothy and the Wizard in Oz*. Reilly & Britton. 1908. 1st ed. 1st state. illus. by John R. Neill. blue cloth. $1,000.00–$1,750.00

Baum, L. Frank. *Father Goose, His Book.* Hill. 1899. 1st ed. 1st prtg. illus. by Denslow.
$1,000.00–$2,500.00

Baum, L. Frank. *Father Goose, His Book.* Hill. 1899. 3rd issue. illus. by Denslow.
$300.00–$500.00

Baum, L. Frank. *Magic of Oz.* Chi. Reilly & Lee. (1919). 1st ed. illus. by Neill.
$400.00–$600.00

Baum, L. Frank. *Tik-Tok of Oz.* Reilly/Britton. (1914). 1st ed. illus. by Neill.
$350.00–$600.00

Baum, L. Frank. *Tin Woodsman of Oz.* Chicago. 1918. 1st ed. 1st printing.
$1,000.00–$1,200.00

Baum, L. Frank. *Wizard of Oz.* Grosset & Dunlap. 1939. $100.00–$175.00

Baum, Vicki. *Grand Hotel.* Lon. Bles. 1930. 1s UK ed. cloth. movie was based on book. dj.
$225.00–$350.00

Baum, Vicki. *Grand Hotel.* NY. Doubleday Doran. 1931. 1st Amer ed. cloth. movie was based on book. dj. $350.00–$500.00

Baum, Vicki. *Grand Hotel.* NY. Doubleday Doran. 1931. 1st Amer ed. cloth. movie was based on book. sgn. dj. $500.00–$750.00

Bayldon, Arthur A. D. *Poems & for Private Circulation Only.* Brisbane. Wendt. (1898). 2nd ed. red cover. blindstamped. $90.00–$100.00

Bayley, Thomas B. *Thoughts on the Necessity and Advantages & in Collecting and Preserving Different Substances for Manure. . . .* Manchester. Nicholson. 1796. 2nd ed. $100.00–$140.00

Bayliss, John F. (ed.). *Black Slave Narratives.* NY. Macmillan. 1970. 1st ed. $20.00–$30.00

Beachey, R. W. *Slave Trade of Eastern Africa, The.* NY. Barnes and Noble. 1976. 1st ed. cloth.
$30.00–$40.00

Bean, L.L. *Hunting-Fishing and Camping.* Freeport. L.L.Bean. 1965. illus. red illus. binding. good cond. $8.00–$20.00

Beard, George. *Practical Treatise on Nervous Exhaustion, A.* NY. Wood. 1880. 1st ed. green cloth. $200.00–$400.00

Beard, James. *Beard on Pasta.* NY. Knopf. 1983. 1st ed. illus. dj. $15.00–$18.00

Beattie, Jessie L. *Black Moses: the Real Uncle Tom.* Tor. Ryerson. 1957. 1st ed. dj.
$40.00–$55.00

Beaumont, William. *Experiments and Observations of the Gastric Juice and the Physiology of Digestion.* Plattsburgh. Allen. 1833. 1st ed. illus. woodcuts. boards. $1,500.00–$2,000.00

Beckett, Samuel. *Lessness.* Lon. 1970. ltd 100 cc. sgn. $1,300.00–$3,000.00

Beckett, Samuel. *Lessness.* Lon. Calder 7 Boyars. 1970. 1st trade ed. $75.00–$150.00

Beckett, Samuel. *North, The.* Lon. 1972. ltd 137 cc. etchings. sgn. $800.00–$1,000.00

Beckett, Samuel. *Waiting for Godot.* Lon. 1956. 1st UK ed. dj. $700.00–$1,000.00

Beckett, Samuel. *Waiting for Godot.* NY. Faber. 1954. 1st ed. dj. $1,500.00–$2,000.00

Bee, Claire. *Home Run Feud.* Grosset & Dunlap. 1964. 1st edition. #22 in the Chip Hilton series. $40.00–$70.00

Beebe, Louis and Charles Clegg. *Trains We Rode, The; Volumes I & II.* Berkeley. Howell-North. 1965. 1st ed. illus. inscrb. photos. djs. $150.00–$200.00

Beebe, Lucius. *High Iron: A Book of Trains.* NY. Appleton-Century. 1943. illus. 4th printing. photos. dj. $15.00–$25.00

Beebe, Lucius. *20th Century.* Berkeley, CA. Howell-North. 1962. 1st ed. illus. luxury train travel. 180 pp. photos. map endpapers. dj. $65.00–$90.00

Beebe, Lucius and Charles Clegg. *Narrow Gauge in the Rockies.* Berkeley, CA. Howell-North. 1958. 1st ed. illus. 250 photos. color paintings. map endpapers. dj. $70.00–$90.00

Beerbohm, Max. *Rossetti and His Circle.* Lon. Heinemann. 1922. 1st ed. illus. 20 color plates. $135.00–$225.00

Beerbohm, Max. *Things New and Old.* Lon. Heinemann. 1923. 1st ed. dj. $50.00–$75.00

Beerbohm, Max. *Zuleika Dobson: an Oxford Love Story.* Lon. Heinemann. 1911. 1st ed. $115.00–$300.00

Beers, D. B. *Atlas of Luzerne County, PA.* Beers & Co. 1873. illus. hand colored maps. $300.00–$750.00

Beers, D. B. *History of Mongomery and Fulton Counties, NY.* NY. Beers. 1878. illus. lithographs. maps. folio. $200.00–$300.00

Beers, F. W. *Atlas of Delaware County.* NY. Beers & Co. 1869. gilt lettering. maps. $150.00–$200.00

Beers, F.W. *Atlas of Windsor Co. Vermont.* New York. Beers, Ellis, Soule. 1869. 1st ed. illus. folio cloth & lea. color plates. $400.00–$600.00

Behan, Brendan. *Borstal Boy.* Lon. Hutchinson. 1958. 1st ed. dj. $50.00–$75.00

Belden, L. Burr. *Mines of Death Valley.* CA. La Siesta Press. 1966. 1st ed. wraps. 71 pp. illus. $20.00–$25.00

Belden, L. Burr. *Old Stovepipe Wells.* CA. Inland Printing and Engraving. 1968. 1st ed. wraps. 12 pp. $12.00–$20.00

Belknap, Michal R. *Federal Law and the Southern Order.* Athens. Univ of Georgia Press. 1987. 1st ed. dj. $20.00–$25.00

Bell Telephone Laboratories. *History of Engineering and Science in the Bell System.* 1975. 1st ed. illus. dj. $50.00–$60.00

Bell, William. *Carpentry Made Easy.* Phil. Howard Challen. 1858. 1st ed. illus. gray cloth, gilt letter on cover. $125.00–$250.00

Bemelmans, Ludwig. *Madeline and the Bad Hat.* NY. Viking. (1957). 1st trade ed. pictorial red cloth. dj. $500.00–$800.00

Bemelmans, Ludwig. *Madeline's Christmas*. NY. Viking. 1985. 1st ed. wraps. illus.
$75.00–$125.00

Bennett, Ella Costello. *Abelard and Heloise*. SF. Elder. (1907). First Edition. frontis.
$18.00–$25.00

Bennett, John C. *History of the Saints, The; or an Expose of Joe Smith and Mormonism*. Bos. Leland & Whiting. 1842. 1st ed. plates. $2,000.00–$3,000.00

Benson, Stella. *The Far-Away Bride*. NY. Reader's Club. 1941. orange cloth. $75.00–$125.00

Berman, S. N. *Pirate, The*. NY. Random House. (1943). 1st ed. dj. $100.00–$150.00

Bernoulli, Daniel. *Hydrodynamica*. Argentorati. 1738. 12 folding engraved plates. rebacked.
$4,000.00–$6,000.00

Berry, Charles Walter. *Viniana*. Lon. Constable. 1934. illus. small red cloth. $5.00–$75.00

Bester, Alfred. *Demolished Man*. Chi. Shasta. 1953. dj. $100.00–$175.00

Bewick, R. M. *The Problem of the Far East*. Lon. 1922–23. green wrps. $40.00–$65.00

Biegeleisen, J. I. and Max Cohn. *Silk Screen Stenciling as a Fine Art*. NY. McGraw-Hill. 1942. 1st ed. illus. by Max Cohn. 8 color plates. $125.00–$200.00

Bierce, Ambrose. *Ambrose Bierce Satanic Reader, The*. NY. Doubleday. 1968. Jerome Hopkins (ed). dj. $20.00–$40.00

Bierce, Ambrose. *Shadow on the Dial*. San Francisco. Robertson. 1909. 1st ed. no dj.
$80.00–$120.00

Bierce, Ambrose. *Shadow on the Dial*. San Francisco. Robertson. 1909. 1st ed. dj.
$200.00–$450.00

Bierce, Ambrose. *Shapes of Clay*. San Francisco. Wood. 1903. $400.00–$650.00

Bierce, Ambrose. *Ten Tales*. Lon. First Editions Club. 1925. $30.00–$100.00

Bierce, Ambrose. *Vision of Doom, A*. RI. Grant. 1980. dj. $15.00–$25.00

Bigelow, John. *Retrospectives on an Active Life*. NY. Baker and Taylor. 1909. 1st ed. 3 vols. teg. $500.00–$650.00

Bilby, Julian W. *Nanook of the North*. NY. Dodd, Mead. 1926. First Edition. dj missing.
$125.00–$150.00

Bingham, Capt. *The Bastille*. NY. Pott & Co. 1901. 2 vols. illus. $75.00–$100.00

Bingham, John. *Trial of Conspirators & Assassination of President Lincoln*. DC. GPO. 1865. 1st ed. wraps. $300.00–$500.00

Bishop, Elizabeth. *North & South*. Bos. Houghton Mifflin. 1946. 1st ed. author's first book. ltd 1000 cc. inscrb. sgn. association copy. dj. $5,000.00–$6,000.00

Bishop, Elizabeth. *North & South*. Bos. Houghton Mifflin. 1946. 1st ed. author's first book. ltd 1000 cc. dj. $800.00–$950.00

Bishop, Elizabeth. *Poems: North & South_ A Cold Spring.* Bos. Houghton Mifflin. 1955. 1st ed. Pulitzer Prize winner. dj. $400.00–$500.00

Bisland, Elizabeth. *Life and Letters of Lafcadio Hearn, The.* Bos. Houghton Mifflin. 1906. 1st ed. illus. 2 vols. photos. $150.00–$200.00

Blackburn, I. *Illus. of Gross Morbid Anatomy of the Brain in the Insane.* DC. GPO. 1908. 1st ed. photos. $150.00–$200.00

Blacker, C. P. *Birth Control and the State.* NY. Dutton. (1926). 1st ed. boards.
$40.00–$60.00

Blackson, Lorenzo D. *Rise and Progress of the Kingdoms of Light and Darkness.* Phil. Nicholas. 1867. 1st ed. illus. frontis. $2,500.00–$4,000.00

Blackstone, William. *Commentaries on the Laws of England.* Lon. Clarendon Press. 1766–79. 4 vols. mixed states. $5,000.00–$5,500.00

Blackstone, William. *Commentaries on the Laws of England.* Lon. Clarendon Press. 1765. 1st ed. 4 vols. 8-page supplement in first volume. restored. $15,000.00–$20,000.00

Blaine, John. *Rocket's Shadow.* NY. Grosset & Dunlap. 1947. Rick Brant #1. dj.
$10.00–$20.00

Blair J. Paul. *Out of the Wind.* NY. Vantage. 1st ed. dj. $45.00–$55.00

Blakeslee, George H. *The Pacific Area: An International Survey.* Bos. World Peace Foundation. 1929. 1st ed. red cloth fold-out map. $10.00–$20.00

Blassingame, John W. *Slave Community, The: Plantation Life in the Antebellum South.* NY. Oxford Univ Press. 1972. 1st ed. dj. $35.00–$45.00

Blassingame, John W. *Slave Community, The: Plantation life in the Antebellum South.* NY. Oxford Univ Press. 1972. 2nd printing. dj. $25.00–$30.00

Blee, Kathleen M. *Women of the Klan.* Berkeley. Univ of California Press. 1991. 1st ed. dj.
$20.00–$25.00

Blegen, Theodore and Sara Davidson (ed.). *Iron Face: the Adventures of Jack Frazer, Frontier Warrior, Scout & Hunter.* Chi. Caxton. 1950. 1st ed. ltd 500 cc. $80.00–$125.00

Bloch, Robert. *Deadbeat.* NY. Simon & Schuster. 1960. 1st ed. dj. $60.00–$75.00

Bloch, Robert. *Lori.* NY. Doherty. 1989. 1st ed. dj. $35.00–$45.00

Bloch, Robert. *Night of the Ripper.* NY. Doubleday. 1981. 1st ed. inscrb. sgn. dj.
$50.00–$70.00

Bloch, Robert. *Psycho.* NY. Simon & Schuster. 1959. 1st ed. sgn. dj. $800.00–$1,200.00

Block, Lawrence. *Burglar Who Liked to Quote Kipling.* NY. Random House. 1979. 1st ed. dj. presentation copy. sgn. $125.00–$145.00

Block, Lawrence. *Burglar Who Painted Like Mondrian.* NY. (1983). 1st ed. dj.
$50.00–$135.00

Block, Lawrence. *Burglar Who Studied Spinoza.* NY. Random House. (1980). 1st ed. dj.
$20.00–$30.00

Block, Lawrence. *Even the Wicked*. Lon. (1996). 1st ed. dj. $25.00–$30.00

Block, Lawrence. *Even the Wicked*. NY. (1997). 1st US ed. sgn. dj. $100.00–$125.00

Block, Lawrence. *Ronald Rabbit is a Dirty Old Man*. Chi. Geis. 1971. 1st ed. dj.
    $100.00–$150.00

Block, Lawrence. *Ticket to the Boneyard*. NY. Morrow. 1990. 1st ed. inscrb. dj.
    $30.00–$50.00

Block, Lawrence. *Two for Tanner*. CT. (1968). 1st ed. wraps. sgn. dj. $30.00–$50.00

Blue Cloud, Peter. *Sketches in Winter, With Crows*. NY. Strawberry Press.1984. First Edition. inscrb. $250.00–$300.00

Blumenthal, Joseph. *Art of the Printed Book 1455–1955*. NY. Pierpont Morgan Library. 1973. 1st ed. illus. 125 b/w plates. fldg plate. Stinehour Press. inscrb. $90.00–$110.00

Blumenthal, Joseph. *Printed Book in America, The*. Lunenberg, VT. Stinehour. 1977. 1st ed. dj. $40.00–$60.00

Boaz, Franz and George Hunt. *Kwakiutl Texts*. American Museum of Natural History. 1902. wraps. $95.00–$125.00

Boell, Jacques. *High Heaven*. Lon. Elek. (1947). 1st ed in English. pictorial dj. illus.
    $20.00–$30.00

Bogue, Thomas. *Treatise on the Structure, Color and Preservation of the Human Hair*. Phil. 1845. 2nd ed. 107 pp. plates. cloth. $90.00–$1,125.00

Bohr, Niels. *Theory of Spectra and Atomic Constitution*. Cambridge Univ Press 1922.
    $50.00–$100.00

Bolton, H. W. *Home and Social Life*. Bos. McDonald & Gill. 1884. $10.00–$15.00

Bond, John W. *Minnesota, the Empire State of the New North-West*. St. Paul. Smyth. 1878. wraps. 88 pp. folding map. $200.00–$300.00

Book of Unusual Cookery, The. Chi. Woman's World. 1928. 1st ed. wraps. illus. tall illus. cover. $10.00–$15.00

Born, Max. *La Constitution de la Matiere*. Paris. 1922. wraps. illus. Nobel Prize–winning author. $40.00–$60.00

Born, Max. *Constitution of Matter, The*. NY. Dutton (1923). 1st US ed. $20.00–$40.00

Bosson, Mrs. Jennie (Hood). *John Hood of Lynn, Massachusetts*. Salem. Essex. 1909. 1st ed. frontis. 44 pp. $50.00–$90.00

Botkin, B.A. (ed.). *A Regional Miscellany*. OK. 1930. 454 pp. dj. very good cond.
    $40.00–$60.00

Bourke-White, Margaret. *Dear Fatherland, Rest Quietly*. NY. 1946. 1st ed. sgn.
    $200.00–$300.00

Bourke-White, Margaret. *One Thing Leads to Another*. Bos/NY. Houghton Mifflin. 1936. 1st ed. blue cloth. dj. $30.00–$50.00

Bourke-White, Margaret. *Say, Is This the USA.* NY. Duell, Sloan. 1941. 1st ed.
$75.00–$125.00

Bourne, G. (ed.). *Cytology and Cell Physiology.* Oxford. Clarendon Press. 1942. 1st ed. dj.
$40.00–$75.00

Bovey, Wilfrid. *The French Canadians Today.* Tor. J.M. Dent. 1938. 1st ed. illus. red cloth. very good cond.
$20.00–$50.00

Bowen, Elizabeth. *House In Paris, The.* Lon. Gollancz. 1935. 1st UK ed. $130.00–$250.00

Bowen, Elizabeth. *House In Paris, The.* NY. Knopf. 1936. 1st US ed. $100.00–$125.00

Bowen, J. J. *Strategy of Robert E. Lee, The.* NY. Neale. 1914. illus. $50.00–$90.00

Bowles, Paul. *Sheltering Sky, The.* Lon. 1949. 1st ed. dj. $6,000.00–$7,000.00

Boy Scout Handbook. NY. Boy Scouts of America. (1936). blue wraps. rev. $70.00–$90.00

Boy Scout Handbook. NY. Boy Scouts of America. 1965. green wraps. rev. $15.00–$20.00

Boyd, Pliny. *Up and Down The Merrimac.* Bos. D. Lothrop. 1879. illus. a small red dec. cover, fair to good cond.
$15.00–$75.00

Boyden, Seth. *Correspondence on the Subject of Atmospheric Electricity . . . .* Newark. private printing. 1868. wraps.
$100.00–$200.00

Boyle, Jack. *Boston Blackie.* NY. Fly. (1919). 1st ed. cloth. no dj. $90.00–$100.00

Boyle, Robert. *Essay of the Great Effects of Even Languid and Unheeded Motion.* Lon. 1685. 1st ed. Boyle's name not on title page.
$2,000.00–$3,000.00

Boyles, Kate and Virgil. *Langford of the Three Bars.* Chi. McClurg. 1907. 1st ed. illus. in color by N.C. Wyeth, tan dec. cloth.
$25.00–$100.00

Boylston, Helen Dore. *Sue Barton, Staff Nurse.* Bos. Little Brown. 1952. 1st ed. dj.
$150.00–$200.00

Brace, Charles L. *Races of the World, The; a Manual of Ethnology.* NY. Scribner. 1863. 1st ed.
$40.00–$55.00

Bracken, Henry, William Taplin and James White. *American Farrier, The.* Troy. Adancourt. 1826. 1st ed. illus. engravings. frontis.
$400.00–$500.00

Bradbury, Ray. *Dandelion Wine.* Garden City. Doubleday. 1957. 1st ed. scarce. dj.
$400.00–$500.00

Bradbury, Ray. *Dark Carnival.* Lon. Hamish Hamilton. 1948. 1st UK ed. dj.
$300.00–$400.00

Bradbury, Ray. *Dark Carnival.* Sauk City. Arkham House. 1947. ltd 3000 cc. sgn.
$600.00–$1,000.00

Bradbury, Ray. *Day It Rained Forever, The.* Lon. Rupert Hart-Davis. 1959. 1st UK ed. dj.
$75.00–$90.00

Bradbury, Ray (ed.). *Futuria Fantasia, Volume 1: 1–4.* Los Angeles. 1939–1940. edited by Bradbury with selections by Bradbury.
$5,000.00–$6,000.00

Bradbury, Ray. *Halloween Tree*. NY. Knopf. (1972). 1st ed. dj. $75.00–$150.00

Bradbury, Ray. *How Not to Burn a Book; or 1984 Will Not Arrive*. KY. Contre Coup. 2002. 1st ed. ltd 27 cc. $500.00–$700.00

Bradbury, Ray. *Long After Midnight*. NY. Knopf. 1976. 1st ed. dj. $40.00–$75.00

Bradbury, Ray. *Martian Chronicles, The*. Garden City. Doubleday. 1950. 1st ed. green cloth. dj. $2,000.00–$3,000.00

Bradbury, Ray. *Martian Chronicles, The*. Garden City. Doubleday. 1950. 1st ed. green cloth. inscrb, dj. $3,500.00–$5,500.00

Bradbury, Ray. *Medicine for Melancholy*. Garden City. Doubleday. 1959. 1st ed.
$150.00–$350.00

Bradbury, Ray. *October Country*. Lon. Rupert Davis. 1956. dj. $100.00–$150.00

Bradbury, Ray. *R is for Rocket*. NY. Doubleday. (1962). 1st ed. dj. $150.00–$250.00

Bradbury, Ray. *S is for Space*. NY. Doubleday. 1966. 1st ed. dj. $50.00–$75.00

Bradbury, Ray. *Where Robot Mice and Robot Men Run Round in Robot Towns*. New York. Knopf. 1977. 1st ed. orange and green cloth, dj, signed. $100.00–$300.00

Bradford, Richard. *Red Sky at Morning*. Phila. Lippincott. (1968). wraps. advance reading copy. $40.00–$65.00

Bradley, Marion Zimmer. *House Between the Worlds*. Garden City. Doubleday. 1980. 1st ed. dj. $35.00–$45.00

Bradley, Marion Zimmer. *House Between the Worlds*. Garden City. Doubleday. 1980. 1st ed. sgn. dj. $75.00–$120.00

Bradley, Omar N. *Soldier's Story, A*. Chi. (1980). 2nd printing. illus. maps. sgn.
$350.00–$400.00

Bradley, Will. *Peter Poodle*. NY. Dodd, Mead. 1906. 1st ed. illus. oversize gray pictorial boards. $300.00–$500.00

Bradley, Will. *Will Bradley, His Chap Book &* . NY. Typophiles. 1955. 650 cc. $45.00–$95.00

Bradshaw, George and Ruth Norman. *Cook Until Done: A Collection of Unexpected Recipes*. NY. Barrows. 1962. 1st ed. cloth. dj. $20.00–$25.00

Brakefield, Tom. *Sportsman's Complete Book of Trophy and Meat Care*. PA. Stackpole. 1975. illus. later printing. buckram. dj. $12.00–$15.00

Brand, Edward. *Illinois Baptists*. Bloomington. Pan. 1930. 1st ed. brown cloth lettering on spine. $25.00–$35.00

Bravery, H. E. *Successful Winemaking at Home*. NY. Gramercy. nd. later printing. 151 pp. drawings. pictorial dj. $12.00–$15.00

Breen, Richard L. *Bibliography of A. Conan Doyle*. Oxford. Clarendon Press. 1983. illus. dj.
$70.00–$80.00

Breen, T. H. and Stephen Innes. *Myne Owne Ground: Race and Freedom on Virginia's Eastern Shore, 1640–1676.* NY. Oxford Univ Press. 1980. dj. $30.00–$70.00

Brenner, Gary. *Naked Grape, The.* Indianapolis. Bobbs Merrill. 1975. 1st ed. illus. maps. drawings. dj. $12.00–$15.00

Breton, Andre, et al. *Yves Tanguy: Une Recueill des ses Oeuvres.* NY. Pierre Matisse. 1963. illus. drawings. $600.00–$750.00

Brewer, A. *History of the Sixty-first Regiment, Pennsylvania Volunteers 1861–65.* Pitt. Art Engraving and Printing. 1911. $100.00–$150.00

Brice, Tony. *So Long.* Chi. Rand McNally. 1937. illus. by Tony Brice, illus. boards.
$20.00–$40.00

Bridges, Tyeler. *The Rise of David Duke.* Jackson. Univ Press of Mississippi. 1994. 1st ed. illus. dj. $15.00–$20.00

Briscoe, T. W. *Orchids for Amateurs.* Lon. Collingridge. 1st ed. illus. green cloth lettering on spine, frontis. $15.00–$30.00

Brodine, Virginia Warner. *Seed of the Fire.* NY. International. 1996. 1st ed. dj.
$10.00–$12.00

Bronson, Ruth Muskrat. *Indians Are People, Too.* NY. Friendship Press. (1944). First Edition. no dj. $65.00–$75.00

Bronte, Charlotte. *Jane Eyre: An Autobiography.* Lon. Smith, Elder & Co. 1848. 3rd ed. 3 vols. original cloth. $4,500.00–$6,000.00

Bronte, Charlotte. *Jane Eyre: An Autobiography.* Lon. Smith, Elder. 1847. 1st ed. 3 vols.
$40,000.00–$50,000.00

Bronte, Emily. *Wuthering Heights.* NY. Harper. 1848. 1st US ed. cloth.
$15,000.00–$20,000.00

Brooks, Gwendolyn. *Annie Allen.* NY. Harper & Row. (1949). 1st ed. first African American Pulitzer Prize winner. inscrb. sgn. lacking dj. $400.00–$450.00

Brooks, Lake. *Science of Fishing.* Ohio. A.R. Harding. 1912. 1st ed. illus. small green dec. binding. good+ cond. $10.00–$20.00

Brothers, Mary Hudson. *Billy the Kid, the Most Hated, The Most Loved &.* Hustler Press. 1949. 1st ed. wraps. $40.00–$50.00

Brown, Ina Corinne. *Story of the American Negro.* NY. Friendship Press. (1936). wraps.
$75.00–$85.00

Brown, Ina Corinne. *Story of the American Negro.* NY. Friendship Press. (1936). 1st ed. cloth.
$150.00–$200.00

Brown, John. *Two Against the Amazon.* NY. Dutton. 1953. 1st ed. maps. dj. $15.00–$22.00

Brown, Richard. *Domestic Architecture.* Lon. 1942. reprint. $400.00–$500.00

Brown, Richard. *Rudiments of Drawing Cabinet and Upholstery. . . .* Lon. 1820.
$2,000.00–$3,000.00

Brown, Theodore M. *Old Louisville*. KY. Univ of Louisville. (1961). 68 pp. illus. photos. map. $25.00–$30.00

Brown, Vinson. *Great Upon the Mountain: The Story of Crazy Horse, Legendary Mystic and Warrior*. NY. Macmillan. 1975. 1st ed. dj. $10.00–$20.00

Brown, William. *That Comical Brown's Budget of Comical Songs, as Sung by Him in His Entertainments Throughout the Country*. Bos. Brown. 1881. wraps. $50.00–$60.00

Browne, Juanita Kennedy. *Tale of Two Cities and a Train*. Nevada City. Nevada County Historical Society. 1987. 1st ed. sgn. 2000 cc. numbered. sgn. illus. photos. no dj as issued. $70.00–$90.00

Browning, Elizabeth Barrett. *Essay on Mind*. Lon. Duncan. 1826. 1st ed. bound by Sangorski & Sutcliffe. tan calf. aeg. $1,000.00–$1,100.00

Browning, Elizabeth Barrett. *Sonnets from the Portuguese*. Boston. Copeland & Day. 1896. ltd 750 cc. $800.00–$1,000.00

Brownlow, John. *Memoranda; or, Chronicles of the Foundling Hospital....* Lon. Sampson Low, Lambs. 1847. 1st ed. litho and engr plates. 3/4 morocco. $200.00–$250.00

Bryant, Charles. *Flora Diaetetica*. Lon. 1783. 1st ed. $300.00–$500.00

Buck, Pearl S. *Good Earth, The*. NY. 1931. 1st ed. 1st printing. John Day copyright. 1st issue binding. dj. $4,000.00–$5,500.00

Budrys, Algis. *Blood & Burning*. Lon. Gollancz. 1979. 1st hardcover ed. dj. $30.00–$40.00

Buell, Augustus. *Paul Jones Founder of the American Navy*. NY. Scribner's. 1905. 2 vols. $50.00–$90.00

Bugbee, Lester Gladstone. *Texas Frontier*. Pa. 1900. $50.00–$75.00

Buist, Robert. *Family Kitchen Gardener*. NY. Saxton. 1855. illus. $80.00–$125.00

Buist, Robert. *Rose Manual*. Phil. 1847. 7th ed. $25.00–$50.00

Bull, J. *Birds of New York State*. NY. Doubleday. 1974. illus. $45.00–$60.00

Bull, Marcus. *Experiments to Determine the Comparative Value of the Principal Varieties of Fuel used in the United States....* Phil. Dobson. 1827. 1st ed. engraved frontis. inscrb. $500.00–$1,000.00

Bull, Rice C. *Soldiering. The Civil War Diary of Rice C. Bull, 123rd Vol. Infantry....* CA. San Rafael Presidio. 1978. dj. $25.00–$50.00

Bunyan, John. *Pilgrim's Progress*. Lon. Henry Frowde. 1903. First Cruikshank edition. illus by George Cruikshank. ltd. 1,000 cc. plates. $200.00–$250.00

Burden, Bill. *Wandering Gastronaut, The*. Dubuque. Tel Graphics. 1975. 1st ed. illus. dj. $20.00–$25.00

Burger, Carl. *Wild Animals and Their Children*. Racine. Whitman. 1934. 1st ed. wraps. illus. tall dec. linen-like finish. $8.00–$20.00

Burgess, Fred W. *Old Prints and Engravings*. New York. G.P. Putnam. 1925. 1st ed. illus. blue decorated cloth gold lettering on spine. $20.00–$25.00

Burgess, Gelett. *Goop Directory*. Stokes. 1913. 1st ed. illus. paper over boards.
$100.00–$200.00

Burgess, Gelett. *Goops and How to Be Them*. Phil. Lippincott. 1928. illus. boards. dj.
$25.00–$75.00

Burgess, Gelett. *Maxims of Methusaleh*. Stokes. (1907). $25.00–$40.00

Burgess, Gelett. *More Goops and How Not to Be Them*. NY. Lippincott. 1931. illus. yellow cloth. $25.00–$50.00

Burgess, Gelett. *Purple Cow and Other Nonsense*. NY. Dover. 1961. illus. $25.00–$45.00

Burgess, Thornton. *Animal Book for Children*. Bos. Little Brown. 1918. 1st ed. illus. by cady.
$60.00–$150.00

Burgess, Thornton W. *Burgess Seashore Book for Children, The*. Bos. Little, Brown. 1929. 1st ed. inscrb. pictorial cloth with pictorial paper on cover. $500.00–$700.00

Burgess, Thornton W. *The Burgess Flower Book For Children*. Bos. Little Brown. 1923. 1st ed. illus. illus cover. col. frontis. $150.00–$250.00

Burnett, C. M. *Insanity Tested by Science &* . Lon. Highley. 1848. 1st ed. sgn.
$200.00–$300.00

Burroughs, Edgar Rice. *Apache Devil*. Tarzana. Burroughs. (1933). 1st ed. dj.
$700.00–$1,000.00

Burroughs, Edgar Rice. *At the Earth's Core*. Lon. Methuen. 1938. 1st UK ed. $35.00–$45.00

Burroughs, Edgar Rice. *Beasts of Tarzan*. McClurg. 1916. 1st ed. illus. by Allen St. John. cloth. $250.00–$500.00

Burroughs, Edgar Rice. *Gods of Mars, The*. CA. Edgar Rice Burroughs. 1940. tan cloth red lettering on cover and spine. $25.00–$35.00

Burroughs, Edgar Rice. *Gods of Mars, The*. Chicago. McClurg. 1918. 1st ed. 1st printing.
$160.00–$200.00

Burroughs, Edgar Rice. *Jungle Tales of Tarzan*. Chi. McClurg. 1919. 1st ed. illus. cloth.
$50.00–$100.00

Burroughs, Edgar Rice. *Llana of Gathol*. Tarzana. Burroughs. (1948). 1st ed. dj.
$150.00–$400.00

Burroughs, Edgar Rice. *New Adventures of Tarzan Pop-Up*. Chi. Pleasure Books. 1935. 1st ed. illus. 3 pop-ups. pictorial boards. $400.00–$450.00

Butler, Ellis Parker. *Philo Gubb; Correspondence-School Detective*. Bos. Houghton Mifflin. 1918. 1st ed. illus. dj. $800.00–$1,000.00

Buxton, Thomas Powell. *The African Slave Trade*. Lon. Murray. 1839. 2nd ed. sgn.
$400.00–$500.00

Bynner, Witter. *New Poems, 1960*. NY. Knopf. (1960). 1st ed. ltd 1750 cc. numbered.
$20.00–$40.00

Byrd, Richard Evelyn. *Little America: Aerial Exploration in the Antarctic; the Flight to the South Pole.* NY. 1930. 1st ed. illus. folding maps. sgn. $275.00–$325.00

Cahan, Abraham. *Rise of David Levinsky, The.* NY. Harper. 1917. 1st ed. dj.
                                                                                                   $120.00–$150.00

Caldecott, Randolph. *Gleanings from the Graphic.* Lon. Routledge. 1889. 1st ed. folio.
                                                                                                   $200.00–$300.00

Calvert, Michael. *Prisoners of Hope.* Lon. Jonathan Cape. 1952. 1st ed. dj. $90.00–$100.00

Calverton, Victor Francis. *Three Strange Lovers.* NY. Macaulay. 1930. 1st ed. intro by Edward J. O' Brien. dj. $200.00–$250.00

Cameron, Peter. *One Way or Another.* NY. Harper & Row. 1986. 1st ed. author's first book. dj.
                                                                                                   $10.00–$15.00

Campbell, John Lord. *Lives of the Chief Justices of England, The.* Lon. Murray. 1849. 1st ed. 2 vols. calf. raised bands. $150.00–$375.00

Campbell, Joseph. *The Hero With a Thousand Faces.* NY. Pantheon. 1949. 1st ed. dj.
                                                                                                   $300.00–$1,000.00

Campbell, Mary Emily. *Attitude of Tennesseans Toward the Union, 1847–1861.* NY. 1961. 1st ed.
                                                                                                   $30.00–$50.00

Camus, Albert. *La Peste (The Plague).* Paris. 1947. 1st ed. wraps. in French. deluxe. ltd 220 cc. $2,500.00–$3,000.00

Camus, Albert. *Stranger, The.* NY. Knopf. 1946. 1st US ed. dj. $900.00–$1,500.00

Cantwell, First Lieut. J.C. *Report of the Operations of the U.S. Revenue Steamer Nunivak on the Yukon River Station, Alaska 1899–1901.* Wash. Government Printing Office. 1902. 1st ed. illus. green cloth. 325pp. $100.00–$250.00

Cantwell, Robert. *Land of Plenty.* 1934. 1st ed. $50.00–$55.00

Cantwell, Robert. *Land of Plenty.* 1934. 1st ed. dj. $200.00–$300.00

Cantwell, Robert. *Real McCoy, The.* NJ. Auerbach. 1971. 1st ed. illus. dj. $50.00–$130.00

Card, Orson Scott. *Ender's Game.* NY/Tor. 1985. 1st ed. scarce. dj. $500.00–$675.00

Cargill, John F. *Big-Horn Treasure: A Tale of Rocky Mountain Treasure.* Chi. McClurg. 1897. 1st ed. illus. frontis. plates. red cloth. $25.00–$35.00

Carpentry and Building. New York. 1881. illus. 3/4 lea. and marbleized bds. folio, vol. 3, #1.
                                                                                                   $150.00–$200.00

Carpentry and Building. New York. 1879. 1st ed. illus. folio, vol. 1, #1. $200.00–$250.00

Carr, Annie E. (ed.). *East of Antelope Island.* Bountiful. Daughters of Utah Pioneers. 1948. 1st ed. $50.00–$90.00

Carroll, Jim. *Living at the Movies.* NY. Grossman. 1973. 1st ed. dj. $300.00–$400.00

Carroll, Jonathan. *Land of Laughs.* NY. Viking. 1980. 1st ed. inscrb. author's first book. dj.
                                                                                                   $300.00–$350.00

Carroll, Jonathan. *Outside the Dog Museum*. NY. Doubleday. 1992. 1st ed. sgn. dj.
$50.00–$60.00

Carroll, Lewis. *Complete Works, The*. Lon. Nonesuch. (1939). 1st ed. thus. cloth. dj.
$60.00–$90.00

Carroll, Lewis. *Hunting of the Snark, The*. Lon. Macmillan. 1876. 1st ed. 1st impression. illus. by Henry Holiday. $1,000.00–$7,500.00

Carruth, Hayden. *Crow & the Heart, 1946–1959*. NY. Macmillan. 1959. 1st ed. author's first trade book. printed wrappers. $90.00–$125.00

Carson, Rachel. *Edge of the Sea*. Bos. 1955. 1st ed. dj. $30.00–$75.00

Carson, Rachel. *Silent Spring*. Bos. Houghton Mifflin. 1962. 1st ed. no dj. $60.00–$90.00

Carson, Rachel. *Silent Spring*. Bos. Houghton Mifflin. 1962. 1st ed. illus. dj.
$200.00–$700.00

Carson, Rachel. *Under the Sea Wind*. NY. 1941. 1st ed. dj. $100.00–$150.00

Carter, Jimmy. *Always a Reckoning*. NY. Times Books. (1995). 1st ed. sgn. dj.
$150.00–$200.00

Carter, Jimmy. *Blood of Abraham, The; Insights into the Middle East*. Bos. Houghton Mifflin. 1985. 1st ed. sgn. dj. $200.00–$300.00

Carter, Jimmy. *Farewell Address of President Jimmy Carter, January 14, 1981*. Winston-Salem. Palaemon Press. 1981. 1st ed. 300 cc. printed and sgn by Carter. blue cloth.
$600.00–$750.00

Carter, Jimmy. *Negotiation: The Alternative to Hostility*. Carl Vinson Memorial Lecture Series, Inaugural Lecture. Macon. Mercer Univ Press. (1984). 1st ed. navy imitation lea. sgn.
$600.00–$625.00

Carter, Jimmy. *Turning Point: A Candidate, a State, and a Nation Come of Age*. NY. Times Books. (1992). 1st ed. illus. photos. inscrb. sgn. dj. $200.00–$300.00

Carter, Jimmy. *Why Not The Best?* Nashville, TN. Broadman. (1977). Presidential Edition. illus. sgn by Jimmy and Rosalynn. case. $400.00–$500.00

Cartier-Bresson, Henri. *From One China to Another*. NY. (1956). 1st ed. dj. $100.00–$150.00

Cartier-Bresson, Henri. *People of Moscow*. NY. Simon & Schuster. 1955. 1st ed. dj.
$50.00–$135.00

Carver, Raymond. *At Night the Salmon Move*. Santa Barbara. Capra Press. 1976. 1st ed. wraps. ltd 1000 cc. $200.00–$250.00

Carver, Raymond. *Cathedral*. NY. Knopf. 1983. 1st ed. inscrb. dj. $300.00–$400.00

Carver, Raymond. *Ultramarine*. NY. Random House. 1986. 1st ed. dj. $50.00–$80.00

Carver, Raymond. *Ultramarine*. NY. Random House. 1986. 1st ed. sgn. dj. $250.00–$350.00

Carver, Raymond. *What We Talk About When We Talk About Love*. NY. Knopf. 1981. 1st ed. sgn. dj. $900.00–$1,200.00

Carver, Raymond. *Will You Please Be Quiet, Please?* NY. McGraw-Hill. (1976). 1st ed. author's first collection of stories. sgn. dj. $2,500.00–$3,000.00

Carver, Raymond. *Will You Please Be Quiet, Please?* NY. McGraw-Hill. (1976). 1st ed. dj. $400.00–$500.00

Carver, Raymond. *Winter Insomnia.* Santa Cruz. Kayak. 1970. 1st ed. ltd 1000 cc. sgn. $500.00–$700.00

Cassidy, Carl. *History of the 775th Bombardment Squadron.* Iowa. 1982. illus. reprint. ltd 300 cc. sgn. $95.00–$125.00

Cather, Willa. *Death Comes for the Archbishop.* NY. Knopf. 1927. 1st ed. green cloth. sgn. lacking dj. $5,000.00–$7,500.00

Cather, Willa. *Death Comes for the Archbishop.* NY. 1927. 1st ed. 303 pp. very good cond. $100.00–$150.00

Cather, Willa. *Lucy Gayheart.* NY. Knopf. 1935. limited. sgn. $150.00–$200.00

Cather, Willa. *Professor's House, The.* NY. Knopf. 1925. 1st ed. ltd 225 cc. numbered and sgn. $900.00–$1,000.00

Cather, Willa. *Sapphira and the Slave Girl.* limited. sgn. dj. $200.00–$300.00

Centennial History of Highland, Ill. Highland. Highland Centennial Asso. 1937. 1st ed. illus. blue silver lettering on cover. $20.00–$40.00

Ceremony of Flag Presentation to Columbia University. Privately Printed by Lafayette Post. 1899. 1st ed. illus. tan cloth, decorated cover, col plates. $20.00–$40.00

Chadwick, Henry. *Spalding's Official Baseball Guide 1907.* New York. American Sports Pub. Co. 1907. wraps. illus. cover loose, rear cover gone. $100.00–$350.00

Chalmers, David M. *Hooded Americans; the First Century of the Ku Klux Klan, 1865–1965.* Garden City. Doubleday. 1965. 1st ed. dj. $30.00–$35.00

Chamberlain, Samuel and Henry N. Flynt. *Historic Deerfield: Houses and Interiors.* NY. Hastings. (1965). illus. dj. $25.00–$35.00

Chambers, Robert W. *Hidden Children, The.* NY/Lon. Appleton. 1914. 1st ed. red cloth. dj. $300.00–$400.00

Chandler, Raymond. *Big Sleep, The.* NY. Knopf. 1939. 1st ed. author's first book. Philip Marlowe. movie based on book. original cloth. pictorial dj. $10,000.00–$15,000.00

Chandler, Raymond. *Big Sleep, The.* NY. Knopf. 1939. 1st ed. author's first book. Philip Marlowe. movie based on book. lacking dj. $800.00–$1,000.00

Chandler, Raymond. *Farewell My Lovely.* NY. Knopf. 1940. 1st ed. orange cloth. some wear. dj. $500.00–$900.00

Chandler, Raymond. *Farewell My Lovely.* NY. Knopf. 1940. 1st ed. orange cloth. fine condition. dj. $1,000.00–$2,000.00

Chandler, Raymond. *Farewell My Lovely.* NY. Knopf. 1940. 1st ed. orange cloth. lacking dj. $200.00–$350.00

Chandler, Raymond. *High Window, The.* NY. Knopf. 1942. 1st ed. dj. $2,000.00–$5,000.00

Chandler, Raymond. *High Window, The.* NY. Pocket Books. (1946). 1st paperback ed.
$500.00–$1,500.00

Chandler, Raymond. *Killer in the Rain.* Lon. Hamish Hamilton. 1964. 1st ed. collection of stories. lacking dj. $500.00–$600.00

Chandler, Raymond. *Lady in the Lake, The.* NY. Knopf. 1943. 1st ed. dj.
$10,000.00–$12,000.00

Chandler, Raymond. *Lady in the Lake, The.* Melbourne. Hamish Hamilton. (1946). 1st Australian ed. dj. $2,000.00–$2,200.00

Chandler, Raymond. *Playback.* Lon. Hamish Hamilton. (1958). 1st ed. dj. $400.00–$500.00

Chandler, Raymond. *Playback.* Bos. Houghton Mifflin. 1958. 1st US ed. dj.
$300.00–$400.00

Chapelle, Howard. *Yacht Designing and Planning.* NY. WW Norton. 1936. 1st ed. illus. gray cloth with lettering on cover and spine. very good. $20.00–$50.00

Chapin, Walter. *The Missionary Gazetteer.* Woodstock. 1825. 1st ed. all leather. lea pastedown with lettering on spine. lacks a hand-colored map. $50.00–$100.00

Chapin, Walter. *The Missionary Gazetteer.* Woodstock. 1825. 1st ed. full calf. hand-colored map. $350.00–$750.00

Chapman, M. Frank. *Color Key to North American Birds.* New York. Appleton & Co. 1912. illus. brown dec. cloth, b/w and col. illus. $8.00–$60.00

Chesnutt, Charles W. *Conjure Woman, The.* NY. Houghton Mifflin. 1899. 1st ed. author's first book. brown cloth. $350.00–$425.00

Chesterton, Gilbert K. *George Bernard Shaw.* NY. John Lane Co. 1909. 1st edition.
$20.00–40.00

Child, Lydia Maria. *American Frugal Housewife, The.* NY. Wood. 1834. 15th edition.
$30.00–$400.00

Child, Lydia Maria. *Right Way, The Safe Way, The.* NY. Negro Univ Press. 1969. reprint of Abolitionist tract. $15.00–$25.00

Child, William. *History of the Fifth Regiment, New Hampshire, A.* Bristol. Musgrove. 1893.
$125.00–$200.00

Child's Book of Abridged Wisdom, A. San Fran. Paul Elder. 1905. 1st ed. illus. grey dec board. exposed cords on spine. Japanese folds. printed endpapers. $85.00–$200.00

Childs, Christopher, ed. *Clear Sky, Pure Light.* Lincoln, MA. Penmaen Press. (1978). 1st ed. ltd. 100 handmade cc. boxed. $150.00–$175.00

Christensen, Mark. *Aloha.* NY. Simon & Schuster. 1994. 1st ed. dj. $10.00–$12.00

Christian Spectator Conducted by an Association of Gentlemen for the Year 1820, The. NY. Howe & Spalding. 1820. 3/4 lea and bds. $65.00–$125.00

Christie, Agatha. *Murder at the Vicarage.* NY. 1930. 1st US ed. green cloth. good to fine condition. dj. $900.00–$3,500.00

Christie, Agatha. *Partners in Crime.* NY. Dodd, Mead & Co. (1929). 1st ed. dj.
$900.00–$1,500.00

Christie's. *Haskell Norman Library of Science and Medicine, Part II.* Christie's Auction. June, 1998. 1st ed. catalogue. $50.00–$110.00

Churchill, Winston. *History of the English-Speaking Peoples.* Lon. Cassell. 1956–58. 1st ed. 4 vols. dj. $200.00–$250.00

Churchill, Winston. *Liberalism and the Social Problems.* Lon. 1909. 1st UK ed.
$400.00–$800.00

Churchill, Winston. *Second World War.* 1948–54. 1st ed. 6 vols. djs. $150.00–$300.00

Churchill, Winston. *World Crisis.* NY. 1931. 1st US ed. charts. maps. illus. $100.00–$175.00

Clancy, Tom., *Hunt for Red October, The.* Annapolis. Naval Institute Press. 1984. 1st ed. 1st issue. movie based on the book starring Sean Connery. $300.00–$700.00

Clancy, Tom. *Hunt for Red October, The.* Annapolis. Naval Institute Press. 1984. 1st ed. 1st issue. movie based on the book starring Sean Connery. $900.00–$1,500.00

Clancy, Tom. *Red Storm Rising.* NY. Putnam's. 1986. 1st ed. dj. $25.00–$30.00

Clancy, Tom. *Red Storm Rising.* NY. Putnam's. 1986. 1st ed. sgn. dj. $75.00–$100.00

Clark, Francis E. *Our Journey Around the World.* Hartford. Worthington. 1896. illus. engr. color map. $30.00–$45.00

Clark, Francis E. *Our Journey Around the World.* Hartford. Worthington. 1894. engr. color map. $40.00–$100.00

Clark, Joseph G. *Lights and Shadows of Sailor Life.* Bos. Putnam. 1847. 1st ed. 2nd issue. frontis. plates. 324 pp. cloth. $600.00–$800.00

Clark, Mary Higgins. *Remember Me.* NY. Simon & Schuster. 1994. 1st ed. dj.
$15.00–$20.00

Clark, Mary Higgins. *Remember Me.* NY. Simon & Schuster. 1994. 1st ed. sgn. dj.
$40.00–$50.00

Clark, Walter Van Tilburg. *Ox-Bow Incident, The.* NY. 1940. 1st ed. wraps. advance reading copy. pictorial dj. $800.00–$1,000.00

Clarke, Arthur C. *Childhood's End.* NY. Ballantine. 1953. 1st ed. in wraps. $50.00–$95.00

Clarke, Arthur C. *Childhood's End.* NY. Harcourt. (1953). 1st ed. sgn. dj
$1,500.00–$3,000.00

Clarke, Arthur C. *Childhood's End.* Lon. Sidgwick & Jackson 1954. 1st UK ed. dj.
$350.00–$500.00

Clarke, Arthur C. *Expedition to Earth.* Ballantine. (1953). 1st ed. wraps. $35.00–$45.00

Clarke, Arthur C. *Exploration of the Moon.* Lon. Frederick Muller. (1954). 1st ed. black cloth. $40.00–$60.00

Clarke, Arthur C. *Sands of Mars.* NY. Gnome Press. (1952). 1st ed. dj. $90.00–$150.00

Clarke, Arthur C. *2001: A Space Odyssey.* Lon. 1968. 1st UK ed. $250.00–$600.00

Clarke, Arthur C. *2001: A Space Odyssey.* NY. New American Library. 1968. 1st ed. dj. $900.00–$1,500.00

Clarke, Arthur C. *2001: A Space Odyssey.* New American Library. (1968). 1st ed. book based on screenplay. no dj present. $250.00–$300.00

Clarke, Arthur C. *2001: A Space Odyssey.* New American Library. (1968). 1st ed. book based on screenplay. dj present. sgn. $1,500.00–$2,500.00

Clarke, Arthur C. *2061: Space Odyssey Three.* NY. Del Rey. 1987. 1st ed. dj. $25.00–$30.00

Clarke, John Henry. *Dictionary of Practical Materia Medica.* Sussex. 1962. 3 vols. $150.00–$200.00

Clarkson, Rosetta E. *Green Enchantment, the Magic Spell of Gardens.* NY. Macmillan. 1940. 1st ed. illus. dj. $10.00–$20.00

Cleaver, Edith Marion. *Kindergarten Work in the Home.* n.p. n.d. 1st ed. wraps. illus. illustrated cover. 16 pages. near fine. $8.00–$15.00

Clements, Thomas. *Geological Story of Death Valley.* CA. Desert Magazine. 1954. 1st ed. 52 pp. illus. photos. map. pictorial wrappers. $12.00–$20.00

Clowes, John. *Dialogues on the Nature, Design, and Evidence of the Theological Writing of the Honourable Emanuel Swedenborg.* NY. 1821. blue paper wrappers. stitched. $80.00–$100.00

Clutterbuck, Richard. *Protest and the Urban Guerrilla.* Lon. Cassell. 1973. 1st ed. dj. $15.00–$20.00

Cobb, W. Mantague. *First Negro Medical Society & District of Columbia 1884–1939.* DC. Associated Publishers. 1939. $40.00–$50.00

Cochin, Augustin. *Results of Emancipation, The.* Bos. Walker, Wise and Company. 1863. rebound. $150.00–$200.00

Codrescu, Andrei. *The Lady Painter.* Bos. Four Zoas Press. 1977. First Edition. ltd. 300cc.wraps. $25.00–$30.00

Coffin, Charles C. *Boys of 1861.* Bos. 1885. $100.00–$120.00

Coffin, Charles C. *Life of Abraham Lincoln.* NY. 1893. $50.00–$80.00

Cohe, Albert K. *Delinquent Boys: The Culture of the Gang.* Illinois. Free Press. (1955). 1st ed. dj. $15.00–$25.00

Colby, Benjamin. *A Guide to Health, being an exposition of the principles of the Thomsonian System of Practice.* . . . Milford, NH. John Burns. 1846. 3rd ed. illus. plates. $100.00–$150.00

Colcord, Joanna. *Roll and Go Songs of American Sailormen.* Indianapolis. Bobbs-Merrill. 1924. illus. gray boards. 118 pp. $20.00–$50.00

Cole, Ralph. *Young Angler's Pocket Companion, The.* Lon. Bassam. 1795. 1st ed. marbled boards backed with sheep. $600.00–$1,000.00

Cole, S. W. *American Fruit Book.* Bos. 1849. 1st ed. $50.00–$80.00

Coleman, Wanda. *Mad Dog Black Lady.* Santa Barbara. Black Sparrow. 1979. 1st ed. ltd. 200 cc. sgn. $90.00–$115.00

Coleridge, S. T. *Friend: A Series of Essays.* Burlington. Chauncy Goodridge. 1831. 1st US ed. $80.00–$150.00

Collins, Stephen, M.D. *Miscellanies.* Phil. Carey and Hart. 1842. 1st ed. green cloth. $70.00–$90.00

Collins, Wilkie. *Armadale.* NY. Harper & Bros. 1870. 1st US ed. $100.00–$300.00

Collodi, Carlo. *Pinocchio.* Akron. (1924). illus. by Frances Brundage. pictorial cover paste-on. $30.00–$50.00

Colomb, Captain R. N. *Slave-Catching in the Indian Ocean.* Lon. Longmans. 1873. 1st ed. illus. frontis. map. plates. original cloth. $3,000.00–$3,500.00

Colomb, Captain R. N. *Slave-Catching in the Indian Ocean.* 1968. illus. reprint. $50.00–$75.00

Colomb, Captain R. N. *Slave-Catching in the Indian Ocean.* Lon. Longmans. 1873. 1st ed. illus. rebacked. $1,200.00–$1,500.00

Colquhoun, Archibald R. *China in Transformation.* NY. Harper. 1899. illus. fldg & pocket maps. $60.00–$75.00

Colquhoun, Archibald R. *Overland to China.* NY. Harper. 1900. illus. clr fldg maps. $75.00–$90.00

Colton, J. H. *Colton's United States Showing the Military Stations &.* NY. Putnam. 1892. $100.00–$120.00

Colton, Walter Rev. *The Sea and The Sailor.* NY. A.S. Barnes & Burr. 1860. brown blind-stamped binding. frontis. $20.00–$50.00

Colum, Padraic. *Creatures.* NY. 1927. 1st ed. illus. by Artzybasheff. $30.00–$50.00

Colum, Padraic. *Girl Who Sat by the Ashes.* NY. 1919. 1st ed. illus. by Dugald Walker. $40.00–$50.00

Commonwealth of Massachusetts. *Memorial of Charles Sumner.* Bos. Wright & Potler. 1874. purple cloth. 316 pp. $20.00–$25.00

Comstock, J. L. *Elements of Chemistry.* NY. Pratt Woodford & Co. 1853. revised ed. leather. $25.00–$35.00

Condon, Richard. *Manchurian Candidate.* NY. McGraw-Hill. 1959. 1st ed. movies based on this title. fine condition. fine dj. sgn. $300.00–$800.00

Condon, Richard. *Manchurian Candidate.* NY. McGraw-Hill. 1959. 1st ed. movies based on this title. fine condition. fine dj. $100.00–$200.00

Connett, Eugene. *Wildfowling in the Mississippi Flyway.* Tor/NY. Van Nostrand. (1949). 1st ed. $80.00–$100.00

Conrad, Joseph. *Victory.* Garden City, NY. Doubleday, Page & Co. 1915. $14.00–$20.00

Conrad, Joseph. *Tales of Hearsay.* NY. Doubleday, Page & Co. 1925. 1st ed. red pub. mark on title page. $25.00–$125.00

Conrad, Joseph. *Last Essays.* NY. Doubleday, Page & Co. 1926. 1st ed. red pub. mark on title page. $25.00–$75.00

Conrad, Joseph. *Nostrodomo.* Lon. 1904. 1st ed. morocco case. $1,500.00–$2,000.00

Conrad, Joseph. *Suspense.* Lon. Dent. 1925. 1st ed. original maroon cloth. dj. $150.00–$500.00

Conroy, Pat. *Great Santini, The.* NY. Houghton Mifflin. 1976. 1st ed. movie based on this title. dj. $125.00–$200.00

Conroy, Pat. *Great Santini, The.* NY. Houghton Mifflin. 1976. 1st ed. movie based on this title. sgn. dj. $400.00–$800.00

Conroy, Pat. *Great Santini, The.* NY. Houghton Mifflin. 1976. 1st ed. movie based on this title. signed by Conroy and his father, who was the model for "Santini." dj. $900.00–$1,100.00

Conroy, Pat. *Prince of Tides, The.* Bos. Houghton Mifflin. 1986. 1st ed. movie based on this title. dj. $25.00–$50.00

Conroy, Pat. *Prince of Tides, The.* Bos. Houghton Mifflin. 1986. 1st ed. movie based on this title. sgn. dj. $350.00–$700.00

Conroy, Pat. *Water Is Wide, The.* NY. Houghton Mifflin. 1972. 1st ed. "Conrack" movie based on this title. sgn. inscrb. dated. dj. $800.00–$1,500.00

Conroy, Pat. *Water Is Wide, The.* NY. Houghton Mifflin. 1972. 1st ed. "Conrack" movie based on this title. dj. $150.00–$400.00

Conway, Sir William Martin. *First Crossing of Spitsbergen, The.* Lon. Dent. 1897. 1st ed. illus. plates. folding maps. photos. brown cloth. teg. $650.00–$950.00

Cook, George C. *Chasm, The.* Stokes. 1911. 1st ed. yellow cloth. $50.00–$90.00

Cook, James. *Explorations of Captain James Cook in the Pacific . . .* 1768–1779. NY. Limited Editions Club. 1957. 1st ed. thus. frontis. illus. endpaper maps. $125.00–$175.00

Cook, John A. *Pursuing the Whale.* Bos. Houghton Mifflin. 1926. 1st ed. gray cloth. $40.00–$80.00

Cook, Philip St. George. *Scenes and Adventures in the Army.* Phil. Lindsay. 1857. $300.00–$600.00

Cook, Roy Bird. *Family and Early Life of Stonewall Jackson.* VA. 1925. 1st ed. $50.00–$75.00

Cooper, Clarence, Jr. *Weed; a Novel.* Evanston. Regency. 1961. 1st ed. wraps. good condition.
$20.00–$30.00

Cooper, James Fenimore. *Deerslayer, The.* NY. Scribner's. 1925. 1st edition illustrated by N. C. Wyeth. dj.
$100.00–$200.00

Cooper, James Fenimore. *Deerslayer, The.* Phil. Lea & Blanchard. 1841. 1st ed. purple cloth.
$1,000.00–$2,000.00

Cooper, James Fenimore. *Pathfinder, The.* Lon. Bentley. 1840. 1st UK ed. 3 vols.
$750.00–$2,500.00

Cooper, James Fenimore. *Pathfinder, The.* Phil. Lea & Blanchard. 1840. 1st ed.
$800.00–$2,000.00

Corelli, Marie. *Secret Power, The.* Lon. Methuen. 1921.
$130.00–$145.00

Cormier, Robert. *Chocolate War, The.* NY. Pantheon. 1974. 1st ed. sgn. dj.
$125.00–$180.00

Cornish, Dudley Taylor. *Sable Arm, Negro Troops in the Union Army, 1861–1865.* NY. 1956.
1st ed.
$50.00–$75.00

Cornwallis, Caroline Francis. *Introduction to Practical Organic Chemistry.* Lon. Pickering.
1843.
$100.00–$175.00

Correl & Gosden. *All About Amos 'n Andy and Their Creators, Correl & Gosden.* NY. Rand McNally. 1929. illus. 1st ed.
$40.00–$80.00

Correspondence Between the Rev. Samuel H. Cox of Brooklyn. . . . NY. Office of the American Anti-Slavery Society. 1846. wraps.
$60.00–$90.00

Coulter, Ellis Merton. *Civil War and Readjustment in Kentucky.* Chapel Hill. Univ NC Press.
1926. 1st ed.
$70.00–$100.00

Coulter, Ellis Merton. *William B. Brownlow, Fighting Parson of the Southern Highlands.*
Chapel Hill. Univ NC Press. 1937. 1st ed.
$45.00–$70.00

Coulton, G.G. *Medieval Panorama.* Cambridge. University Press. 1939. illus. green decorated cover, lettering on spine.
$10.00–$18.00

Courlander, Harold. *Negro Folk Music USA.* NY. Columbia Univ Press. 1963. dj.
$50.00–$75.00

Cox, Palmer. *Brownies at Home.* NY. Century. 1893. illus.
$100.00–$300.00

Coyle, Kathleen. *There Is A Door.* Paris. Edward W. Titus. 1931. 1st ed. pink and beige cloth 524/525cc. sgn by author.
$50.00–$125.00

Craig, Neville B. *History of Pittsburgh, with a Brief Notice of Its Facilities. . . .* Pittsburgh.
Mellor. 1851. 1st ed. frontis. maps. cloth.
$150.00–$225.00

Crane, Hart. *Seven Lyrics.* Cambridge. Ibex Press. 1st ed. ltd 250 cc. wraps.
$125.00–$150.00

Crane, Stephen. *Monster and Other Stories.* NY/Bos. Harpers. 1899. 1st ed.
$200.00–$250.00

Crane, Stephen. *Open Boat and Other Stories.* Lon. 1898. 1st ed. green cloth.
$195.00–$230.00

Crane, Stephen. *Red Badge of Courage, The.* NY. Appleton. 1896. 1st ed. $125.00–$200.00

Crane, Walter. *Absurd ABC.* Lon. Routlege & Sons. 1st ed. red leather. $350.00–$400.00

Crane, Walter. *Flora's Feast of Flowers.* Lon. 1889. 1st ed. illus. 40 pp. pictorial boards.
$90.00–$150.00

Creole Cookery Book. New Orleans. Thomason. 1885. 1st ed. by Christian Woman's Exchange.
$100.00–$150.00

Crews, Harry. *All We Need of Hell.* NY. Harper. 1987. 1st ed. dj. $40.00–$50.00

Crews, Harry. *Blood and Grits.* NY. Harper. (1979). 1st ed. dj. $40.00–$50.00

Crews, Harry. *Feast of Snakes.* Lon. Atheneum. (1977). 1st UK ed. dj. $75.00–$125.00

Crews, Harry. *Naked in Garden Hills.* NY. Morrow. 1969. 1st ed. dj. $75.00–$200.00

Crichton, Michael. *Andromeda Strain.* NY. Knopf. 1969. 1st ed. 1st issue. dj.
$100.00–$200.00

Crichton, Michael. *Andromeda Strain.* NY. Knopf. 1969. 1st ed. 1st issue. sgn. dj.
$400.00–$700.00

Crichton, Michael (Michael Douglas). *Dealing or the Berkeley-to-Boston Forty-Brick Lost-Bag Blues.* NY. Knopf. 1971. 1st ed. written with Crichton's brother, Douglas. dj.
$100.00–$250.00

Crichton, Michael. *Jurassic Park.* NY. Knopf. 1990. 1st ed. dj. $30.00–$45.00

Crichton, Michael. *Jurassic Park.* NY. Knopf. 1990. 1st ed. sgn. dj. $125.00–$350.00

Crite, Allan Rohan. *All Glory.* Mass. Society of Saint John the Evangelist. 1947. 1st ed. illus. blue cloth gold lettering on spine, signed presentation copy no dj. $50.00–$75.00

Crosman, J. S. *Annual Report of the Warden of the Nevada State Prison, for the Fiscal Year Ending Dec. 31, 1866.* Carson City. Eckley. 1867. wraps. folding table. $400.00–$600.00

Crothers, Samuel McChord. *Children of Dickens.* NY. Scribner's. 1925. 1st ed. illus. by Jessie Wilcox Smith. dj. $200.00–$350.00

Crouch, Nathaniel. *Unhappy Princess, The.* Lon. Crouch. 1710. 1st ed. engraved frontis. woodcuts. early children's book on historical figures. $1,000.00–$1,250.00

Cruise of the Revenue Steamer Corwin in Alaska. DC. GPO. 1883. illus. color and b/w plates.
$300.00–$350.00

Cubas, Antonia Garcia (trans by Henderson). *Republic of Mexico in 1876, The.* Mexico. La Ensenanza. 1876. wraps. illus. color plates. maps. 8 leaves of music. $250.00–$300.00

Cullen, Countee. *Black Christ, The.* New York. Harper & Bros. 1929. 1st ed. illus. blue boards, black spine, paper label with lettering on cover and spine. $25.00–$40.00

Cullin, Mitch. *Cosmology of Bing, The.* Sag Harbor. Permanent. 2001. 1st ed.
$10.00–$15.00

Culpeper, Nicholas. *Pharmacopoeia Londinensis; or The London Dispensary &* . Bos. John Allen. 1720. 1st medical book printed in America. $17,000.00–$22,000.00

cummings, e. e. *CIOPW.* NY. Covici Friede. 1931. 1st ed. illus. by cummings. ltd 391 cc. numbered. sgn. $500.00–$850.00

cummings, e. e. *eimi.* NY. Covici Friede. 1933. 1st ed. ltd 1381 cc. numbered. sgn. dj. $700.00–$750.00

cummings, e. e. *Enormous Room, The.* NY. Boni and Liveright. 1922. 1st ed. 1st issue. points. inscrb. restored dj. $3,500.00–$4,500.00

cummings, e. e. *No Thanks.* NY. Golden Eagle Press. (1935). 1st ed. blue cloth. 990 deluxe edition cc. sgn. $900.00–$1,000.00

Cummings, Ray. *Explorers into Infinity.* NY. Avalon. 1965. 1st ed. dj. $60.00–$75.00

Cunningham, Michael. *Flesh and Blood.* NY. Farrar, Straus & Giroux. 1995. 1st ed. dj. $10.00–$15.00

Curie, Madam Marie. *Radioactivité.* Paris. 1935. wraps. $500.00–$1,200.00

Currie, William. *Historical Account of the Climate and Diseases of the United States.* Phil. Dobson. 1792. 1st ed. rebound. $600.00–$800.00

Curtis, John. *Harvey's Views on the Circulation of Blood.* NY. Columbia Univ Press. 1915. $50.00–$75.00

Curtis, Matoon. *Book of Snuff and Snuff Boxes.* NY. 1935. illus. dj. $25.00–$40.00

Curtis, Natalie (ed. and compiler). *Indians' Book.* NY. Harper. 1907. 1st ed. illus. $250.00–$400.00

Curtis, Newton. *From Bull Run to Chancellorsville.* NY. 1906. $90.00–$100.00

Curtis, Paul. *Sportsmen All.* Derrydale Press. (1938). ltd 950 cc. illus. $100.00–$125.00

Curtis, William Eleroy. *Egypt, Burma and British Malaysia.* Chi. Revel. 1905. 1st ed. illus. maps. $35.00–$100.00

Curwood, James. *Danger Trail.* Bobbs-Merrill. (1910). 1st ed. $20.00–$30.00

Curwood, James. *Plain of Abraham.* NY. 1928. 1st ed. dj. $20.00–$30.00

Cushing, Harvey. *Consecratio Medici.* 1928. 1st ed. $50.00–$160.00

Cushing, Harvey. *From a Surgeon's Journal, 1915–1918.* Bos. 1936. 1st ed. $50.00–$75.00

Cushing, Harvey. *Life of Sir William Osler.* Oxford. Clarendon Press. 1925. 1st ed. illus. 2 vols. 4th impression. $90.00–$375.00

Cussler, Clive. *Night Probe!.* NY. Bantam. 1981. 1st ed. dj. $80.00–$100.00

Cussler, Clive. *Night Probe!.* NY. Bantam. 1981. 1st ed. sgn. dj. $125.00–$200.00

Custer, Elizabeth. *Boots and Saddles.* NY. Harper. 1885. 1st ed. 2nd issue. map. portrait. $75.00–$200.00

Custer, General G. A. *Life on the Plains.* NY. 1874. 1st ed. illus. $250.00–$400.00

Cutter, Donald. *California Coast, The.* Norman. Univ Oklahoma Press. (1969). reprint of 1891 edition. illus. photos and facsimiles. $40.00–$50.00

Cutter, Donald. *Malaspina in California.* San Francisco. Howell. 1960. 1st ed. illus. ltd 1000 cc. plates. tan cloth. $90.00–$125.00

Dahl, Roald. *Charlie and the Chocolate Factory.* NY. Knopf. 1964. 1st ed. first state. dj. $1,500.00–$2,500.00

Dahl, Roald. *Charlie and the Chocolate Factory.* NY. Knopf. 1964. early issue. dj. $40.00–$50.00

Dahl, Roald. *Charlie and the Chocolate Factory.* NY. Knopf. 1964. 1st ed. first state. dj. $900.00–$2,000.00

Dahl, Roald. *Charlie and the Chocolate Factory.* NY. Knopf. 1964. 1st ed. first state. sgn. dj. $5,000.00–$9,000.00

Dahl, Roald. *James and the Giant Peach.* London. George Allen & Unwin. 1967. 1st UK edition. dj. $350.00–$400.00

Dahl, Roald. *James and the Giant Peach.* NY. Alfred A. Knopf. 1961. First edition. dj. $750.00–$1,500. 00

Dahl, Roald. *James and the Giant Peach.* NY. Knopf. later edition. $5.00–$40.00

Daley, Brian. *Han Solo at Star's End.* NY. Del Rey. 1979. 1st ed. dj. $100.00–$130.00

Dali, Salvador. *Secret Life of Salvador Dali.* NY. Dial Press. 1942. 1st US ed. dj. $200.00–$250.00

Dampier, Robert. *To the Sandwich Islands on H. M. S. Blonde.* Honolulu. Univ of Hawaii Press. 1971. illus. drawings. $45.00–$60.00

Dana, Charles. *Eastern Journeys.* NY. Appleton. 1898. teg. $40.00–$75.00

Dana, Charles. *Life of Ulysses S. Grant.* Gurdon Bell. 1868. $50.00–$60.00

Dana, Charles L. *Peaks of Medical History: Outline of the Evolution of Medicine.* NY. Hoeber. 1926. 1st ed. illus. plates. $100.00–$120.00

Dana, Richard Henry, Jr. *Two Years Before the Mast.* Chi. Lakeside. 1930. illus. ltd 1000 cc. slipcase. $150.00–$200.00

Dana, Richard Henry, Jr. *Two Years Before the Mast.* NY. Limited Editions Club. 1947. 1/1500 cc. Intro by W. McFee. illus. and sgn by H. A. Mueller. slipcase. $50.00–$75.00

Dana, Richard Henry, Jr. *Two Years Before the Mast.* Harper. 1840. 1st ed. $2,000.00–$2,500.00

Daniel, Charles S. *Ai. A Social Vision.* Phil. Miller. 1892. 1st ed. utopian literature. presentation copy. blue cloth. $125.00–$175.00

Daniels, Jonathan. *Man of Independence, The.* Phil. Lippincott. (1950). later edition. inscrb. by Truman. dj. $600.00–$900.00

Darrow, Clarence. *Story of My Life, The.* NY. 1932. ltd 1st ed. 294 cc. numbered. sgn. illus. plates. $2,000.00–$2,500.00

Darrow, Clarence. *Story of My Life.* NY. Scribner's. 1932. 1st ed. sgn. dj. $400.00–$700.00

Darwin, Charles. *Descent of Man.* Lon. Murray. 1871. 1st ed. illus. 2 vols.
$3,000.00–$5,000.00

Darwin, Charles. *Descent of Man.* NY. Appleton. 1871. 1st US ed. 2 vols.
$900.00–$1,100.00

Darwin, Charles. *Descent of Man.* Lon. Murray. 1871. 2nd issue. 2 vols.
$1,500.00–$2,500.00

Darwin, Charles. *Effects of Cross and Self Fertilization.* NY. 1889. later edition.
$100.00–$200.00

Darwin, Charles. *Naturalist's Voyage . . . of HMS Beagle.* Lon. John Murray. 1890. later edition. 500 pp. $100.00–$200.00

Darwin, Charles. *On the Origin of Species by Means of Natural Selection.* Lon. 1859. 1st ed. 1st issue. $50,000.00–$95,000.00

Darwin, Charles. *On the Origin of Species.* Lon. Murray. 1860. 2nd ed. 2nd issue. green cloth.
$7,000.00–$10,000.00

Darwin, Charles. *On the Origin of Species by Means of Natural Selection.* NY. Appleton. 1871. 5th ed. $300.00–$400.00

Davidson, George. *Alaska Boundary.* San Francisco. Alaska Packers Association. 1903. 1st ed. illus. maps. brown cloth. $500.00–$600.00

Davies, Charles. *Translated from the French by A. M. Legendre, by David Brewster.* A.S. Barnes & Co. Phila. 1842. $35.00–$100.00

Davis, Christopher. *Joseph and the Old Man.* St. Martin's. 1986. 1st ed. author's first book. dj.
$20.00–$25.00

Davis, George. *Recollections of a Sea Wanderer's Life.* NY. 1887. 1st ed. illus. pictorial cloth.
$250.00–$300.00

Davis, Hassoldt. *Land of the Eye . . . Burma, China, India and the Lost Kingdom of Nepal.* NY. Holt. (1940). 1st ed. illus. photos. $20.00–$50.00

Dawson, Nicholas. *Narrative of Nicholas Cheyenne Dawson.* San Francisco. Grabhorn. 1933. 2nd ed. ltd 500 cc. cloth-backed decorated boards. $100.00–$125.00

Dawson, William Leon. *Birds of California.* San Diego. Moulton. 1923. deluxe ltd ed. 4 vols. teg. morocco. $1,500.00–$2,000.00

De Angeli, Marguerite. *Book of Nursery & Mother Goose Rhymes.* Garden City. Doubleday. 1954. illus. Caldecott Honor book. dj. $45.00–$250.00

De Angeli, Marguerite. *Petite Suzanne.* Doubleday Doran. 1937. 1st ed. illus. by De Angeli. dj. $50.00–$90.00

De Angeli, Marguerite. *Up the Hill.* Doubleday Doran. 1942. 1st ed. illus. by De Angeli. dj.
$30.00–$50.00

De Blacam, Aodh. *Old Wine: Verses from the Irish, Spanish and Latin.* . . . Dublin. Three Candles. 1st ed. inscrb. wraps.
$70.00–$90.00

De Brunhoff. *Babar and Zephir.* Random House. 1937. 1st US ed. illus.
$40.00–$60.00

De Brunhoff, Jean. *Babar the King.* Smith and Haas. 1935. 1st US ed.
$700.00–$900.00

De Brunhoff. *Serafina the Giraffe.* World. (1961). 1st ed.
$60.00–$75.00

De Camp, L. *Sprague. Great Fetish, The.* Garden City. Doubleday. 1978. 1st ed. dj.
$25.00–$35.00

De La Rue, Sidney. *Land of the Pepper Bird: Liberia, The.* NY. Putnam's Sons. 1930. illus. photos.
$20.00–$30.00

Dean, James. *Alphabetical Atlas, An; or Gazeteer of Vermont.* Montpelier. Godd. 1808. 1st ed. wraps. sole edition.
$100.00–$150.00

Dean, Leon W. *Guns Over Champlain.* NY, Tor. Rinehart and Co. 1946. 1st ed. rust color cloth binding. very good cond.
$10.00–$20.00

Dean, Mallette. *Journal of Julius Rodman.* San Francisco. Colt. 1947. ltd 500 cc. Grabhorn.
$70.00–$90.00

Decker, Amelia Stickney. *That Ancient Trail.* Trenton. By Author. 1962. illus. black cloth with gilt lettering on cover.
$45.00–$155.00

Defoe, Daniel. *History of the Great Plague in London.* Lon. Noble. 1754. 3/4 morocco.
$500.00–$600.00

Defoe, Daniel. *Life and Adventures of Robinson Crusoe.* Chi. Saalfeld. 1924. illus. by Francis Brundage.
$60.00–$90.00

Defoe, Daniel. *Life and Adventures of Robinson Crusoe.* NY. Cosmopolitan. 1920. illus. by Wyeth.
$150.00–$500.00

DeGolyer, E. *Antiquity of the Oil Industry.* Texas. Peripatetic Press. 1946. 1st ed. ltd 300 cc. light green wrappers.
$90.00–$100.00

Deitz, August. *Star Wars Dark Forces.* Putnam. 1997. 1st ed. dj.
$15.00–$20.00

Delaplaine, Edward S. *Francis Scott Key: Life and Times.* NY. 1937. 1st ed. ltd 500 cc. numbered. sgn. folding plates. teg. slipcase.
$125.00–$175.00

Dellengaugh, Frederick. *North Americans of Yesterday, A Comprehensive Study of North-American Indian Life.* . . . NY. Putnam's. 1901. 1st ed. illus. photos. tan cloth.
$100.00–$175.00

Dellengaugh, Frederick. *Romance of the Colorado River, The.* NY. Putnam's. 1909. 3rd ed. tan cloth.
$85.00–$120.00

Denman, Thomas. *An Introduction to the Practice of Midwifery.* Brattleborough, Vt. William Fessenden. 1807. later US edition.
$200.00–$275.00

Denslow, W. W. *Mother Goose.* NY. McClure. 1901. illus. paper boards. $100.00–$200.00

Denslow, W. W. *Pearl and the Pumpkin, The.* NY. Dillingham. 1904. 1st ed. illus. green cloth. $100.00–$200.00

Denslow, W. W. *Scarecrow and the Tin-Man.* Dillingham. (1904). $150.00–$300.00

Denslow, W. W. *When I Grow Up.* Century. 1909. 1st ed. illus. 24 color plates. $100.00–$150.00

Derby, George H. (John Phoenix). *Squibob Papers, The.* NY. Carleton. 1865. 1st ed. 4 pp ads. blind-stamped gray cloth. $125.00–$175.00

Derleth, August (ed.). *Arkham Collector, The.* Sauk City. Arkham House. 1970. printed self wrappers. #6, winter. 2500 cc printed. $20.00–$40.00

Derleth, August (ed.). *Arkham Collector, The.* Sauk City. Arkham House. 1968. printed self wrappers. #2, winter. 2500 cc printed. $20.00–$40.00

Derleth, August (ed.). *Arkham Collector, The.* Sauk City. Arkham House. 1967–1971. 10 vols. printed self wrappers. $200.00–$250.00

Derleth, August. *Bright Journey.* NY. Scribner's. 1940. 1st ed. inscrb. $50.00–$90.00

Derleth, August. *Casebook of Solar Pons.* Sauk City. Mycroft & Moran. 1965. 1st ed. dj. $90.00–$125.00

Derleth, August. *Dark Mind, Dark Heart.* Sauk City. Arkham House. 1962. sgn. dj. $80.00–$120.00

Derleth, August. *Mask of Cthulhu, The.* UK. Spearman. 1974. 1st UK ed. dj. $40.00–$60.00

Derleth, August. *Mask of Cthulhu, The.* Sauk City. Arkham. 1958. 1st ed. dj. $100.00–$250.00

Derleth, August. *Not Long For This World.* Sauk City. Arkham House. 1948. 1st ed. dj. $75.00–$250.00

Derleth, August. *Over the Edge.* Sauk City. Arkham House. 1964. 1st ed. dj. $40.00–$60.00

Derleth, August. *Restless Is the River.* NY. Scribner's. 1939. 1st ed. dj. $75.00–$100.00

Derleth, August. *Thirty Years of Arkham House.* NY. Scribner's. 1970. 1st ed. dj. $50.00–$85.00

Derleth, August (ed.). *Time to Come: Science Fiction Stories of Tomorrow.* NY. Farrar Straus & Young. 1954. 1st ed. dj. $50.00–$90.00

Devoluy, Pierre and Pierre Borel. *French Riviera, The.* Bos. Hale, Cushman & Flint. 160 pp. illus. $10.00–$15.00

Dewees, William. *Compendious System of Midwifery.* Phil. Carey & Lea. 1824. 1st ed. $150.00–$300.00

Dewees, William. *Treatise on the Diseases of Females.* Phil. Carey & Lea. 1826. 1st ed. illus. morocco. plates. $1,000.00–$1,500.00

D' Ewes, J. *Sporting in Both Hemispheres.* Lon. 1858. 2nd ed. $100.00–$125.00

Dick and Jane: Fun With Dick and Jane. 1940. $50.00–$120.00

Dick and Jane: More Dick and Jane Stories. 1934. 1st ed. $70.00–$170.00

Dick and Jane: Now We Read. 1965. wraps. $50.00–$75.00

Dick and Jane: We Look and See. 1946–47. wraps. $100.00–$120.00

Dick, Philip K. *Days of Perky Pat.* NY. Ziff Davis (1963). in Amazing Fact and Science Fiction, vol. 37, no. 1. sgn. $250.00–$300.00

Dick, Philip K. *Do Androids Dream of Electric Sheep?* Garden City. Doubleday. 1968. 1st ed. basis for movie "Blade Runner." dj. $5,000.00–$7,500.00

Dick, Philip K. *Do Androids Dream of Electric Sheep?* Garden City. Doubleday. 1968. 1st ed. basis for movie "Blade Runner." ex lib in good condition. dj. $1,000.00–$1,500.00

Dick, Philip K. Dr. *Futurity.* NY. Ace. (1960). 1st ed. wraps. $25.00–$35.00

Dick, Philip K. *Man in the High Castle, The.* NY. Putnam Sons. (1962). 1st ed. Hugo Winner. dj. $500.00–$1,500.00

Dick, Philip K. *World Jones Made, The.* NY. Ace Double. 1956. 1st ed. wraps. bound with Agent of the Unknown. $40.00–$50.00

Dickens, Charles. *Christmas Carol, A.* Lon. Chapman & Hall. 1843. 1st ed. 2nd issue. rebound. $3,000.00–$5,000.00

Dickens, Charles. *Christmas Carol, A.* Lon. Chapman & Hall. 1843. 1st ed. red-brown cloth. fair to good condition. $12,000.00–$30,000.00

Dickens, Charles. *Dombey & Sons.* Lon. Bradbury and Evans. 1848. $500.00–$1,000.00

Dickens, Charles. *Life and Adventures of Nicholas Nickelby.* Lon. Chapman and Hall. 1839. 1st ed. illus. by Phiz. frontis. plates. rebound. $750.00–$1,200.00

Dickens, Charles. *Little Dorrit.* Lon. 1857. illus. 1st ed in book form. engr. ½ calf. marbled boards. $500.00–$1,200.00

Dickens, Charles. *Martin Chuzzlewit.* Lon. Chapman & Hall. 1844. 1st ed. illus. original boards. $1,000.00–$1,750.00

Dickens, Charles. *Posthumous Papers of the Pickwick Club.* Lon. Chapman and Hall. 1837. 1st ed in book form. good condition. points. $600.00–$3,000.00

Dickens, Charles. *Tale of Two Cities, A.* Lon. Chapman and Hall. 1859. 1st ed. 1st state. points. scarce. $10,000.00–$18,000.00

Dickens, Charles. *Tale of Two Cities, A.* Lon. Chapman and Hall. 1859. 1st ed. 2nd or mixed state. $1,200.00–$5,000.00

Dickey, James. *Drowning with Others.* Middletown, CT. Wesleyan Univ Press. (1962). 1st ed. sgn. dj. $200.00–$300.00

Dickinson, Robert L. And L. Beam. *The Single Woman*. Baltimore. Williams & Wilkins. 1949. rprnt. $30.00–$40.00

Dictionary of the Kalispel of Flat-head Indian Language, Compiled by the Missionaries of the Society of Jesus. Montana. St. Ignatius. 1877–8-9. 1st ed. 2 vols. wraps. approx. 100 cc. $1,200.00–$1,500.00

Diehl, Edith. *Bookbinding*. NY. Rinehart. 1946. 1st ed. illus. 2 vols. 93 plates. $150.00–$200.00

Diescher, Victor. *Book of Good Manners, The*. New York. Social Culture. 1923. brn cl. $5.00–$20.00

Diringer, David. *Alphabet, The: A Key to the History of Mankind*. Funk & Wagnalls. 1968. 3rd ed. 2 vols. slipcase. $150.00–$200.00

Disch, Thomas. *On Wings of Song*. NY. St. Martins. 1979. 1st US ed. Nebula nominee. Hugo nominee. dj. $25.00–$45.00

Disch, Thomas M. *Castle of Indolence*. NY. Picador. 1995. 1st ed. sgn. dj. $25.00–$35.00

Disney Studios. *Pop-Up Mickey Mouse*. NY. Blue Ribbon Books. 1933. 1st ed. illus. by Disney Studios. 3 pop-ups. pictorial boards. $400.00–$700.00

Dixon, Franklin W. *Arctic Patrol Mystery*. Grosset & Dunlap. 1969. 1st ed. Hardy Boys series. pictorial cover. $10.00–$15.00

Dixon, Franklin W. *Clue of the Screeching Owl*. Grosset & Dunlap. 1962. 1st ed. Hardy Boys series. pictorial cover. $10.00–$15.00

Dixon, Franklin W. *Mystery at Devil's Paw*. Grosset & Dunlap. 1959. 1st ed. Hardy Boys series. dj. $20.00–$25.00

Dixon, Franklin W. *Mystery of the Desert Giant*. Grosset & Dunlap. 1961. 1st ed. Hardy Boys series. dj. $20.00–$25.00

Dixon, Franklin W. *Secret of Skull Mountain*. NY. Grosset & Dunlap. (1948). #28. later printing. dj. $25.00–$30.00

Dixon, Franklin W. *Secret of the Lost Tunnel*. Grosset & Dunlap. 1950. 1st ed. Hardy Boys. dj. $30.00–$70.00

Dixon, Franklin W. *Secret of Wildcat Swamp, The*. Grosset & Dunlap. 1952. 1st ed. Hardy Boys series. dj. $25.00–$30.00

Dobie, J. Frank. *Longhorns, The*. Bos. Little Brown. 1941. 1st ed. dj. $40.00–$70.00

Dobie, J. Frank. *Man, Bird and Beast*. Austin. 1930. 1st ed. cloth. $35.00–$75.00

Dobie, J. Frank. *Tales of Old Time Texas*. Bos. Little Brown. 1955. dj. $45.00–$55.00

Dobie, J. Frank. *Voice of the Coyote, The*. Bos. Little Brown. 1949. 1st ed. illus. by Murie. sgn. dj. $400.00–$500.00

Dobie, J. Frank. *Wild and Wily*. Flagstaff. Northland Press. 1980. 1st ed. dj. $30.00–$45.00

Doctorow, E. L. *Billy Bathgate*. Franklin Center. Franklin Library. 1989. ltd. sgn. morocco. aeg. frontis. $100.00–$200.00

Dodge, Henry Nehemiah. *Mystery of the West*. Bos. Badger. 1906. 1st ed. green cloth.
$30.00–$55.00

Doig, Ivan. *English Creek*. NY. Atheneum. 1984. 1st ed. dj. $50.00–$70.00

Doig, Ivan. *Heart Earth*. NY. Atheneum. 1993. 1st ed. dj. $20.00–$30.00

Doig, Ivan. *Ride with Me, Mariah Montana*. NY. Atheneum 1990. 1st ed. dj.
$15.00–$20.00

Doig, Ivan. *Ride with Me, Mariah Montana*. NY. Atheneum. 1990. 1st ed. sgn. dj.
$25.00–$30.00

Doig, Ivan. *Sea Runners, The*. NY. Atheneum. 1982. 1st ed. dj. $90.00–$125.00

Dollard, John. *Caste and Class in a Southern Town*. New Haven. The Institute of Human Relations. 1938. brown cloth with gilt border. $20.00–$45.00

Donnelly, Ignatius. *Atlantis: The Antediluvian World*. New York. Harper. 1910. 1st ed. illus. green cloth. $50.00–$60.00

Donovan, Dick. *In the Face of the Night*. Lon. Long. 1908. 1st ed. $50.00–$90.00

Dooley, Mrs. James H. *Dem Good Ole Times*. NY. Doubleday, Page. 1906. 1st ed. cloth. plates. $75.00–$85.00

Dore Bible Gallery. Phil. 1883. illus. $50.00–$80.00

Dorsey, James Owen and John R. Swanton. *Dictionary of the Biloxi and Ofo Languages*. DC. GPO. 1912. 1st ed. $30.00–$60.00

Dorsey, Sarah A. *Recollections of Henry Watkins Allen & Confederate Army*. NY. 1866. 1st ed. lea. $125.00–$200.00

Dos Passos, John. *1919*. NY. Harcourt Brace. (1932). 1st ed. dj. $100.00–$200.00

Dos Passos, John. *1919*. NY. Harcourt Brace. (1932). 1st ed. sgn. dj. $150.00–$200.00

Dos Passos, John. *State of the Nation*. NY. Houghton Mifflin. 1944. 1st ed. dj.
$200.00–$400.00

Dossenbach, Monique and Hans. *Great Stud Farms of the World*. NY. William Morrow. 1978. 1st Amer ed. illus. dj. $50.00–$140.00

Doughty, Charles M. *Wanderings in Arabia*. Lon. Duckworth. (1923). 2 vols. maps.
$75.00–$100.00

Doughty, Charles M. *Wanderings in Arabia*. Lon. Duckworth. 1939. 607 pp. frontis. fldg map. $20.00–$30.00

Douglas, Norman. *In the Beginning*. Florence. Private Printing. 1927. 1st ed. ltd 700 cc. numbered. sgn. $150.00–$275.00

Douglas, Norman. *In the Beginning*. NY. 1928. 1st Amer ed. dj. $20.00–$50.00

Douglas, Norman. *Nerinda*. Florence. Orioli. 1929. 1st ed. ltd 475 cc. inscrb.
$3,000.00–$4,000.00

Douglas, Norman. *South Wind*. NY. Limited Editions Club. 1932. ltd. 1.500 cc. numbered and signed by illustrator C. Petrina. $70.00–$80.00

Douglas, Norman. *South Wind*. NY. Dodd, Mead. 1928. 1st ed. thus. illus. by V. Angelo. boxed. dj. $150.00–$170.00

Douglas, Norman. *South Wind*. Chi. Argus. 1920. 1st ed. 2 vols. illus by John Austen. partially unopened. untrimmed. dj. boxed. $250.00–$275.00

Douglass, Frederick. *Life and Times of Frederick Douglass, written by Himself.* . . . Hartford. Park Publishing. 1882. illus. 2nd printing. cloth. $200.00–$400.00

Douglass, Frederick. *My Bondage and My Freedom*. NY. Miller, Orton and Mulligan. 1855. 1st ed. illus. frontis. cloth. fair condition. $400.00–$600.00

Douglass, Frederick. *My Bondage and My Freedom*. NY. Miller, Orton and Mulligan. 1855. 1st ed. illus. frontis. cloth. very good condition. $1,000.00–$1,500.00

Douglass, Frederick. *My Bondage and My Freedom*. NY. Miller, Orton and Mulligan. 1855. 1st ed. frontis. inscrb by Douglass. $20,000.00–$30,000.00

Douglass, Frederick. *Oration of Frederick Douglass Delivered on the Occasion of the Unveiling of the Freedmen's Monument.* . . . DC. Gibson. 1876. 1st ed. wraps. 21 pp. $5,000.00–$7,000.00

Dow, George Francis. *Slave Ships and Slaving*. Salem, MA. Marine Research Society. 1927. 1st ed. illus. plates. good condition, good dj. $300.00–$500.00

Dow, George Francis. *Slave Ships and Slaving*. Salem, MA. Marine Research Society. 1927. 1st ed. illus. plates. no dj. $25.00–$100.00

Downes, T. W. *History of and Guide to the Wanganui River*. Wanganui. Wanganui Herald Newspaper Co. 1923. wraps. illus. tan pictorial wrps. $20.00–$30.00

Downing, A. G. *Architectural Heritage of Newport, R.I.* NY. 1967. 2nd ed. dj. $15.00–$25.00

Downing, A. J. *Fruits and Fruit Trees of America*. NY. 1846. cloth. $250.00–$500.00

Downing, A. J. *Horticulturists, The*. Albany. July, 1846. 1st ed. $125.00–$175.00

Downing, A. J. *Rural Essays*. NY. 1853. illus. $125.00–$150.00

Downing, A. J. *Treatise on the Theory and Practice of Landscape Gardening, A*. NY. 1854. later ed. illus. fair condition. $80.00–$275.00

Downing, A. J. *Treatise on the theory and practice of landscape gardening adapted to North America . . . , A*. NY. 1849. later ed. illus. good condition. $300.00–$400.00

Downing, Andrew Jackson. *Architecture of Country Houses, The*. NY/Lon. Appleton. 1850. 1st ed. pictorial cloth. $145.00–$200.00

Dowsett, H. M. *Wireless Telephony and Broadcasting*. 1924. 1st ed. illus. $90.00–$100.00

Doyle, Arthur Conan. *Adventures of Sherlock Holmes*. NY. Harper. (1892). 1st Amer ed.
$750.00–$1,250.00

Doyle, Arthur Conan. *Adventures of Sherlock Holmes.* Lon. Newnes 1892. 1st ed.
$1,750.00–$2,000.00

Doyle, Arthur Conan. *Case-book of Sherlock Holmes.* Lon. Murray. 1927.
$750.00–$1,000.00

Doyle, Arthur Conan. *Croxley Master, The.* NY. Doran. (1925). 1st Amer ed.
$90.00–$100.00

Doyle, Arthur Conan. *Hound of the Baskervilles.* NY. 1902. 1st Amer ed. 1st issue.
$1,000.00–$3,000.00

Doyle, Arthur Conan. *Hound of the Baskervilles.* Lon. Newnes. 1902. 1st ed. 1st state, with "you" for "your" on page 13, line 3. $4,000.00–$10,000.00

Doyle, Arthur Conan. *Lost World.* NY. Hodder & Stoughton. (1912). 1st Amer ed.
$75.00–$300.00

Doyle, Arthur Conan. *Maracot Deep, The.* NY. Doubleday Doran. 1929. 1st US ed. black cloth. $100.00–$200.00

Doyle, Arthur Conan. *New Revelation, The.* NY. Doran. (1918). 1st US ed. brown cloth.
$100.00–$150.00

Doyle, Arthur Conan. *Our American Adventure.* NY. Doran. nd. 1st American ed. brown cloth with green lettering. $150.00–$200.00

Doyle, Arthur Conan. *Return of Sherlock Holmes, The.* Lon. Newnes. 1905. 1st ed.
$800.00–$900.00

Doyle, Arthur Conan. *Sign of Four.* Lon. Newnes. 1893. 3rd ed. red pictorial covers.
$200.00–$300.00

Doyle, Arthur Conan. *Valley of Fear.* NY. Doran. (1914). 1st ed. soiled. missing dj.
$100.00–$200.00

Doyle, Arthur Conan. *Valley of Fear, The.* NY. (1914). 1st ed. red cloth. scarce dj.
$300.00–$700.00

Doyle, Arthur Conan. *Valley of Fear.* Lon. Smith Elder. 1915. 1st UK ed. frontis.
$750.00–$1,400.00

Doyle, Arthur Conan. *White Company.* NY. Cosmopolitan. 1922. illus. by N. C. Wyeth. dj.
$200.00–$400.00

Doyle, Lily. *Bound in Khaki. . . .* Lon. Elliot Stock. 1916. 1st ed. tan cloth. 63 pp.
$40.00–$50.00

Drago, Harry Sinclair. *Out of the Silent North.* NY. Macaulay. 1923. 1st ed. frontis. dj.
$80.00–$100.00

Drake, Benjamin. *Life of Tecumseh and of His Brother the Prophet. . . .* Cinc. 1856. 1st ed. xlib. $100.00–$190.00

Drake, Benjamin. *Life of Tecumseh and of His Brother the Prophet. . . .* Cinc. 1856. 1st ed.
$200.00–$250.00

Drake, D. Dr. *Daniel Drake's Letters on Slavery*. NY. 1940. 1st ed. ltd 250 cc. dj.
$150.00–$195.00

Drake, Samuel. *Indian Biography*. Bos. Drake. 1832. 1st ed. $125.00–$270.00

Drane, Maude Johnson. *History of Henry County, Kentucky*. 1948. 1st ed. $60.00–$75.00

Dreiser, Theodore. *An American Tragedy*. NY. Boni & Liveright. 1925. 1st ed. 1st issue. 2 vols. dj. $900.00–$1,000.00

Dreiser, Theodore. *Gallery of Women*. NY. Liveright. 1929. 1st ed. 2 vols. djs.
$125.00–$250.00

Dreiser, Theodore. *Plays of the Natural and the Supernatural*. Lon/NY. Lane/Bodley Head. 1916. 1st ed. 1st issue. green paper boards. printed label. $100.00–$250.00

Dreiser, Theodore. *Sister Carrie*. Lon. Heinemann. 1901. 1st UK ed. pictorial cloth.
$1,000.00–$1,200.00

Dreiser, Theodore. *Sister Carrie*. NY. Doubleday. 1900. 1st ed. author's first novel. pictorial cloth. $3,500.00–$8,000.00

Drinker, Frederick E. *Booker T. Washington: The Master Mind of a Child of Slavery*. np. 1915. 1st ed. illus. photos. $75.00–$125.00

Drinker, Frederick E. and James G. Lewis. *Radio, Miracle of the 20th Century*. 1922. 1st ed. illus. $25.00–$60.00

Drummond, H. *Tropical Africa*. NY. Scribner. 1889. 1st US ed. $100.00–$200.00

Drummond, H. *Tropical Africa*. Lon. 1888. 1st ed. $150.00–$200.00

Drury, Clifford. *Marcus and Narcissa Whitman and the Opening of the Old Oregon*. Glendale. Clark. 1973. 1st ed. 2 vols. illus. blue cloth. inscrb. $125.00–$150.00

Drury, John. *Old Illinois Houses*. Illinois. State Historical Society. 1948. later issue. illus. 21 plates. $10.00–$40.00

Drury, John. *Old Illinois Houses*. Illinois. State Historical Society. 1948. 1st ed. illus. 21 plates.
$120.00–$150.00

Dryden, Adam. *Hints to Anglers*. 1862. 1st ed. fldg maps. half morocco and cloth.
$150.00–$250.00

Dryden, John. *Songs and Poems of John Dryden*. Lon. Golden Cockerel Press. 1957. ltd 500 cc. numbered. Special copy with extra sets of color plates and drawings. $1,000.00–$1,200.00

Du Bois, W. E. B. *Dark Princess*. NY. Harcourt. 1928. 1st ed. near fine. $150.00–$175.00

Du Bois, W. E. B. *Darkwater*. NY. Harcourt, Brace and Howe. 1920. 1st ed. dark blue cloth.
$40.00–$175.00

Du Bois, W. E. B. *Dusk to Dawn*. NY. Harcourt Brace. (1940). 1st ed. $300.00–$1,000.00

Du Bois, W. E. B. *In Battle for Peace*. NY. Masses & Mainstream. 1952. 1st ed. sgn. dj.
$750.00–$1,000.00

Du Chaillu, Paul. *Land of the Midnight Sun*. NY. Harper. (1881). 2 vols. 1st ed. illus wood engr. pocket map. $175.00–$500.00

Du Chaillu, Paul. *Land of the Midnight Sun*. NY. Harper. 1881. 2 vols. later printing. illus wood engr. pocket map. $60.00–$75.00

Du Chaillu, Paul. *Lost in the Jungle*. NY. 1869. 1st ed. $40.00–$100.00

Du Chaillu, Paul. *Stories of the Gorilla Country*. NY. 1868. 1st ed. illus. inscrb. $200.00 $300.00

Du Chaillu, Paul. *Stories of the Gorilla Country*. NY. 1868. 1st ed. illus. $40.00–$60.00

Du Voisin, Roger. *All Aboard*. New York. Grosset & Dunlap. 1935. 1st ed. wraps. illus. by author, tall dec bd cover, dj. $35.00–$85.00

Dubois, Abbe J. *Hindu Manner, Customs & Ceremonies*. Oxford. Clarendon. 1899. 1st ed. 2nd revised, corrected and enlarged ed. 732 pp. $50.00–$75.00

Dubois, Donald. *Fisherman's Handbook of Trout Flies*. NY. 1960. 1st ed. illus. color plates. dj. $25.00–$50.00

Dubourg, George. *Violin, The*. Lon. 1852. 4th ed. $20.00–$60.00

Dubus, Andre. *All the Time in the World*. NY. Knopf. 1996. 1st ed. $25.00–$40.00

Dubus, Andre. *Finding a Girl in America*. Bos. Godine. 1980. 1st ed. inscrb. dj. $175.00–$495.00

Dubus, Andre. *Lieutenant, The*. NY. Dial. 1967. 1st ed. author's first book, dj. $125.00–$150.00

Duchassois, P. *Mid Snow and Ice: the Apostles of the North-West*. Lon. 1923. 1st ed. illus. $45.00–$85.00

Duchow, John Charles. *Duchow Journal: A Voyage from Boston to California, 1852*. Mallette Dean. 1959. ltd 200 cc. handmade paper. cloth backed decorated boards. $200.00–$300.00

Dufur, S. M. *Over the Dead Line or Tracked by Bloodhounds*. Burlington, VT. 1902. $75.00–$125.00

Duke, Basil. *History of Morgan's Cavalry*. Cinn. 1867. $150.00–$200.00

Dulac, Edmund. *Daughters of the Stars*. Lon. 1939. dj. $50.00–$75.00

Dulac, Edmund. *Stories from Hans Anderson*. Doran. nd. 1st ed. illus. by Dulac. color plates. $100.00–$150.00

Dulac, Edmund. *Stories from the Arabian Nights*. NY. Hodder & Stoughton. 1907. illus. color plates. $900.00–$1,000.00

Dumas, Alexandre. *Le Comte de Monte-Cristo (The Count of Monte-Cristo)*. Brussels. 1845–46. in French. 1st trade ed. 5 vols. $5,000.00–$6,500.00

Dumas, Lt-Gen. M. *Memoirs of His Own Time Including the Revolution*. Phil. 1839. 2 vols. $150.00–$200.00

Dumay, Raymond. *Guide du Vin.* 1967. written in French. $15.00–$20.00

Dumond, Dwight L. *Secession Movement, The.* NY. Macmillan. 1931. 1st ed. dj.
     $40.00–$50.00

Dumont, Henrietta. *Lady's Oracle.* Phil. Peck & Bliss. 1853. 270 pp. aeg. $50.00–$75.00

Dunaway, W. F. *Reminiscences of a Rebel.* NY. Neale. 1913. $200.00–$225.00

Dunbar, Alice Moore. *Masterpieces of Negro Eloquence.* NY. 1914. $180.00–$200.00

Dunbar, Paul Laurence. *Folks From Dixie.* NY. Dodd Mead. 1926. illus. by Kemble.
     $55.00–$90.00

Dunbar, Paul Laurence. *Folks From Dixie.* NY. Dodd Mead. 1898. 1st ed. illus. by Kemble.
     $200.00–$450.00

Dunbar, Paul Laurence. *Howdy Honey Howdy.* NY. Dodd Mead. 1905. 1st ed. illus. photos.
     $400.00–$700.00

Dunbar, Paul Laurence. *Jest of Fate, The.* Lon. Jarrold. 1902. 1st English ed.
     $1,000.00–$1,500.00

Dunbar, Paul Laurence. *Li' l Gal.* 1904. 1st ed. photos. $100.00–$150.00

Dunbar, Paul Laurence. *Li' l Gal.* NY. Dodd Mead. 1904. 1st ed. dj. $600.00–$900.00

Dunbar, Paul Laurence. *Lyrics of Love and Laughter.* NY. Dodd Mead. 1903. 1st ed. teg.
     $75.00–$250.00

Dunbar, Paul Laurence. *Lyrics of Love and Laughter.* NY. Dodd Mead. 1903. 1st ed. inscrb.
     $3,500.00–$6,000.00

Dunbar, Paul Laurence. *Lyrics of Lowly Life.* NY. Dodd Mead. 1901. later printing.
     $50.00–$100.00

Dunbar, Paul Laurence. *Lyrics of Lowly Life.* NY. Dodd Mead. 1897. 1st ed.
     $250.00–$400.00

Dunbar, Paul Laurence. *Oak and Ivy.* OH. United Brethren. 1893. 1st ed. blue cloth.
     $2,000.00–$5,000.00

Dunbar, Paul Laurence. *Poems of Cabin and Field.* NY. Dodd Mead. 1899. 1st ed. illus. by
Hampton Institute. $150.00–$175.00

Dunbar, Paul Laurence. *When Malindy Sings.* NY. Dodd Mead. 1903. 1st ed. illus. cloth. sgn.
     $1,000.00–$2,000.00

Dunbar, Paul Laurence. *When Malindy Sings.* NY. Dodd Mead. 1903. later prtg. illus.
cloth. teg. $175.00–$250.00

Duncan Brothers. *United States Homeopathic Pharmacopoeia.* Chi. 1878. 1st ed. 281 pp.
     $50.00–$75.00

Duncan, F. Martin. *Plant Traps and Decoys.* Henry Frowde. $75.00–120.00

Duncan, Isadora. *My Life.* NY. 1927. illus. ltd. 650 cc. $40.00–$65.00

Dunlap, Roy. *Ordnance Went Up Front.* South Carolina. Small Arms Tech Pub. 1948. 1st ed. illus. green cloth, lettering on cover and spine. $45.00–$200.00

Dunlop, William. *History of American Theatre.* NY. 1832. $250.00–$350.00

Dunn, Finley Peter. *Mr. Dooley in Peace and in War.* Bos. Small, Maynard. 1898. 1st ed. green cloth. $65.00–$100.00

Dunn, William Edward. *Spanish and French Rivalry in the Gulf Region of the United States 1678–1702.* Austin. 1917. wraps 238 pp. 5 maps (1 folding). $100.00–$140.00

Dunne, Peter M. *Early Jesuit Missions in Tarahumara.* Berkely. 1948. 1st ed. illus. folding map. $50.00–$75.00

Dunning, John. *Booked to Die.* NY. Scribner's. (1992). 1st ed. fine condition. sgn. dj. $1,200.00–$1,400.00

Dunning, John. *Booked to Die.* NY. Scribner's. (1992). 1st ed. good condition. dj. $400.00–$600.00

Dunning, John. *Bookman's Wake.* NY. Scribner's. 1995. 1st ed. dj. $40.00–$50.00

Dunning, John. *Deadline.* NY. Fawcett. 1981. 1st ed. wraps. $50.00–$90.00

Dunsany, Lord. *Blessing of Pan, The.* Lon. Putnam. 1927. 1st ed. 287 pp. frontis. blue cloth. no dj. $30.00–$90.00

Dunsany, Lord. *Blessing of Pan, The.* Lon. Putnam. 1927. 1st ed. frontis. blue cloth. dj. $100.00–$230.00

Dunsany, Lord. *Blessing of Pan, The.* NY/Lon. Putnam. 1928. frontis. blue cloth. no dj. $50.00–$60.00

Dunsany, Lord. *Chronicles of Rodriguez, The.* NY. Putnam. 1922. 1st ed. dj. $200.00–$600.00

Dunsany, Lord. *Chronicles of Rodriguez, The.* NY. Putnam. 1922. ltd. 55 cc. teg. illus by Sime. sgn by Dunsany and Sime. $350.00–$800.00

Dunsany, Lord. *Fourth Book of Jorkens.* Arkham House. 1948. 1st ed. dj. $80.00–$150.00

Dunsany, Lord. *His Fellow Men.* Lon. Heinemann. 1952. 1st ed. dj. $125.00–$400.00

Dunsany, Lord. *Rory and Bran.* Putnam. 1937. 1st ed. green cloth. dj missing. $40.00–$50.00

Dunsany, Lord. *Selections from the Writings.* Churchtown. Cuala Press. 1912. 1st ed. ltd 250 cc. $125.00–$150.00

Dunsany, Lord. *Sword of Welleran.* Lon. 1908. 1st ed. illus. sgn. $150.00–$200.00

Dunsany, Lord. *Sword of Welleran.* Lon. 1908. 1st ed. illus. $75.00–$100.00

Dunsany, Lord. *Tales of War.* Dub. Talbot. 1918. 1st ed. dj. $130.00–$325.00

Dunsany, Lord. *Time and the Gods.* Lon. Heinemann. 1906. 1st ed. 1st issue. $200.00–$375.00

Dunston, W. Herbert. *Rigging of a Texan.* Austin. Texas State Historical Association. 1943. illus. $30.00–$50.00

Durant, Will. *Philosophy and the Social Problem.* NY. 1917. $35.00–$40.00

Durrell, Lawrence. *Numquam.* Lon. Faber. (1970). 1st ed. dj. $25.00–$30.00

Durrell, Lawrence. *Zero & Asylum in the Snow: Two Excursions into Reality.* Berkeley. Circle. 1947. 1st ed. dj. $40.00–$55.00

Dustin, Fred. *Custer Tragedy.* Ann Arbor. (1965). reprint. $85.00–$150.00

Dustin, Fred. *Custer Tragedy.* Ann Arbor. 1939. ltd. 200 cc. sgn. maps. $1,500.00–$2,000.00

Dustin, Fred. *Saginaw Treaty of 1819 between Gen. Louis Cass and Chippewa Indians.* Saginaw. 1919. $50.00–$75.00

Dwiggins, W. A. *Technique for Dealing with Artists.* NY. Woolly Whale. 1941. wraps. illus. 954 cc. $35.00–$50.00

Dwight, N. *Lives of the Signers of the Declaration of Independence.* NY. 1851. 1st ed. $50.00–$90.00

Dwight, S. E. *Hebrew Wife.* Glasgow. Gallie. 1837. 1st Glasgow ed. 148 pp. $125.00–$150.00

Dwight, Theodore. *History of the Hartford Convention.* NY. White. 1833. 1st ed. original cloth and paper label. $75.00–$100.00

Eames, Wilberforce. *Early New England Catechisms.* Worcester. Hamilton. 1898. 1st ed. wraps. presentation copy. $200.00–$300.00

Earhart, Amelia. *Last Flight.* NY. 1937. 1st ed. illus. dj. $80.00–$150.00

Earle, Alice Morse. *Child Life in the Colonial Days.* NY. Macmillan. 1899. 1st ed. illus. $45.00–$65.00

Earle, Alice Morse. *Sun Dials and Roses of Yesterday.* NY. 1902. 1st ed. illus. $75.00–$120.00

Earle, Alice Morse. *Two Centuries of Costumes in America.* NY. 1903. 2 vols. 1st ed. illus. bumped. soiled. $25.00–$50.00

Earle, Alice Morse. *Two Centuries of Costumes in America.* NY. 1903. 1st ed. illus. 2 vols. $90.00–$125.00

East of the Sun and West of the Moon. NY. 1922. illus. by Kay Nielsen. tipped in color plates. dj. $150.00–$300.00

Eastlake, William. *Child's Garden of Verses for the Revolution.* NY. Grove Press. 1970. 1st ed. dj. $25.00–$40.00

Eastlake, William. *Go in Beauty.* NY. (1956). 1st ed. author's first book. dj. $100.00–$200.00

Eastman, Charles A. *Indian Boyhood.* NY. 1902. illus. $75.00–$90.00

Eastman, E. F. *History of the State of New York.* NY. White. 1829. 1st ed. lea.
$60.00–$150.00

Eastman, M. E. *East of the White Hills.* N. Conway, NH. (1900). 1st ed. illus. $45.00–$75.00

Eastman, Mrs. Mary H. *American Aboriginal Portfolio.* Phil. 1853. 84 pp. 26 engr. large 4to. aeg. gold stamped boards. rare. $500.00–$750.00

Eastman, Mrs. Mary H. *Aunt Phillis's Cabin or Southern Life as It Is.* Phil. Lippincott. 1852.
$90.00–$120.00

Eaton, Allen. *Handicrafts of the Southern Highlands.* 1937. illus. 2nd printing. dj.
$50.00–$125.00

Eaton, Allen. *Handicrafts of the Southern Highlands.* 1937. 1st ed. illus. dj. $100.00–$300.00

Eaton, Elon Howard. *Birds of New York.* Albany. 1914. 2nd ed. $50.00–$75.00

Eaton, Elon Howard. *Birds of New York.* Albany. 1910. 2 vols. illus. color plates.
$100.00–$200.00

Eaton, Faith. *Dolls in Color.* NY. Macmillan. (1975). illus. 1st US ed. color photos.
$20.00–$30.00

Eaton, Faith. *Miniature House.* NY. Abrams. (1991). illus. 1st Amer ed. $40.00–$50.00

Eaton, John H. *Life of Andrew Jackson.* Phil. 1824. 2nd ed. $50.00–$100.00

Eaton, John P. & Charles A. Haas. *Titanic.* NY. 1986. illus. dj. $25.00–$35.00

Eaton, Seymour. *Traveling Bears in Outdoor Sports.* Barse & Hopkins. 1915. illus.
$100.00–$125.00

Eberstadt, Edward and Sons. *Northwest Coast: A Century of Personal Narratives of Discovery . . . 1741–1841.* NY. Eberstadt. (1941). 1st ed. frontis. plates. blue pictorial wrappers.
$50.00–$90.00

Eckert, A. and Karalus. *Owls of North America.* Doubleday. 1974. ltd 250 cc. sgn.
$250.00–$500.00

Eckert, Allan. *Great Auk, The.* Bos. Little Brown. 1963. 1st ed. dj. $30.00–$50.00

Eckert, Allan. *Savage Journey.* Bos. Little Brown. 1979. 1st ed. inscrb. dj. $30.00–$50.00

Eckert, Allan. *Song of the Wild.* Bos. Little Brown. 1980. 1st ed. sgn. dj. $50.00–$75.00

Eddington, A. S. *Space Time and Gravitation.* Camb. 1921. 1st ed. $50.00–$75.00

Eddison, E. R. *Worm of Ouroboros, The.* Lon. Cape. (1922). 1st ed. dj. $1,200.00–$1,700.00

Eddy, Clyde. *Down the World's Most Dangerous River.* NY. Stokes. 1929. illus.
$150.00–$175.00

Eddy, Richmond. *History of the 60th Regiment, New York State Volunteers.* Phil. 1864.
$200.00–$400.00

Edison, Judith. *Dolls From Kewpie to Barbie and Beyond.* NY. Smithmark. (1994). 1st ed. illus. color and black and white. dj. $20.00–$30.00

Edison Swan Co. *Pageant of the Lamp.* 1948. 1st ed. illus. $50.00–$60.00

Edmonds, Harfield H. and Norman N. Lee. *Brook and River Trouting: A Manual.* . . . Bradford. pub by authors. (1916). 1st ed. illus. ltd 1000 cc. color plates. buckram.
                                                                    $150.00–$175.00

Edmonds, J. M. *Sappho Revocata.* Lon. Peter Davie. 1928. 1st ed. ltd. 350 cc. numbered.
                                                                    $70.00–$100.00

Edmonds, Walter. *Chad Hanna.* Bos. Little Brown. (1940). 1st ed. dj. $30.00–$45.00

Edmonds, Walter. *Chad Hanna.* Bos. Little Brown. (1940). 1st ed. no dj. $10.00–$15.00

Edmonds, Walter. *Drums Along the Mohawk.* Bos. 1936. 1st ed. 1st state. $200.00–$300.00

Edmonds, Walter. *Drums Along the Mohawk.* Bos. 1936. 1st ed. later printing.
                                                                    $30.00–$45.00

Edmonds, Walter. *In the Hands of the Senecas.* Bos. Little Brown. (1947). 1st ed. dj.
                                                                    $30.00–$50.00

Education of a French Model. NY. Boar's Head. 1950. illus. 186 pp. photos by Man Ray. reprint. dj. $50.00–$75.00

Edward, Ruth Dudley. *Victor Gollancz: A Biography.* Lon. Gollancz. 1987. 1st ed. dj.
                                                                    $40.00–$50.00

Edward, Ruth Dudley. *Victor Gollancz: A Biography.* Lon. Gollancz. 1987. 1st ed. dj.
                                                                    $30.00–$70.00

Edwards, Albert. *Comrade Yetta.* NY. Macmillan. 1913. blue boards. $50.00–$60.00

Edwards, Amelia. *Pharoahs, Fellahs and Explorers.* NY. Harper. 1891. 1st Amer ed. illus.
                                                                    $50.00–$70.00

Edwards, Amelia. *Thousand Miles Up the Nile.* NY. 2nd ed. cloth. $30.00–$50.00

Edwards, Arthur. *Treatise on the Principles and Practice of Medicine, A.* NY. Lea & Febiger. 1909. 2nd ed. illus. plates. $35.00–$40.00

Edwards, E. and J. Rattray. *Whale Off.* NY. 1932. 1st ed. illus. dj. $50.00–$100.00

Edwards, E. I. *Desert Harvest.* Los Angeles. Westernlore. 1962. 1st ed. ltd 600 cc. cloth. pictorial dj. $60.00–$100.00

Edwards, E. I. *Desert Voices, A Descriptive Bibliography.* Los Angeles. Westernlore. 1958. 1st ed. plates. photos. map. tan cloth. 500 cc. pictorial dj. $75.00–$200.00

Edwards, E. I. *Enduring Desert, The.* LA. Ward Ritchie. 1969. 1st ed. cloth. slipcase.
                                                                    $100.00–$150.00

Edwards, E. I. *Lost Oases along the Carrizo.* Los Angeles. Westernlore. 1961. 1st ed. plates. photos. endpaper map. tan cloth. 500 cc. pictorial dj. $125.00–$200.00

Edwards, E. I. *Valley Whose Name is Death, The.* Pasadena. San Pasqual Press. 1940. 1st ed. ltd. $40.00–$70.00

Edwards, Gladys Brown. *Anatomy and Conformation of the Horse.* Croton-on-Hudson. Dreenan. 1980. wraps. illus. photos. drawings. $30.00–$35.00

Edwards, Jonathan. *Freedom of the Will.* NY. 1858. $35.00–$50.00

Edwards, Lionel. *Fox, The.* NY. Scribner's. nd. illus. $50.00–$125.00

Edwards, Lionel. *Getting to Know Your Pony.* NY. 1948. 1st Amer ed. illus.
$35.00–$40.00

Edwards, Philip Leget. *Diary of Philip Leget Edwards: the Great Cattle Drive....* SF. Grabhorn. 1932. illus. ltd 500 cc. $50.00–$75.00

Edwards, William B. *Civil War Guns.* Harrisburg. 1962. illus. dj. $35.00–$50.00

Edwards, William B. *Story of Colt's Revolver, The.* 1953. 1st ed. sgn. dj. $75.00–$150.00

Ehrenreich, Barbara and Deirdre English. *Witches, Midwives, and Nurses.* Westbury, NY. Feminist Press. 1973. later edition. wraps. $8.00–$12.00

Ehrlich, Gretel. *Heart Mountain.* NY. Viking. 1988. 1st ed. sgn. dj. $35.00–$45.00

Ehwa, Carl, Jr. *Book of Pipes and Tobacco, The.* NY. Random House/Ridge Press. 1978. 1st ed. illus. dj. $50.00–$65.00

Eidinoff, Maxwell Leigh and Hyman Ruchliss. *Atomics for the Millions.* NY. McGraw-Hill. 1947. 1st ed. illus. by Maurice Sendak. statement of paper quality on copyright page. sgn.
$175.00–$350.00s

Eidinoff, Maxwell Leigh and Hyman Ruchlis. *Atomics for the Millions.* NY/Lon. 1947. 1st ed. illus. by Maurice Sendak. $100.00–$120.00

Eikemeyer, Carl. *Among the Pueblo Indians.* NY. 1895. $40.00–$50.00

Einstein, Albert. *Relativity, the Special and General Theory.* Lon. Methuen (1920). red cloth gilt. $1,500.00–$2,000.00

Einstein, Albert. *Relativity.* NY. Holt. 1920. 1st ed. 1st printing. blue cloth. no dj.
$2,000.00–$3,000.00

Einstein, Albert. *Relativity.* NY. Holt. 1920. 1st ed. 1st printing. blue cloth. dj.
$8,000.00–$10,000.00

El Museo Del Oro. *Bogota.* Del Banco De La Republica. 1948. 1st ed. wraps. illus. white wrps. gilt letter on cover. $25.00–$40.00

Eliot, Charles. *Charles Eliot Landscape Architect.* Houghton Mifflin, Bos. and New York. 1902. $125.00–$175.00

Eliot, George. *Mill on the Floss.* Phil. 1860, 3 vols. purple cloth. $400.00–$1,500.00

Eliot, George. *Mill on the Floss.* Phil. 1860. 1st ed. 1st state binding. points. 3 vols.
$2,000.00–$4,000.00

Eliot, George. *Romola.* Lon. 1863. Blackwood. 1st ed. $600.00–$875.00

Eliot, George. *Romola.* NY. 1863. 1st US ed. $125.00–$300.00

Eliot, George. *Silas Marner.* Edin/Lon. 1861. 1st ed. $600.00–$1,200.00

Eliot, T. S. *Ash-Wednesday.* NY/Lon. Fountain Press/Faber & Faber. 1930. 1st ed. ltd 600 cc. numbered. $1,000.00–$1,200.00

Eliot, T. S. *Dante.* Lon. Faber & Faber. (1929). 1st ed. dj. $100.00–$250.00

Eliot, T. S. *Elder Statesman.* NY. 1959. 1st US ed. dj. $50.00–$60.00

Eliot, T. S. *Poems.* NY. Knopf. 1920. 1st Amer ed. dj. $3,000.00–$4,000.00

Eliot, T. S. *Prufrock: and Other Observations.* Lon. Egoist. 1917. 1st ed. wraps. one of 500 cc. author's first book. sgn. slipcase. $25,000.00–$40,000.00

Eliot, T. S. *Sacred Wood, The.* Lon. Methuen. (1920). 1st ed. 1st state. blue cloth. dj. $2,000.00–$3,000.00

Eliot, T. S. *Waste Land, The.* Richmond. Hogarth. 1923. 1st English ed. ltd 460 cc. no dj issued. $5,000.00–$5,500.00

Eliot, T. S. *Waste Land, The.* NY. Boni & Liveright. 1922. 2nd ed. ltd 1,000 cc. numbered. $2,800.00–$3,200.00

Elliott, Franklin Reuben. *Hand Book of Practical Landscape Gardening.* Rochester. Dewey. 1885. 3rd ed. illus. wood engravings. cloth. $400.00–$500.00

Ellis, Havelock. *Kanga Creek.* Berkshire. Golden Cockerel Press. 1922. 1st UK ed. dj. $50.00–$90.00

Ellison, Harlan. *Beast that Shouted Love at the Heart of the World.* NY. Avon. 1969. 1st ed. dj. $30.00–$50.00

Ellison, Harlan. *Stalking the Nightmare.* Phantasia Press. 1982. 1st ed. ltd 750 cc. sgn. $80.00–$90.00

Ellison, Harlan. *Strange Wine.* NY. Harper & Row. (1978). 1st ed. dj. $50.00–$75.00

Ellison, Ralph. *Going to the Territory.* NY. 1986. 1st ed. dj. $45.00–$75.00

Ellison, Ralph. *Invisible Man.* NY. 1952. 1st ed. dj. $1,000.00–$4,000.00

Ellison, Ralph. *Invisible Man, The.* NY. Random House. (1952). 1st ed. sgn. dj. $6,000.00–$15,000.00

Ellwanger, H. B. *Rose, The.* Lon. Heinemann. rev. 310 pp. $60.00–$75.00

Elwes, H. J. *Memoirs of Travel, Sport and Natural History.* Lon. 1930. $25.00–$40.00

Embick, Milton. *Military History of the Third Division, 9th Corp, Army of the Potomac.* np. 1913. 1st ed. illus. $50.00–$90.00

Embrey, Alvin. *History of Fredericks-burg Virginia.* Richmond. Old Dominion Press. 1937. 1st ed. illus. dark blue cloth. lettering on cover. $30.00–$50.00

Emerson, Adaline. *Ralph Emerson, Jr: Life and Letters.* Edited by His Mother. Rockford. 1891. 1st ed. illus. $100.00–$125.00

Emerson, Ralph Waldo. *Society and Solitude.* Bos. 1870. 1st ed. small 8vo. $50.00–$75.00

Emerson's Turbine Record. Holyoke. 1874. 1st ed. wraps. illus. periodical on turbines, well illus. very good cond. $25.00–$30.00

Emilio, Luis Fenollosa. *Emilio Collection of Military Buttons, The.* Salem. The Essex Institute. 1942. illus. red cloth, lettering on spine, brown dj. reprint of 1911 ed. 500 cc.
$75.00–$120.00

Emilio, Luis Fenollosa. *Emilio Collection of Military Buttons, The.* Mass. The Essex Institute. 1911. illus. red cloth gold lettering on spine. ltd. ed. 500 cc. 264 pp. paper dust jacket.
$100.00–$200.00

Emory, W. H. *Notes of a Military Reconnaissance. . . . Washington.* Congress. 1848. 1st ed. 2nd Senate issue. 416 pp. brown cloth. folding map. litho plates. $500.00–$1,500.00

Encyclopedia Britannica, 11th Edition. 1910. 20 vols. $500.00–$900.00

Endore, Guy. *Crime at Scottsboro, The.* CA. Hollywood Scottsboro Committee. pictorial wrappers. 1st ed. inscrb. by Endore. $300.00–$350.00

England, George Allan. *Air Trust, The.* St Louis. Wagner. 1915. 1st ed. $100.00–$250.00

England, George Allan. *Darkness and Dawn.* 1916. 1st ed. $100.00–$150.00

England, George Allan. *Golden Blight, The.* NY. Fly. 1916. 1st ed. $25.00–$80.00

Ensko, Stephen. *American Silversmiths.* 1989. 1st ed. illus. dj. $35.00–$40.00

Erdrich, Louise. *Bingo Palace, The.* NY. HarperCollins. 1994. 1st ed. dj. $15.00–$20.00

Erdrich, Louise. *Crown of Columbus, The.* NY. HarperCollins. 1991. 1st ed. sgn. dj.
$20.00–$25.00

Esquivel, Laura. *Like Water for Chocolate.* NY. Doubleday. 1989. 1st ed. dj. $40.00–$75.00

Eustis, Helen. *Fool Killer.* Garden City. Doubleday. 1954. 1st ed. dj. $90.00–$100.00

Evans, Frederick William. *Egyptian Sphinx.* Mt Lebanon. nd. wraps. $80.00–$110.00

Evans, John. *History of Jewelry, 1100–1870.* NY. (1953). illus. dj. $100.00–$125.00

Evans, Nicholas. *Horse Whisperer, The.* NY. Delacorte. 1995. 1st ed. dj. $40.00–$50.00

Everett, Fred. *Fun with Trout.* Harrisburg. Stackpole. 1952. 1st ed. illus. $70.00–$100.00

Ewart, John. *History of Two Cases of Ulcerated Cancer of the Mamma.* Bath. Cruttwell. 1794. 1st ed. illus. $600.00–$800.00

Exposition of the African Slave Trade, from the year 1840 to 1850. NY. Books for Libraries. 1971. facsimile. $20.00–$40.00

Eyre, J. W. H. *Elements of Bacterial Technique.* Phil. Saunders. 1913. 2nd ed.
$15.00–$20.00

Faber, Elmer. *Behind The Law.* Greensburg. Chas. M. Henry. 1933. illus. red decorated cloth. $45.00–$75.00

Fairfield, Asa Merrill. *Fairfield's Pioneer History of Lassen County, California*. San Francisco. Crosker. 1916. 1st ed. red cloth. $175.00–$200.00

Farley, Walter. *Black Stallion's Courage, The*. NY. Random House. (1956). 1st ed. 1st printing. $35.00–$40.00

Farley, Walter. *Son of Black Stallion*. NY. Random House. (1947). later printing. $12.00–$16.00

Farmer, Philip Jose. *Dark Design, The*. NY. Berkley/Putnam. 1977. 1st ed. sgn. dj. $80.00–$120.00

Farmer, Philip Jose. *Dark is the Sun*. NY. Del Rey. 1979. 1st ed. sgn. dj. $50.00–$75.00

Farmer, Philip Jose. *Magic Labyrinth*. NY. Berkley/Putnam. 1980. 1st ed. sgn. dj. $45.00–$60.00

Farquhar, Francis P. *Yosemite, the Big Trees and the High Sierra.* . . . Berkeley. Univ of California Press. 1948. 1st ed. dj. $150.00–$250.00

Farquhar, J. B. *Farquhar's Official Directory of Bedford County, Pennsylvania*. Bedford. Inquirer. (1879). 1st ed. rebound. $175.00–$200.00

Farrell, James T. *Gas-House McGinty*. NY. Vanguard. 1933. 1st ed. dj. $125.00–$150.00

Farrell, James T. *Judgment Day*. Vanguard. 1935. 1st US ed. $50.00–$70.00

Farrell, James T. *Studs Lonigan*. Lon. Constable. 1936. 1st UK ed. no dj. $25.00–$40.00

Farrer, Reginald. *Alpines & Bog Plants*. Lon. Edward Arnold. 1908. illus. green cloth, gold lettering on cover and spine, b/w plates. $60.00–$250.00

Farrington, Frank. *John Martin's Clerks: A Tale of the Store*. Merchants Helps Pub. Co. NY. 1907. $10.00–18.00

Faulkner, John. *Cabin Road*. NY. Fawcett Gold Medal. 1951. 1st ed. wraps. #178. $25.00–$40.00

Faulkner, John. *Dollar Cotton*. NY. Harcourt Brace. 1942. 1st ed. sgn. dj. $250.00–$300.00

Faulkner, John. *Men Working*. NY. Harcourt Brace. 1941. 1st ed. stated first, dj. $75.00–$150.00

Faulkner, John. *My Brother Bill*. NY. Trident. (1963). 1st ed. dj. $25.00–$50.00

Faulkner, William. *As I Lay Dying*. NY. Jonathan Cape. (1930). 1st ed. 1st issue. points. dj. $4,500.00–$9,000.00

Faulkner, William. *Go Down, Moses, and Other Stories*. NY. Random House. 1942. 1st ed. 1st state binding. dj. $1,200.00–$2,500.00

Faulkner, William. *Hamlet, The*. NY. Random House. 1940. 1st trade ed. dj. $2,500.00–$5,000.00

Faulkner, William. *Reivers, The*. NY. Random House. (1962). 1st ed. Pulitzer Prize winner. cloth. dj. $300.00–$400.00

Faulkner, William. *Reivers, The.* NY. Random House. (1962). 1st ed. Pulitzer Prize winner. ltd 500 cc. numbered. sgn. dj. $2,000.00–$2,500.00

Faulkner, William. *Requiem for a Nun.* NY. Random House. (1951). ltd 750 cc. cloth. sgn. $1,000.00–$1,500.00

Faulkner, William. *Sound and the Fury, The.* NY. Jonathan Cape. (1926). 1st ed. rebound. $900.00–$1,200.00

Feder, Norman. *American Indian Art.* NY. Abrams. nd. 1st ed. illus. dj $125.00–$150.00

Feiffer, Jules. *Ackroyd.* NY. Simon & Schuster. 1977. 1st ed. inscrb. dj. $40.00–$50.00

Ferguson, James. *Easy Introduction to Astronomy for Young Gentlemen and Ladies. . . .* Phil. Warner, Green. 1819. $90.00–$100.00

Ferrel, Mallory Hope. *Tweetsie Country: The East Tennessee & Western North Carolina Railroad.* CO. Pruett. 1973. 1st ed. illus. diagrams. photos. dj. $90.00–$110.00

Ferro, Robert. *Others, The.* NY. Scribner's. 1977. 1st ed. dj. $40.00–$50.00

Fielding, Helen. *Bridget Jones: the Edge of Reason.* NY. Viking. 1999. 1st ed. sgn. dj. $35.00–$45.00

Fillmore, John Comfort. *Lessons in Musical History.* Phil. Presser. 1888. 1st ed. illus. blue cloth. $15.00–$35.00

Fisher, M. F. K. *Alphabet for Gourmets, An.* NY. Viking. 1949. 1st ed. illus. dj. $90.00–$125.00

Fisher, M. F. K. *Sister Age.* NY. Knopf. 1983. 1st ed. dj. $100.00–$150.00

Fitzgerald, F. Scott. *Great Gatsby, The.* NY. Scribner's. 1925. 1st ed. points including sick in tired on page 205. green cloth. some wear. dj missing. $2,000.00–$3,000.00

Fitzgerald, F. Scott. *Great Gatsby, The.* NY. Scribner's. 1925. 1st ed. points include sick in tired on page 205. green cloth. fine condition. dj. $5,000.00–$10,000.00

Fitzgerald, F. Scott. *Great Gatsby, The.* NY. Scribner's. 1925. 1st ed. points including sick in tired on page 205. green cloth. sgn. dj. $50,000.00–$125,000.00

Fitzgerald, F. Scott. *Great Gatsby, The.* Lon. Chatto and Windus. 1926. 1st UK ed. morocco. $2,000.00–$3,000.00

Fitzgerald, F. Scott. *Great Gatsby, The.* NY. Modern Library. 1934. dj. $800.00–$1,000.00

Fitzgerald, F. Scott. *This Side of Paradise.* NY. 1920. 1st ed. 1st state. $5,000.00–$10,000.00

Fitzgerald, Zelda. *Save Me the Waltz.* Scribner's. 1932. Zelda's first book. dj. $2,000.00–$2,500.00

Five Slave Narratives. NY. Arno Press. 1968. sgn. $30.00–$40.00

(Flagg, Edmund T.). *The Far West or A Tour Beyond the Mountains.* NY. Harper & Bros. 1838. 1st ed. 2vols. cloth. paste-down on spine. Howes F169. $300.00–$600.00

Fleming, Ian. *Casino Royale.* Lon. Jonathan Cape. (1953). 1st ed. morocco. slipcase. author's first 007 novel. $4,500.00–$10,000.00

Fleming, Ian. *Casino Royale.* NY. Macmillan. 1954. 1st Amer ed. fair condition. dj. $250.00–$900.00

Fleming, Ian. *Casino Royale.* NY. Macmillan. 1954. 1st Amer ed. author's first 007 novel. good to fine conditon. dj. $900.00–$2,000.00

Fleming, Ian. *Casino Royale.* NY. Macmillan. 1954. 1st Amer ed. author's first 007 novel. chips and minor tears. dj. $200.00–$400.00

Fleming, Ian. *Dr. No.* Jonathan Cape. 1958. 1st ed. cloth. dj. $900.00–$1,500.00

Follett, Ken. *Dangerous Fortune, A.* NY. Delacorte. 1993. 1st ed. dj. $25.00–$30.00

Follett, Ken. *Place Called Freedom, A.* NY. Crown. 1995. 1st ed. $20.00–$25.00

Follett, Ken. *Triple.* NY. Arbor House. 1979. 1st ed. dj. $11.00–$15.00

Foner, Philip S. (ed.). *Life and Writings of Frederick Douglass, early years....* NY. International. 1950. 1st ed. 2 vols. frontis. $50.00–$80.00

Foner, Philip S. (ed.). *Life and Writings of Frederick Douglass, early years....* NY. International. 1952. $25.00–$35.00

Foote, Shelby. *Civil War, The: A Narrative.* NY. 1958–74. 3 vols. maps. sgn. $400.00–$475.00

Forbes, Allan. *Yankee Ships Sailing Cards.* Bos. 1952. wraps. illus. 3 vols. $75.00–$100.00

Forbes, R. B. *Appeal to Merchants and Shipowners, An.* Bos. 1854. 1st ed. $50.00–$80.00

Ford, Gerald. *Time to Heal: The Autobiography of Gerald Ford.* NY. 1979. ltd 250 cc. illus. slipcase. sgn. $1,500.00–$1,750.00

Ford, Richard. *Independence Day.* NY. Knopf. 1995. 1st ed. Pulitzer Prize winner. dj. $40.00–$50.00

Ford, Richard. *Sportswriter, The.* NY. Vintage. 1986. 1st ed. wraps. $15.00–$20.00

Ford, Richard. *Wildlife.* NY. Atlantic Monthly. 1990. 1st ed. dj. $25.00–$30.00

Forester, C. S. *African Queen, The.* NY. Modern Library. (1940). 1st Modern Library ed. dj. $50.00–$75.00

Forester, C. S. *Captain Horatio Hornblower.* Bos. 1939. 1st US ed. illus by Wyeth. dj. $45.00–$50.00

Forester, C. S. *Hornblower Companion.* Bos. Little Brown. (1964). 1st ed. red cloth. $170.00–$350.00

Forester, C. S. *Lord Hornblower.* Bos. Little Brown. 1946. 1st ed. $20.00–$30.00

Forester, C. S. *Sky and Forest.* Lon. Michael Joseph. (1948). 1st UK ed. dj. $20.00–$30.00

Forester, Frank. *Hints to Horse-Keepers.* NY. 1859. $50.00–$60.00

Forster, E. M. *Passage to India, A.* Lon. Arnold. 1924. 1st ed. deluxe issue. ltd 200 cc. sgn.
$3,000.00–$9,000.00

Forster, E. M. *Passage to India, A.* Lon. Arnold. 1924. 1st ed. dj. $900.00–$1,500.00

Forster, E. M. *Room With a View, A.* Lon. 1908. 1st ed. 2000 cc. $800.00–$900.00

Fowler, Harlan D. *Camels to California, A Chapter in Western Transportation.* CA. Stanford Univ Press. (1950). 1st ed. illus. plates. endpaper map. tan cloth. pictorial dj. $40.00–$65.00

Fowler, O.S. and L.N. Fowler. *The Phrenological and Physiological Almanac 1846.* NY. Fowler & Wells. 1845. wraps. illus. wrps. small pamphlet. 48 pp. illus. $75.00–$150.00

Fowler, Thomas. *Medical Reports of the Effects of Tobacco in the Cure of Dropsies and Dysuries. . . .* Lon. private. 1788. 2nd ed. gray boards. $500.00–$750.00

Fowles, John. *Collector, The.* 1963. 1st ed. 1st state. author's first book. $100.00–$150.00

Francis, Dick. *Flying Finish.* Lon. Michael Joseph. 1966. 1st ed. dj. $200.00–$400.00

Francis, Dick. *For Kicks.* Lon. Michael Joseph. 1965. 1st ed. dj. $300.00–$900.00

Francis, Dick. *High Stakes.* Lon. Michael Joseph. 1966. 1st ed. dj. $60.00–$90.00

Francis, Dick. *Knock Down.* Lon. Michael Joseph. 1974. 1st ed. dj. $100.00–$125.00

Francis, Dick. *Lester, The Official Biography.* Lon. Michael Joseph. 1986. 1st ed. dj.
$30.00–$50.00

Francis, Francis. *By Lake and River.* Lon. Field Office. 1874. 1st ed. ½ morocco. raised bands. $300.00–$400.00

Francis, Francis and A. W. Cooper. *Sporting Sketches with Pen and Pencil.* Lon. Field Office. 1879. 1st ed. illus. wood-engravings. morocco and cloth. aeg. $200.00–$300.00

Francis, Jean. *Dolls I Have Known and Loved.* Canada. private printing. 1980. illus. ltd 1000 cc. pictorial boards. sgn by author. $40.00–$60.00

Frank, P. *Alas, Babylon.* Phila. Lippincott. 1959. 1st ed. dj. $400.00–$500.00

Franklin, John. *Narrative of a Journey to the Shores of the Polar Sea 1819–22.* Lon. Murray. 1823. 1st ed. illus. maps. plates. $1,500.00–$2,000.00

Fraser, Chelsea. *Heroes of the Air.* Crowell. 1928. illus. revised. 550 pp. $30.00–$40.00

Fraser, George MacDonald. *Flashman and the Angel of the Lord.* NY. Knopf. (1994). 1st ed. dj. $25.00–$30.00

Fraser, George MacDonald. *Flashman and the Dragon.* NY. Knopf. (1986). 1st ed. dj.
$35.00–$50.00

Fraser, George MacDonald. *Flashman and the Mountain of Light.* Lon. Collins Harvill. (1990). 1st UK ed. dj. $50.00–$90.00

Fraser, George MacDonald. *Flashman and the Redskins.* NY. Knopf. (1982). 1st ed. ddj.
$25.00–$35.00

Fraser, George MacDonald. *General Danced at Dawn, The.* NY. Knopf. (1973). 1st ed. white cloth. dj. $75.00–$100.00

Frazier, Charles. *Cold Mountain.* NY. Atlantic Monthly. (1997). 1st ed. 1st state. cloth and boards. points. dj. sgn. $300.00–$500.00

Frazier, Charles. *Cold Mountain.* NY. Atlantic Monthly. (1997). 1st ed. 1st state. cloth and boards. points. dj. $200.00–$300.00

Frazier, Don. *Recognizing Derrydale Press Books.* np. private printing. 1983. illus. 23 color plates, ltd 347 cc. brown leather. $500.00–$600.00

Frederick, J. V. *Ben Holladay, the Stagecoach King.* CA. Clark. 1940. 1st ed. ltd 1016 cc. inscrb. by publisher, Clark. $100.00–$150.00

Fredericks, J. Page. *Green-Pipes.* New York. Macmillan. 1929. illus. by Fredericks, tall green cl. b/w and col plates. $35.00–$65.00

Freece, Hans P. *Letters of an Apostate Mormon to His Son.* NY. private printing. 1908.
                                                                                                                                    $80.00–$100.00

Freece, Hans P. *Letters of an Apostate Mormon to His Son.* Elmira. Chemung. (1908). 2nd ed. frontis. illus. $35.00–$50.00

Freeman, Douglas Southall. *Lee's Lieutenants: A Study in Command.* NY. 1944. 3 vols. illus. maps. inscrb. sgn. $650.00–$700.00

Freeman, Douglas Southall. *Lee's Lieutenants: A Study in Command.* Scribner's. 3 vols. b/w illus. maps. $200.00–$225.00

Freeman, Douglas Southall. *Robert E. Lee, a Biography.* NY. 1934–35. 4 vols. illus.
                                                                                                                                    $95.00–$250.00

Freeman, Harry C. *Brief History of Butte, Montana.* Shepard. 1900. 1st ed. $75.00–$125.00

Freeman, Larry and Jane Beaumont. *Early American Plated Silver.* Watkins Glen. Century House. 1947. 1st ed. $50.00–$60.00

Freligh, Martin. *Homeopathic Practice of Medicine.* NY. Lamport, Blakeman & Law. 1854. maps. $125.00–$250.00

Fremont, Capt. J. C. *Report of the Exploring Expedition to the Rocky Mountains. . . .* DC. 1842. maps. $125.00–$250.00

Fremont, John. *Life of Col.* Fremont. NY. 1856. 1st ed. 32 pp. sewn. portrait. two illus.
                                                                                                                                    $100.00–$120.00

French, John C. *Passenger Pigeon in Pennsylvania.* Altoona. Altoona Tribune. 1919. 1st ed. wraps. illus. $100.00–$150.00

Freud, Sigmund. *General Introduction to Psychoanalysis, A.* NY. Boni and Liveright. 1920. 1st ed. blue cloth. $500.00–$700.00

Freud, Sigmund. *Interpretation of Dreams.* NY. 1937. dj. $50.00–$60.00

Freud, Sigmund. *Interpretation of Dreams.* Macmillan. 1913. $1,200.00–$2,000.00

Freud, Sigmund. *Modern Sexual Morality and Modern Nervousness.* NY. Eugenics. 1931.
$40.00–$75.00

Friedan, Betty. *Feminine Mystique, The.* NY. 1963. 1st ed. dj. $100.00–$150.00

Friedman, Bruce Jay. *Black Angels.* NY. (1966). 1st ed. dj. $35.00–$45.00

Fritchey, Alfred James. *Blue-Dragon Ballads, The.* LA. Fritchey. (1922). 1st ed. paper on boards. 69 pp. $15.00–$25.00

Frizell, Richard. *Christianity Proved, by the Miracle of Christianity Itself. . . .* Barnstaple. Syle. (1819). wraps. disbound. 20 pp. $200.00–$300.00

Froiseth, Jennie Anderson. *Women of Mormonism.* Detroit. 1887. illus. $90.00–$120.00

Frost, A. B. *Stuff and Nonsense.* NY. Scribner's. (1884). illus. original pictorial boards.
$80.00–$120.00

Frost, John. *American Naval Biography.* Phila. 1844. illus. 3/4 morocco. $90.00–$200.00

Frost, John. *Book of Travels in Africa.* NY/Phil. 1848. illus. $50.00–$80.00

Frost, John. *Pictorial History of Mexico and the Mexican War.* Phil. 1849. maps.
$40.00–$60.00

Frost, John. *Thrilling Adventures Among the Indians.* Bos. L.P. Crown. illus. engravings. col. frontis. $45.00–$100.00

Frost, Robert. *Boy's Will, A.* NY. Holt. 1915. 1st ed. points. dj. $2,500.00–$3,000.00

Frost, Robert. *Boy's Will, A.* Lon. Nutt. 1913. 1st ed. wraps. 1st issue. points. author's first book. cream paper cover with 8-petal flower ornament. $1,500.00–$3,500.00

Frost, Robert. *Collected Poems.* NY. Holt. 1939. sgn and dated. dj. $500.00–$1,000.00

Frost, Robert. *Collected Poems.* NY. Holt. (1930). 1st trade ed. Pulitzer Prize winner. 1000 cc. numbered. inscrb. no dj. $1,100.00–$2,500.00

Frost, Robert. *Further Range, A.* NY. Holt. 1936. 1st ed. dj. $40.00–$100.00

Frost, Robert. *Further Range, A.* NY. 1936. ltd 802 cc. sgn. $300.00–$500.00

Frost, Robert. *Masque of Mercy, A.* NY. Holt. 1947. 1st ed. 39 pp. $50.00–$80.00

Frost, Robert. *Mountain Interval.* New York. Henry Holt. 1916. 1st ed. blue cloth, errata pgs. 88 and 93. $200.00–$500.00

Frost, Robert. *New Hampshire.* NY. 1923. 1st ed. $150.00–$200.00

Frost, Robert. *North of Boston.* NY. Holt. 1915. 1st Amer ed. points. dj.
$1,000.00–$1,200.00

Frost, Robert. *North of Boston.* Lon. Nutt. (1914). 1st ed. 1st issue. points. inscrb.
$5,000.00–$5,500.00

Frost, Robert. *Steeple Bush.* NY. Holt. 1947. 1st ed. ltd 750 cc. sgn. dj. $200.00–$400.00

Froud, Nina. *Cooking the Japanese Way*. Lon. Spring Books. 1963. 1st ed. illus. dj.
$12.00–$15.00

Fry, Christopher. *Lady's Not for Burning, The*. Lon. 1949. dj. $30.00–$40.00

Fryer, Jane E. *Mary Frances Cook Book*. Phil. Winston. 1912. 1st ed. illus. $100.00–$200.00

Fryer, Jane E. *Mary Frances Sewing Book*. Phil. 1913. 1st ed. illus. patterns.
$150.00–$225.00

Fuentes, Carlos. *Aura*. NY. 1965. 1st UK ed. dj. $100.00–$120.00

Fugitives. The Story of Clyde Barrow and Bonnie Parker. Dallas. 1934. 1st ed. $50.00–$90.00

Fulghum, David. *Vietnam Experience*. Boston Pub. (1981). 21 vols. $200.00–$300.00

Fuller, Claud E. and Richard D. Steuart. *Firearms of the Confederacy, the Shoulder Arm, Pistols and Revolvers of the Confederate Soldier*. Huntington, W. Va. Standard. 1944. 1st ed. dj.
$200.00–$350.00

Fuller, J. F. C. *Generalship of Ulysses S. Grant*. NY. 1929. $40.00–$50.00

Fuller, Metta. *Fresh Leaves from Western Woods*. Buffalo. 1852. 1st ed. 2 vols.
$25.00–$30.00

Fuller, R. Buckminster. *Nine Chains to the Moon*. Phil. 1938. 1st ed. author's first book. dj.
$90.00–$120.00

Fulton, Frances. *To and Through Nebraska*. Lincoln. 1884. 1st ed. 273 pp. $100.00–$145.00

Fulton, Robert. *Treatise on the Improvement of Canal Navigation. . . .* Lon. 1796. illus. plates. original boards.
$2,500.00–$3,500.00

Fun With Dick and Jane. Scott Foresman. early editions (1950s). $45.00–$100.00

Furlong, Charles W. *Let er Buck*. NY. 1921. 1st ed. fair condition. sgn. $60.00–$80.00

Furling, Charles Wellington. *Let er Buck: A Story of the Passing of the Old West*. NY. Putnam's. 1921. 1st ed. frontis. inscrb.
$100.00–$150.00

Fuzzlebug, Fritz (John H. Dunkle). *Prison Life During the Rebellion*. Singer's Glen, VA. 1869. 1st ed. wraps.
$130.00–$175.00

Gade, John. *Book Plates Old and New*. NY. 1898. illus. $50.00–$75.00

Gage, S. H. *The Microscope*. Ithaca. Comstock. 1936. $50.00–$100.00

Gage, W. L. *Palestine: Historical and Descriptive*. Bos. 1883. illus. $80.00–$100.00

Galbraith, John Kenneth. *How to Get Out of Vietnam*. NY. Signet. 1967. 1st ed. wraps.
$25.00–$35.00

Gallant, Mavis. *Other Paris*. Bos. Houghton Mifflin. 1956. 1st ed. author's first book. dj.
$50.00–$80.00

Gallaudet, Thomas. *Plan of a Seminary for the Education of Instructers of Youth*. Bos. Cummings, Hilliard & Co. 1825. 1st ed. illus. 39 pp.
$75.00–$90.00

Gallery of Famous English and American Poets, A. Phil. Butler. 1860. illus. brown morocco. embossed in gilt and black. aeg. $90.00–$120.00

Gallico, Paul. *Snow Goose, The.* 1941. 1st ed. dj. $225.00–$250.00

Gallo, Miguel M. *Gold of Peru, The.* Germany. 1959. 1st Ed in English. dj. $275.00–$300.00

Galsworthy, John. *Eldest Son, The.* NY. Scribner's. 1912. 1st US ed. green cloth. $20.00–$35.00

Galsworthy, John. *Forsythe Saga.* Lon. Heinemann. 1922. 1st ed. leather. aeg. $200.00–$400.00

Galsworthy, John. *Slaughter of Animals for Food, The.* Lon. Society for Prevention of Cruelty to Animals. nd. wraps. $25.00–$30.00

Galsworthy, John. *Swan Song.* NY. Scribner's. 1928. 1st US ed. dj. $40.00–$60.00

Galton, Francis. *Memories of My Life.* Lon. Methuen. (1908). 1st ed. blue cloth. Darwin's cousin. $700.00–$900.00

Games of the Xth Olympiad: Los Angeles 1932. Los Angeles. Xth Olympiad Committee. 1933. 1st ed. orange cloth covered boards. $350.00–$400.00

Gammons, Rev. John G. *Third Massachusetts Regiment Volunteers . . . 1861–1863.* Prov. 1906. 1st ed. illus. $50.00–$80.00

Gandhi, Mahatma. *My Appeal to the British.* NY. John Day. (1942). 1st US ed. cloth. dj. $80.00–$100.00

Gandhi, M. K. *Story of My Experiments with Truth, The.* Ahmedebad. Navajivan Press. 1927. 1st English language ed. no dj. $850.00–$950.00

G.A.R. *Souvenir Book of Boston.* Bos. Commonwealth Pub. 1st ed. wraps. illus. small wrps. $20.00–$40.00

Garces, Francisco. *Record of Travels in Arizona and California, 1775–1776.* San Francisco. Howell. translated by John Galvin. ltd 1250 cc. $60.00–$80.00

Garcia Marquez, Gabriel. *In Evil Hour.* NY. Harper & Row. (1979). 1st US ed. dj. $60.00–$100.00

Garcia Marquez, Gabriel. *One Hundred Years of Solitude.* Lon. Cape. (1970). 1st UK ed. Nobel–Prize winning author. dj. $300.00–$800.00

Garcia Marquez, Gabriel. *One Hundred Years of Solitude.* NY. 1970. 1st ed. in English. author's first novel. dj. points. $1,500.00–$2,500.00

Garcia Marquez, Gabriel. *One Hundred Years of Solitude.* Buenos Aires. 1967. 1st ed. Spanish. Nobel Prize winning author. $6,000.00–$10,000.00

Garcia Marquez, Gabriel. *Solitude of Latin America, The.* NY. Targ. 1984. galleys of Nobel Prize speech. $850.00–$2,000.00

Gardiner, Howard C. *In Pursuit of the Golden Dream: Reminiscences of San Francisco.* . . . MA. Western Hemisphere. 1970. 1st ed. illus. 8 plates. 2 maps. 1 folding. $60.00–$90.00

Gardner, Erle Stanley. *Case of the Careless Cupid.* NY. William Morrow. 1968. 1st ed. dj.
$50.00–$70.00

Gardner, Erle Stanley. *Case of the Ice-Cold Hands.* NY. William Morrow. 1962. 1st ed. dj.
$50.00–$60.00

Gardner, Erle Stanley. *Case of the Screaming Woman.* NY. William Morrow. 1957. 1st ed. dj.
$35.00–$45.00

Gardner, Erle Stanley. *Case of the Substitute Face.* NY. William Morrow. 1938. 1st ed. dj.
$350.00–$400.00

Gardner, Erle Stanley. *D.A. Breaks an Egg.* NY. William Morrow. 1949. 1st ed. dj.
$40.00–$50.00

Gardner, John. *Grendel.* NY. Knopf. 1971. 1st ed. dj. $500.00–$750.00

Gardner, John. *King's Indian: Stories and Talks.* NY. Knopf. 1974. 1st ed. dj. $35.00–$50.00

Gardner, John. *October Light.* NY. Knopf. 1976. 1st ed. dj. $45.00–$50.00

Gardner, John. *Resurrection, The.* NY. New American Library. (1966). 1st ed. sgn. dj.
$900.00–$1,750.00

Gardner, John. *Sunlight Dialogues.* NY. 1972. 1st ed. dj. $60.00–$70.00

Garis, Howard. *Uncle Wiggily's Automobile.* NY. Platt & Munk. (1939). $45.00–$55.00

Garis, Howard R. *Uncle Wiggily's Picture Book.* Platt & Munk. 1932. 1st ed. dj.
$75.00–$90.00

Garner, R.L. *Apes and Monkeys.* Lon., Bos. The Athenaeum Press. 1900. 1st ed. illus. blue decorated cloth, gold lettering on cover and spine. $20.00–$55.00

Garner, T. and A. Stratton. *Domestic Architecture of England during the Tudor Period.* NY. (1929). 2nd ed. 2 vols. 210 plates. $150.00–$200.00

Garnett, David. *First Hippy Revolution.* Cerillos, NM. 1970. 1st ed. wraps. sgn.
$40.00–$50.00

Garnett, Porter (ed.). *Papers of San Francisco Vigilance Committee of 1851.* Berkeley. Univ of California Press. 1910. wraps. $40.00–$70.00

Garnett, Theodore Stanford. *J. E. B. Stuart (Major General) Commander of the Cavalry Corps.* NY/DC. Neale Publishing Co. 1907. 1st ed. illus. plates. $200.00–$250.00

Garrard, Lewis H. *Wah-T-Yah and the Taos Trail.* Palo Alto. American West. 1968. reprint of 1936 ed. dj. $30.00–$50.00

Garrison, Fielding H. *Introduction to the History of Medicine.* Saunders. 1914. 763 pp.
$90.00–$125.00

Gask, Norman. *Old Silver Spoons of England.* Lon. 1926. illus. rebound. ¼ leather.
$75.00–$125.00

Gass, Patrick. *Journal of the Voyages and Travels of a Corps of Discovery under the Comnand of Capt. Lewis. . . .* Minn. Ross & Haines. 1958. illus. ltd 2000 cc. photos. folding endpaper map. cloth. $50.00–$100.00

Gass, William. *Omensetter's Luck.* NY. New Amsterdam Library. (1966). 1st ed. author's first novel. dj $60.00–$125.00

Gass, William H. *In the Heart of the Heart of the Country.* NY. Harper. 1968. 1st ed. dj.
$100.00–$125.00

Gaster, M. *Hebrew Illuminated Bibles of the 9th and 10th Centuries.* Lon. 1901. folio. plates.
$85.00–$125.00

Gasthoff's Parade Floats & Decorations. Tampa, Fl. Gasthoff's Display Service. 1937–38. pictorial wraps. illus. 24 pp. $40.00–$50.00

Gatty, Mrs. A. *Book of Sun Dials, A.* Lon. 1872. 1st ed. illus. plates. $100.00–$200.00

Gault, William Campbell. *Cat and Mouse.* NY. St. Martin's. 1988. 1st ed. sgn. dj.
$20.00–$30.00

Gauvreau, Charles. *Reminiscences of the Spanish American War.* Rouses Point, NY. Author's Publishing Company. 1915. 1st ed. illus. presentation copy. sgn. small blue cloth, gold lettering. $300.00–$400.00

Gauvreau, Charles F. *Reminiscences of the Spanish American War.* Rouses Point. Authors Pub. 1915. 1st ed. illus. blue cl. lettering on cover. $100.00–$200.00

Gavin, Charles Murray. *Royal Yachts.* Lon. Rich & Cowan. 1932. ltd 1000 cc. color plates.
$500.00–$750.00

Gay, John. *Beggar's Opera.* Paris. 1937. illus. ltd 1500 cc. slipcase. $65.00–$75.00

Gay, Joseph R. *Progress and Achievements of the Colored People.* DC. 1913. 1st ed. 434 pp.
$60.00–$90.00

Gay, Wanda. *Growing Pains.* Coward. 1940. 1st ed. illus. author's first book. dj.
$200.00–$300.00

Genet, Jean. *Thief's Journal.* NY. Grove. 1964. 1st ed. dj. $30.00–$40.00

Gerstaecker, Frederick. *Frank Wildman's Adventures on Land and Water.* Phil. Lippincott & Co. 1878. brown decorated cloth. $15.00–$50.00

Gibbs, James. *Book of Architecture, A.* Lon. the author. 1728. 1st ed. engr plates. folio.
$15,000.00–$18,000.00

Gibbs, James. *Book of Architecture, A.* Lon. Innys. 1739. 2nd ed. engr plates.folio.
$1,500.00–$2,000.00

Gilbert, Edward M. *Panamint Legend.* Los Angeles. Hesperus. 1st ed. 16 pp. illus. drawings. pictorial wrappers. $50.00–$100.00

Gilbert, W. S. *Bab Ballads, The.* Lon. Hotten. 1869. 1st ed. illus. 4 pp ads. green cloth.
$200.00–$300.00

Gilchrist, Ellen. *Annunciation, The.* Bos. Little Brown. 1983. 1st ed. author's first novel. dj.
$50.00–$75.00

Gilchrist, Ellen. *Annunciation, The.* Bos. Little Brown. 1983. 1st ed. author's first novel. sgn. dj.
$90.00–$125.00

Gilchrist, Ellen. *Drunk with Love.* Bos. Little Brown. 1986. 1st ed. inscrb. dj. $30.00–$50.00

Gillespie, Dizzy (with Al Frazer). *To Be or Not to Bop.* Garden City. Doubleday. 1979. 1st ed. dj.
$200.00–$250.00

Gillies' Family Almanac. NY. Wright Gillies' & Bros. 1870. 1st ed. wraps. illus. very good. teas, coffee and spices.
$10.00–$25.00

Gilpin, W. S. *Practical Hints upon Landscape Gardening; with some remarks on Domestic Architecture as connected with Scenery.* Lon. Cadell. 1835. 2nd ed.
$400.00–$600.00

Gingrich, Arnold. *The Well-Tempered Angler.* NY. Knopf. 1966. red cloth. lettering on spine.
$5.00–$20.00

Ginsberg, Allen. *Fall of America.* San Francisco. 1972. wraps.
$30.00–$50.00

Ginsberg, Allen. *Planet News.* CA. City Lights. 1968. 1st ed. wraps. dj.
$50.00–$90.00

Ginsberg, Allen. *Reality Sandwiches.* (1963). 1st ed. wraps.
$50.00–$60.00

Girardi, Robert. *Madeleine's Ghost.* NY. 1995. 1st ed. author's first novel. sgn. dj.
$100.00–$150.00

Girardi, Robert. *Pirate's Daughter, The.* NY Delacorte. 1997. 1st ed. sgn. dj.
$50.00–$90.00

Girouard, Desire. *Supplement to Lake St. Louis.* Montreal. Poirier, Bessette & Co. 1903. illus. red cloth, very good.
$75.00–$100.00

Glasgow, Ellen. *They Stooped to Folly.* Garden City. Literary Guild. 1929. 1st ed. 1st ed after ltd ed. dj.
$60.00–$90.00

Glass, Julia. *Three Junes: A Novel.* NY. Pantheon. 2002. 1st ed. 1st issue dj. National Book Award Winner.
$50.00–$75.00

Glass, Julia. *Three Junes.* NY. Pantheon. (2002). 1st ed. author's first novel. National Book Award winner. sgn. dj.
$90.00–$100.00

Glass, Montague. *Potash and Perlmutter.* Phil. Altemus. nd. 1st ed. author's first book. illus. red cloth.
$50.00–$75.00

Glasse, Hannah. *Art of Cookery, made Plain and Easy.* Lon. Straham. 1784. calf.
$500.00–$600.00

Glasse, Hannah. *Art of Cookery, made Plain and Easy.* Lon. Prospect. 1983. facsimile.
$25.00–$40.00

Glazier, Captain Willard. *Headwaters of the Mississippi*. Chi/NY. Rand, McNally. 1894. illus. blue decorated cloth. $35.00–$100.00

Gloag, John. *Guide to Western Architecture*. NY. Macmillan. 1958. illus. red cloth. 407 pp. plates. dj. $35.00–$45.00

Glover, Jack. *Bobbed Wire: An Illustrated Guide to the Identification and Classification of Barbed Wire*. Wichita Falls. Terry Bros. 1966. 1st ed. wraps. sgn. $35.00–$45.00

Godwin, Gail. *Finishing School, The*. Franklin Center. Franklin Library. 1984. 1st ed. sgn. lea. raised bands. $20.00–$30.00

Gold, Glen David. *Carter Beats the Devil*. Lon. Sceptre. 2001. 1st ed. sgn. author's first book. dj. $30.00–$45.00

Gold Mines East of the Rocky Mountains. . . . DC. House of Representatives Ex. Doc. No. 92. 1867. wraps. 28 pp. $225.00–$300.00

Goldberg, Whoopi. *Whoopi Goldberg Book*. NY. Weisbach/Morrow. 1997. 1st ed. sgn. dj. $45.00–$60.00

Golding, William. *Brass Butterfly, The*. NY. Faber and Faber. 1958. 1st ed. dj. $100.00–$125.00

1959 Indian Artists Exhibition: Museum of New Mexico Art Gallery. Santa Fe. 1959. illus. catalog. wraps. $20.00–$30.00

Golding, William. *Darkness Visible*. NY. Farrar Straus. 1979. 1st ed. dj. $40.00–$50.00

Golding, William. *Lord of the Flies*. NY. Coward-McCann. 1955. 1st ed. dj. $300.00–$1,100.00

Golding, William. *Lord of the Flies*. Lon. Faber & Faber. (1954). 1st UK ed. dj. $2,000.00–$7,000.00

Goldsmith, Oliver. *History of the Earth and Animated Nature*. . . . Edinburgh. Fullerton. nd. illus. 72 hand-colored plates. $600.00–$800.00

Goldwater, Barry. *Arizona*. 1978. 1st ed. $40.00–$60.00

Goodrich, Mary. *On the Old Calaveras Road*. np. private printing. 1929. 1st ed. illus. green pictorial wrappers. $30.00–$40.00

Gordimer, Nadine. *Lying Days*. NY. Simon & Schuster. 1953. 1st Amer ed. dj. $75.00–$125.00

Gordimer, Nadine. *Lying Days*. Lon. Gollancz. 1953. 1st ed. sgn. dj. $300.00–$400.00

Gordimer, Nadine. *Soft Voice of the Serpent*. NY. Simon & Schuster. (1952). 1st ed. sgn. dj. $400.00–$650.00

Gordimer, Nadine. *Soft Voice of the Serpent*. NY. Simon & Schuster. (1952). 1st ed. dj. $200.00–$275.00

Gordimer, Nadine. *Something Out There*. Lon. Jonathan Cape. (1984). 1st ed. 1st UK ed. sgn. dj. $40.00–$50.00

Gordimer, Nadine. *Something Out There*. NY. Viking. (1984). 1st US ed. dj. $25.00–$40.00

Gordon, A. C. and Page Thomas Nelson. *Befo' De War*. NY. Scribner's. 1888. 1st ed. Gordon's first book. Nelson's 2nd book. buckram. $135.00–$250.00

Gordon, A. C. and Page Thomas Nelson. *Befo' De War*. NY. Scribner's. 1888. 1st ed. Gordon's first book. Nelson's 2nd book. buckram. ltd. sgn. $250.00–$300.00

Gordon, Armistead Churchill. *Jefferson Davis*. NY. Scribner. 1918. 1st ed. sgn.
$45.00–$70.00

Gordon, Elizabeth. *Bird Children*. Volland. 1912. illus. later editions. $50.00–$150.00

Gordon, Elizabeth. *Bird Children*. Volland. 1912. illus. early editions. $100.00–$300.00

Gordon, Elizabeth. *Flower Children*. Volland. 1910. illus. later editions. $20.00–$50.00

Gordon, Elizabeth. *Flower Children*. Volland. 1910. illus. early editions. $75.00–$250.00

Gordon, Elizabeth. *Loraine and the Little People of the Ocean*. Chi. Rand McNally. 1922. 1st ed. illus. dj. $125.00–$175.00

Gordon, Gen. John B. *Reminiscences of the Civil War*. NY. Scribner's. 1904. Memorial ed.
$95.00–$150.00

Gordon, Thomas. *Gazetteer of the State of New Jersey*. Trenton. 1834. 1st ed. frontis. lea.
$250.00–$450.00

Gordon, Thomas. *Gazetteer of the State of Pennsylvania*. Phila. 1832. 1st ed. map. lea.
$150.00–$200.00

Gorey. *Gambling, Gaming Supplies*. Chi. Evans Co. 1929. wraps. $80.00–$100.00

Gorey, Edward. *Blue Aspic*. NY. Meredith Press. (1968). 1st ed. black paper over boards. dj.
$75.00–$225.00

Gorey, Edward. *Broken Spoke, The*. NY. Dodd. (1976). 1st ed. dj. $75.00–$150.00

Gorey, Edward. *Broken Spoke, The*. NY. Dodd. (1976). 1st ed. sgn. dj. $250.00–$400.00

Gorey, Edward. *Dancing Cats & Neglected Murderesses*. NY. Workingman Publishing. 1980. 1st ed. wraps. $60.00–$95.00

Gorey, Edward. *Dancing Cats & Neglected Murderesses*. NY. Workingman Publishing. 1980. 1st ed. sgn. $90.00–$140.00

Gorey, Edward. *Dracula, A Toy Theatre*. NY. Scribners. 1979. 1st ed. wraps. spiral bound folio. sgn. $350.00–$425.00

Gorey, Edward. *Eclectic Abecedarium*. Bos. 1983. 1st ed. ltd 300 cc. sgn. $300.00–$400.00

Gorey, Edward. *Eclectic Abecedarium*. NY. Adams. (1983). 1st ed. 1st trade ed. glossy boards. sgn. $250.00–$300.00

Gorey, Edward. *Haunted Tea-Cozy, The*. Harcourt. 1997. 1st ed. $25.00–$35.00

Gorey, Edward. *Listing Attic, The*. NY/Bos. Duell, Sloan and Pearce/Little, Brown. (1954). 1st ed. wraps. dj. $135.00–$225.00

Gorey, Edward. *Loathsome Couple, The*. Dodd Mead. 1977. 1st ed. illus. dj. $40.00–$75.00

Gorey, Edward. *Unstrung Harp, The*. Duell Sloan & Pearce. 1953. 1st ed. Author's first book. dj. $300.00–$500.00

Gorey, Edward. *Unstrung Harp, The*. Duell Sloan & Pearce. 1953. 1st ed. Author's first book. dj. $600.00–$950.00

Gorey, Edward. *Water Flowers*. NY. Congdon and Weed. (1982). 1st ed. dj. $40.00–$60.00

Gorey, Edward. *Water Flowers*. NY. Congdon and Weed. (1982). 1st ed. sgn. dj. $250.00–$350.00

Goulart, Ron. *Nemo*. Lon. Hale. 1979. 1st hardcover ed. dj. $25.00–$40.00

Gould, John. *Toucans*. Lon. 1852–54. folio. hand colored plates. $20,000.00–$35,000.00

Gould, Marcus. *Report of the Trial of Friends*. Phil. 1829. ¼ morocco. $100.00–$150.00

Government Printing Office. *1907*. 1st ed. wraps. tan wrps in brown paper dust jacket. 95pp. fold-out map frontis—Vermont. $20.00–$35.00

Grady, Thomas E. *Grady's Directory, Guide and Reference Book of Montgomery, PA....* Montgomery. Grady. 1897. ¼ lea. cloth boards. map. pictorial ads. $75.00–$100.00

Graffagnino, J. K. *Shaping of Vermont*. Rutland. 1983. illus. $40.00–$50.00

Grafton, Sue. *A is for Alibi*. NY. Holt Rinehart & Winston. 1982. 1st ed. sgn. dj. $1,200.00–$2,000.00

Grafton, Sue. *A is for Alibi*. Lon. Macmillan. 1982. 1st UK ed. dj. $250.00–$300.00

Grafton, Sue. *A is for Alibi*. NY. Bantam. 1987. wraps. illus. 1st paperback ed. $5.00–$10.00

Grafton, Sue. *B is for Burglar*. Lon. Macmillan. 1986. 1st ed. sgn. dj. $500.00–$800.00

Grafton, Sue. *C is for Corpse*. NY. 1986. 1st ed. sgn. dj. $400.00–$500.00

Grafton, Sue. *D is for Deadbeat*. NY. Holt. (1987). 1st ed. sgn. dj. $300.00–$400.00

Grafton, Sue. *E is for Evidence*. NY. Holt. (1988). 1st ed. sgn. dj. $250.00–$300.00

Grafton, Sue. *K is for Killer*. NY. Holt. (1994). 1st ed. sgn. dj. $50.00–$75.00

Grahame, Kenneth. *Golden Age*. Lon/NY. 1900. illus. by Maxfield Parrish. $90.00–$110.00

Grahame, Kenneth. *Wind in the Willows*. Lon. Methuen. (1908). 1st ed. ¼ morocco. $5,000.00–$10,000.00

Grainge, William. *Daemonologia, Discourse on Witchcraft*. Harrogate. 1882. $30.00–$50.00

Grant, Blanche C. (ed.). *Kit Carson's Own Story of His Life*. Taos. 1926. wraps. $75.00–$90.00

Grass, Gunter. *Cat and Mouse*. NY. Harcourt Brace and World. 1965. 1st US ed. dj. $20.00–$25.00

Grass, Gunter. *Dog Years*. NY. 1965. 1st ed. dj. $25.00–$35.00

Graves, Robert. *Lawrence and the Arabian Adventure*. Garden City. Doubleday. 1949. 1st ed. dj. $50.00–$75.00

Graves, Robert. *On English Poetry.* Lon. Heinemann. 1922. 1st ed. $150.00–$200.00

Graves, Robert. *Poems.* Seizin Press. Lon. 1929. $150.00–$200.00

Green, Anna Katherine. *Difficult Problem, A.* NY. Lupton. 1900. 1st ed. green cloth.
$100.00–$150.00

Green, Edwin L. *Indians of South Carolina.* Columbia. (1904). 1st ed. $50.00–$65.00

Greenaway, Kate. *A Apple Pie.* Lon. Routledge. 1886. $300.00–$400.00

Greenaway, Kate. *Almanack for 1883.* Lon. Routlege. (1882). illus. by Greenaway.
$200.00–$750.00

Greenaway, Kate. *Almanack for 1883.* Lon. Routlege. (1882). illus. by Greenaway. presentation. $3,000.00–$5,000.00

Greenaway, Kate. *Greenaway's Babies.* Akron, Ohio. Saalfield. 1907. illus. full color. limp cloth. $150.00–$300.00

Greenaway, Kate. *Mother Goose.* Lon. Frederick Warne. (1881). $150.00–$250.00

Greene, Graham. *Human Factor.* Lon. 1978. 1st UK ed. dj. $40.00–$60.00

Greene, Graham. *Our Man in Havana.* Lon. 1958. dj. $85.00–$100.00

Greenwood, Grace. *New Life in New Lands.* NY. J.B. Ford. 1873. brown pictorial cloth gilt lettering on cover and spine. $20.00–$30.00

Gregory, Isabella Augusta, Lady. *Seven Short Plays.* Bos. Luce. (1909). 1st ed. buckram. blue boards. printed paper label. frontis portrait. $50.00–$90.00

Grenfell, Wilfred, Thomason. *A Labrador Doctor.* Bos. Houghton Mifflin. 1919. 1st ed. illus. green cloth with gold lettering on cover and spine. presentation copy signed by author.
$40.00–$55.00

Grey Owl. *Tales of an Empty Cabin.* Lovat. Lon. 1936. illus. brown cl. very good.
$20.00–$40.00

Grey, Zane. *Call of the Canyon.* NY. Harper. (1924). 1st ed. dj. $90.00–$250.00

Grey, Zane. *Call of the Canyon.* NY. Harper. (1924). 1st ed. presentation. dj.
$1,500.00–$3,000.00

Grey, Zane. *Hash Knife Outfit, The.* NY. Grosset & Dunlap. (1940). dj. $30.00–$40.00

Grey, Zane. *Tales of Southern Rivers.* NY. Harper. 1924. 1st ed. green cloth. 249 pp.
$150.00–$225.00

Grey, Zane. *Tales of the Angler's El Dorado.* NY. Grosset & Dunlap. 1926. illus. photos. dj.
$50.00–$75.00

Grey, Zane. *Thundering Herd.* NY. 1925. 1st ed. dj. $50.00–$125.00

Grey, Zane. *West of the Pecos.* NY. Harper. 1937. 1st ed. dj. $80.00–$100.00

Grey, Zane. *Wild Horse Mesa.* NY/Lon. Harper. 1928. 1st ed. blue cloth. dj. $75.00–$90.00

Grey, Zane. *Wildfire.* NY. Grosset & Dunlap. 1945. dj. $10.00–$15.00

Griffin, John S. *Doctor Comes to California, A: the Diary of John S. Griffin, Assistant Surgeon with Kearny's Dragoons, 1846–1847.* San Francisco. California Historical Society. 1943. 1st ed. thus. 97 pp. frontis portrait. red cloth. $50.00–$100.00

Griffith, D. W. *Rise and Fall of Free Speech in America, The.* LA. 1916. 1st ed. author's first book. $300.00–$400.00

Grimes, Martha. *Anodyne Necklace, The.* Bos. Little Brown. (1983). 1st ed $25.00–$125.00

Grimkè, A. E. *Appeal to the Christian Women of the South.* NY. 1836. 1st ed. wraps. author's first book. $500.00–$600.00

Grimsley, Jim. *My Drowning.* Chapel Hill. Algonquin. 1997. 1st ed. sgn. dj. $30.00–$40.00

Grimsley, Jim. *Winter Birds.* Chapel Hill. Algonquin. 1994. 1st ed. sgn.dj. $45.00–$55.00

Grinnell, George Bird. *Blackfoot Lodge Tales.* NY. 1892. 1st ed. $50.00–$85.00

Grinnell, George Bird. *Indians of Today.* NY. 1915. 3rd printing. plates. $50.00–$100.00

Grisham, John. *A Time to Kill.* NY. 1993. ltd 350 cc. lea. slipcase. sgn. $700.00–$850.00

Grisham, John. *A Time to Kill.* NY. Wynwood. (1989). 1st ed. author's first book. cloth. sgn. dj. $2,000.00–$3,800.00

Grisham, John. *Client, The.* NY. Doubleday. 1993. 1st ed. dj. $30.00–$60.00

Grisham, John. *Firm, The.* NY. 1991. 1st ed. dj. $90.00–$130.00

Gruelle, Johnny. *Cruise of the Rickety Robin.* Manning. 1931. 1st ed. wraps. illus. by Gruelle. $200.00–$300.00

Gruelle, Johnny. *Friendly Fairies.* NY. Johnny Gruelle Co. 1949. dj. $30.00–$40.00

Gruelle, Johnny. *Friendly Fairies.* NY. Volland. (1919). illus. in color by Gruelle. black pictorial boards. $45.00–$90.00

Gruelle, Johnny. *Johnny Gruelle's Golden Book.* Donohue. (1929). illus. by Gruelle. $80.00–$100.00

Gruelle, Johnny. *Raggedy Andy Stories.* Volland. (1920). 1st ed. illus. by Gruelle. $100.00–$200.00

Gruelle, Johnny. *Raggedy Ann and Andy and the Camel with the Wrinkled Knees.* Chi. Donohue. 1924. pictorial endpapers. unpaginated. $50.00–$125.00

Gruelle, Johnny. *Raggedy Ann Goes Sailing.* McLoughlin. (1941). 1st ed. illus. by Gruelle. $50.00–$75.00

Gruelle, Johnny. *Raggedy Ann in Cookie Land.* McLoughlin. 1940. 1st ed. illus. by Gruelle. $50.00–$75.00

Gruelle, Johnny. *Raggedy Ann in the Magic Book.* NY. Johnny Gruelle Co. 1939. dj. $25.00–$90.00

Gruelle, Johnny. *Raggedy Ann's Alphabet Book*. NY. Volland. 1925. illus. by Gruelle.
$45.00–$50.00

Gruelle, Johnny. *Raggedy Ann Stories*. Volland. (1918). 1st ed. illus. by Gruelle.
$150.00–$225.00

Gruelle, Justin. *Mother Goose Parade*. Volland. (1929). 1st ed. illus. by Justin Gruelle.
$75.00–$100.00

Guild, F. N. *The Mineralogy of Arizona*. Easton. Chemical Pub. Co. 1910. 1st ed. illus. small dark green cl. 103 pp. $35.00–$60.00

Gunnison, J. W. *Mormons, The: or Latter-Day Saints in the Valley of the Great Salt Lake*. Phil. Lippincott. 1852. 1st ed. frontis. brown cloth. blindstamped. $200.00–$300.00

Gussow, H. T. and W. S. Odell. *Mushrooms and Toadstools*. Ottawa. Minister of Agriculture. 1927. 1st ed. illus. green cloth with gold lettering on cover and spine, color frontis and black and white illus. $25.00–$40.00

Guterson, David. *Snow Falling on Cedars*. NY. Harcourt Brace. 1994. 1st ed. sgn. dj.
$200.00–$450.00

H. H. (Jackson). *Bits of Travel at Home*. Bos. Roberts Bros. 1891. small green cloth. blind-stamp decorations on cover. frontis. $15.00–$40.00

Habberton, John. *Scripture Club of Valley Rest, The*. NY. Putnam's. 1877. 1st ed. green cloth.
$40.00–$60.00

Haggadah Seder Shel Pesach. NY. Hebrew Publishing. (1908). illus. woodcuts. New York State Bank ads. new ed. $750.00–$950.00

Haggard, H. Rider. *Ayesha*. NY. 1905. 1st ed. $40.00–$130.00

Haggard, H. Rider. *Regeneration*. Lon. Longmans Green. 1910. 1st ed. $100.00–$150.00

Haggard, H. Rider. *The Virgin of the Sun*. NY. Grosset & Dunlap. 1922. blue cloth, frontis.
$5.00–$15.00

Haggard, Howard W. *The Doctor on History*. NY. Dorset Press. (1989). First printing. illus. woodcuts, engr, dj. $10.00–$12.00

Haggard, H. Rider. *When the World Shook*. L. Longmans Green. 1919. 1st ed.
$40.00–$65.00

Haig-Brown, Roderick. *Western Angler*. William Morrow. 1947. $25.00–$35.00

Haig-Brown, Roderick. *Western Angler*. William Morrow. 1947. $25.00–$35.00

Haines, Francis. *Nez Perce*. Univ of Oklahoma Press. (1955). 1st ed. dj. $40.00–$75.00

Haining, Peter. *Movable Books: An Illustrated History*. Lon. New English Library Limited. 1979. $125.00–$150.00

Hale, Edward Everett. *Man Without A Country, The*. Bos. Ticknor and Fields. 1865.
$500.00–$700.00

Hale, Edward Everett. *Man Without A Country*. Bos. Roberts. 1889. illus. by Merrill.
$35.00–$50.00

Hall, Bernard. *Hell In a Very Small Place*. Phil. 1966. 1st ed. dj. $40.00–$50.00

Hall, Bernard. *Street Without Joy*. Harrisburg. Stackpole. 1961. 1st ed. dj. $300.00–$400.00

Hall, Carroll D. *Bierce and the Poe Hoax*. San Francisco. Book Club of California. 1934. 1st
ed. frontis. ltd 250 cc. sgn. $200.00–$300.00

Hall, Charles. *Regiments and Armories of Massachusetts*. Bos. Potter & Co. 1901. illus. green
cloth, 3/4 leather, marbleized endpps. t.e.g. dec. cover and spine. $200.00–$275.00

Hall, Thorne. *Odyssey of Death Valley*. CA. Pacific Coast Odyssey. 1962. 1st ed. 36 pp. illus.
photos. map. pictorial wrappers. $15.00–$30.00

Hallard, James Henry. *Gallica and Other Essays*. Lon. Longman, Green. 1895. 1st ed. light
brown cloth. $30.00–$40.00

Haller, John S., Jr. And Robin M. Haller. *The Physician and Sexuality in Victorian America*.
Urbana, IL. University of Illinois. 1974. dj. $25.00–$30.00

Halliday, Brett. *She Woke In Darkness*. NY. Torquil. 1954. 1st ed. dj. $50.00–$75.00

Hallock, Charles. *Our New Alaska*. NY. Forest and Stream. 1886. 1st ed. illus. red decorated
cloth with gold lettering on cover and spine. $40.00–$100.00

Hammett, Dashiell. *Adventures of Sam Spade*. Cleve. World. (1945). 1st ed. dj.
$100.00–$300.00

Hammett, Dashiell. *Big Knockover, The*. NY. Random House. (1966). 1st ed. dj.
$60.00–$100.00

Hammett, Dashiell. *Dain Curse, The*. NY. Knopf. 1st ed. no dj. $300.00–$1,200.00

Hammett, Dashiell. *Maltese Falcon*. NY. Knopf. 1930. 1st ed. tan cloth. $500.00–$1,000.00

Hammett, Dashiell. *Maltese Falcon*. NY. Knopf. 1930. 1st ed. tan cloth. dj.
$5,000.00–$10,000.00

Hammett, Dashiell. *Red Harvest*. NY. Knopf. 1929. 1st ed. author's first novel. dj.
$1,000.00–$2,000.00

Hammett, Dashiell. *Thin Man*. NY. 1934. 1st ed. soiled. no dj. $400.00–$600.00

Hammond, William A. *Insanity and Its Relation to Crime: A Text and Commentary*. NY. Appleton. 1873. 1st ed. sgn. $575.00–$650.00

Hampton, Lionel (with James Haskins). *Hamp*. NY. Warner. 1989. 1st ed. illus. 16 pp photos. sgn by Hampton. dj. $100.00–$200.00

Hanaford, Phoebe. *Daughters of America*. Augusta. True and Co. 1882. illus. $20.00–$30.00

Handy, W. C. *Blues: An Anthology*. NY. Albert & Charles Boni. 1926. 1st ed. illus. 1st printing of author's first book. intro by Abbe Niles. $150.00–$200.00

Handy, W. C. *Blues: An Anthology*. NY. Albert & Charles Boni. 1926. illus. by Miguel Covar-
rubias. pink and black cloth. $65.00–$125.00

Hannah, Barry. *Airships*. NY. Knopf. 1978. 1st ed. sgn. dj. $100.00–$135.00

Hannah, Barry. *Nightwatchmen*. NY. Viking. 1973. 1st ed. dj. $100.00–$200.00

Hansen, Ron. *Atticus*. NY. Harper-Collins. 1996. 1st ed. sgn. dj. $40.00–$50.00

Hansen, Ron. *Mariette in Ecstasy*. NY. HarperCollins. 1991. 1st ed. sgn. dj. $20.00–$30.00

Hardy, Deborah. *Land and Freedom: The Origins of Russian Terrorism, 1876–1879*. NY. Greenwood. 1987. 1st ed. dj. $30.00–$40.00

Harland, Marion and Virginia Van De Water. *Everyday Etiquette*. Indianapolis. Bobbs-Merrill. 1907. green cl. $7.00–$9.00

Harmer, S. F. *Report on Cetacea*. Lon. British Museum. 1927. illus. maps. 91 pp. $100.00–$125.00

Harold, Childe. *A Child's Book of Abridged Wisdom*. SF. Paul Elder & Co. 1905. illus. decorated gray boards, spine partly exposed with cord ties. $35.00–$50.00

Harper's Weekly Journal of Civilization. NY. Harper & Co. 1864. 1st ed. wraps. illus. by Brady, A. R. Waud. General Grant's Campaign by Waud. $44.00–$75.00

Harris, Albert W. *Cracker Tales*. np. private. (1912). 1st ed. presentation copy. frontis. cloth. $40.00–$50.00

Harris, Joel Chandler. *Aaron in the Wildwood*. Bos. 1897. 1st ed. $75.00–$100.00

Harris, Joel Chandler. *Little Union Scout*. NY. McClure. 1904. 1st ed. illus. green cloth. $75.00–$200.00

Harris, Joel Chandler. *Tar Baby and Other Rhymes of Uncle Remus*. NY. Appleton. 1904. 1st ed. illus. orange cloth. $100.00–$250.00

Harris, Thomas. *Silence of the Lambs*. NY. 1988. 1st ed. sgn. dj. $60.00–$80.00

Harrison, Harry. *Men from P.I.G. and R.O.B.O.T., The*. NY. Atheneum. 1978. 1st US ed. dj. $40.00–$50.00

Harrison, Jim. *Legends of the Fall*. NY. Delacorte. (1979). 1st ed. one volume trade edition of three novellas. movies based on first two novellas. dj. $150.00–$175.00

Harrison, Jim. *Legends of the Fall*. NY. Delacorte. (1979). 1st ed. one volume trade edition of three novellas. movies based on first two novellas. signed. dj. $190.00–$250.00

Harrison, Jim. *Locations*. NY. Norton. (1968). 1st ed. hardcover. sgn. dj. $600.00–$800.00

Harrison, Jim. *Plain Song*. NY. Norton. (1965). 1st ed. author's first book. 1500 cc. wrappers. $500.00–$800.00

Harte, Bret. *Heathen Chinee, The*. San Francisco. John Henry Nash. 1934. illus. illustrated boards. slipcase. $75.00–$90.00

Harte, Bret. *Millionaire of Rough-and-Ready, A*. Kentfield. Allen. 1955. brown boards. dj. $100.00–$120.00

Harte, Bret. *Salomy Jane*. Bos. Houghton Mifflin. 1910. 1st ed. dj. $75.00–$150.00

Harte, Bret. *Story of Enriquez, The*. San Francisco. Rothchild. 1924. batik boards. 100 cc.
$100.00–$200.00

Haskins, Charles Homer. *Normans in European History, The*. Bos. Houghton Mifflin. 1915.
$20.00–$30.00

Hawkins, Richard. *Observations of Sir Richard Hawkins*. Lon. Argonaut. 1933. 1st ed. thus. frontis map. folding maps. vellum and buckram. blindstamped. $100.00–$150.00

Hawthorne, Nathaniel. *Doctor Grimshawe's Secret*. Osgood. 1883. 1st ed. $100.00–$300.00

Hawthorne, Nathaniel. *House of Seven Gables, The*. Bos. Ticknor, Reed & Fields. 1851. 1st ed. 1st issue. brown cloth. first issue points. $2,000.00–$4,000.00

Hawthorne, Nathaniel. *Scarlet Letter, The*. Bos. Ticknor, Reed & Fields. 1850. first edition points: "March 1, 1850" ads; "reduplicate" for "repudiate" on page 21. $5,000.00–$12,000.00

Hayes, Charles. *Treatise on Fluxion: or, An Introduction to Mathematical Philosophy. . . .* Lond. Midwinter. 1704. 1st ed. 1st English work on calculus. folio. woodcuts.
$2,000.00–$3,500.00

Haymond, Creed. *Central Pacific Railroad Co., Its Relation to the Government. . . .* SF. Crocker. 1888. reprint with corrections. cloth with gilt lettering. $190.00–$210.00

Heap, Gwinn Harris. *Central Route to the Pacific, from the Valley of the Mississippi to California*. Phil. Lippincott. 1854. 1st ed. brown cloth over boards. $1,000.00–$1,200.00

Hearn, Lafcadio. *Glimpses of Unfamiliar Japan*. Bos/NY. Houghton Mifflin. (1894). illus. 2 vols. ltd 1000 cc. teg. slipcase. $250.00–$600.00

Hearn, Lafcadio. *Japan*. NY. 1904. 1st ed. 1st issue. teg. dj. $200.00–$250.00

Hearn, Lafcadio. *Karma*. NY. 1918. 1st ed. $100.00–$150.00

Hearn, Lafcadio. *Koharo*. Bos. 1896. 1st ed. $50.00–$75.00

Hearn, Lafcadio. *Out of the East*. Bos. (1895). 1st ed. $75.00–$200.00

Hearn, Lafcadio. *Romance of the Milky Way, The*. Bos. Houghton Mifflin. 1905. 1st ed. cloth.
$250.00–$400.00

Hedrick, U. P. *Cyclopedia of Hardy Fruits*. New York. Macmillan. 1922. 1st ed. illus. green cl. col frontis. b/w and colored plates. $50.00–$75.00

Heinlein, Robert. *Assignment in Eternity*. PA. Fantasy Press. (1953). 1st ed. 2nd issue. green. dj. $200.00–$250.00

Heinlein, Robert. *Door Into Summer*. Garden City. Doubleday. 1957. 1st ed. dj.
$200.00–$1,000.00

Heinlein, Robert. *Green Hills of Earth, The*. Chicago. Shasta. (1951). 1st ed. dj.
$150.00–$200.00

Heinlein, Robert. *Grumbles from the Grave*. NY. Ballantine. (1989). 1st ed. dj.
$20.00–$25.00

Heinlein, Robert. *Red Planet*. NY. Scribner's. 1949. x-lib. $10.00–$15.00

Heinlein, Robert A. *Cat Who Walks Through Walls, The*. NY. 1985. 1st ed. dj.
$50.00–$100.00

Heinlein, Robert A. *Farnham's Freehold*. NY. Putnam. 1964. 1st ed. dj. $220.00–$600.00

Heinlein, Robert A. *Friday*. NY. Holt Rinehart and Winston [1982]. 1st edition. limited to 500 copies. numbered and signed. slipcase. $300.00–$650.00

Heinlein, Robert A. *Grumbles from the Grave*. NY. Del Rey. 1990. 1st ed. edited by Virginia Heinlein. dj. $15.00–$25.00

Heinlein, Robert A. *Job: A Comedy of Justice*. NY. Del Rey. 1984. 1st ed. dj. $10.00–$15.00

Heinlein, Robert A. *Rocket Ship Galileo*. NY. Scribner's. 1947. 1st ed. illus. by Voter.
$250.00–$350.00

Heinlein, Robert A. *Rocket Ship Galileo*. NY. 1947. 1st ed. author's first novel. dj.
$900.00–$1,500.00

Heinlein, Robert A. *Stranger in a Strange Land*. NY. Putnam's. (1961). 1st ed. pictorial dj. Hugo Award–winning novel. $2,000.00–$5,000.00

Heinlein, Robert A. *Waldo and Magic, Inc*. Garden City. 1950. 1st ed. dj. $250.00–$500.00

Heizer, Robert F. *Indians of California, A Critical Bibliography*. Indiana. Indiana Univ Press. (1976). 1st ed. wraps. 68 pp. $15.00–$20.00

Heller, Joseph. *God Knows*. NY. 1984. 1st ed. dj. $30.00–$40.00

Heller, Joseph. *Catch-22*. NY. Simon & Schuster. 1961. 1st ed. author's first book. sgn. dj.
$10,000.00–$12,000.00

Heller, Joseph. *Catch-22*. NY. Simon & Schuster. 1961. 1st ed. author's first book. dj.
$3,500.00–$5,000.00

Hellman, Lillian. *Children's Hour*. NY. 1934. 1st ed. dj. $350.00–$750.00

Hellman, Lillian. *Little Foxes*. NY. 1939. 1st ed. dj. $100.00–$200.00

Helprin, Mark. *Ellis Island and Her Stories*. NY. Delacorte Press. (1981). 1st ed. dj.
$50.00–$60.00

Helprin, Mark. *Winter's Tale*. NY. 1983. 1st ed. sgn. dj. $60.00–$75.00

Hemenway, Abby Maria. *Abby Hemenway's Vermont*. VT. Green. 1972. dj. $10.00–$15.00

Hemenway, Abby Maria. *Local History of Ancover, VT*. NY. 1921. reprint. $30.00–$40.00

Hemenway, Abby Maria. *Vermont Historical Gazeteer* . . . Vol III. NH. 1877. illus.
$300.00–$425.00

Hemenway, Abby Maria. *Vermont Historical Gazeteer* . . . Vol V. Brandon. 1891. illus.
$400.00–$450.00

Hemingway, Ernest. *Death in the Afternoon*. NY. 1932. 1st ed. dj. $750.00–$1,250.00

Hemingway, Ernest. *Death in the Afternoon*. NY. 1932. 1st ed. dj. $2,000.00–$3,000.00

Hemingway, Ernest. *Farewell to Arms, A.* NY. Scribner's. 1929. 1st ed. 1st issue. dj.
$8,000.00–$9,000.00

Hemingway, Ernest. *Farewell to Arms, A.* NY. Scribner's. 1929. 1st ed. 1st issue. sgn. dj.
$20,000.00–$30,000.00

Hemingway, Ernest. *Farewell to Arms, A.* Franklin Library. 1975. aeg. $90.00–$125.00

Hemingway, Ernest. *For Whom the Bell Tolls.* NY. Scribner's. 1940. 1st ed. dj.
$1,500.00–$3,000.00

Hemingway, Ernest. *For Whom the Bell Tolls.* NY. Scribner's. 1940. 1st ed. dj.
$200.00–$500.00

Hemingway, Ernest. *For Whom the Bell Tolls.* NY. Scribner's. 1940. no dj. $40.00–$50.00

Hemingway, Ernest. *Green Hills of Africa.* NY. 1935. 1st ed. dj. $2,500.00–$3,500.00

Hemingway, Ernest. *Old Man and the Sea.* NY. Scribners. (1952). 1st ed. dj.
$1,000.00–$4,000.00

Hemingway, Ernest. *Old Man and the Sea.* NY. Scribners. (1952). 1st ed. sgn. dj.
$20,000.00–$25,000.00

Hemingway, Ernest. *Old Man and the Sea.* Lon. Jonathan Cape. (1952). 1st UK ed.
$200.00–$300.00

Henderson, Peter. *Garden and Farm Topics.* New York. Peter Henderson. 1884. 1st ed. illus. small reddish brown cloth decorative gold lettering on cover, portrait frontis.
$15.00–$25.00

Hendrick, Burton J. *Lees of Virginia, The.* Bos. Little Brown. 1935. 1st ed. blue cloth. portraits. fold-out table. $30.00–$40.00

Herbert, Frank. *Dune.* Phil. Chilton. 1965. 1st ed. Hugo and Nebula Award winner.
$3,000.00–$5,000.00

Herbert, Frank. *God Emperor of Dune.* NY. 1981. 1st ed. sgn. dj. $100.00–$200.00

Herbert, Frank. *Heretics of Dune.* NY. (1984). 1st US ed. 1500 cc. sgn. slipcase.
$100.00–$200.00

Herbert, Frank. *White Plague.* NY. (1982). 1st ed. ltd 500 cc. numbered. sgn.
$90.00–$125.00

Herbert, Frank. *White Plague.* NY. (1982). 1st ed. $25.00–$75.00

Herbst, Josephine. *Starched Blue Sky.* NY. Harper. 1991. 1st ed. dj. $20.00–$50.00

Herne, B. *Tanzania Safaris.* NY. 1981. illus. ltd 1000 cc. numbered and sgn. slipcase.
$300.00–$400.00

Herne, B. *Uganda Safaris.* NJ. 1979. ltd. 1000 cc. numbered and sgn. author's first book. slipcase. $300.00–$400.00

Hersey, John. *Wall, The.* NY. Knopf. 1950. 1st ed. inscrb. dj. $500.00–$900.00

Hesse, Herman. *Siddhartha*. NY. New Directions. 1951. 1st edition in English. dj.
$200.00–$1,000.00

Higgins, Anthony and Bayard Wooten. *New Castle, Delaware, 1651–1939*. Boston. Houghton Mifflin. 1939. 1st ed. illus. ltd. 47 plates. folio. $75.00–$100.00

Hill, Emma Shepard. *Dangerous Crossing and What Happened on the Other Side, A*. Denver. private printing. 1914. 1st ed. $1,000.00–$2,000.00

Hill, Emma Shepard. *Dangerous Crossing and What Happened on the Other Side, A*. Denver. private printing. 1914. 1st ed. sgn. $2,500.00–$3,000.00

Hinman, Wilbur. *Corporal Si Klegg and His Pard*. Ohio. Hamilton & Co. 1890. illus. red dec. cover. gilt lettering on cover. $40.00–$80.00

Hirsch, Irving. *Manufacture of Whiskey, Brandy and Cordials*. Newark. Sherman Eng' r' g co. 1937. illus. blue cloth. lettering on cover. 183 pp. $90.00–$120.00

History of Ashtabula County, Ohio . . . 1798–1878. Phila. 1878. rebacked. $200.00–$225.00

History of the Connecticut Valley in Massachusetts. Phil. 1879. 2 vols. $75.00–$90.00

History of the Ordinance of 1787 and the Old Northwest Territory. Ohio. NW Territory Celebration Comm. 1937. 1st ed. wraps. illus. blue wrps. Fed. Writer's Project.
$30.00–$50.00

Hitchcock, Henry-Russel. *Boston Architecture 1637–1954*. NY. Reinhold. (1954). 1st ed. illus. photos. maps. $20.00–$30.00

Hitchens, Robert. *Near East*. Century. 1913. 1st ed. 268 pp. plates. $60.00–$75.00

Hoagland, Edward. *Cat Man*. Bos. Houghton Mifflin. 1955. 1st ed. author's first book. dj.
$50.00–$90.00

Hobbes, Thomas. *Leviathan, or the Matter, Forme, & Power of a Common-Wealth Ecclesiasticall and Civill*. Lon. Crooke. 1651. 1st ed. folio. folding table. 396 pp. rebacked.
$9,000.00–$10,000.00

Hocker, Edward W. *Germantown 1683–1933*. Phil. By author. 1933. 1st ed. black cloth, gilt lettering on cover. $35.00–$50.00

Hodge, O. J. *Reminiscences*. Ohio. The Brooks Co. 1910. 1st ed. small red decorated cloth gold lettering on cover and spine. $25.00–$35.00

Hodgson, Fred T. *Practical Cabinet Maker, The*. Chi. Frederick J. Drake. 1910. 1st ed. illus. green cloth, black lettering on cover and spine, frontis. $25.00–$45.00

Holden, George H. *Canaries and Cage-Birds*. NY. Holden. 1888. illus. 2nd ed. chromolithographs. $350.00–$500.00

Holder, Charles Frederick. *Big Game at Sea*. Lon. 1908. 1st UK ed. $200.00–$250.00

Holder, Charles Frederick. *Ivory King, The: A Popular History of the Elephant. . . .* NY. Scribner's. 1886. 1st ed. frontis. gray cloth. $350.00–$475.00

Holland, J. G. *Nicholas Minturn*. NY. Scribner, Armstrong. 1877. 1st ed. 2 pp ads. green cloth. $50.00–$65.00

Holley, Marietta. *Samantha in Europe*. NY. Funk and Wagnalls. 1896. illus. green decorated cloth. decorated spine. $20.00–$60.00

Holling, Holling C. *Minn of the Mississippi*. Bos. Houghton Mifflin. 1951. 1st ed. illus. by Holling. Newberry Award winner. dj. $100.00–$150.00

Holling, Holling C. *Pagoo*. Bos. Houghton Mifflin. 1957. 1st ed. illus. by Holling C. Holling and Lucille Webster Holling. inscrb. dj. $200.00–$250.00

Holling, Holling C. *Tree in the Trail*. Bos. Houghton Mifflin. 1942. 1st ed. illus. by Holling. sgn. dj. $200.00–$250.00

Holmes, George, ed. *Transactions of the Institution of Naval Architects*. Lon. Henry Sotheran & Co. 1893. illus. grn. dec cover. gilt lettering on cover. fold-out plates in rear of book. $85.00–$125.00

Holmes, W. D. *Square in the Arctic Circle, A*. CT. 1960. illus. dj. $100.00–$200.00

Hood's Practical Cook's Book. C.I. Hood & Co., Mass. 1897. $15.00–$50.00

Hoover, Herbert. *Ordeal of Woodrow Wilson, The*. NY. (1958). ltd 500 cc. numbered. sgn. illus. $600.00–$700.00

Hope, Anthony. *Prisoner of Zenda, The*. New York. Grosset & Dunlap. illus. blue cloth, illus. dj. photoplay edition. $20.00–$45.00

Hope, Laura Lee. *Bobbsey Twins and The Country Fair Mystery*. NY. Grosset & Dunlap. 1960. 1st ed. pictorial cover. $10.00–$15.00

Hope, Laura Lee. *Bobbsey Twins at Big Bear Pond*. NY. Grosset & Dunlap. 1958. 1st ed. pictorial cover. $10.00–$12.00

Hope, Laura Lee. *Bobbsey Twins in a Radio Play*. Grosset & Dunlap. 1937. dj. $20.00–$30.00

Hope, Laura Lee. *Bobbsey Twins in Echo Valley*. Grosset & Dunlap. 1943. cloth. dj. $15.00–$20.00

Hope, Laura Lee. *Bobbsey Twins on an Airplane Trip, The*. NY. Grosset & Dunlap. (1933). dj. $15.00–$20.00

Hope, Laura Lee. *Six Little Bunkers at Mammy June's*. NY. Grosset & Dunlap. (1922). 1st ed. later dj. $40.00–$50.00

Horgan, Paul. *Under the Sangre De Cristo*. Santa Fe. Rydal. 1985. ltd 20 sgned and lettered cc. slipcase. $175.00–$200.00

Hornaday, W. T. *Campfires in the Canadian Rockies*. NY. 1906. 1st ed. illus. 353 pp. $200.00–$300.00

Horsford, Professor. *Horsford Cook Book, The: Containing Practical Recipes*. . . . Providence. Rumford Chemical Works. nd. wraps. 32 pp. advertising. $30.00–$40.00

Houdini, Beatrice. *Houdini*. New York. Harcourt Brace. 1928. illus. red cloth.
$15.00–$20.00

Hough, Walter. *Moki Snake Dance, The*. Santa Fe Route. 1898. 1st ed. illus. rebound with original pictorial wraps. $100.00–$150.00

How Columbus Discovered America. Lon. Bancroft. 1961. 1st ed. illus. Pop-up Book.
$150.00–$200.00

Howell, Father A.E. *Leaves From A White Father's Diary*. Lon. Catholic Book Club. 1941. wraps. illus. decorated wrps. map. $18.00–$50.00

Hoyem, Andrew. *Andrew Hoyem Picture/Poems*. San Francisco. Arion Press. 1975. 1st ed. illus. catalogue. ltd 500 cc. sgn. $100.00–$200.00

Hoyem, Andrew. *First Poet Travels to the Moon, The*. San Francisco. Arion Press. 1975. 1st ed. wraps. ltd 500 cc. sgn. $20.00–$35.00

Hubbard, L. Ron. *Dianetics: the Modern Science of Mental Health*. NY. Hermitage House. (1950). 1st ed. dj. $200.00–$250.00

Hubbard, L. Ron. *Kingslayer, The*. LA. Fantasy Publishing. 1949. 1st ed. dj.$85.00–$200.00

Hubbard. L. Ron. *Slaves of Sleep*. NY. Lancer. 1967. 1st paperback ed. wraps.
$12.00–$18.00

Hubbard, L. Ron. *Slaves of Sleep*. Chi. Shasta Pub. 1948. 1st ed. dj. $100.00–$150.00

Hudson River Day Line. New York. 1903. wraps. illus. gray wrps. pictorial paste-down on cover, 41pp. $35.00–$85.00

Hudson, W. H. *Birds of La Plata*. NY. Dutton. 1920. illus. 1st US ed. 2 vols. color plates. ltd 1500 sets. djs. $225.00–$250.00

Hughes, Langston. *Jim Crow's Last Stand*. Atlanta. Negro Publication Society. (1943). 1st ed. wraps. $175.00–$225.00

Hughes, Richard. *High Wind in Jamaica, A*. Lon. Chatto & Windus. 1929. ltd 150 cc. numbered. sgn. no dj issued. $700.00–$800.00

Humphreys, G. R. *List of Irish Birds, A*. Dublin. The Stationery Office. 1937. wraps. illus. 75 pp. green wrps. $8.00–$15.00

Hungerford, Edward. *Transport for War, 1942–1943*. NY. Dutton. 1943. 1st ed. dj.
$40.00–$60.00

Hunt, Lynne Bogue. *Our American Game Birds*. NY. Doubleday Doran. 1941. illus. dj.
$35.00–$65.00

Hunter, Beatrice Trum. *Natural Foods Cookbook, The*. NY. Simon & Schuster. 1961. 1st ed. dj. $20.00–$25.00

Hunter, Dard. *Literature of Papermaking 1890–1800*. Chilicothe. Mountain House. 1925. folio. ltd 190 cc. numbered. sgn. $2,500.00–$3,000.00

Hunter, Dard. *Papermaking Through Eighteen Centuries.* NY. Rudge. 1930. 1st ed. illus. teg. folding illustrations. dj. $200.00–$250.00

Hunter, J. A. *Tales of the African Frontier.* NY. 1954. 1st ed. illus. endpaper maps. dj.
                                                                                   $50.00–$90.00

Hunter, J. A. *White Hunter. CA.* 1986. reprint. ltd 1000 cc. numbered. slipcase.
                                                                                  $175.00–$200.00

Hunter, John D. *Memoirs of a Captivity Among the Indians of North America. . . .* Lon. Longmans. 1824. 3rd ed. frontis. rebound. $450.00–$500.00

Hurst, Fannie. *Back Street.* NY. Cosmopolitan. 1931. 1st ed. movie. dj. $200.00–$250.00

Hurston, Zora Neale. *Their Eyes Were Watching God.* Phil. Lippincott. 1937. 1st ed. dj.
                                                                             $5,000.00–$10,000.00

Huxley, Aldous. *After Many a Summer Dies the Swan.* NY. Harper. 1st US ed. dj.
                                                                                  $300.00–$400.00

Huxley, Aldous. *Brave New World.* Lon. 1932. 1st ed. deluxe. ltd 324 cc. numbered. sgn. slipcase. $4,000.00–$6,500.00

Huxley, Aldous. *Little Mexican and Other Stories.* Lon. Chatto. 1924. 1st ed. sgn. dj.
                                                                                  $200.00–$300.00

Huxley, Aldous. *Most Agreeable Vice, The.* Los Angeles. Zeitlin. 1938. 8 pp. unbound. 1st ed. 550 cc. $300.00–$400.00

Huxley, Aldous. *Words and Their Meanings.* Los Angeles. Zeitlin. (1940). ltd 100 cc. sgn. dj.
                                                                                  $500.00–$600.00

Huxley, Leonard. *Life and Letters of Sir Joseph Dalton Hooker.* Lon. Murray. 1918. 1st ed. 2 vols. blue cloth. inscrb. $700.00–$950.00

Ibsen, Henrik. *Peer Gynt, A Dramatic Poem.* Lon. Harrap. 1936. 1st ed. thus. illus and sgn by Rackham. vellum. slipcase. $1,500.00–$4,000.00

Illustrated Catalogue of United States Cartridge Company's Collection of Firearms. Lowell. U.S. Cartridge Co. 1903. wraps. illus. gray illus. cover 140 pp. $45.00–$168.00

Illustrations of Contra Costa Co., California. Sacramento. 1952. illus. facsimile reprint of 1879 ed. 54 pp. 72 plates. $50.00–$75.00

Indian School at Carlisle Barracks. DC. GPO. 1880. wraps. $75.00–$90.00

Inman, Col. Henry and Col. William F. Cody. *Great Salt Lake Trail, The.* New York. MacMillan Co. 1898. 1st ed. illus. brown illustrated cloth, full page plates by Clarke.
                                                                                   $42.00–$150.00

Irving, John. *Cider House Rules, The.* NY. Morrow. (1985). 1st ed. sgn. dj. $250.00–$300.00

Irving, John. *Hotel New Hampshire.* 1981. 1st ed. dj. $35.00–$50.00

Irving, John. *Hotel New Hampshire.* NY. Dutton. (1981). 1st ed. sgn. dj. $100.00–$200.00

Irving, John. *My Movie Business.* NY. Random House. 1999. 1st ed. sgn. dj. $45.00–$60.00

Irving, John. *150-Pound Marriage, The.* NY. Random House. (1974). 1st ed. author's 3rd book. small printing. dj. $200.00–$300.00

Irving, John. *Setting Free the Bears.* NY. Random House. (1968). dj. $900.00–$2,000.00

Irving, John. *World According to Garp, The.* NY. Dutton. 1978. 1st ed. no dj.
$50.00–$100.00

Irving, John. *World According to Garp, The.* NY. Dutton. (1978). 1st ed. dj. $300.00–$350.00

Irving, John. *World According to Garp, The.* NY. Dutton. (1978). 1st ed. dj.
$850.00–$1,200.00

Irving, Washington. *Astoria.* Phil. Carey Lea & Blanchard. 1836. 1st ed. 2 vols. red cloth binding. folding map. $450.00–$500.00

Irving, Washington. *Rip Van Winkle.* McKay. (1921). illus. by N. C. Wyeth.
$100.00–$125.00

Irving, Washington. *Tour on the Prairies, A.* Phil. 1835. $100.00–$300.00

Irving, William, J. K. Paulding, and Washington Irving. *Salmagundi.* NY. Putnam. 1860. frontis. green decorated leather. raised bands on spine. $25.00–$60.00

Irwin, Inez Haynes. *The Story of the Woman's Party.* NY. Harcourt Brace. 1921. 1st ed.
$250.00—$300.00

Irwin, Jim. *To Rule the Night: the Discovery Voyage of Astronaut Jim Irwin.* Phila/NY. Holman. (1973). presentation. inscrb. dj. $125.00–$175.00

Irwin, Will. *House that Shadows Built: the Story of Adolph Zukor.* . . . NY. Doubleday Doran. 1928. 1st ed. illus. photos. inscrb by Zukor. $400.00–$500.00

Isherwood, Christopher. *All the Con-spirators.* NY. New Directions. 1958. 1st US ed. sgn. dj.
$200.00–$250.00

Isherwood, Christopher. *Condor and the Cows.* NY. 1949. 1st ed. $40.00–$50.00

Isherwood, Christopher. *Goodbye to Berlin.* NY. Random House. 1939. 1st US ed. dj.
$500.00–$900.00

Isherwood, Christopher. *Goodbye to Berlin.* Lon. Hogarth. 1939. 1st ed. dj.
$2,500.00–$7,500.00

Isherwood, Christopher. *Intimate Journals of Charles Baudelaire, The.* Hollywood. Rodd. 1947. 1st US ed. dj. $60.00–$80.00

Isherwood, Christopher. *Prater Violet.* Lon. Methuen. 1946. 1st ed. dj. $50.00–$75.00

Ishiguro, Kazuo. *Remains of the Day, The.* NY. Knopf. 1989. 1st US ed. sgn. review copy. movie based on book. dj. $200.00–$300.00

Ishiguro, Kazuo. *Unconsoled, The.* Faber. 1995. 1st ed. dj. $45.00–$60.00

Jack the Giant Killer. NY. Blue Ribbon. 1933. illus. by Lentz. Pop-up Book.
$300.00–$800.00

Jackson, Helen Hunt. *Ramona.* Los Angeles. Limited Editions Club. 1959. ltd 1500 cc. numbered. slipcase. $80.00–$100.00

Jackson, Helen Hunt. *Ramona.* Roberts Bros. 1884. 1st ed. green cloth. $150.00–$375.00

Jackson, James R. *History of Littleton New Hampshire.* Cambridge. For the Town. 1905. 1st ed. illus. 3 vols. in green cloth. lettering on spine. $200.00–$350.00

Jackson, Joseph. *Encyclopedia of Philadelphia.* Harrisburg. National Historical Association. 1931. illus. burgundy cloth. $200.00–$300.00

Jackson, Joseph. *Iconography of Philadelphia.* Phil. Kynett. 1934. 1st ed. illus. 26 pp. blue boards. pictorial paper cover. slipcase. $30.00–$40.00

Jackson, Shirley. *Haunting of Hill House.* NY. 1959. 1st ed. dj. $100.00–$300.00

Jackson, Shirley. *Lottery, The.* 1953. Chi. stage adaptation. 1st ed. $40.00–$50.00

Jackson, Shirley. *Lottery, The.* NY. Farrar Straus. 1949. 1st ed. dj. $1,500.00–$2,000.00

Jackson, Shirley. *Lottery, The.* Lon. Gollancz. 1950. 1st UK ed. dj. $800.00–$900.00

Jackson, Shirley. *We Have Always Lived in the Castle.* NY. Viking. (1962). 1st ed. dj. $65.00–$85.00

Jacobs, William. *Jew's Reason for Believing in One God Only, The.* NY. Vale. 1848. 1st ed. original printed wraps. $600.00–$700.00

Jacques, Brian. *Castaways of the Flying Dutchman.* NY. Philomel. 2001. 1st ed. sgn. $30.00–$40.00

Jaffray, Robert. *King Arthur and the Holy Grail.* NY/Lon. Putnam's Sons. 1928. 1st ed. frontis. $50.00–$70.00

James, George Wharton. *California Romantic and Beautiful.* Bos. Page. 1914. 1st ed. illus. photos. pictorial Art Nouveau binding. $200.00–$250.00

James, George Wharton. *Indian Blankets and Their Makers.* Chi. McClurg. 1914. 1st ed. illus. 95 plates. $250.00–$300.00

James, Henry. *Ambassadors, The.* NY. 1903. 1st ed. dj. $150.00–$400.00

James, Henry. *Bostonians, The.* Lon/NY. Macmillan. (1886). 1 vol. $150.00–$250.00

James, Henry. *Bostonians, The.* Lon. 1886. 3 vols. $1,000.00–$1,800.00

James, Henry. *Daisy Miller.* Lon. Macmillan. 1879. 1st UK ed. 2 vols. $300.00–$400.00

James, Henry. *Finer Grain, The.* NY. Scribner's. 1910. 1st ed. teg. $100.00–$300.00

James, Henry. *Finer Grain.* Lon. Methuen. (1910). 1st UK ed. presentation stamp on title page. $50.00–$100.00

James, Henry. *Little Tour in France, A.* B. Osgood. 1885. 1st ed. brown cloth. $60.00–$80.00

James, Henry. *Most Unholy Trade, A.* Scarab Press. 1923. ltd 100 cc. numbered. $300.00–$350.00

James, Henry. *Washington Square.* NY. Harper. 1881. 1st ed. illus. by George Du Maurier.
$100.00–$275.00

James, P. D. *Black Tower, The.* Lon. Faber & Faber. 1975. 1st ed. dj. $100.00–$150.00

James, P. D. *Certain Justice, A.* NY. Knopf. 1997. 1st US ed. sgn. dj. $45.00–$60.00

James, P. D. *Skull Beneath the Skin, The.* NY. 1982. 1st ed. dj. $15.00–$30.00

James, P. D. *Taste for Death, A.* NY. Knopf. 1986. 1st US ed. dj. $15.00–$25.00

James, P. D. *Taste for Death.* Lon. 1986. 1st ed. sgn. dj. $75.00–$100.00

James, Walter. *Wine, a Brief Encyclopedia.* NY. Knopf. 1960. illus. pictorial dj.
$18.00–$22.00

James, Will. *Scorpion.* NY. Scribner's. 1936. 1st ed. illus. in pen-and-ink by James. color
frontis. dj. $100.00–$150.00

Jameson, Mrs. *History of Our Lord as Exemplified in Works of Art.* Lon. Longmans. 1865.
illus. 2nd ed. ½ half. morocco spine. plates. $150.00–$175.00

Jamison, James K. *By Cross and Anchor.* Paterson. St. Anthony Guild. 1946. 1st ed. illus. dark
blue cl. lettering on cover. $10.00–$40.00

Jamsheed, F. L. *Wild Tribes of the Soudan.* NY. 1883. illus. folding maps. decorative gilt
cover. $300.00–$450.00

Jeffers, Robinson. *Give Your Heart to the Hawks.* NY. Random House. 1933. ltd 200 cc. slipcase. sgn. $250.00–$325.00

Jeffers, Robinson. *Such Counsels You Gave to Me & Other Poems.* NY. Random House/Spi-
ral. (1937). ltd 300 cc. sgn. slipcase. $250.00–$300.00

Jeffries, David. *Treatise on Diamonds and Pearls,. . . .* Lon. Ackers. 1751. 2nd ed. engr plates.
$1,200.00–$2,000.00

Jehl, Francis. *Menlo Park: Reminiscences.* Dearborn. Edison Institute. 1936. 2 parts in 1 volume. 430 pp. dj. $60.00–$85.00

Jekyll, Gertrude. *Children and Gardens.* Lon. 1908. $35.00–$50.00

Jekyll, Gertrude. *Gardener's Testament.* Lon. Country Life. (1937). 1st ed. illus.
$75.00–$90.00

Jekyll, Gertrude. *Old West Surrey.* Lon. 1904. 1st ed. photos. $100.00–$150.00

Jellicoe, Viscount. *Crisis of the Naval War.* NY/Lon. 1920. illus. plates. pocket charts.
$70.00–$150.00

Jewitt, Llewellynn and S. C. Hall. *Stately Homes of England, The.* Lon. Virtue. 1874. 2 vols.
aeg. illus. $60.00–$80.00

Jin, Ha. *Waiting.* NY. Pantheon. (1999). 1st ed. National Book Award winner. dj.
$50.00–$90.00

Jocelyn, Stephen Perry. *Mostly Alkall.* Caldwell. Caxton. 1953. 1st ed. illus. photos. foldout
illustration. dj. $120.00–$130.00

John Brown's Raid. National Park Service. 1974. wraps. illus. $10.00–$20.00

Johnson, George Lindsay. *Photography in Colours.* NY. Dutton. 1917. revised ed. illus. 14 plates. green cloth. $20.00–$30.00

Johnson, Hank. *They Felled the Redwoods.* Los Angeles. Trans-Anglo Books. 1966. 1st ed. illus. photos. maps. map endpapers. dj. $75.00–$90.00

Johnson, Lionel. *Twenty-one Poems.* Maine. Mosher. 1908. ltd 950 cc. gray boards.
     $40.00–$65.00

Johnson, Lyndon Baines. *Vantage Point, The.* NY. Holt Rinehart and Winston. 1971. 1st ed. memoirs. inscrb. dj. $250.00–$300.00

Johnson, Merle. *High Spots of American Literature.* NY. Bennet. 1929. 1st ed. 3/4 blue morocco. teg ltd 700 cc. $40.00–$60.00

Johnson, Mrs. S.O. *Every Woman Her Own Flower Gardener.* Henry T. Williams. N.Y. 1871. 1st edition. $55.00–$100.00

Johnson, Stephen. *Everlasting Punishment of the Ungodly, The.* New London. Green. 1786. 1st ed. $500.00–$600.00

Johnson, T. B. *Tramps Around the Mountains of the Moon and Through the Back Gate of the Congo State.* Lon. 1908. illus. folding map. blue decorated cloth. 316 pp. $500.00–$650.00

Johnston, D. *Phrenology Exemplified and Illustrated . . . For the Year 1837.* Boston. 2nd ed.
     $200.00–$250.00

Jolly Jump-Ups Favorite Nursery Stories. McLoughlin. 1942. illus. Pop-up Book.
     $50.00–$75.00

Jonas, Dennis. *Landscape Gardener, The; Comprising the History and Principles of Tasteful Horticulture.* Lon. Ridgeway. 1835. 1st ed. green cloth. $1,000.00–$1,500.00

Jones, Archer. *Art of War in the Western World, The.* Lon. Harrop. 1988. 1st ed. illus. maps. dj. $45.00–$60.00

Jones, James. *From Here to Eternity.* NY. Scribner's. 1951. Academy Award–winning movie. dj. $650.00–$800.00

Jones, Robert Tyre. *Golf is My Game.* Garden City. Doubleday. 1960. 1st ed. illus. photos. sgn. dj. $3,000.00–$4,000.00

Jones, Tristan. *Yarns.* Bos. Sail Books. 1983. dj. $15.00–$25.00

Jones, William. *Credulities Past and Present.* Lon. Chatto and Windus. 1880. frontis.
     $60.00–$80.00

Jong, Erica. *Fear of Flying.* NY. Holt Rinehart. 1973. 1st ed. sgn.dj. $100.00–$135.00

Jong, Erica. *Fear of Flying.* NY. 1973. dj. $35.00–$45.00

Jong, Erica. *How to Save Your Own Life.* NY. Holt, Rinehart & Winston. (1977). 1st ed. dj.
     $20.00–$30.00

Joyce, James. *Chamber Music.* NY. Huebsch. 1923. $40.00–$50.00

Joyce, James. *Dubliners.* Lon. 1914. 1st ed. 740 cc. dj. $50,000.00–$80,000.00

Joyce, James. *Portrait of the Artist as a Young Man.* NY. (1948). wraps. $50.00–$75.00

Joyce, James. *Portrait of the Artist as a Young Man, A.* NY. Huebsch. 1916. 1st ed.
$1,500.00–$4,000.00

Joyce, James. *Ulysses.* NY. Random House. 1934. 1st Amer ed. dj. $4,000.00–$5,000.00

Joyce, James. *Ulysses.* NY. Limited Editions Club. 1935. illus. by Matisse. ltd 1500 cc. numbered. 250 cc sgn by Joyce and Matisse. slipcase. $20,000.00–$30,000.00

Joyce, James. *Ulysses.* Shakespeare and Company. 1922. 1st ed. ltd 1000 cc. 750 cc numbered.
½ morocco. $7,000.00–$10,000.00

Joyce, James. *Ulysses.* NY. Random House. 1934. 1st Amer ed. sgn. dj.
$13,000.00–$14,000.00

Jung, Carl. *Contributions to Analytical Psychology.* Harcourt. 1928. 1st US ed.
$60.00–$75.00

Kabat-Zinn, Jon. *Coming to Our Senses, Healing ourselves and the world through mindfulness.*
NY. Hyperion. (2005). First Edition. dj. $10.00–$20.00s

Kael, Pauline. *Going Steady.* Bos. Little Brown. (1970). sgn and dated by author.
$90.00–$200.00

Kael, Pauline. *Reeling.* Bos. Little Brown. (1976). inscrb. dj. $200.00–$250.00

Kafka, Franz. *Great Wall of China, The.* Lon. Secker. 1933. 1st English language ed. dj.
$375.00–$475.00

Kafka, Franz. *Metamorphosis, The.* NY. Vanguard. 1946. 1st US ed. dj.
$500.00–$1,500.00

Kafka, Franz. *Metamorphosis, The.* Lon. Parton 1937. 1st English ed. $2,000.00–$5,000.00

Kahn, David. *Hitler's Spies. German Military Intelligence in World War II.* NY. Macmillan.
(1978). 1st ed. illus. photos. maps. dj. $20.00–$30.00

Kaiser, Charles. *Gay Metropolis 1940–1996, The.* Bos/NY. Houghton Mifflin. 1997. 1st ed. dj.
$40.00–$50.00

Kane, Elisha Kent. *Arctic Explorations: The Second Grinnell Expedition in Search of Sir John Franklin. . . .* Phil. Childs & Peterson. 1856. 1st ed. illus. 2 vols. plates. maps.
$800.00–$1,000.00

Karch, R. Randolph. *Printing and the Allied Trades.* New York. Pitman. 1939. illus. blue
cloth. $8.00–$20.00

Kayser, C. *Physiology of Natural Hibernation.* NY. 1961. $50.00–$75.00

Kearton, Cherry. *In the Land of the Lion.* New York. National Travel Club. 1929. illus.
black cloth red lettering on cover. $5.00–$12.00

Keate, George. *Account of the Pelew Islands. . . .* Phil. Crukshank. 1789. 1st US ed.
$700.00–$850.00

Keeler, James Edward. *Publications of the Lick Observatory . . . Vol VIII: Nebulae and Clusters. . . .* Sacramento. Univ of California. 1908. illus. black cloth. gilt decoration.
$1,900.00–$2,200.00

Keene, Carolyn. *Bungalow Mystery, The.* NY. Grosset & Dunlap. 1930. 1st ed. Nancy Drew #3. blue cloth. dj.
$60.00–$75.00

Keene, Carolyn. *By the Light of the Study Lamp.* NY. Grosset & Dunlap. 1934. Dana Girls. later printing green cloth. illus frontis. dj.
$20.00–$25.00

Keene, Carolyn. *Circle of Footprints.* NY. Grosset & Dunlap. 1937. 1st ed. Dana Girls #6. dj.
$200.00–$300.00

Keene, Carolyn. *Clue in the Old Album, The.* NY. Grosset & Dunlap. 1947. Nancy Drew. blue cloth. dw.
$15.00–$20.00

Keene, Carolyn. *Clue in the Old Stagecoach, The.* NY. Grosset & Dunlap. 1960. 1st ed. Nancy Drew #47.
$75.00–$100.00

Keene, Carolyn. *Clue of the Black Keys.* Grosset & Dunlap. 1951. 1st ed. Nancy Drew series. dj.
$30.00–$40.00

Keene, Carolyn. *Secret at Lone Tree Cottage, The.* Lon. Sampson Low. 1934. 1st ed. Dana Girls series.
$15.00–$25.00

Keene, Carolyn. *Secret at Lone Tree Cottage, The.* NY. Grosset & Dunlap. 1934. Dana Girls series. dj.
$7.00–$10.00

Keene, Carolyn. *Secret of the Old Clock.* NY. Grosset & Dunlap. 1959. Nancy Drew #1. dj.
$40.00–$50.00

Keene, Carolyn. *Secret of the Old Clock.* NY. Grosset & Dunlap. 1959. Nancy Drew #1. dj. later printings.
$12.00–$40.00

Keene, Carolyn. *Secret of the Wooden Lady.* Grosset & Dunlap. 1950. 1st ed. Nancy Drew series. dj.
$30.00–$40.00

Keene, Carolyn. *Three Cornered Mystery.* NY. Grosset & Dunlap. 1935. Dana Girls. dj.
$20.00–$30.00

Keene, Carolyn. *Witch Tree Symbol.* NY. Grosset & Dunlap. 1955. Nancy Drew #33.
$10.00–$15.00

Keillor, Garrison. *Leaving Home.* NY. Viking. 1987. 1st ed. ltd 1500 cc. numbered and sgn. green cloth. slipcase.
$30.00–$40.00

Keillor, Garrison. *Old Man Who Loved Cheese, The.* Bos. Little Brown. 1996. 1st ed. illus. sgn. dj.
$30.00–$40.00

Keller, Helen. *Our Duties to the Blind.* Bos. 1904. 1st ed. wraps. author's first book.
$75.00–$125.00

Keller, Helen. *Out of the Dark.* Garden City. 1913. 1st ed. dj. $750.00–$800.00

Keller, Helen. *Story of My Life.* NY. Doubleday. 1902. 1st ed. 441 pp. $35.00–$50.00

Kellerman, Jonathan. *Butcher's Theater.* NY. Bantam. 1988. 1st ed. dj. $18.00–$35.00

Kellerman, Jonathan. *Time Bomb.* NY. Bantam. 1990. 1st ed. dj. $25.00–$35.00

Kellog, Vernon. *Nuova the New Bee.* NY. (1920). illus. by Milo Winter. scarce dj.
$25.00–$40.00

Kelly, Charles. *Outlaw Trail.* NY. 1959. $25.00–$35.00

Kelly, Charles. *Outlaw Trail: a History of Butch Cassidy. . . .* Salt Lake City. printed by author. 1938. 1st ed. illus. 500 cc. photos. plates. brown cloth. gilt lettering. $300.00–$600.00

Kelly, Emmett. *Clown.* NY. Prentice Hall. 1953. 1st ed. wraps. $40.00–$100.00

Kelly, Fanny. *Narrative of My Captivity Among the Sioux Indians.* Hartford. 1871. 1st ed. illus.
$100.00–$125.00

Kelly, H. *Medical Gynecology.* NY/Lon. 1908. 1st ed. illus. $50.00–$200.00

Kelly, L. V. *Range of Men; the Story of the Ranchers and Indians of Alberta.* Tor. Briggs. 1913. 1st ed. illus. frontis. teg. $350.00–$700.00

Kelly, Robert. *Cruise of the Pnyx.* Barrytown. 1979. 1st ed. wraps. $25.00–$35.00

Kelly, Robert. *Cruise of the Pnyx.* Barrytown. 1979. 1st ed. wraps. inscrb. $60.00–$75.00

Kelly, Walt. *Incompleat Pogo.* NY. Simon & Schuster. 1954. 1st ed. wraps. $30.00–$35.00

Kelly, Walt. *Pogo Peek-a-Book.* NY. Simon & Schuster. 1955. 1st ed. wraps. $45.00–$65.00

Kelly, Walt. *Songs of the Pogo.* NY. Simon & Schuster. 1956. 1st ed. illus. dj. $30.00–$50.00

Kelly, Walt. *Uncle Pogo So-So Stories.* NY. Simon & Schuster. 1977. dj. $25.00–$35.00

Kelly, Walt. *Uncle Pogo So-So Stories.* NY. Simon & Schuster. 1953. wraps. $50.00–$70.00

Kelly's Hand Forged Bits and Spurs. El Paso. Kelly Bros Mfg. nd. wraps. catalogue.
$70.00–$100.00

Kelso, Isaac. *Stars and Bars or The Reign of Terror in Missouri.* Bos. 1863. 1st ed.
$75.00–$90.00

Kemelman, Harry. *Friday the Rabbi Slept Late.* NY. Crown. (1964). 1st ed. dj.
$30.00–$60.00

Kemelman, Harry. *Nine Mile Walk.* NY. Putnam. 1967. 1st ed. dj. $30.00–$60.00

Kemelman, Harry. *Nine Mile Walk.* NY. Penguin. 1971. paperback. good condition.
$5.00–$8.00

Kemelman, Harry. *One Fine Day the Rabbi Bought a Cross.* NY. William Morrow. 1987. 1st ed. dj. $10.00–$20.00

Kemelman, Harry. *Saturday the Rabbi Stayed Home.* NY. 1969. 1st ed. dj. $8.00–$15.00

Kemelman, Harry. *Saturday the Rabbi Went Hungry.* NY. Crown. 1966. Book Club ed. dj.
$9.00–$15.00

Kempis, Thomas. *Christian Pattern, The; or The Imitation of Jesus Christ. . . .* Germantown. Sowr. 1749. 1st American printing. $5,000.00–$6,000.00

Kendall, J. B. *Treatise on the Horse and His Diseases.* VT. 1891. $40.00–$60.00

Kendrick, Herbert. *Barnum: The Mahomet of Humbug.* Liverpool. Marples. 1933. wraps. 25 pp. 1st ed. presentation copy. inscrb. $50.00–$90.00

Keneally, Thomas. *Family Madness, A.* NY. Simon & Schuster. 1986. 1st ed. sgn. dj. $40.00–$55.00

Keneally, Thomas. *Office of Innocence, The.* Hodder & Stoughton. 2002. 1st ed. sgn. dj. $60.00–$75.00

Keneally, Thomas. *Schindler's List.* Lon. Hodder and Stoughton. (1982). 1st ed. sgn. $200.00–$400.00

Keneally, Thomas. *To Asmara.* NY. Warner. 1989. 1st ed. sgn. dj. $40.00–$55.00

Kennan, George. *Siberia and the Exile System.* NY. Century. 1891. 1st ed. 2 vols. illus. maps. woodcuts. 409 pp. 575 pp. $200.00–$250.00

Kennan, George. *Tent Life in Siberia.* NY. Putnam. 1870. 1st ed. $80.00–$110.00

Kennedy, Edward. *Our Day and Generation.* NY. Simon & Schuster. 1979. 1st ed. dj. $15.00–$30.00

Kennedy, John. *History of Steam Navigation.* Liverpool. 1903. illus. $130.00–$140.00

Kennedy, John F. *Profiles in Courage.* NY. Harper & Bros. (1956). 1st ed. dj. $90.00–$600.00

Kennedy, John F. *Profiles in Courage.* NY. Harper & Bros. (1956). 1st ed. slipcase. presentation. sgn. $10,000.00–$12,000.00

Kennedy, John F. *Profiles in Courage.* NY. Harper & Bros. (1956). 1st ed. illus. sgn. dj. $2,500.00–$6,000.00

Kennedy, Joseph P. *I'm for Roosevelt.* NY. Reynal & Hitchcock. (1936). 1st ed. green cloth. dj. $120.00–$160.00

Kennedy, Michael S. (ed.). *Red Man's West. . . .* NY. Hastings House. 1965. 1st ed. illus. ltd 199 cc. buckskin with silk screen Indian Shield on cover. $25.00–$50.00

Kennedy, Robert F. *To Seek a Newer World.* Garden City. Doubleday. 1967. 1st ed. sgn. dj. $900.00–$1,000.00

Kennedy, Sen. John F. *Strategy of Peace.* NY. 1960. 1st ed. inscrb. sgn. dj. $2,000.00–$2,500.00

Kennedy, Sen. John F. *Strategy of Peace.* NY. 1960. 1st ed. dj. $200.00–$300.00

Kennedy, William. *Quinn's Book.* NY. Viking. (1988). 1st ed. illus. inscrb. dj. $50.00–$75.00

Kennell, Frances. *Folk Medicine: Fact and fiction.* NY. Crescent Books. 1976. dj. $12.00–$18.00

Kenrick, William. *American Silk Grower's Guide.* Bos. 1839. 2nd ed. illus. $60.00–$100.00

Kent, Alexander. *Inshore Squadron.* NY. Putnam. 1979. 1st Amer ed. dj. $40.00–$50.00

Kent, Rockwell. *Northern Christmas.* NY. 1941. 1st ed. dj. · $50.00–$90.00

Kent, Rockwell. *Salomina.* NY. 1935. 1st ed. dj. $100.00–$150.00

Kent, Rockwell. *Seven Ages of Man, The.* NY. 1918. 1st ed. $250.00–$350.00

Kent, Rockwell. *This is My Own.* NY. Duell, Sloan & Pearce. (1940). 1st ed. inscrb. dj.
$125.00–$225.00

Kent, Rockwell. *This is My Own.* NY. Duell, Sloan & Pearce. (1940). 1st ed. dj.
$65.00–$100.00

Kent, Rockwell. *Voyaging Southward from the Straits of Magellan.* NY. 1924. 1st ed. blue
buckram. dj. $500.00–$600.00

Kepes, Gyorgy. *Art in Science.* Simon & Schuster. 1954. illus. plates. boxed. $40.00–$70.00

Kephart, Horace. *Our Southern Highlanders.* NY. Macmillan. 1929. illus. red cloth. lettering
on cover and spine. $25.00–$40.00

Kerouac, Jack. *Desolation Angels.* NY. Coward, McCann. 1965. 1st ed. dj.
$300.00–$400.00

Kerouac, Jack. *Doctor Sax/Faust Part Three.* NY. Grove. (1959). 1st ed. ltd 26 lettered cc. sgn.
original clear jacket. $5,000.00–$7,000.00

Kerouac, Jack. *Lonesome Traveler.* McGraw-Hill. 1960. illus. dj. $150.00–$200.00

Kerouac, Jack. *On the Road.* NY. Viking. 1957. 1st ed. 1st printing. dj. $3,500.00–$4,500.00

Kerouac, Jack. *Satori in Paris.* NY. Grove. (1966). 1st ed. dj. $250.00–$350.00

Kerouac, Jack. *Subterraneans, The.* NY. Grove. (1958). 1st ed. deluxe. ltd 100 numbered and
sgn cc. gray boards. original glassine jacket. $4,000.00–$5,000.00

Kerouac, Jack. *Visions of Cody.* NY. McGraw-Hill. (1972). 1st ed. pictorial dj.
$80.00–$100.00

Kerr, Walter. *Tragedy and Comedy.* NY. Simon and Schuster. (1967). 1st ed. dj.
$15.00–$25.00

Kesey, Ken. *One Flew Over the Cuckoo's Nest.* NY. 1962. 1st ed. author's first book. dj.
$6,000.00–$8,000.00

Kesey, Ken. *Sometimes A Great Notion.* NY. Viking. (1964). 1st ed. with logo on half-title
page. dj. $500.00–$600.00

Keynes, John Maynard. *Economic Consequences of the Peace.* Lon. 1919. 1st ed. dj.
$800.00–$1,000.00

Keynes, John Maynard. *Economic Consequences of the Peace.* Lon. 1919. 1st ed. dj missing.
$150.00–$200.00

Keynes, John Maynard. *Treatise on Money, A.* NY. (1930). 2 vols. $500.00–$800.00

Keynes, John Maynard. *Treatise on Money, A.* Lon. 1930. 1st ed. 2 vols. green cloth.
$1,000.00–$1,200.00

Khayyam, Omar (trans by Edward Fitzgerald). *Rubaiyat of Omar Khayyam*. Phil. McKay. (1942). 1st ed. illus. by Willy Pogany. morocco. $400.00–$500.00

Kilbourn, John. *Ohio Gazeteer, or Topographical Dictionary*. Columbus. 1816.
$3,500.00–$4,500.00

Kilmer, Joyce. *Summer of Love*. NY. 1911. 1st ed. teg. points. author's first book.
$450.00–$550.00

Kilmer, Joyce. *Trees and Other Poems*. NY. (1914). 1st ed. teg. tan boards. $200.00–$300.00

Kincaid, Jamaica. *Autobiography of My Mother, The*. NY. Farrar, Straus and Giroux. 1996. 1st ed. sgn. dj. $50.00–$75.00

Kincaid, Jamaica. *Autobiography of My Mother, The*. NY. Farrar, Straus and Giroux. 1996. 1st ed. dj. $20.00–$30.00

Kincaid, Jamaica. *Lucy*. NY. Farrar Straus & Giroux. 1990. 1st ed. dj. $20.00–$30.00

Kincaid, Jamaica. *Small Place, A*. NY. Farrar, Straus and Giroux. 1988. 1st ed. green cloth. dj. $40.00–$60.00

Kincaid, Jamaica. *Small Place, A*. NY. Farrar, Straus and Giroux. 1988. 1st ed. green cloth. sgn. dj. $75.00–$90.00

Kincaid, Zoe. *Kabuki, The Popular Stage of Japan*. Lon. Macmillan. 1925. 1st ed. illus. color frontis. dj. $200.00–$250.00

King, Laurie. *The Beekeeper's Apprentice*. St. Martin's. 1994. 1st ed. author's second book, based on the character of Sherlock Holmes in retirement. dj. $150.00–$200.00

King, Laurie. *The Beekeeper's Apprentice*. St. Martin's. 1994. 1st ed. author's second book, based on the character of Sherlock Holmes in retirement. sgn. dj. $300.00–$450.00

King, Stephen. *Carrie*. Garden City. Doubleday. 1974. 1st ed. author's first book. dj.
$2,500.00–$7,500.00

King, Stephen. *Dark Tower, The Gunslinger*. West Kingston. Grant. 1982. 1st ed. sgn.
$1,000.00–$1,200.00

King, Stephen. *Dark Tower, The Gunslinger*. NY. New American. 1982. wraps.
$25.00–$30.00

King, Stephen. *Shining, The*. Garden City. Doubleday. 1977. 1st ed. dj. $500.00–$800.00

King, Stephen. *Stand, The*. Garden City. Doubleday. 1978. 1st ed. dj. good condition.
$500.00–$800.00

Kingsolver, Barbara. *Bean Trees, The*. NY. Harper. 1988. 1st ed. author's first book. dj.
$100.00–$200.00

Kingsolver, Barbara. *High Tide in Tucson*. NY. Harper. (1995). 1st ed. illus. dj.
$30.00–$40.00

Kingsolver, Barbara. *Pigs in Heaven*. NY. Harper. (1993). 1st ed. dj. $20.00–$30.00

Kinkle, Roger D. *Complete Encyclopedia of Popular Music and Jazz 1900–1950*. CT. Arlington House. 1974. 1st ed. 4 vols. djs. $175.00–$200.00

Kinnell, Galway. *Black Light*. Bos. Houghton Mifflin. 1966. review copy. dj. review slip laid in. $60.00–$90.00

Kinsella, W. P. *Shoeless Joe*. Bos. Houghton Mifflin. 1982. 1st ed. dj. $200.00–$400.00

Kipling, Rudyard. *American Notes*. Brown & Company Boston. 1899. $20.00–$45.00

Kipling, Rudyard. *Captains Courageous*. NY. Century. 1897. 1st US ed. green cloth. teg.
                                                                          $250.00–$750.00

Kipling, Rudyard. *The Jungle Book* and *The Second Jungle Book*. 1894 and 1895. 1st ed. sgn.
                                                                      $2,000.00–$2,500.00

Kipling, Rudyard. *Just So Stories*. Lon. 1902. 1st ed. $400.00–$750.00

Kipling, Rudyard. *Kim*. Lon. Macmillan. 1901. 1st ed. illus with plates by J. Lockwood Kipling. red cloth. $200.00–$500.00

Kipling, Rudyard. *Puck of Pook's Hill*. NY. Doubleday Page. 1906. 1st ed. illus. green dec. cloth. color plates by Arthur Rackham. $250.00–$300.00

Kipling, Rudyard. *Sea and Sussex From Rudyard Kipling's Verse*. Garden City. Doubleday Page. 1926. color plates. $500.00–$600.00

Kipling, Rudyard. *The Light That Failed*. Doubleday & McClure Co. NY. 1899.
                                                                           $20.00–$35.00

Kipling, Rudyard. *They*. Lon. Macmillan. 1905. 1st separate ed. illus by Townsend. white cloth with gilt vignette. illus. color plates. $200.00–$350.00

Kipling, Rudyard. *Traffics and Discoveries*. Lon. Macmillan. 1904. 1st ed. of this collection. red cloth. points. $80.00–$90.00

Kirby, William and William Spence. *Introduction to Entomology, An*. Lon. Longman. 1828. 5th ed. 4 vols. raised bands. marbled endpapers. $500.00–$700.00

Kirke, Edmund. *Among the Pines*. NY. Gilmore. 1862. 1st ed. $45.00–$55.00

Kirkup, James. *Paper Windows*. Poems from Japan. Lon. Dent. 1968. 1st ed. dj.
                                                                           $15.00–$20.00

Kissinger, Henry. *Years of Upheaval*. Bos. Little Brown. 1982. 1st ed. ltd 1500 cc. numbered. sgn. slipcase. $250.00–$400.00

Knight, John Alden. *Field Book of Fresh-Water Angling*. NY. G.P. Putnam. 1944. illus. small, narrow blue cloth binding. $15.00–$30.00

Koehler, O. *Ku Winda (To Hunt)*. San Antonio. private printing. 1956. illus. photographic endpapers. Kenya and Tanzania. 99 pp. imitation snake binding. $150.00–$225.00

Kornbluth, C. M. *Mile Beyond the Moon, A*. NY. MacFadden. 1962. wraps. 1st paperback ed.
                                                                           $12.00–$18.00

Kosinski, Jerzy. *Being There*. NY. Harcourt Brace. 1970. 1st ed. dj. $30.00–$45.00

A copy of *Puck of Pook's Hill*, N.Y.: Doubleday Page, 1905, illustrated by Rackham; *Live Boys, or Charlie and Nasho in Texas,*by Arthur Morecamp, Boston: Lee & Shepard, 1879, first edition. Difficult to find, the book was written by Thomas Pilgrim under a pseudonym and is one of the earliest to mention "cowboys"; *The Poor White or The Rebel Conscript*, Boston: Graves & Young, 1864, first edition, a Civil War novel.
Digital photography by Jonathan Draudt, Tamarac Arts.

Kosinski, Jerzy. *Steps.* NY. Random House. (1968). 1st ed. National Book Award winner. dj.
$175.00–$250.00

Kourier *The Magazine of Americanism.* Vol. 5 #1. Knights of the KKK. Atlanta, Ga. 1928.
$18.00–$25.00

Kraus-Boelte, Maria. *The Kindergarten Guide.* New York. E. Steiger & Co. 1906. illus. 2 vols. brown cl. gilt lettering.
$75.00–$125.00

Krauss, Ruth. *How To Make An Earthquake.* Harper & Bros. N.Y. 1954. $20.00–$50.00

Kreipe, Werner et al. *Fatal Decisions.* Lon. Joseph. 1956. dj. $20.00–$45.00

Kuralt, Charles. *Southerners.* AL. Oxmoor. 1986. 1st ed. illus. folio. illus. buckram. pictorial dj.
$20.00–$30.00

Kurutz, Gary F. *California Gold Rush, The: A Descriptive Bibliography.* . . . SF. Book Club of California. 1997. 1st ed. ltd 1000 cc. dj. $200.00–$275.00

La Farge, Oliver. *As Long As the Grass Shall Grow.* NY & Toronto. Alliance Book Corp. 1940. 1st ed. tan cloth, brn. lettering. pres. signed. $100.00–$200.00

La Fontaine, Jean de. *Fables of La Fontaine.* NY. Viking. 1954. ltd 400 cc.
$200.00–$300.00

La Gallienne, Richard. *Romance of Perfume.* NY. 1928. 1st ed. illus. by Barbier. color plates, Richard Hudnut brochure in rear pocket. dj. $60.00–$90.00

La Vogue The Standard of Style. Cleveland. 1911. 1st ed. wraps. illus. small color illus. cover.
$10.00–$20.00

Laboyteaux, W. H. *Handbook for Masters.* New York. American Steamship Owners. 1919.
black cloth, fold-out plan. $7.00–$20.00

LaBranche, George. *Salmon and the Dry Fly.* Bos. Houghton. 1924. ltd. $150.00–$200.00

Lamb, Dana. *On Trout Streams and Salmon Rivers.* Massachusetts. 1963. 1st ed. ltd 1500 cc.
$100.00–$400.00

Lamb, Dana. *On Trout Streams and Salmon Rivers.* Meadow Run. 1996. no dj issued.
$40.00–$80.00

L' Amour, Louis. *Fair Blows the Wind.* NY. Dutton. 1978. 1st ed. dj. $70.00–$150.00

L' Amour, Louis. *Jubal Sackett.* NY. Bantam. (1985). 1st ed. dj. $30.00–$40.00

L' Amour, Louis. *Law of the Desert Born.* NY. Carroll & Graf. 1983. reprint. dj.
$20.00–$25.00

L' Amour, Louis. *Outlaws of Mesquite, The.* NY. Bantam. (1990). 1st ed. dj. $25.00–$35.00

L' Amour, Louis. *Rivers West.* NY. Dutton. 1975. 1st ed. dj. $100.00–$250.00

L' Amour, Louis. *Sackett's Land.* NY. Dutton. 1974. 1st ed. dj. $80.00–$100.00

Landstrom, Bjorn. *Bold Voyages and Great Explorers.* NY. Doubleday. 1964. illus. maps. cj.
$30.00–$40.00

Lane, Mark. *Rush to Judgement.* NY. Holt Rinehart. 1966. 1st ed. dj. $69.00–$80.00

Lardner, Dionysius and Henry Kater. *Treatise on Mechanics, A.* Phil. 1831. 1st US ed. illus.
plates. $400.00–$500.00

Lathrop, Elise. *Historic Homes of Early America.* NY. Tudor. 1937. photos. dj.
$100.00–$130.00

Laumer, Keith. *Retief to the Rescue.* NY. Timescape. 1983. 1st ed. dj. $30.00–$45.00

Laumer, Keith. *Star Colony.* NY. St. Martins. 1981. 1st ed. dj. $20.00–$35.00

Laverty, Maura. *Cookery Book.* Lon. Longmans, Green. (1948). 1st ed. $40.00–$50.00

Lavigne, Frank C. *Crimes, Criminals and Detectives.* Helena. State Publishing. (1921). 1st ed.
wraps. frontis. $500.00–$800.00

Lawrence, D. H. *Aaron's Rod.* NY. Seltzer. 1922. dj. $100.00–$200.00

Lawrence, D. H. *Lady Chatterley's Lover.* NY. Knopf. 1932. 1st US ed. orange cloth. dj.
$130.00–$150.00

Lawrence, D. H. *Lady Chatterley's Lover.* NY. Grove. 1959. Unexpurgated version. dj.
$150.00–$200.00

Lawrence, D. H. *Lady Chatterley's Lover.* Florence. Private Printing. 1928.
$100.00–$200.00

Lawrence, D. H. *Nettles*. Lon. Faber. (1930). 1st ed. wraps. $20.00–$30.00

Lawrence, D. H. *Pansies*. Lon. Secker. (1929). ltd 2600 cc. $50.00–$60.00

Lawrence, D. H. *Virgin and the Gypsy, The*. Lon. Secker. (1930). 1st trade ed. dj.
$80.00–$90.00

Lawrence, John. *Slavery Question, The*. Dayton. United Brethren in Christ. 1854. 1st ed.
brown cloth. blindstamped. 224 pp. $250.00–$350.00

Lawrence, T. E. *Oriental Assembly*. Lon. Williams and Norgate. (1939). 1st ed. brown cloth.
291 pp. dj. $60.00–$75.00

Lawrence, T. E. *Secret Despatches from Arabia*. Lon. Golden Cockerel Press. (1939). 1st ed.
ltd 1000 cc. 173 pp. ¼ morocco. teg. slipcase. $700.00–$800.00

Lawson, Marie A. *Dragon John*. NY. Viking. 1943. 1st ed. dj. $40.00–$55.00

Lawson, Robert. *Ben and Me*. Bos. Little Brown. 1944. dj. $50.00–$60.00

Lawson, Robert. *Rabbit Hill*. NY. 1944. 1st ed. $45.00–$100.00

Lawton, Harry. *Willie Boy: A Desert Manhunt*. CA. Paisano Press. (1960). 1st ed. plates. photos. illustrations. endpaper map. pictorial dj. $50.00–$75.00

Lawton, Herbert A. *Historic Newport*. RI. Chamber of Commerce. 1933. wraps. 61 pp.
plates. photos. $15.00–$25.00

Lay, Shawn (ed.). *Invisible Empire in the West, The*. Urbana. Univ of Illinois Press. 1992. dj.
$15.00–$20.00

Layard, Austen Henry. *Discoveries in the Ruins of Nineveh and Babylon. . . .* Lon. John Murray. 1853. illus. plates. folding maps. ½ morocco. marbled boards. teg. $300.00–$350.00

Layard, Austen Henry. *Nineveh and Its Remains*. Lon. John Murray. 1849. illus. 2 vols.
plates. maps. ½ morocco. teg. $300.00–$350.00

Layton, Jean (trans.). *Medieval Costume, Armour and Weapons (1350–1450)*. Lon. Hamlyn.
1962. 2nd printing. dj. $100.00–$130.00

Le Blanc, Maurice. *From Midnight to Morning*. Macaulay. 1933. 1st ed. dj. $75.00–$100.00

Le Blond, Mrs. Aubrey. *True Tales of Mountain Adventure*. NY. Dutton. 1903. illus. 1st US
ed. blue cloth. teg. $75.00–$90.00

Le Carré, John. *Call for the Dead*. NY. Walker. 1962. 1st US ed. author's first book. sgn.
$900.00–$1,500.00

Le Carré, John. *Looking-Glass War, The*. Lon. Heinemann. (1965). sgn. dj.
$400.00–$600.00

Le Carré, John. *Perfect Spy, A*. NY. Knopf. 1986. 1st US ed. sgn. dj. $50.00–$150.00

Le Carré, John. *Russia House*. NY. Knopf. 1989. 1st ed. dj. $15.00–$18.00

Le Carré, John. *Smiley's People*. Lon. Hodder & Stoughton. 1979. 1st ed. dj. $75.00–$300.00

Le Carré, John. *Tinker, Tailor, Soldier, Spy*. Lon. 1974. 1st UK ed. dj. $40.00–$50.00

Le Fanu, Sheridan. *In a Glass Darkly*. Lon. Davies. 1929. orange cloth. dj. first collectin thus.
$300.00–$400.00

Le Guin, Ursula. *Dispossessed*. NY. (1974). 1st ed. dj. $50.00–$60.00

Le Guin, Ursula K. *Fisherman of the Inland Sea, A*. NY. Harper. (1944). 1st ed. advanced reading copy. blue cloth. $30.00–$40.00

Le Guin, Ursula K. *Fisherman on the Inland Sea, A*. NY. HarperPrism. 1994. ltd 1500 cc.
$50.00–$100.00

Le Guin, Ursula. *Lathe of Heaven*. Lon. 1972. 1st UK ed. dj. $30.00–$85.00

Le Guin, Ursula K. *Malafrena*. NY. Putnam. 1979. 1st ed. dj. $30.00–$45.00

Le May, Curtis. *Mission with Le May: My Story*. NY. 1965. photos. $15.00–$25.00

Le Queux, William. *On the Polar Star in the Arctic Sea*. Lon. Hutchinson & Co. 1903. 1st ed. illus. 2 volumes, green decorated cloth lettering on spine, 16 full page photogravure plates, 2 panoramas. $250.00–$400.00

Lea, Elizabeth. *Domestic Cookery*. Balt. 1878. $75.00–$90.00

Lea, Tom. *King Ranch*. Little Brown. (1957). 2 vols. 1st ed. $75.00–$100.00

Leaf, Munro. *Story of Ferdinand*. Lon. Hamish Hamilton. (1937). illus. by Robert Lawson. 1st UK ed. $40.00–$60.00

Leakey, M. D. *Excavation of Burial Mounds in Ngorongoro Crater*. Dar es Salaam. reprint. blue wraps. sgn. $30.00–$45.00

Least Heat-Moon, William. *Prairy Erth*. Bos. Houghton Mifflin. 1991. 1st ed. sgn. dj.
$50.00–$100.00

Least Heat-Moon, William. *Prairy Erth*. Bos. Houghton Mifflin. 1991. 1st ed. dj.
$30.00–$50.00

LeBlond, Mrs. Aubrey. *True Tales of Mountain Adventure*. NY. Dutton. 1903. illus. 1st Amer ed. teg. $50.00–$100.00

Lecture on Palestine and Scripture History. NY. wraps. broadside for lecture by Mr. Holt. good plus. $45.00–$65.00

Ledger, Edmund. *Sun: Its Planets and Their Satellites*. Lon. Edward Stanford. 1881. illus. 3 Woodburytypes. 1 color lithograph. wood engravings in text. $125.00–$175.00

Lee, Art. *Fishing Dry Flies for Trout on Rivers and Streams*. NY. 1982. 1st ed. $30.00–$50.00

Lee, Irving H. *Negro Medal of Honor Men*. NY. Dodd Mead. (1969). dj. $20.00–$45.00

Lee, Harper. *To Kill a Mockingbird*. Lippincott. 1960. rebound. inscrb.
$10,000.00–$12,000.00

Lee, Harper. *To Kill a Mockingbird*. Lippincott. 1960. near fine, inscrb.
$20,000.00–$28,000.00

Lee, Robert. *Clinical Midwifery*. Phil. 1849. 1st ed. $125.00–$150.00

Lee, William F. *Stan Kenton*. CA. Creative Press. 1980. 1st ed. illus. photos. dj.
$80.00–$100.00

Lees, Willis T. *Stories in Stone*. NY. Chatauqua Press. 1927. illus. photos. dj. $40.00–$50.00

Leeson, F. *Identification of Snakes of the Gold Coast*. Lon. 1950. illus. $50.00–$75.00

Leffingwell, William Bruce. *Shooting on Upland Marsh and Stream*. Rand McNally. 1895. 1st ed. slipcase. $165.00–$225.00

Leffingwell, William Bruce. *Wild Fowl Shooting*. Rand McNally. 1890. 1st ed.
$75.00–$100.00

Legends of Shasta Spring of California. SF. nd. 1st ed. wraps. $50.00–$75.00

Leger, Jacques Nicholas. *Haiti. Her History and Her Detractors*. NY/DC. 1907. 1st ed.
$100.00–$150.00

Leiber, Fritz. *Bazaar of the Bizarre*. Kingston. 1st ed. ltd 1300 cc. $20.00–$30.00

Leiber, Fritz. *Heroes and Horrors*. Whispers Press. 1978. 1st ed. dj. $25.00–$35.00

Leiber, Fritz. *Two Sought Adventure*. NY. Gnome. 1957. 1st ed. 1st binding. dj.
$45.00–$50.00

Leibovitch, J. *Ancient Egypt*. Cairo. 1938. 1st ed. wraps. illus. $30.00–$50.00

Leighton, Clare. *Country Matters*. NY. Macmillan Co. 1937. 1st ed. illus. by Clare Leighton, maroon oversize cloth. $20.00–$50.00

Leighton, Clare. *Four Hedges*. NY. 1935. illus. sgn. dj. $75.00–$100.00

Leighton, Clare. *Growing New Roots: an Essay with Fourteen Wood Engravings*. Book Club of California. 1979. ltd 500 cc. sgn. $50.00–$90.00

Leighton, Clare. *Where Land Meets Sea*. NY. (1954). illus. dj. $20.00–$30.00

L' Engle, Madeleine. *Dance in the Desert*. Farrar Straus. (1969). 1st ed. sgn. dj.
$50.00–$75.00

L' Engle, Madeleine. *Ladder of Angels*. Seabury. 1970. 1st ed. illus. dj. $25.00–$35.00

L' Engle, Madeleine. *Wrinkle in Time, A*. NY. (1962). $45.00–$65.00

L' Engle, Madeleine. *Wrinkle in Time, A*. Ariel. (1962). 1st ed. sgn. dj. $75.00–$125.00

Lennon, John. *In His Own Write*. Lon. 1964. 1st ed. $60.00–$75.00

Lennon, John. *Spaniard in the Works*. Lon. 1965. $85.00–$90.00

Lenski, Lois. *Blue Ridge Billy*. Phil. Lippincott. (1946). illus. by Lenski. dj. $75.00–$100.00

Lenski, Lois. *Blue Ridge Billy*. Phil. Lippincott. (1946). illus. by Lenski. no dj.
$20.00–$35.00

Lenski, Lois (illus). *Blue Ridge Billy*. NY. Dell. 1975. paperback. $15.00–$20.00

Lenski, Lois. *Cowboy Small*. NY. Oxford Univ Press. 1949. 1st ed. illus. no dj.
$50.00–$75.00

Lenski, Lois. *Cowboy Small.* NY. Oxford Univ Press. 1949. 1st ed. illus. sgn. dj.
$300.00–$550.00

Lenski, Lois. *Deer Valley Girl.* Phil. Lippincott. 1968. 1st ed. illus. by Lenski. xlib. dj.
$40.00–$75.00

Lenski, Lois. *Deer Valley Girl.* Phil. Lippincott. 1968. 1st ed. illus. by Lenski. dj.
$150.00–$175.00

Lenski, Lois. *High-Rise Secret.* Phil. Lippincott. 1966. 1st ed. illus. dj. $15.00–$30.00

Lenski, Lois. *Jack Horner's Pie.* NY. Harper. 1927. 1st ed. illus. $20.00–$35.00

Lenski, Lois. *Little Fire Engine.* 1946. 1st ed. $30.00–$100.00

Lenski, Lois. *Lois Lenski's Christmas Stories.* Phil. Lippincott. 1968. 1st ed. illus. red cloth. dj.
$45.00–$60.00

Lenski, Lois. *Mama Hattie's Girl.* Phil, NY. J.B. Lippincott. 1953. 1st ed. illus. by author. green cloth. illus. endpapers, dj. very good cond. $45.00–$150.00

Lenski, Lois. *Papa Small.* NY. Oxford Univ Press. 1951. 1st ed. illus. cloth. dj.
$75.00–$125.00

Lenski, Lois. *Prairie School.* Phil. Lippincott. (1951). 1st ed. illus. dj. $100.00–$150.00

Lenski, Lois. *Shoo-Fly Girl.* Phil. Lippincott. 1963. 1st ed. $50.00–$90.00

Lenski, Lois. *Skipping Village.* NY. 1927. 1st ed. illus. by author. $35.00–$100.00

Lenski, Lois. *Songs of Mr. Small.* NY. Oxford Univ Press. 1954. 1st ed. illus. dj.
$70.00–$90.00

Lenski, Lois. *We Live by the River.* Phil. Lippincott. 1956. 1st ed. illus. dj. $15.00–$20.00

Lenski, Lois. *We Live in the Country.* Phil. Lippincott. 1960. 1st ed. illus. dj. $30.00–$40.00

Lenton, H. T. *Warships of WWII.* Lon. 1968. illus. $35.00–$45.00

Lentz, Harold. *Pop-up Pinocchio.* NY. 1932. $100.00–$120.00

Leonard, Elmore. *City Primeval.* NY. Arbor House. 1980. 1st ed. dj. $25.00–$30.00

Leonard, Elmore. *Elmore Leonard Sampler.* NY. Dell. (1993). sgn. $40.00–$50.00

Leonard, Elmore. *Gunsights.* NY. Bantam. 1979. 1st ed. wraps. $60.00–$80.00

Leonard, Elmore. *Killshot.* NY. Arbor House. 1989. 1st ed. dj. $35.00–$45.00

Leonard, Elmore. *Mr. Majestyk.* NY. Dell. 1974. 1st ed. wraps. $50.00–$70.00

Leonard, Elmore. *Stick.* NY. Arbor House. 1983. 1st ed. sgn. dj. $20.00–$50.00

Leonard, Elmore. *Swag.* NY. Delacorte. 1976. 1st ed. dj. $20.00–$50.00

Leonard, Elmore. *Switch, The.* Lon. Secker & Warburg. 1979. 1st hardcover ed. dj.
$100.00–$250.00

Leonhardt, Olive. *New Orleans Drawn and Quartered.* Richmond. Dale Press. 1938. illus.
$35.00–$50.00

Leopold, Aldo. *Report on a Game Survey of the North Central States.* Madison. American Game Association. 1931. 1st ed. illus. $35.00–$50.00

Lesley, J. P. *Geological Hand Atlas of the Sixty-Seven Counties of Pennsylvania . . . 1874 to 1884.* Harrisburg. Commonwealth of Pennsylvania. 1885. 1st ed. ½ lea. $200.00–$350.00

Leslie, Frank. *Famous Leaders and Battle Scenes of the Civil War.* NY. 1896. 1st ed. folio. $140.00–$175.00

Leslie, Frank. *Illustrated History of the Civil War.* 1895. illus. repaired. $50.00–$100.00

Leslie, Frank. *Leslie's Famous War Pictures: Portfolio of War and Nation–Civil War.* DC. War Dept. 1906. illus. rebound folio. $175.00–$200.00

Leslie, Frank. *Leslie's Famous War Pictures: Portfolio of War and Nation–Civil War.* DC. War Dept. 1906. illus. 582 pp. folio. $225.00–$300.00

Leslie, Frank. *Scenes and Portraits of the Civil War.* NY. (1894). $200.00–$300.00

Leslie, J. *et al. Narrative of Discovery and Adventure in the Polar Seas and Regions.* Edin. Oliver & Boyd. 1830. 1st ed. fldg maps. ½ lea. $375.00–$500.00

Leslie, Miss. *75 Receipts for Pastry, Cakes and Sweetmeats.* Bos. Munroe and Francis. 1836. later ed. author's first cookbook. $175.00–$250.00

Leslie, Miss. *Directions for Cookery.* Phil. 1863. 59th ed. $20.00–$30.00

Leslie, Miss. *Directions for Cookery.* Phila. Carey & Hart. 1839. eighth ed. $125.00–$200.00

Leslie, Miss. *Miss Leslie's Behavior Book.* Peterson. 1859. 1st ed. $60.00–$80.00

Leslie, Miss. *Miss Leslie's New Recipes for Cooking.* Phil. 1854. $90.00–$125.00

Lessing, Doris. *African Stories.* NY. Simon & Schuster. (1965). 1st US ed. xlib. dj. $30.00–$50.00

Lessing, Doris. *African Stories.* NY. Simon and Schuster. 1965. 1st US ed. dj. $40.00–$75.00

Lessing, Doris. *African Stories.* Lon. Michael Joseph. (1964). 1st ed. dj. $75.00–$125.00

Lessing, Doris. *Fifth Child.* NY. 1988. 1st ed. dj. $20.00–$25.00

Lessing, Doris. *Fifth Child, The.* NY. Knopf. 1988. 1st Amer ed. dj. $20.00–$25.00

Lessing, Doris. *Fifth Child, The.* Lon. Jonathan Cape. 1st UK ed. dj. $25.00–$30.00

Lessing, Doris. *Under My Skin: Volume One of My Autobiography, to 1949.* NY. Harper-Collins. (1994). 1st US ed. illus. photos. sgn. dj. $70.00–$80.00

Lester, J. C. and D. L. Wilson. *Ku Klux Klan.* Nashville. 1884. wraps. $700.00–$1,000.00

Letters of John James Audubon 1826–1840. Bos. 1930. 2 vols. ltd 225 cc. slipcase. $400.00–$450.00

Letters of John James Audubon, 1826–1840. Kraus. reprint. $80.00–$100.00

Levin, Ira. *Rosemary's Baby.* Lon. Michael Joseph. 1st UK ed. dj. $40.00–$80.00

Levin, Ira. *Rosemary's Baby.* NY. Random House. 1967. 1st ed. dj. $50.00–$100.00

Levin, Ira. *Rosemary's Baby.* NY. Random House. 1967. 1st ed. sgn. dj. $400.00–$1,000.00

Levin, Ira. *Stepford Wives.* NY. Random House. 1972. 1st ed. dj. $60.00–$100.00

Levin, Meyer. *Citizens.* NY. Viking. 1940. 1st ed. dj. $35.00–$45.00

Levin, Meyer. *Citizens.* NY. Viking. 1940. 1st ed. no dj. $20.00–$25.00

Levin, Meyer. *Citizens.* NY. Viking. 1940. 1st ed. sgn. dj. $50.00–$150.00

Levin, Meyer. *Compulsion.* NY. Simon & Schuster. 1956. 1st ed. $50.00–$100.00

Levin, Meyer. *Settlers, The.* NY. Simon & Schuster. (1972). 1st ed. $25.00–$75.00

Levi-Strauss, Claude. *Introduction to a Science of Mythology: The Raw and the Cooked and From Honey to Ashes.* NY. Harper & Row. 1969. 2 vols. 1st US ed. dj. $100.00–$135.00

Levy, D. A. *North American Book of the Dead.* Cleveland. Free Lance Press. 1965. association copy inscrb to a friend. stapled wrappers. $675.00–$800.00

Lewis, C. S. *Pilgrim's Regress, The.* Lon. Dent. (1933). brown cloth. map endpapers. dj.
$1,000.00–$2,000.00

Lewis, John. *Life of the Learned and Right Reverend Reynold Pecock. . . .* Oxford. Clarendon. 1820. 2nd ed. green boards. $150.00–$200.00

Lewis, Matthew G. *Monk, The.* NY. Moore & Jackson. 1845. 1st US ed. 127 pp.
$35.00–$45.00

Lewis, Sinclair. *Arrowsmith.* NY. Harcourt Brace. (1925). 1st ed. sgn. blue boards. teg.
$400.00–$900.00

Lewis, Sinclair. *Babbitt.* NY. Harcourt Brace. (1925). 1st ed. 1st printing. blue cloth. dj.
$500.00–$800.00

Lewis, Sinclair. *Dodsworth.* NY. Harcourt Brace. (1929). 1st ed. blue cloth. dj.
$600.00–$1,400.00

Lewis, Sinclair. *Dodsworth.* NY. Grosset & Dunlap. (1929). dj. $30.00–$50.00

Lewis, Sinclair. *Dodsworth.* Lon. Jonathan Cape. (1929). 1st UK ed. blue cloth.
$50.00–$75.00

Lewis, Sinclair. *Elmer Gantry.* NY. Harcourt Brace. (1927). presentation copy. sgn. blue cloth. dj. $1,400.00–$1,900.00

Lewis, Sinclair. *Elmer Gantry.* NY. Harcourt Brace. (1927). 1st ed. dj. $1,000.00–$1,200.00

Lewis, Sinclair. *Elmer Gantry.* NY. Harcourt Brace. (1927). 1st ed. 1st binding. points. sgn. blue cloth. dj. $1,500.00–$2,500.00

Lewis, Sinclair. *Main Street.* NY. Harcourt Brace. (1921). later printing. black cloth. dj.
$75.00–$150.00

Lewis, Sinclair. *Main Street.* Chi. Limited Editions Club. 1937. illus. by Grant Wood. ltd 1500 cc. sgn. cloth. slipcase. $100.00–$200.00

Lewis, Sinclair. *Man Who Knew Coolidge, The*. NY. Harcourt Brace. (1928). 1st ed. blue cloth. dj. $200.00–$300.00

Lewis, Sinclair. *Mantrap*. NY. Harcourt Brace. (1926). 1st ed. blue cloth, dj.
$700.00–$1,500.00

Lewis, Sinclair. *Mantrap*. Lon. Jonathan Cape. (1926). 1st UK ed. blue cloth. $30.00–$45.00

Liggett, John. *The Human Face*. NY. Stein and Day. (1974). illus. dj. $25.00–$35.00

Lincoln, Abraham. *Proclamation of Emancipation by the President of the United States,. . . .* Bos. Forbes. (1862). 1st edition in pamphlet. 7 pp. wraps. $15,000.00–$22,000.00

Lincoln, Mrs. D. A. *Boston School Kitchen Text-book*. Bos. Little Brown. 1905.
$30.00–$45.00

Lincoln, Mrs. D. A. *Mrs. Lincoln's Boston Cook Book*. Bos. Roberts. 1891. cloth and boards. rebound. $40.00–$75.00

Lindbergh, Anne Morrow. *Dearly Beloved*. Harcourt Brace. 1962. sgn. dj. $40.00–$50.00

Lindbergh, Anne Morrow. *North to the Orient*. Harcourt Brace. 1935. 1st ed. dj.
$50.00–$65.00

Lindbergh, Charles. *Of Flight and Life*. NY. Scribner's. 1948. 1st ed. dj. $50.00–$60.00

Lindbergh, Charles. *Spirit of St. Louis*. NY. Scribner's. 1953. 1st ed. illus. decorated endpapers. blue cloth. dj. $50.00–$120.00

Lindbergh, Charles A. *Wartime Journals of Charles A. Lindbergh, The*. NY. Harcourt Brace Jovanovich. 1970. 1st ed. dj. slipcase. $2,000.00–$3,000.00

Lindsay, Charles. *Fly Fishing in the West*. NY. Aperture. 2000. 1st ed. dj. $25.00–$40.00

Lindsay, David Moore. *A Voyage to the Arctic in the Whaler Aurora*. Bos. Dana Estes. 1911. 1st ed. illus. blue decorated cloth red lettering on cover and spine. $35.00–$100.00

Lipsey, John J. *Incompleat Angler, The; or A Week-end on the Platte with Rod, Fly and Minnow in South Park*. Colorado Springs. private printing. 1948. 1st ed. wraps. ltd 250 cc. inscrb.
$10.00–$20.00

Little Red Riding Hood. NY. Blue Ribbon. 1933. illus. by Lentz. Pop-up Book.
$300.00–$400.00

Livermore, Mary A. *The Story of My Life*. Worthington & Co. 1898. $50.00–$100.00

Loewy, Raymond. *The Locomotive*. Lon. New York. The Studio. 1937. illus. gray cloth black lettering on cover and spine. Review Copy. $65.00–$200.00

Lofting, Hugh. *Doctor Dolittle in the Moon*. NY. Stokes. (1928). 1st ed. illus. by author.
$150.00–$200.00

Lofting, Hugh. *Doctor Dolittle's Circus*. NY. (1924). 1st ed. $40.00–$50.00

Lofting, Hugh. *Doctor Dolittle's Zoo*. NY. Stokes. (1925). 1st ed. $30.00–$40.00

Lofting, Hugh. *Voyages of Doctor Dolittle.* NY. Stokes. (1922). illus. 2nd printing.
$60.00–$90.00

London, Jack. *Call of the Wild, The.* NY. Macmillan. 1903. 1st ed. illus. green cloth. teg. dj.
$8,000.00–$10,000.00

London, Jack. *Call of the Wild, The.* NY. 1903. 1st ed. 1st state. original dj.
$10,000.00–$12,000.00

London, Jack. *Children of the Frost.* NY. Macmillan. 1902. 1st ed. cloth. $350.00–$500.00

London, Jack. *Game, The.* NY. Macmillan. 1905. 1st ed. 2nd issue. restored.
$500.00–$600.00

London, Jack. *Hearts of the Tree.* NY. McClure. 1920. 1st ed. $225.00–$500.00

London, Jack. *Iron Heel, The.* NY. 1908. 1st ed. $350.00–$500.00

London, Jack. *John Barleycorn.* NY. Century. 1913. 1st ed. plates. green cloth.
$90.00–$180.00

London, Jack. *Love of Life and Other Stories.* NY. Macmillan. 1907. 1st ed. blue cloth. bumped corners. rubbed. $300.00–$400.00

London, Jack. *Moon-Face.* NY. Macmillan. 1906. 1st ed. 4 pp ads. blue cloth.
$500.00–$750.00

London, Jack. *White Fang.* NY. Macmillan. 1906. 1st ed. 2nd issue. plates. $50.00–$100.00

Long, Mason. *Life of Mason Long, The Converted Gambler, The.* Chi. Donnelly, Loyd. 1878. 1st ed. frontis. $70.00–$90.00

Longfellow, Henry Wadsworth. *Courtship of Miles Standish and Other Poems.* Bos. Ticknor & Fields. 1858. 1st US ed. first state. $200.00–$350.00

Longfellow, Henry Wasdsworth. *Golden Legend.* Bos. Ticknor, Reed & Fields. 1851. 1st ed. brown cloth. $100.00–$150.00

Longfellow, Henry W. *Hyperion: A Romance.* . . . Lon. Bennet. 1865. illus. photos. morocco.
$600.00–$2,000.00

Lopez, Antonio. *Antonio's Girls.* NY. Congreve. 1982. 1st ed. illus. drawings. sgn and dated. dj. $300.00–$350.00

Lord, John. *Life of Emma Willard, The.* NY. Appleton. 1873. 1st ed. gray pictorial cloth. frontis. $80.00–$90.00

Lougheed, Victor. *Vehicles of the Air.* Chi. Reilly and Britton Co. 1910. illus. blue cloth with decorative cover. 514pp. $90.00–$200.00

Lovecraft, H. P. *At the Mountains of Madness.* Sauk City. Arkham House. 1964. 1st ed. dj.
$125.00–$250.00

Lovecraft, H. P. *Dagon and Other Macabre Tales.* Sauk City. Arkham House. 1965. 1st ed.
$100.00–$150.00

Lovecraft, H. P. *Dunwich Horror, The.* Sauk City. Arkham House. 1945. 1st ed. wraps.
$100.00–$125.00

Lovell, Jim and Jeffrey Kluger. *Lost Moon. The Perilous Voyage of Apollo 13.* Norwalk, CT. Easton. 1994. ltd ed. illus. aeg. $500.00–$800.00

Lowie, Robert H. *Indians of the Plains.* NewYork. McGraw-Hill. 1954. illus. black cloth.
$20.00–$45.00

Lowry, Malcolm. *Under the Volcano.* NY. Reynal & Hitchcock. 1947. 1st ed. uncorrected proof. $2,000.00–$2,750.00

Lucey, Donna M. *Photographing Montana 1894–1928.* NY. Knopf. 1990. 1st ed. illus. dj.
$175.00–$225.00

Luchetti, Cathy. *Medicine Women, the story of early-American women doctors.* NY. Crown. (1998). First Edition. illus. dj. $45.00–$60.00

Ludlum, Robert. *Osterman Weekend, The.* NY. World. (1972). 1st ed. blue cloth. $6.98 price and A3918 on back panel of dj. $125.00–$175.00

Ludlum, Robert. *Osterman Weekend, The.* NY. World. (1972). 1st ed. blue cloth. $6.98 price and A3918 on back panel of dj. sgn. $500.00–$600.00

Ludlum, Robert. *Scarlatti Inheritance.* Lon. Hart-Davis. (1971). 1st ed. author's first book. presentation copy. dj. $800.00–$1,000.00

Ludlum, Robert. *Scarlatti Inheritance.* Lon. Hart-Davis. (1971). 1st ed. author's first book. dj.
$75.00–$200.00

Ludlum, Robert. *Scarlatti Inheritance.* NY. World. (1971). 1st ed. author's first book. no dj.
$25.00–$35.00

Luling, Elizabeth. *Do Not Disturb.* Lon NY Tor. Oxford University. 1937. 1st ed. illus. cloth backed pictorial boards. $25.00–$95.00

Lydekker, R. L. *Catalogue of the Heads and Horns of Indian Game.* Lon. 1913. illus. 45 pp. photos. $100.00–$150.00

Lyell, Charles. *Travels in North American; with Geological Observations on the United States, Canada, and Nova Scotia.* Lon. Murray. 1845. 1st ed. illus. 2 vols. maps. plates. cloth.
$600.00–$700.00

Lyell, Denis D. *Memories of an African Hunter.* Lon. Unwin. (1924). illus. 2nd ed. plates.
$650.00–$900.00

Lynch, Bernard. *Guide to Health Through the Various Stages of Life.* Lon. private printing. 1744. 1st ed. $550.00–$650.00

Lynch, V. E. *Trails to Successful Trapping.* A.R. Harding Pub. 1935. illus. yellow illustrated binding. 2nd ed. $20.00–$30.00

Lynn, Elizabeth A. *Watchtower.* NY. Berkley/Putnam. 1979. uncorrected proof. blue wrappers. inscrb. $90.00–$110.00

Mably, Gabriel Bonnot de. *Observations on the Government and Laws of the United States of America.* . . . Lon. JFR & Co. 1784. translation of the French. gray paper over boards.
$600.00–$700.00

MacDonald, Eileen. *Shoot the Women First.* NY. Random House. 1991. 1st ed. dj.
$30.00–$40.00

MacDonald, George. *Dealings With the Fairies.* NY. Routledge. nd. 1st hardcover ed. illus. brown cloth.
$800.00–$1,000.00

MacDonald, John D. *Darker than Amber.* Lon. Hale. 1966. 1st UK ed. dj.
$1,000.00–$2,000.00

MacDonald, John D. *Executioners, The.* NY. Simon & Schuster. 1958. 1st ed. dj.
$800.00–$1,000.00

MacDonald, John D. *Good Old Stuff, The.* NY. Harper & Row. 1982. 1st ed. sgn. dj.
$300.00–$450.00

MacDonald, John D. *Pale Gray for Guilt.* Phil. Lippincott. 1971. 1st US ed. dj.
$800.00–$850.00

MacDermot, Violet. *Cult of the Seer in the Ancient Middle East, The.* Berkeley. Univ of California Press. 1971. 1st US ed. dj.
$65.00–$90.00

Machen, Arthur. *One Hundred Merrie & Delightsome Stories.* NY. 1924. illus. silk covered boards. ltd ed. 2vols.
$125.00–$160.00

MacKee, Seumas. *I was a Franco Soldier.* Lon. United Editorial. 1938. wraps. $50.00–$60.00

Mackie, J. L. *Cement of the Universe, The; a Study of Causation.* Oxford Univ Press. 1974. 1st ed. dj.
$60.00–$75.00

MacLagan, A. *White Hunter's Life, A.* NJ. 1983. illus. ltd 1000 cc. numbered and sgn. slipcase.
$150.00–$250.00

MacLean, Alistair. *Ice Station Zebra.* Lon. Collins. 1963. 1st ed. dj. $40.00–$50.00

MacLean, Norman. *River Runs Through It, A.* Chi. 1976. 1st ed. wraps. illus. dj.
$50.00–$60.00

MacLean, Norman. *River Runs Through It, A.* Chi. 1976. 1st ed. cloth. dj. $400.00–$1,000.00

MacLeish, Archibald. *Conquistador.* Bos/NY. Houghton Mifflin. 1932. 1st ed. no dj.
$20.00–$35.00

Maclure, Wiliam. *Opinions on Various Subjects, Dedicated to the Industrious Producers.* Indiana. School Press. 1831. 2 vols in one.
$1,000.00–$1,250.00

Macomb, Alexander. *Treatise on Martial Law and Courts Martial, A.* . . . Charleston, SC. Hoff. 1809. rebacked. 340 pp.
$800.00–$1,000.00

Macquoid, Percy. *History of English Furniture.* NY. Putnam's. 1904–1908. 1st US eds. 4 vols. illus.
$400.00–$500.00

Macy, Jesse. *Institutional Beginnings in a Western State*. Baltimore. N. Murray Pub. 1884. 1st ed. bound in black and white marblized bds and cloth. x-lib.　　　$19.00–$25.00

Madison, James. *Message from the President of the United States, Requesting Information Touching & Barbary Powers*. DC. 1815. 1st ed. 14 pp.　　　$75.00–$80.00

Mailer, Norman. *Naked and the Dead, The*. 1948. 1st ed. author's first book. dj.
　　　$900.00–$1,000.00

Malamud, Bernard. *Magic Barrel, The*. NY. Farrar Straus & Cudahy (1958). dj.
　　　$100.00–$175.00

Malamud, Bernard. *Natural, The*. NY. Harcourt Brace. (1952). 1st ed. blue, red or gray binding. dj.　　　$2,500.00–$4,000.00

Malamud, Bernard. *Natural, The*. NY. Harcourt Brace & Co. (1952). 1st ed. blue, red or gray binding. sgn. dj.　　　$3,000.00–$7,500.00

Malamud, Bernard. *Natural, The*. Lon. Eyre & Spottiswoode. 1963. 1st UK ed.
　　　$200.00–$600.00

Malamud, Bernard. *Natural, The*. NY. Harcourt Brace & Co. (1952). 1st ed. blue, red or gray binding. inscrb & sgn by author. dj.　　　$7,500.00–$10,000.00

Malory, Sir Thomas. *Arthur Pendragon of Britain*. New York. Putnam. 1943. 1st ed. illus. by Andrew Wyeth.　　　$60.00–$200.00

Malory, Sir Thomas. *Boy's King Arthur, The*. New York. Scribner's Sons. 1922. illus. by N.C.Wyeth, black illustrated paste-down on front cover.　　　$30.00–$200.00

Malory, Thomas. *Boy's King Arthur, The*. Lon. 1880. 1st ed.　　　$400.00–$500.00

Malthus, Thomas Robert. *Essay on the Principle of Population, An*. Lon. Johnson Good. 1806. 3rd ed. 2 vols.　　　$700.00–$800.00

Mamet, David. *Cabin, The*. San Francisco. Arion Press. 1992. 1st ed. wraps. ltd 500 cc. title essay. engraving. sgn.　　　$125.00–$300.00

Mann, H.C. *A Brief Account of the Indians in the Township of North Hempstead and their Dealings with the White Settlers*. Ira J. Friedman, N.Y. 1949. Reprint.　　　$10.00–$18.00

Mann, Thomas. *Magic Mountain*. Lon. Secker. (1927). 1st English language ed. 2 vols. by Nobel Prize–winning author. dj.　　　$5,500.00–$7,000.00

Mann, Thomas. *Nocturnes*. sgn.　　　$130.00–$145.00

Mann, Zane B. *Fair Winds and Far Places*. Minneapolis. Dillon. 1978. illus. color photos.
　　　$20.00–$30.00

Manning, Reg. *From Tee to Cup*. Arizona. Reganson. 1954. 1st ed. illus. by author, illus. cl over bds.　　　$8.00–$34.00

Margolis, Joseph A. (ed.). *Strange and Fantastic Stories; Fifty Tales of Terror, Horror and Fantasy*. NY. Whittlesey House. 1946. 1st ed. dj.　　　$75.00–$100.00

Marinaro, Vincent. *Modern Dry Fly Code, A*. NY. Putnam. 1950. 1st ed. illustrated. blue cover. dj.　　　$90.00–$300.00

Marinaro, Vincent. *Modern Dry Fly Code, A*. NY. Putnam. 1950. 1st ed. sgn. dj.
$250.00–$375.00

Markham, B. *West with the Night*. 1942. 1st US ed. dj. $375.00–$425.00

Marks, John. *Search for the Manchurian Candidate*. NY. McGraw-Hill. 1980. wraps.
$10.00–$15.00

Marquis, Don. *Prefaces*. NY/Lon. Appleton. 1919. 1st ed. points. presentation. inscrb.
$90.00–$120.00

Marsalis, Wynton and Carl Vigeland. *Jazz in the Bittersweet Blues of Life*. MA. Da Capo Press. 2001. 1st ed. sgn. dj. $45.00–$55.00

Marsh, Ngaio. *False Scent*. Lon. Collins Crime Club. 1960. 1st ed. dj. $25.00–$40.00

Marsh, Ngaio. *Off With His Head*. Lon. Collins Crime Club. 1957. 1st ed. dj. $45.00–$60.00

Marsh, Ngaio. *Scales of Justice*. Lon. Collins Crime Club. 1955. 1st ed. dj. $35.00–$40.00

Marshall, A. J. *Bower Birds*. Clarendon Press. 1954. dj. $75.00–$90.00

Marshall, John. *Opinion of the Supreme Court of the United States, at January Term 1832, . . . in the Case of Samuel A. Worcester . . . versus The State of Georgia. . . .* DC. Gales and Seaton. 1832. 1st ed. 39 pp. disbound treatise on Indian treaties. $200.00–$350.00

Marshall, Paule. *Brown Girl, Brownstones*. NY. Random House. 1959. 1st ed. dj.
$200.00–$550.00

Martin, Ralph G. *Man for All People, A: Hubert H. Humphrey*. NY. (1968). 1st ed. illus. inscrb by Humphrey. dj. $125.00–$150.00

Mather, Cotton. *Essays to Do Good*. KY. Skillman. 1822. later printing. $250.00–$300.00

Mather, Increase. *Brief History of the War with the Indians in New England, A. . . .* Lon. Chiswell. 1676. 1st English ed. $14,000.00–$16,500.00

Mathews, W. S. B. *Pronouncing Dictionary and Condensed Encyclopedia*. Phil. Theodore Presser. 1880. 1st ed. illus. green decorated cloth. gold lettering on cover. $10.00–$20.00

Matthiessen, Peter. *Shorebirds of North America, The*. NY. Viking. 1967. 1st ed. illus. ltd 350 cc. numbered. sgn by editor, author and illustrator. tan calf. slipcase. $600.00–$800.00

Maugham, W. Somerset. *Constant Wife, The*. NY. Baker and Taylor. 1909. 1st US ed. frontis of Ethel Barrymore. dj. $800.00–$900.00

Maugham, W. Somerset. *Don Fernando*. Lon. Heinemann. 1935. 1st ed. inscrb. dj.
$800.00–$1,000.00

Maugham, W. Somerset. *Razor's Edge, The*. Lon. Heinemann. 1944. 1st UK ed. dj.
$900.00–$1,000.00

Maugham, W. Somerset. *Strictly Personal*. Garden City. Doubleday Doran. 1941. 1st ed. ltd 515 cc. sgn. slipcase. $700.00–$750.00

Maurois, Andre. *Chelsea Way*. Elkin Mathews & Marrot. London. 1930. signed.
$35.00–100.00

Maxwell, Hu. *Jonathan Fish and His Neighbors.* West Virginia. Acme. 1902. 1st ed. green cloth. gilt lettering. presentation copy. inscrb and dated. $40.00–$55.00

Maxwell Leigh Eidinoff. *Atomics for the Millions.* NY. McGraw Hill. 1947. 1st edition.
$700.00–$1,200.00

May, Earl Chapin. *Model Railroad in the Home.* NY. Funk & Wagnalls. 1939. 1st ed. dj.
$50.00–$75.00

Mayes, James Russell. *Small Favors.* Bos. Alyson. 1994. 1st ed. dj. $20.00–$25.00

Mayor, Archer. *Occam's Razor.* NY. Mysterious Press. 1999. 1st ed. dj. $15.00–$25.00

Mayor, Archer. *Skeleton's Knee, The.* NY. Mysterious Press. (1993). 1st ed. dj. $25.00–$45.00

Mayor, Archer. *Skeleton's Knee, The.* NY. Mysterious Press. (1993). 1st ed. sgn. dj.
$40.00–$65.00

McAdam, Roger Willams. *Priscilla of Fall River.* NY. Stephen Daye Press. 1956. 2nd ed. illus. Fall River Line Steamer Service. dj. $20.00–$40.00

McAlmon, Robert. *Hasty Bunch, A.* Paris. Contact. 1922. 1st ed. wraps. 288 pp. lacks broadside laid in. $250.00–$300.00

McCabe, James D. *New York by Sunlight and Gaslight.* NY. Union Pub. House. 1881.
$20.00–100.00

McCabe, James D. *Illustrated History of the Centennial Exhibition, The.* Phil. National Publishing. (1876). 1st ed. illus. fold-out plates. red cloth. $80.00–$100.00

McCaffrey, Anne. *Freedom's Landing.* NY. Ace/Putnam. 1995. 1st ed. dj. $18.00–$22.00

McCarthy, Cormac. *All the Pretty Horses.* NY. 1992. 1st ed. illus. $40.00–$50.00

McCarthy, Cormac. *Blood Meridian.* NY. Random House. 1985. 1st ed. dj.
$700.00–$1,000.00

McCarthy, Cormac. *Blood Meridian.* NY. Random House. 1985. 1st paperback ed.
$75.00–$150.00

McCarthy, Cormac. *Orchard Keeper, The.* NY. Random House. (1965). 1st ed. sgn. dj.
$5,000.00–$7,000.00

McCarthy, Cormac. *Outer Dark.* NY. Random House. (1968). 1st ed. sgn. dj.
$4,000.00–$5,000.00

McCarthy, Cormac. *Stonemason, The.* Ecco Press. 1994. 1st ed. $15.00–$20.00

McCarthy, Cormac. *Suttree.* NY. Random House. (1979). 1st ed. sgn. dj.
$4,000.00–$4,500.00

McCarthy, Don (ed.). *Language of the Mosshorn: A Glossary of Cowboy Lingo. . . . Billings.* Gazette Publishing. 1936. 1st ed. wraps. illus. by Will James. $250.00–$300.00

McCarthy, Eugene. *Other Things and the Aardvark.* Garden City. Doubleday. (1970). 1st trade ed. inscrb. $25.00–$50.00

McClellan, George B. *Report of the Secretary of War.* DC. GPO. 1864. $100.00–$150.00

McClintock, John S. *Mormon Settlement in Arizona.* Phoenix. 1921. illus. photos. folding map. bibliography. $60.00–$85.00

McClintock, John S. *Pioneer Days in the Black Hills.* Deadwood. 1939. 1st ed.
$100.00–$200.00

McCorkle, Samuel. *Incident on the Bark Columbia . . . 1860–1862.* MA. (1941). 1st ed. ltd 300 cc. $150.00–$200.00

McCracken, Harold. *God's Frozen Children.* Garden City. Doubleday Doran. 1930. 1st ed. illus. inscrb. dj. $100.00–$130.00

McCullers, Carson. *Member of the Wedding, A.* Bos. Houghton Mifflin. 1946. 1st ed.
$50.00–$100.00

McCutcheon, John T. *History of Indiana.* Indianapolis. Bobbs Merrill. (1911). 1st ed. illus. by author. red cloth. $50.00–$75.00

McDaniel, Ruel. *Vinegarroon; the Saga of Judge Roy Bean The Law West of the Pecos.* Kingsport. Southern. 1936. 1st ed. no dj as issued. $40.00–$60.00

McGreevy, Thomas. *Thomas Stearns Eliot: A Study.* Lon. Chatto & Windus. 1931. 1st ed. pictorial dj. presentation copy. inscrb. dj. $55.00–$75.00

McIntosh, Charles. *Greenhouse, Hot House, and Stove.* Lon. Orr. 1849. 2nd ed. illus. litho plates. $400.00–$600.00

McLaughlin, Christian. *Glamorpuss.* NY. Dutton. 1994. 1st ed. review copy. author's first novel. $10.00–$15.00

McLure, J. B. *Edison and His Inventions.* 1879. 1st ed. illus. $100.00–$150.00

McMurtry, Larry. *Buffalo Girls.* NY. Simon & Schuster. (1990). 1st ed. dj. $15.00–$25.00

McMurtry, Larry. *Desert Rose.* NY. Simon & Schuster. 1983. 1st ed. ltd ed. dj.
$100.00–$200.00

McMurtry, Larry. *Evening Star, The.* NY. Simon & Schuster. (1992). 1st ed. dj.
$15.00–$25.00

McMurtry, Larry. *Last Picture Show.* NY. Dial. 1966. 1st ed. dj. $500.00–$1,000.00

McMurtry, Larry. *Lonesome Dove.* NY. Simon & Schuster. 1985. 1st ed. $125.00–$300.00

McMurtry, Larry. *Terms of Endearment.* NY. Simon & Schuster. (1975). 1st ed. dj.
$50.00–$75.00

McPhee, John. *Curve of Binding Energy.* NY. Farrar Straus & Giroux. (1974). dj.
$90.00–$125.00

McPhee, John. *Encounters with the Archdruid.* NY. Farrar Straus & Giroux. (1971). dj.
$200.00–$300.00

McPhee, John. *Headmaster.* NY. Farrar Straus & Giroux. 1966. 1st ed. illus. photos. dj.
$100.00–$120.00

McPhee, John. *Levels of the Game.* NY. Farrar Straus & Giroux. (1969). review copy. dj.
$150.00–$200.00

McPhee, John. *Roomful of Hovings.* NY. 1968. dj. $90.00–$120.00

McQuire, Hunter. *The Confederate Cause.* Richmond. 1907. $100.00–$125.00

Mead, Margaret. *Male and Female.* NY. 1st ed. dj. $50.00–$100.00

Mellinkoff, Ruth. *Horned Moses of Medieval Art and Thought, The.* Berkeley. Univ California Press. 1970. 1st ed. insrb. dj. $50.00–$75.00

Meltzer, Milton. *Dorothea Lange: A Photographer's Life.* NY. Farrar, Straus, Giroux. (1978). 1st ed. illus. cloth. dj. $25.00–$35.00

Melville, Herman. *Journal Up The Straits.* NY. The Colophon. 1935. 1st ed. marbleized boards. 182 pp. $45.00–$150.00

Melville, Herman. *Mardi.* NY. Harper. 1849. 2 vols. cloth. $2,500.00–$4,500.00

Melville, Herman. *Mardi.* London. Bentley. 1849. 3 vols. precedes U.S. edition.
$6,500–$8,000

Memoirs and Letters of Dolly Madison. Bos/NY. 1886. 1st ed. teg. 4 pp ads. $90.00–$120.00

Mencken, H. L. *Book of Prefaces, A.* NY. Knopf. 2nd ed. no dj. $80.00–$900.00

Mencken, H. L. *Book of Prefaces, A.* NY. Knopf. 1917. 1st ed. no dj. $100.00–$120.00

Mencken, H. L. *Book of Prefaces, A.* NY. Knopf. 1917. 1st ed. collection of stories. dj.
$800.00–$900.00

Mencken, H. L. *Christmas Story.* NY. Knopf. 1946. 1st ed. illus. sgn. dj. $500.00–$550.00

Mencken, H. L. *George Bernard Shaw: His Plays.* Bos. Luce. 1905. 1st ed. lacking dj.
$200.00–$225.00

Mencken, H. L. *Gist of Nietzsche, The.* Bos. Luce. 1910. 1st ed. burgundy cloth.
$450.00–$550.00

Mencken, H. L. *Heathen Days, 1890–1936.* NY. Knopf. 1943. 1st ed. inscrb. dj.
$300.00–$350.00

Mencken, H. L. *Mencken and Sara.* NY. McGraw-Hill. 1987. 1st ed. inscrb by editor, Rodgers. dj. $50.00–$70.00

Mencken, H. L. *Menckeniana, a Schimpflexikon.* NY. Knopf. 1928. 1st ed. sgn. slipcase.
$800.00–$900.00

Mencken, H. L. *Notes on Democracy.* NY. Knopf. (1926). 1st ed. ltd 235 cc. 200 numbered and sgn. lacking slipcase. $500.00–$600.00

Mencken, H. L. *Treatise on the Gods.* NY. Knopf. 1930. 1st ed. ltd 375 cc. numbered. sgn. vellum. $300.00–$400.00

Mencken, H. L. *Treatise on the Gods*. NY. Knopf. 1930. 1st ed. ltd 375 cc. sgn. dj. slipcase.
$800.00–$900.00

Mencken, H. L. *Treatise on Wright and Wrong*. NY. Knopf. 1934. 1st ed. inscrb. sgn. dj.
$250.00–$450.00

Mendelson. *Early Auden*. NY. Viking. (1981). 1st ed. brown cloth. dj. $20.00–$30.00

Mercer, H. *Lenape Stone or the Indian and the Mammoth*. NY/Lon. Putnam's. 1885. illus.
$100.00–$125.00

Meyer, Joseph E. *Nature's Remedies: Early History and Uses of Botanic Drugs*. . . . IN. Indiana Botanic Gardens. 1934. 1st ed. blue cloth. $45.00–$50.00

Meynell, Francis. *My Lives*. NY. Random House. (1971). 1st ed. founder of Nonesuch Press. dj. $15.00–$20.00

Meynell, Francis. *Seventeen Poems*. NY. Nonesuch Press. 1945. 1st ed. ltd 1000 cc. sgn.
$35.00–$70.00

Michaux, F. *Travels to the Westward of the Allegany Mountains, . . . in the year 1802*. Lon. Sultzer. 1805. illus. early printing. folding map. $500.00–$950.00

Michener, James A. *Drifters, The*. NY. Random House. 1971. 1st ed. wraps. ltd 500 cc. sgn. dj. $200.00–$250.00

Michener, James A. *Hawaii*. NY. Random House. 1959. 1st ed. dj. $200.00–$350.00

Michener, James. *Kent State*. NY. Random House. (1971). 1st ed. illus. photos. sgn.
$300.00–$400.00

Michener, James. *Kent State*. NY. Random House. (1971). 1st ed. illus. photos.
$30.00–$40.00

Michener, James A. *Space*. NY. Random House. 1982. 1st ed. ltd 500 cc. sgn.
$150.00–$200.00

Michener, James A. *Texas*. NY. Random House. (1985). 1st ed. dj. $15.00–$20.00

Middleton, William D. *Interurban Era, The*. Milwaukee. Kalmbach. 1961. 1st ed. illus. photos. dj. $80.00–$110.00

Middleton, William D. *Time of the Trolley, The*. Milwaukee. Kalmbach. 1967. 1st ed. illus. photos. dj. $100.00–$150.00

Middleton, William D. *When the Steam Railroads Electrified*. Milwaukee. Kalmbach. 1967. 1st ed. illus. photos. maps. dj. $80.00–$100.00

Milam, B. J. *Honest Farmer from Arkansaw on a Lark Seein' the West, The*. 1st ed. illus. frontis portrait. photos. plates. red embossed and gild stamped cloth. $1,750.00–$2,000.00

Milhous, Katherine. *Appolonia's Valentine*. NY. Scribner's. (1954). 1st ed. illus. sgn. dj.
$30.00–$40.00

Mill, John Stuart. *Autobiography*. Lon. Longmans, Green, Reader, and Dyer. 1873. 1st ed. 2nd issue. $90.00–$110.00

Mill, John Stuart. *The Subjection of Women*. Phil. Lippincott. 1869. 1st ed. brown pebbled cloth. 1st US ed. 174 pp. 6 pp. ads. $250.00–$500.00

Millay, Edna St. Vincent. *Ballad of the Harp-Weaver, The*. NY. 1922. 1st ed. ltd 500 cc. illus. pictorial wraps. $175.00–$225.00

Millay, Edna St. Vincent. *Harp-Weaver and Other Poems, The*. NY. 1923. 1st ed.
$200.00–$250.00

Millay, Edna St. Vincent. *Lamp and the Bell, The*. NY. Shay. 1921. cloth in pictorial wrapper.
$75.00–$90.00

Miller, Arthur. *All My Sons*. NY. (1947). 1st ed. dj. $600.00–$800.00

Miller, Arthur. *Crucible*. The. NY. 1953. 1st ed. dj. $600.00–$800.00

Miller, Arthur. *Homely Girl, A Life*. NY. Viking. (1995). 1st ed. sgn. dj. $40.00–$75.00

Miller, Henry. *Money and How it Gets That Way*. Paris. Booster. (1938). 1st ed. wraps.
$500.00–$600.00

Miller, Henry. *My Life and Times*. NY. Playboy Press. (1975). 1st ed. sgn. ltd 500 cc. slipcase.
$800.00–$900.00

Miller, Henry. *Tropic of Cancer*. Grove. 1961. dj. $20.00–$50.00

Miller, Henry. *Tropic of Cancer*. NY. Grove. (1961). 1st ed. brown cloth. ltd 100 cc. sgn.
$3,000.00–$4,000.00

Miller, Hugh, *The Cruise of the Betsey or A Summer Ramble Among the Fossiliferous Deposits of the Hebrides*. Gould and Lincoln. Bos. 1858. 524 pp. $50.00–$90.00

Miller, Joaquin. *First Fam'lies of the Sierras*. Chi. Jansen, McClurg. 1876. 1st US ed. blind-stamped cover. gilt lettering. $80.00–$110.00

Miller, Olive Beaupre. *My Book House, The Treasure Chest*. Chi. 1920. illus. $30.00–$50.00

Miller, Olive Beaupre. *Tales Told in Holland*. Bookhouse for Children. (1952).
$20.00–$30.00

Miller, Thomas. *Common Wayside Flowers, 1869,. . . .* Lon. Routledge. 1860. 1st ed. illus. wood engravings. $500.00–$700.00

Milne, A. A. *Christopher Robin Birthday Book*. Lon. Methuen. (1930). illus. by Shepard.
$150.00–$300.00

Milne, A. A. *Gallery of Children, A*. Phil. McKay. (1925). 1st US ed. illus by Saida. 105 pp. blue cloth. $75.00–$100.00

Milne, A. A. *House at Pooh Corner*. Lon. Methuen. (1928). 1st ed. illus. by Shepard. pink cloth. pictorial dj. $2,000.00–$3,500.00

Milne, A. A. *Now We Are Six*. Lon. 1927. 1st ed. illus. teg. $200.00–$300.00

Milne, A. A. *Toad of Toad Hall*. Lon. 1929. 1st ed. dj. $75.00–$110.00

Minarik, Else Holmelund. *Little Bear*. Harper & Row. 1st ed. illus. by Sendak. dj.
$75.00–$100.00

Minot, George (ed.). *Statutes at Large and Treaties of the United States of America . . . 1854–1855*. Bos. Little, Brown. 1855. wraps. 3 vols in one. $40.00–$60.00

Mitchell, Joseph. *Missionary Pioneer, The & the Life, Labours, and Death of John Stewart (Man of Colour)*. . . . NY. Mitchell. 1827. 1st ed. $2,500.00–$3,000.00

Mitchell, Margaret. *Gone With the Wind*. NY. 1936. 1st ed. appears on copyright page. pictorial dj. $4,000.00–$7,500.00

Mitchell, Margaret. *Gone With the Wind*. NY. Macmillan. 1936. 1st ed. sgn. later dj.
$8,500.00–$10,000.00

Mitchell, S. Augustus. *Mitchell's Travellers Guide Through the United States*. Phil. Mitchell. 1834. rebacked. folding map in color. $1,200.00–$1,500.00

Mitchell, S. Augustus. *System of Modern Geography, A*. Phil. Cowperthwait, Desilver & Butler. 1854. illus. 4th ed. paper over bds. lea. spine. $20.00–$75.00

Modern Locomotives: Illustrations, Specifications and Details of Typical American and European Steam and Electric Locomotives. NY. Railroad Gazette. 1897. 1st ed. illus. 448 pp. photos. drawings. diagrams. rebound. $1,000.00–$1,500.00

Montanaro, Ann R. *Pop-up and Movable Books: A Bibliography*. Metuchen, N.J. Scarecrow Press. 1993. $90.00–$200.00

Moody, William Vaughn. *Great Divide, The; A Play in Three Acts*. NY. Macmillan. 1909. 1st ed. blue cloth. $20.00–$30.00

Moon, William. *Light for the Blind*. Lon. Longman. 1875. original blue cloth. aeg.
$700.00–$800.00

Moorcock, Michael. *Behold the Man*. Lon. Allison and Busby. 1969. 1st ed. dj.
$40.00–$50.00

Moore, A. Y. *Life of Schuyler Colfax, The*. Phil. Peterson. (1868). 1st ed. $50.00–$75.00

Moore, George. *Story-Teller's Holiday*. NY. Liveright. 1928. 2 vols. sgn. $20.00–$25.00

Morgan, Dale. *Jedediah Smith and the Opening of the West*. Indianapolis. Bobbs Merrill. (1953). 1st ed. frontis portrait. plates. endpaper maps. navy cloth. pictorial dj.
$100.00–$130.00

Morgan, James Morris. *Recollections of a Rebel Reefer*. Bos. Houghton Mifflin. 1917. illus. 491 pp. $100.00–$125.00

Morgenthau, Henry, Jr. *Germany is Our Problem*. NY/Lon. Harper. (1945). 1st ed. sgn. dj.
$80.00–$100.00

Morison, Samuel Eliot. *Admiral of the Ocean Sea*. Bos. Little Brown. 1942. 1st ed. 2 vols. dj.
$40.00–$65.00

Morris, D. *Washing of the Spears, The*. NY. 1965. 1st ed. illus. endpaper maps. Zulu War of 1879. dj. $100.00–$150.00

Morris, Rob. *Miniature Monitor, The: Containing all the Monitorial Instructions in Blue Lodge Masonry*. . . . Chicago. Bailey. 1864. 15th ed. 176 pp. $100.00–$120.00

Morris, Wright. *Plains Song*. NY. Harper & Row. (1980). inscrb. dj. $250.00–$325.00

Morris, Wright. *Plains Song*. NY. Harper & Row. (1980). dj. $45.00–$70.00

Morrison, J. S. and R. T. Williams. *Greek Oared Ships, 900–322* B. C. Cambridge Univ Press. 1968. illus. cloth. dj. $100.00–$150.00

Morrison, Toni. *Beloved*. NY. Knopf. 1987. 1st ed. wraps. uncorrected proof. Pulitzer Prize Winning novel. $175.00–$200.00

Morrison, Toni. *Beloved*. NY. Knopf. 1987. 1st ed. sgn. Pulitzer Prize Winning novel.
        $300.00–$500.00

Morrison, Toni. *Dancing Mind, The*. NY. Knopf. 1996. 1st ed. sgn. dj. $100.00–$125.00

Morrison, Toni. *Song of Solomon*. NY. Knopf. 1977. 1st ed. dj. $350.00–$400.00

Morrison, Toni. *Song of Solomon*. NY. Knopf. 1977. 1st ed. sgn. dj. $500.00–$900.00

Morrison, Toni. *Sula*. NY. Knopf. 1974. 1st ed. dj. $900.00–$1,000.00

Morrison, Toni. *Tar Baby*. PA. Franklin Library. 1981. 1st ed. ltd. lea. $400.00–$450.00

Morse, I and J. *Yankee in Africa*. MA. 1936. illus. 297 pp. sgn by both authors. dj.
        $100.00–$150.00

Mother Goose. NY. Blue Ribbon. 1934. illus. by Lentz. Pop-up Book. $275.00–$350.00

Moulton, Gary E. (ed). *Atlas of the Lewis & Clark Expedition*. Lincoln. Univ of Nebraska Press. (1983). 1st ed. maps. blue cloth. $1,000.00–$1,500.00

Mourell, Francisco Antonio. *Voyage of the Sonora in the Second Bucarelli Expedition to Explore the Northwest Coast. . . .* San Francisco. Russell. 1920. 1st US ed. frontis portrait. folding map. blue pictorial boards. teg. paper spine label. 230 cc. sgn by publisher.
        $250.00–$350.00

Mudge, Zacariah Atwell. *Missionary Teacher, The*. NY. Lane & Tippett. 1848. 1st ed. frontis. plates. cloth. $400.00–$450.00

Muir, John. *Writing of John Muir*. NY. Houghton Mifflin. (1924). Sierra edition. 10 vols. illus. photos. maps. $500.00–$750.00

Municipal Register City of Bridgeport for 1875. Gould & Stiles. Bridgeport 1875.
        $25.00–$100.00

Munro, Dana Carleton and Merrick Whitcomb. *Medieval and Modern History*. Appleton. 1903. $20.00–$30.00

Munroe, Kirk. *Derrick Sterling: A Story of the Mines*. NY. Harper & Bros. 1888. 1st ed. illus. pictorial green cloth. frontis. $40.00–$50.00

Munroe, Kirk. *Through Swamp and Glade: A Tale of the Seminole War*. NY. Scribner's. 1896. 1st ed. illus. 353 pp. pictorial gray cloth. frontis. plates. $25.00–$35.00

Murder of Union Soldiers. Washington. U.S. Congress. 1867. wraps. $70.00–$75.00

Murray, Hugh. *African Continent, The*. Lon. Nelson and Sons. 1853. illus. maps. plates.
        $60.00–$100.00

Naipaul, V. S. *Among the Believers: An Islamic Journey.* NY. Knopf. 1981. 1st ed. dj.
$20.00–$30.00

Narrow Gauge Railways in America. Oakland. Hardy. 1949. 1st ed thus. sgn. deluxe issue. 950 cc. numbered and sgn by eds. reprint of 1875 ed. 139 pp. dj. $125.00–$175.00

NASA. *Gemini Program, Flight Summary Report, 1966.* NASA. 1966. wraps. tables, charts.
$150.00–$300.00

NASA. *Geologic Setting of the Lunar Samples Returned with Apollo XI.* NASA. 1969. wraps. 93 pp. stapled. $800.00–$1,000.00

Nasar, Sylvia. *Beautiful Mind, A.* NY. Simon & Schuster. 1998. 1st ed. dj. $100.00–$125.00

Nash, Jay Robert. *Among the Missing, an Anecdotal History of Missing Persons. . . .* NY. Simon and Schuster. 1978. illus. $10.00–$15.00

Nasmyth, James and James Carpenter. *Moon, The: Considered as a Planet, a World, and a Satellite.* Lon. John Murray. 1874. illus. blue cover with gold relief drawing.
$1,000.00–$1,300.00

National Agricultural Workers Union. *Disinherited Speak, The: Letters from Sharecroppers.* NY. Workers Defense League. 1st ed. wraps. $100.00–$150.00

National Broom Manufacturer's Association. *Code for Fair Competition for the Broom Manufacturing Industry.* Illinois. Nation Broom Manufacturing Association. 1934. wraps. 15 pp. New Deal regulations. $25.00–$45.00

Naylor, Wilson. *Daybreak in the Dark Continent.* NY. Young People's Missionary Movement. 1905. 1st ed. illus. maps. red decorated cloth. $15.00–$35.00

Nearing, Scott. *Free Born.* NY. 1932. 1st ed. wraps. $150.00–$250.00

Neihardt, John G. *Black Elk Speaks.* NY. Morrow. 1932. 1st ed. dj. $900.00–$1,000.00

Neill, Patrick. *Journal of a Horticultural Tour Through Some Parts of Flanders, Holland and the North of France in the Autumn of 1817.* Edinburgh. Bell & Bradfute. 1823. 1st ed. illus. folding plates. $800.00–$1,000.00

Neumann, John von. *Computer and the Brain, The.* New Haven. Yale Univ Press. 1958. 1st ed. dj. $400.00–$550.00

New York Fraud, The: The Conspiracy of the Office Unmasked. Bos. Harrison Club. (1840). 24 pp. $200.00–$275.00

Nichols, John. *Milagro Beanfield War, The.* NY. Holt Rinehart Winston. (1974). dj.
$450.00–$550.00

Nicholson, Meredith. *The Hoosiers.* NY. Macmillan. 1916. small blue cloth. lettering on spine. regional, Indiana. $7.00–$15.00

Nielsen, Kay. *East of the Sun and West of the Moon.* NY. Hodder & Stoughton. 1914. illus. by Kay Nielsen. 1st trade ed. $2,000.00–$3,500.00

Nietzsche, Frederich. *Thus Spake Zarathustra.* NY/Lon. Macmillan. 1896. 1st US ed. green boards. $900.00–$1,200.00

Nin, Anais. *Ladders to Fire.* NY. Dutton. 1946. 1st ed. inscrb. dj. $200.00–$300.00

Niven, Larry. *Integral Trees, The.* NY. Ballantine. 1984. 1st ed. sgn. dj. $30.00–$40.00

Niven, Larry. *World Out of Time, A.* NY. Holt Rinehart Winston. 1979. 1st ed. inscrb. dj. $30.00–$50.00

Nixon, Richard M. *Memoirs of Richard Nixon.* NY. Grosset & Dunlap. (1978). 1st ed. illus. sgn. slipcase. $500.00–$700.00

Nixon, Richard M. *Six Crises.* NY. 1962. 1st ed. inscrb. sgn. dj. $600.00–$700.00

Noble, Joseph. *From Cab to Caboose: Fifty Years of Railroading.* Norman, OK. Univ of Oklahoma Press. 1964. 1st ed. illus. photos. dj. $40.00–$60.00

Norris, Frank. *Deal in Wheat and Other Stories of the New and Old West, A.* NY. Doubleday Page. 1903. 1st ed. original gilt decorated cloth. frontis and 3 plates. $160.00–$190.00

Norris, Frank. *Surrender of Santiago.* San Francisco. Elder. 1917. 1st ed. wraps. frontis portrait. $45.00–$55.00

North, S. N. D., director. *Heads of Families First Census of the United States 1790.* Wash. Government Printing Office. 1907. 1st ed. wraps. tan wrps in brown paper dust jacket. 146pp. folding map frontis—New Hampshire. $20.00–$30.00

Norwood, Gilbert. *Euripides and Shaw With Other Essays.* Methuen & Co. Lon. 1921. 1st ed. $15.00–$20.00

Norton, Frank H. (ed.). *Frank Leslie's Historical Register of the United States Centennial Exposition.* NY. Leslie's. 1877. 1st ed. subscription ed. folio. ¾ morocco. $800.00–$1,000.00

Nourse, Alan. *Psi High and Others.* Lon. Faber. 1967. 1s UK ed. dj. $20.00–$25.00

Noyes, Alfred. *Accusing Ghost.* Lon. Gollancz. 1957. 1st ed. $20.00–$25.00

Noyes, Alfred. *Wine-Press, The: A Tale of War.* Edinburgh. Blackwood. 1913. 1st ed. teg. $20.00–$30.00

N' Zau, B. *Travel and Adventure in the Congo Free State and Its Big Game Shooting.* Lon. 1894. illus. foldout map. cloth. $900.00–$1,200.00

Oates, Joyce Carol. *Cybele.* Santa Barbara. Black Sparrow. 1979. 1st ed. ltd 300 cc. numbered. sgn. dj. $100.00–$150.00

Oates, Joyce Carol. *Daisy.* Santa Barbara. Black Sparrow. 1977. 1st ed. ltd 60 cc, numbered. sgn. dj. $300.00–$400.00

Oates, Joyce Carol. *Goddess and Other Women.* Vanguard. 1974. 1st ed. dj. $25.00–$30.00

Oates, Joyce Carol. *Snowfall.* Bost. Hall. (1977). 1st ed. wraps. 12mo. Stinehour Press greeting. $25.00–$50.00

Oates, Stephen B. *To Purge This Land with Blood; a Biography of John Brown.* NY. Harper & Row. 1970. 1st ed. dj. $30.00–$40.00

O' Brien, Patrick. *Reverse of the Medal, The.* Lon. Collins. 1986. 1st ed. dj. $200.00–$600.00

O' Brien, Patrick. *Wind at My Back, The.* Garden City. Doubleday. 1964. 1st ed. inscrb. dj. $40.00–$60.00

O' Brien, Patrick. *H.M.S. Surprise.* Phil. Lippincott. (1973). 1st ed. dj. $125.00–$200.00

O' Brien, Tim. *In the Lake of the Woods.* Bos. Houghton Mifflin. (1994). 1st ed. wraps. advanced reading copy. $30.00–$45.00

O' Brien, Tim. *Nuclear Age, The.* NY. Knopf. 1985. 1st ed. sgn. dj. $60.00–$90.00

O' Brien, William. *Irish Ideas.* Lon. Longmans, Green and Co. 1893. 1st ed. small green cloth. lettering on cover. $30.00–$50.00

O' Cathasaigh, P. *Story of the Irish Citizen Army.* Dublin. 1919. 1st ed. wraps. $200.00–$300.00

O' Connor, Flannery. *Complete Stories, The.* NY. Farrar Straus & Giroux. (1971). National Book Award winner. dj. $200.00–$300.00

O' Connor, Flannery. *Good Man is Hard to Find, A.* NY. Harcourt Brace. (1955). 1st ed. dj. $400.00–$600.00

O' Connor, Flannery. *Habit of Being, The.* NY. Farrar, Straus & Giroux. 1979. 1st ed. dj. $45.00–$60.00

O' Connor, Flannery. *Habit of Being, The.* NY. Farrar, Straus & Giroux. 1979. 1st ed. damaged dj. $25.00–$50.00

O' Connor, Flannery. *Habit of Being, The.* NY. Farrar, Straus & Giroux. 1979. 1st ed. sgn. dj. $150.00–$250.00

O' Connor, Flannery. *Wise Blood.* NY. 1952. 1st ed. dj. $350.00–$700.00

O' Connor, J. *Big Game Animals of North America.* 1977. 2nd printing. folio. dj. $50.00–$75.00

O' Connor, J. *Sheep and Sheep Hunting.* Winchester Press. 1974. 1st ed. illus. dj. $150.00–$250.00

Odets, Clifford. *Golden Boy.* NY. 1937. 1st ed. sgn. $500.00–$700.00

Odets, Clifford. *Paradise Lost: A Play in Three Acts.* NY. Random House. 1936. 1st ed. chipped dj. $50.00–$150.00

Odets, Clifford. *Paradise Lost: A Play in Three Acts.* NY. Random House. 1936. 1st ed. play. boards. dj. $150.00–$300.00

O' Flaherty, Liam. *Fairy Goose and Two Other Stories, The.* NY. Crosby Gaige. 1927. 1st ed. ltd 1190 cc. sgn. no dj. $70.00–$80.00

Ogden, George W. *Letters from the West, Comprising a Tour Through the Western Country, and a Resident of Two Summers in the States of Ohio, and Kentucky. . . .* New Bedford. Melcher & Rogers. 1823. 1st ed. rebound. $1,750.00–$2,000.00

Ogden, George W. *Men of the Mesquite*. NY. Dodd Mead. 1932. 1st ed. dj. $100.00–$150.00

O' Hanlon, Redmond. *Joseph Conrad and Charles Darwin: The Influence of Scientific Thought on Conrad's Fiction*. NJ. Humanities Press. 1984. 1st US ed. 1st state. errata slip. facsimile dj.
$400.00–$500.00

O' Hara, John. *Appointment in Samarra*. NY. Harcourt Brace. (1934). 1st ed. dj.
$12,000.00–$14,000.00

O' Hara, John. *Butterfield 8*. NY. Harcourt Brace. 1935). 1st ed. dj. $1,500.00–$2,000.00

O' Hara, John. *From the Terrace*. NY. Random House. (1958). 1st ed. dj. $40.00–$75.00

O' Hara, John. *From the Terrace*. NY. Duell, Random House. (1958). 1st ed. inscrb. dj.
$600.00–$750.00

O' Hara, John. *Hope of Heaven*. NY. Harcourt Brace. (1930). dj. $100.00–$500.00

O' Hara, John. *Pal Joey*. NY. Duell, Sloan and Pearce. (1940). 1st ed. first issue dj without movie connection. $900.00–$1,200.00

O' Hara, John. *Rage to Live*. NY. Random House. (1949). 1st ed. dj. $75.00–$90.00

O' Hara, John. *Ten North Frederick*. NY. Random House. (1955). 1st ed. dj.
$60.00–$75.00

O' Hara, John. *Waiting for Winter*. NY. Random House. (1966). 1st ed. ltd 300 cc. teg. sgn. slipcase. $50.00–$80.00

O' Hara, Larry. *Turning Up the Heat; MI5 After the Cold War*. Lon. Phoenix. 1994.
$25.00–$30.00

Olby, Robert. *Path to the Double Helix, The*. Seattle. Univ of Washington Press. (1984). 1st ed. foreword by Francis Crick. sgn by Crick. dj. $500.00–$900.00

Old Manors Old Houses. *Quebec*. Ls. A. Proulx. 1927. 1st ed. illus. red cloth.
$40.00–$90.00

Oliver, Paul. *Blues Fell This Morning*. NY. Horizon. 1961. 1st Us ed. dj. $80.00–$100.00

Ondaatje, Michael. *Anil's Ghost*. NY. Knopf. 2000. 1st ed. sgn and dated. dj. $50.00–$75.00

Ondaatje, Michael. *Collected Works of Billy the Kid*. Tor. Anansi. 1970. 1st ed. wraps. sgn.
$275.00–$300.00

Ondaatje, Michael. *Collected Works of Billy the Kid*. Lon. Boyard. 1981. wraps. 1st UK ed. sgn. dj. $200.00–$300.00

Ondaatje, Michael. *Collected Works of Billy the Kid*. Tor. Anansi. 1970. 1st ed. dj.
$250.00–$400.00

Ondaatje, Michael. *Collected Works of Billy the Kid*. NY. Norton. 1974. 1st US ed.
$100.00–$200.00

Ondaatje, Michael. *Collected Works of Billy the Kid*. Tor. Anansi. 1970. 1st ed. hardcover. sgn. dj. $1,000.00–$1,500.00

One Hundred & Fiftieth Anniversary of Lancaster New Hampshire, The. Pub by the Committee. 1914. 1st ed. illus. limited ed. 447/1000 cc. very good cond. $25.00–$50.00

O' Neill, Eugene. *Ah, Wilderness!* NY. Random House. 1933. 1st ed. dj. $150.00–$300.00

O' Neill, Eugene. *Anna Christie.* NY. 1930. illus. ltd 775 cc. sgn. $100.00–$200.00

O'Neill, Eugene. *The Hairy Ape.* NY. Liveright. 1929. ltd 750 cc. sgn. $200.00–$250.00

O' Neill, Eugene. *Strange Interlude.* NY. Boni & Liveright. 1928. 1st ed. ltd 775 cc. sgn. slip-case. $200.00–$300.00

O' Neill, Eugene. *Strange Interlude.* NY. Boni & Liveright. 1928. 1st ed. dj. $40.00–$90.00

O' Reilly, John, M.D. *Placenta, the Organic Nervous System, the Blood, the Oxygen. . . .* NY. Wood. 1861. 2nd ed. illus. red cloth. $150.00–$200.00

Ormsbee, Thomas Hamilton. *The Story of American Furniture.* The Macmillan Co, N.Y. 1934. Illustrated. $10.00–$20.00

O' Rourke, Frank. *Thunder on the Buckhorn.* NY. Random House. (1949). 1st ed. dj. $35.00–$50.00

Orwell, George. *Animal Farm.* Lon. 1945. 1st ed. good condition. dj. $800.00–$1,000.00

Orwell, George. *Animal Farm.* Lon. 1945. 1st ed. fine condition. dj. $2,500.00–$3,000.00

Osler, William. *Alabama Student and Other Biographical Essays.* Oxford. 1908. $75.00–$150.00

Osler, William. *On Humanities and the New Science.* Bos. 1920. dj. $75.00–$140.00

Osler, Sir William. *Biblioteca Osleriana: A Catalogue of Books Illustrating the History of Medicine and Science.* McGill–Queen's Univ Press. 1929. 1st ed. $400.00–$500.00

Osler, Sir William. *Lectures on the Diagnostics of Abdominal Tumors.* NY. 1895. $75.00–$120.00

Osler, Sir William. *Principles and Practice of Medicine.* NY. Appleton. 1899. $100.00–$130.00

Oswell, W. *William Cotton Oswell: Hunter and Explorer.* Lon. 1900. 2 vols. illus. maps. Oswell guided Livingstone. $900.00–$1,200.00

Our Cook Book. Burlington. Park Press. 1898. 1st ed. poor white cloth lettering on cover. $10.00–$25.00

Outhwaite, Leonard. *Atlantic Circle.* NY. Scribner. 1931. illus. 309 pp. $20.00–$30.00

Owen, David Dale. *Mineral Lands of the United States.* DC. House Document. 1840. 1st ed. folding maps. charts. plates. $750.00–$1,000.00

Owens, William A. *Slave Mutiny; the Revolt on the Schooner Amistad.* Lon. Peter Davies. 1953. 1st UK ed. dj. $30.00–$40.00

Owens, William A. *Slave Mutiny; the Revolt on the Schooner Amistad.* NY. John Day. (1953). 1st ed. sgn. dj. $45.00–$75.00

Owens, William A. *Slave Mutiny; the Revolt on the Schooner Amistad.* NY. John Day. 1953. 1st ed. dj. $30.00–$45.00

Packman, Ana Begue de. *Early California Hospitality.* CA. Clark. 1938. 1st ed. ltd 1019 cc. inscrb. lacking dj. $90.00–$100.00

Page, Thomas Nelson. *Burial of the Guns, The.* NY. Scribner's. 1894. 1st ed. cream cloth. gilt lettering. $50.00–$75.00

Page, Thomas Nelson. *Captured Santa Claus, A.* NY. Scribner's. 1902. 1st edition thus. illus. $20.00–$25.00

Page, Thomas Nelson. *Gordon Keith.* Lon. Heinemann. 1903. 1st UK ed. green boards. $30.00–$40.00

Page, Thomas Nelson. *Santa Claus's Partner.* NY. Scribner's. 1899. 1st ed. sgn. $100.00–$200.00

Page, Thomas Nelson. *Social Life in Old Virginia Before the War.* NY. Scribner's. 1897. new edition. illus. $40.00–$50.00

Paine, Thomas. *Agrarian Justice, Opposed to Agrarian Law, and to Agrarian Monopoly.* Phil. Folwell. (1797). 1st US ed. 32 pp. wraps. $300.00–$400.00

Paley, William. *Principles of Moral and Political Philosophy.* Bos. Lincoln. 1801. 4th US ed. $40.00–$55.00

Palgrave. *Palgrave's Dictionary of Political Economy.* NY. Reprints. 1963. 3 vols. buckram. $150.00–$200.00

Palliser, John. *Solitary Rambles and Adventures of a Hunter in the Prairies.* Lon. Murray. 1853. 1st ed. frontis. illus. ½ calf. teg. $600.00–$750.00

Palmer, Dr. and Mrs. *Four Years in the Old World....* NY. Foster & Palmer. 1866. maroon cloth. gilt. $35.00–$50.00

Palmer, J. *Grizzly Bear in the Canadian Rockies.* Waukesha. private printing. 1936. illus. original printed wraps. $150.00–$200.00

Palmer, J. *Kodiak Bear Hunt.* NY. private printing. 1958. illus. dj. $200.00–$300.00

Pangborn, Edgar. *Davy.* NY. St. Martin's. 1964. 1st ed. review slip laid in. Hugo and Nebula nominee. dj. $150.00–$225.00

Pangborn, Edgar. *Mirror for Observers, A.* Garden City. Doubleday. 1954. 1st ed. International Fantasy Award winner. dj. $175.00–$250.00

Panger, Daniel. *Black Ulysses.* Athens. Ohio Univ Press. 1st ed. dj. $25.00–$30.00

Parker, Arthur C. (Gawaso Wanneh). *Skunny Wundy and Other Indian Tales.* NY. Doran. (1926). 1st ed. illus. plates. tan cloth. pictorial label. $50.00–$75.00

Parker, Dorothy. *Not So Deep as a Well.* NY. Viking. 1936. 1st ed. ltd 485 cc. sgn. lacking slipcase. $500.00–$600.00

Parker, Dorothy. *Sunset Gun.* NY. Boni & Liveright. 1928. 1st trade ed. blue cloth.
$40.00–$100.00

Parker, Dorothy. *Sunset Gun.* NY. Boni & Liveright. 1928. 1st trade ed. blue cloth. sgn. dj.
$600.00–$1,000.00

Parks, Gordon. *Choice of Weapons, A.* NY. Harper & Row. 1966. 1st ed. dj. $40.00–$75.00

Parks, Gordon. *Choice of Weapons, A.* NY. Harper & Row. 1966. 1st ed. sgn. dj.
$80.00–$100.00

Parr, Samuel (ed.). *Metaphysical Tracts by English Philosophers of the Eighteenth Century.* Lon. Lumley. 1837. 1st ed. 2 vols in one. brown cloth. $80.00–$100.00

Parrish, Maxfield. *Poems of Childhood.* Scribner's. 1904. 1st ed. $125.00–$150.00

Pascal, Blaise. *Thoughts on Religion and Other Curious Subjects.* Lon. Tonson. 1727. translated by Kennet. calf. raised bands. $400.00–$600.00

Pasteur, Lois. *Etudes sur la Biere (Studies on Beer).* Paris. 1876. 1st ed. illus. engraved plates.
$800.00–$950.00

Patchen, Kenneth. *First Will and Testament.* Norfolk. New Directions. 1939. 1st ed. inscrb. dj.
$175.00–$250.00

Pater, Walter. *Marius the Epicurean.* Lon. Macmillan. 1885. 1st ed. 2 vols. blue cloth.
$50.00–$75.00

Pater, Walter. *Miscellaneous Studies.* Lon. Macmillan. 1895. 1st ed. blue cloth.
$35.00–$50.00

Paterson, James Medill. *Little Brother of the Rich.* Chicago. Reilly & Britton. 1908. 1st ed.
$25.00–$40.00

Patriot, The: A Collection of Essay, upon Topics of Government. Dublin. Watts, Law. 1792–1793. 1st ed. disbound. $400.00–$500.00

Pattengill, Henry R. *The Civil Government of Michigan.* Pattengill, Pub. Michigan. 1887.
$35.00–$50.00

Patterson, J. H. *Man-Eating Lions of Tsavo, The.* Chi. Field Museum. 1925. wraps. 43 pp.
$100.00–$200.00

Paulsen, Gary. *Eastern Sun, Winter Moon.* NY. Harcourt Brace Jovanovich. 1st ed. inscrb.
$25.00–$35.00

Pearce, James. *Narrative of the Life of James Pearce. . . .* Rutland. Fay. 1825. 1st ed.
$600.00–$800.00

Peck, Bradford. *World a Department Store, The: A Story of Life Under a Cooperative System.* Main. Peck. (1900). 1st ed. illus. folding frontis. plates. $60.00–$75.00

Percy, Walker. *Last Gentleman.* Farrar, Straus & Giroux. 1966. 1st ed. dj.
$100.00–$130.00

Percy, Walker. *Love in the Ruins.* 1971. dj. $35.00–$55.00

Percy, Walker. *Moviegoer, The.* NY. Knopf. 1961. review copy of author's first book. National Book Award winner. dj. $7,500.00–$9,000.00

Perelman, S. J. *Chicken Inspector.* Simon & Schuster. 1966. 1st ed. dj. $35.00–$50.00

Perelman, S. J. *Ill-Tempered Clavicord.* Simon & Schuster. 1952. 1st ed. dj. $60.00–$90.00

Perkins, Edna Brush. *White Heart of the Mojave, The: An Adventure with the Outdoors of the Desert.* NY. Boni and Liveright. 1st ed. 229 pp. frontis. plates. photos. endpaper map. blue cloth. printed paper labels. $75.00–$100.00

Perkins, Lucy Fitch. *Indian Twins.* Houghton. 1920. illus. $18.00–$35.00

Perkins, Lucy Fitch. *Japanese Twins.* Houghton. 1912. illus. $30.00–$60.00

Pesci, David. *Amistad.* NY. Marlowe. (1997). 1st ed. dj. sgn. $50.00–$100.00

Peters, Ellis. *One Corpse Too Many.* Lon. Macmillan. 1979. 1st ed. dj. $800.00–$900.00

Peters, Frazier Forman. *Houses of Stone.* New York. Putnam's Sons. 1933. 1st ed. illus. tall, black cloth gold lettering on cover. $175.00–$125.00

Phillips, Christopher. *Damned Yankee: The Life of General Nathaniel Lyn.* MO. (1990). 1st ed. illus. dj. $40.00–$50.00

Phillips, Wendell. *Speeches, Lectures and Letters.* Bos. Lee and Shepard. 1884. later edition. $35.00–$50.00

Phillips, Wendell. *Speeches, Lectures and Letters.* Bos. Redpath. 1863. 1st ed. $75.00–$250.00

Phillips, Wendell. *Speeches, Lectures and Letters.* Bos. Redpath. 1863. 1st ed. sgn. $400.00–$800.00

Pickney, James D. *Reminiscences of Catskill.* Catskill. Hall. 1868. 1st ed. green cloth. $150.00–$200.00

Pinderton, Robert E. *The Canoe.* NY. Outing Pub. 1914. 1st ed. illus. gold illustrated binding. $25.00–$50.00

Pinkham, Lydia. *Text Book Upon Ailments Peculiar to Women.* Lynn, MA. Lydia Pinkham Medicine Co. wraps. fronts. 79 pp. $75.00–$90.00

Pinkowski, Edward. *John Siney, The Miners' Martyr.* Phil. Sunshine. 1963. 1st ed. illus. dj. $45.00–$50.00

Pinkwater, Daniel. *Last Guru, The.* NY. Bantam. (1978). wraps. $8.00–$12.00

Pinkwater, Daniel. *Return of the Moose.* NY. Dodd Mead. dj. $20.00–$30.00

Pinkwater, Daniel. *Uncle Melvin.* NY. Macmillan. 1989. 1st ed. dj. $15.00–$25.00

Pittenger, Peggy. *Morgan Horses.* So Brunswick. Barnes. 1977. 1st ed. $50.00–$75.00

Plath, Sylvia. *Ariel.* NY. Harper. (1966). 1st ed. dj. $85.00–$100.00

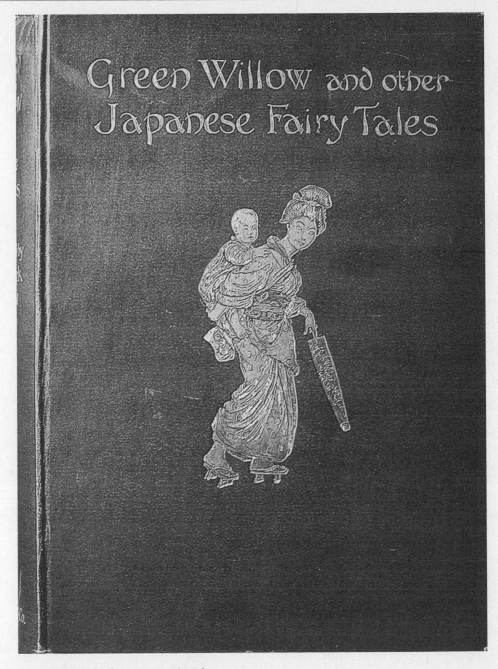

Green Willow and Other Japanese Fairy Tales,
London: Macmillan, 1910. Decorated cloth with
gilt cover illustration. $100.00–$150.00.

Plath, Sylvia. *Bell Jar, The.* Lon. Heinemann. (1963). 1st ed. cloth. dj. by Victoria Lucas.
$1,000.00–$2,000.00

Poe, Edgar Allan. *Fall of the House of Usher, The.* Cheshire House. 1931. illus. by Abner Epstein. ltd 1200 cc. tan cloth. $50.00–$70.00

Poe, Edgar Allan. *Journal of Julius Rodman, Being an Account of the First Passage across the Rocky Mountains of North America.* . . . Phil. Burton. 1840. 1st ed. $500.00–$700.00

Poe, Edgar Allan. *Tales of Mystery and Imagination.* NY. Brentano's. (1923). 1st ed. thus. illus. by Harry Clarke. pictorial label. $75.00–$100.00

Poe, Edgar Allan. *Works of.* . . . Chi. Stone & Kimball. 1894. 10 vols. illus. 36 plates. teg. green cloth. $300.00–$400.00

Poe, Edgar Allan. *Works of Edgar A. Poe, The.* NY. 1902. 10 vols. $100.00–$125.00

Poetry of the Beat Generation. NY. Mitchell. nd. wraps. Gaslight Poetry Review.
$30.00–$50.00

Pogany, Willy. *Wimp and the Woodle and Other Stories, The.* Los Angeles. Sutton. 1935. 1st ed. illus. dj. $300.00–$450.00

Pogany, Willy. *Wimp and the Woodle and Other Stories, The.* Los Angeles. Sutton. 1935. 1st ed. illus. dj missing. $100.00–$150.00

Pogany, Willy and Elaine. *Golden Cockerel.* NY. Thomas Nelson. 1938. 1st ed. illus. by W. Pogany. red cloth. $100.00–$200.00

Pohl, Frederik. *Jem.* NY. St. Martins. 1979. 1st ed. inscrb. dj. $30.00–$45.00

Pokagon, Chief. *O-Gi-Maw-Kew Mit-I-Gwa-Ki.* Michigan. Engle. 1901. illus. photos. gray pictorial wraps. $60.00–$100.00

Pokagon, Chief. *Red Man's Rebuke, The.* Michigan. Engle. (1893). ribbon tie.
$3,500.00–$5,000.00

Polk, James. *Treaty with Mexico.* . . . 30th Congress. 1st session. 1848. House Executive Document No 69. 74 pp. $150.00–$200.00

Poole, Ernest. *Harbor, The.* NY. Macmillan. 1915. 1st ed. $50.00–$90.00

Pop-up Minnie Mouse. NY. Blue Ribbon. 1933. 1st ed. illus. Pop-up Book. $600.00–$750.00

Pop-Up Mother Goose, The. Chi. Pleasure Books. 1934. 1st ed. illus. by Lentz. 3 pop-ups. pictorial boards. $150.00–$300.00

Pop-up Pinocchio, The. Blue Ribbon Books. 1932. 1st ed. illus. four color pop-ups. illustrated cover and spine. $100.00–$300.00

Porter, Katherine Anne. *Collected Essays.* NY. Delacorte. 1970. 1st ed. ltd 250 cc. marbled boards. frontis. slipcase. $200.00–$250.00

Portis, Charles. *True Grit.* NY. Simon & Schuster. 1968. 1st ed. dj. $75.00–$100.00

Potter, Beatrix. *Fairy Caravan.* McKay. (1929). 1st ed. $400.00–$600.00

Potter, Beatrix. *Tale of Jemima Puddleduck.* Warne. 1908. 1st ed. $500.00–$700.00

Potter, Beatrix. *Peter Rabbit.* Graham. (1914). illus. by Francis Brundage.
$100.00–$200.00

Potter, Beatrix. *Tale of Peter Rabbit.* Warne. 1910. 1st trade ed. $500.00–$700.00

Potter, Beatrix. *Tale of Pigling Bland.* Lon. Warne. 1913. illus. plates. $100.00–$400.00

Pound, Ezra. *Spirit of Romance.* NY. Dutton. nd. 1st US ed. ltd. 300 cc. $75.00–$90.00

Powell, Anthony. *Fisher King, The.* NY. Norton. (1986). 1st ed. $20.00–$30.00

Powell, E. Alexander. *The Last Frontier.* NY. Scribner's. 1912. illus. red-brown decorated. cloth. maps. $10.00–$30.00

Powell, E. Henry. *Edward Henry Powell.* Burlington, VT. 1938. 1st ed. wraps. illus. 84 pp. wrps. $10.00–$15.00

Powell, Lawrence Clark. *Books West Southwest.* Los Angeles. Ward Ritchie. 1957. 1st ed. 2000 cc. inscrb. $40.00–$50.00

Powell, Lawrence Clark. *Philosopher Pickett.* CA. Univ of California Press. 1942. 1st ed. dj. $50.00–$75.00

Powys, John Cowper. *In Defence of Sensuality.* NY. Simon & Schuster. 1930. 1st US ed.
$25.00–$40.00

Prairie Crusoe; or Adventures in the Far West, The. Bos. Lee and Shepard. 1875. illus. brown dec. cloth, gold lettering on spine. 277pp. $10.00–$20.00

Prairie Crusoe, The. Bos. Lee and Shepard. 1875. illus. brown decorated cloth.
$10.00–$20.00

Price, Francis. *British Carpenter, The: a Treatise on Carpentry. . . .* Lon. Ackers. 1735. illus. 2nd enlarged ed. 2 frontis. engr plates. $2,000.00–$2,500.00

Prime, W.C. *I Go A-Fishing.* NY. Harper & Bros. 1873. small brown cloth. paste-down lettering on spine. $20.00–$75.00

Pritchard, V. *English Medieval Graffiti.* Cambridge. Univ Press. 1967. illus. black cloth. dj. $50.00–$75.00

Private Bookplates, 1939. Bookplate Collectors Club. $25.00–$40.00

Proctor, Richard A. *Chance and Luck.* Lon. Longmans Green. 1887. 1st ed.
$300.00–$490.00

Proulx, E. Annie. *Shipping News, The.* NY. Scribner's. (1993). National Book Award winner. Pulitzer Prize winner. uncorrected proof. dj. $300.00–$600.00

Proulx, E. Annie. *Shipping News, The.* NY. Scribner's. (1993). National Book Award winner. Pulitzer Prize winner. sgn dj. $400.00–$800.00

Pushkin, Alexander. *Gabriel, A Poem in One Song.* NY. Covici-Friede. 1929. ltd 750 cc. illus by Rockwell Kent. $50.00–$100.00

Puss in Boots. NY. Blue Ribbon. 1934. illus. by Cloud and Lentz. Pop-up Book.
$200.00–$300.00

Pynchon, Thomas. *Gravity's Rainbow.* NY. Viking. (1973). 1st ed. National Book Award winner. dj.
$2,500.00–$3,500.00

Pynchon, Thomas. *Mason & Dixon.* NY. Holt. (1997). 1st ed. dj. $15.00–$25.00

Pynchon, Thomas. *Slow Learner.* Bos. Little Brown. (1984). 1st ed. dj. $30.00–$40.00

Pynchon, Thomas. *V.* Phil. Lippincott. 1963. 1st ed. author's first book. dj.
$2,000.00–$4,000.00

Pynchon, Thomas. *Vineland.* Bos. Little Brown. (1990). 1st ed. 1st printing. dj.
$40.00–$100.00

Pynchon, Thomas. *Vineland.* Bos. Little Brown. (1990). 1st ed. review copy. dj.
$125.00–$200.00

Quaife, Miles Milton. *Flag of the United States, The.* NY. (1942). 1st ed. illus. dj.
$20.00–$25.00

Quaritch, Bernard. *Catalogue of Illuminated and Other Manuscripts. . . .* Lon. Quaritch. 1931. illus. frontis. plate.
$40.00–$60.00

Queeny E. *Cheechako: The Story of an Alaska Bear Hunt.* NY. 1941. ltd 1200 cc. photos. cloth.
$100.00–$150.00

(Rackham, Arthur). *Arthur Rackham Fairy Book.* Phila. Lippincott. 1933. illus. by author. 7 color plates.
$125.00–$350.00

(Rackham, Arthur). *Arthur Rackham Fairy Book.* Lon. Harrap. 1933. illus. 1st ed.
$500.00–$750.00

(Rackham, Arthur). *Arthur Rackham Fairy Book.* Lon. Harrap. 1933. illus. 1st ltd ed. 460 cc. teg. sgn.
$1,500.00–$5,000.00

Raddclyffe, C. *Big Game Shooting in Alaska.* Lon. Ward. 1904. illus. map in rear pocket.
$1,000.00–$1,500.00

Ragan, W. H. *Transactions of the Mississippi Valley Horticultural Society.* Indianapolis. Carlon & Hollenbeck. 1884. illus. brown cloth. portrait frontis. $15.00–$25.00

Ramsey, J. G. M. *Annals of Tennessee, The.* Kingsport. 1926. black blind-stamped cloth, gilt lettering on spine, frontis pull-out map. $100.00–$150.00

Rand, Ayn. *Objectivist, The, Vols 5–10.* 69 issues in set. $700.00–$900.00

Randolph, Vance and George P. Wilson. *Down in the Holler: A Gallery of Ozark Folk Speech.* Normal. Univ of Oklahoma Press. (1953). 1st ed. dj. $60.00–$75.00

Ranlett, William. *Architect, The.* NY. 1849. designs, plans, details. 2 vols. folio.
$350.00–$700.00

Ransom, John Crowe. *Selected Poems.* NY. Knopf. 1945. 1st ed. dj. $35.00–$50.00

Ransome, Arthur. *Aladdin and His Wonderful Lamp*. Lon. Nisbet. (1919). 1st ed. illus. by Mackenzie. $350.00–$500.00

Ransome, Arthur. *Aladdin and His Wonderful Lamp*. Brentano's. (1920). 1st Amer ed. illus. by Mackenzie. $200.00–$300.00

Ransom's Family Receipt Book. *Buffalo*. D. Ransom & Son. n.d. 1st ed. wraps. illus. small orange illustrated cover, 32 pp. $5.00–$15.00

Raspe, Rudolph Erich. *The Adventures of Baron Munchausen*. Phil. Altemus. 1903. illus. small dec cover. $12.00–$30.00

Rath, E. J. *Something For Nothing*. NY. Grosset & Dunlap. 1928. red cloth. illustrated dj. $5.00–$15.00

Rawlings, Marjorie. *Cross Creek*. NY. Grosset & Dunlap. 1942. green decorated cover. dj. $12.00–$20.00

Rawlings, Marjorie Kinnan. *Yearling, The*. NY. Scribner's. 1938. 1st ed. illus. by Shenton. dj. $100.00–$350.00

Rawlings, Marjorie K. *Yearling, The*. NY. Scribner's Sons. 1938. 1st ed. dj. $400.00–$1,000.00

Rawlings, Marjorie K. *Yearling, The*. NY. Scribner's Sons. 1938. 1st ed. dj. inscrb. $1,500.00–$2,000.00

Rawlings, Marjorie K. *Yearling, The*. NY. Scribner's Sons. 1939 ltd. illus. by Wyeth. sgn by author and illustrator. $2,500.00–$4,500.00

Rawstorne, Lawrence. *Gamonia*. Lon. Methuen. 1905. illus. color plates., small red cloth with paste-down on spine. $25.00–$75.00

Redway, Major G. W. *War of Secession, 1861–1862: Bull Run to Malvern Hill*. Lon. 1910. 1st ed. 12 folding maps. map pocket. $200.00–$250.00

Reeve, Carl, and Ann Barton Reeve. *James Connolly and the United States*. NJ. Humanities. 1978. dj. $30.00–$35.00

Regulations for the Army of the Confederate States. Authorized edition. Richmond. 1862. $500.00–$600.00

Reichard, Gladys. *Navajo Medicine Man*. NY. Augustin. 1939. 1st ed. ltd 500 cc. illus. color serigraphs. $400.00–$500.00

Reiss, Winold. *Blackfeet Indians of Glacier National Park*. St. Paul, MN. Great Northern Railroad. 1940. 1st ed. illus. portfolio of paintings. self wrappers. $350.00–$400.00

Remsburg, John E. *Thomas Paine, the Apostle of Religious and Political Liberty*. Boston. Mendum. 1881. frontis. 27 pp supplement. maroon cloth. $50.00–$100.00

Report of the Warren Commission on the Assassination of President Kennedy. NY. (1964). illus. maps. sgn by Gerald Ford below the presidential seal. $550.00–$600.00

Report to the Board of Commissioners of the Department of Public Parks . . . New York. Albany. 1871. wraps. fldg maps. $350.00–$400.00

Revere, Joseph Warren. *Tour of Duty in California*. NY. 1849. 1st ed. rebacked. folding map. lithos. $750.00–$850.00

Reynolds, John S. *Reconstruction in South Carolina 1865–1877*. Columbia. The State Co. 1905. 1st ed. brown cloth lettering on spine. $150.00–$250.00

Rhoades, Lt. Henry. *Around the World With the Blue Jackets*. Bos. D Lothrop. 1890. illus. x-lib. $30.00–$40.00

Rhoades, Lt. Henry E. *Around the World With the Blue Jackets*. Bos. Lothrop Co. 1890. illus. blue cloth rebound. $25.00–$90.00

Rice, Anne. *Lasher*. NY. Knopf. 1993. 1st ed. sgn. dj. $60.00–$125.00

Rice, Anne. *Queen of the Damned, The*. NY. Knopf. 1988. 1st ed. sgn. dj. $100.00–$150.00

Rice, Anne. *Queen of the Damned, The*. NY. Knopf. 1988. 1st ed. dj. $30.00–$75.00

Rice, Anne. *Vampire Lestat, The*. NY. Knopf. 1985. 1st ed. sgn.dj. $100.00–$400.00

Richards, Laura E. *Silver Crown*. Little Brown. 1906. illus. $20.00–$30.00

Richardson, Albert. *Beyond the Mississippi*. Conn. American Pub. Co. 1869. illus. brown, blind-stamp and gilt lettering on cover and spine. 2-page map. $20.00–$100.00

Riis, Jacob A. *Theodore Roosevelt the Citizen*. NY. Outlook Company. 1904. illus. mustard cloth. sgn by author and Roosevelt. $4,500.00–$5,000.00

Rimmel, Eugene. *Book of Perfumes, The*. Lon. Chapman & Hall. 1865. purple cloth. aeg. $500.00–$600.00

Rinehart, Mary Roberts. *Dangerous Days*. NY. Doran Co. 1919. gray, lettered cover, illus. dj. $10.00–$18.00

Rinehart, Mary Roberts. *Tenting To-Night*. Bos. Houghton Mifflin. 1918. 1st ed. illus. $40.00–$50.00

Rivera, Diego. *Frescoes*. NY. (1929). $65.00–$90.00

Rivers, Laurel. *Little Dandy and Other Child Verse*. LA. Rex. 1913. 1st ed. wraps. 35 pp. presentation copy. $20.00–$25.00

Rivkin, Sadie H. (ed). *Mama's Meichulim: Traditional Jewish Cooking Made Easy*. NY. Yoseloff. 1960. 1st ed. dj. $20.00–$22.00

Roberts, Keith. *Grain Kings, The*. Lon. Hutchinson. 1976. 1st ed. dj. $60.00–$80.00

Roberts, Keith. *Kiteworld*. Lon. Gollancz. 1985. 1st ed. sgn. dj. $40.00–$60.00

Robertson, James D. *Great American Beer Book*. Ottawa. Caroline House. 1978. 1st ed. frontis. illus. dj. $25.00–$40.00

Robinson, Roland E. *In New England Fields and Woods*. Rutland. Charles E. Tuttle. 1937. green decorated binding. dj. $14.00–$30.00

Robinson, W. Heath. *Some Frightful War Pictures*. Lon. Duckworth. (1916). $150.00–$210.00

Robinson, William M. Jr. *Justice in Grey: A History of the Judicial System of the Confederate States of America.* Cambridge. 1941. 1st ed. map. $300.00–$350.00

Rodgers, William Ledyard. *Greek and Roman Naval Warfare.* US Naval Institute. 1937. illus. dj. $75.00–$90.00

Roehm, Marjorie Catlin. *Letters of George Catlin and His Family.* CA. Univ of CA Press. 1966. 1st ed. dj. $20.00–$60.00

Rogers, Henry C. *History of The Town of Paris and The Valley of the Sauquoit.* Utica. White & Floyd. 1881. 1st ed. brown decorated cloth, lettering on spine. $50.00–$75.00

Rogers, James H. *Toy Shop Sketches.* Phil. Theodore Presser. 1915. 1st ed. wraps. illus. tall dec wrps. $20.00–$25.00

Rogers, Will. *There's Not a Bathing Suit in Russia & Other Bare Facts.* NY. 1927. 1st ed. illus. by Herb Roth. $800.00–$900.00

Rohmer, Sax. *Bat Flies Low.* NY. 1935. 1st ed. $35.00–$50.00

Rohmer, Sax. *Green Eyes of Bast.* NY. 1920. 1st ed. $45.00–$75.00

Rohmer, Sax. *Grey Face.* NY. Doubleday. 1924. 1st ed. $15.00–$40.00

Rohmer, Sax. *Hand of Fu Manchu.* McBride. 1917. 1st ed. $50.00–$100.00

Rohmer, Sax. *Island of Fu Manchu.* Garden City. 1941. 1st ed. Crime Club. dj. $100.00–$450.00

Rohmer, Sax. *Moon of Madness.* Garden City. 1927. 1st ed. $75.00–$150.00

Rohmer, Sax. *Tales of Chinatown.* NY. Doubleday. 1922. 1st ed. $30.00–$60.00

Rohmer, Sax. *White Velvet.* Garden City. 1937. inscrb & sgn. dj. $900.00–$1,000.00

Rolfe, William. *A Satchel Guide to Europe.* Bos & NY. Houghton Mifflin. 1929. small red gold lettered with maps. $5.00–$15.00

Romero, P. B. *Mexico and Africa from the Sights of My Rifle.* private printing. nd. 1st ed. ltd 1000 cc. 322 pp. illus. photos. photographic endpapers. sgn. dj. $150.00–$200.00

Rood, Henry Edward. *Company Doctor, The.* NY. Merriam. 1895. 1st ed. cloth. $125.00–$150.00

Roosevelt, Eleanor. *On My Own.* NY. Harper. (1958). 1st ed. illus. photos. sgn. dj. $600.00–$700.00

Roosevelt, Eleanor. *This I Remember.* NY. Harper & Bros. 1949. 1st ed. illus. blue cloth. lettering on spine. cover faded. $20.00–$77.00

Roosevelt, Franklin D. *Democratic Book, 1936, The.* Phil. 1936. 1st ed. illus. folio. ltd ed bound. original wrappers bound in. sgn. $2,500.00–$3,000.00

Roosevelt, T. *African Game Trails.* NY. 1909. 1st ed. rare dj present. $1,000.00–$1,500.00

Roosevelt, Theodore. *African Game Trails.* NY. 1910. 1st ed. $100.00–$175.00

Roosevelt, Theodore. *Outdoor Pastimes of an American Hunter.* NY. 1905. 1st ed. illus.
$150.00–$400.00

Roosevelt, T. *Ranch Life and the Hunting Trail.* NY. 1888. 1st ed. illus. by Remington. original cloth.
$2,000.00–$3,000.00

Roosevelt, T. *Through the Brazilian Wilderness.* NY. 1914. 1st ed. illus. foldout map.
$300.00–$325.00

Rosenberg, Harold. *Anxious Object.* NY. Horizon. 1966. 2nd ed. sgn. dj. $45.00–$65.00

Rosenberg, Harold. *Re-Definition of Art.* NY. Horizon. (1972). 1st ed. inscrb. illus. dj.
$45.00–$65.00

Rosetti, Christina. *Goblin Market.* Lon. Macmillan. 1893. 1st ed. $300.00–$400.00

Ross, Ishbel. *Through the Lich-Gate: A Biography of the Little Church Around the Corner.* NY. 1931. ltd 175 cc. illus.
$40.00–$60.00

Ross, Sir John. *Narrative of a Second Voyage in Search of a North-West Passage....* Lon. Webster. 1835. 1st ed. frontis.
$1,500.00–$2,000.00

Rossell, Leonard. *Tracks ... Trails.* Boy Scouts of America. 1928. 1st ed. illus. green decorated. boards and cloth spine.
$15.00–$30.00

Roth, Henry. *Call It Sleep.* San Francisco. Arion. 1995. ltd 300 cc. sgn by Roth.
$500.00–$600.00

Roth, Philip. *Goodbye, Columbus.* Bos. Houghton Mifflin. 1959. 1st ed. author's first book. dj.
$800.00–$1,000.00

Rowling, J. K. *Harry Potter and the Sorcerer's Stone.* Scholastic Press. 1998. 1st U.S. ed. Book Club.
$300.00–$400.00

Rowling, J. K. *Harry Potter and the Sorcerer's Stone.* Scholastic Press. 1998. 1st US ed. 1st printing. dj.
$900.00–$1,200.00

Rowling, J. K. *Harry Potter and the Sorcerer's Stone.* Scholastic Press. 1998. 1st US ed. 1st printing. sgn. dj.
$1700.00–$2500.00

Rowling, J. K. *Harry Potter and the Goblet of Fire.* NY. Scholastic. 2000. 1st ed. one of 25 cc containing color drawing by GrandPre. dj.
$1,750.00–$2,250.00

Ruark, R. *Horn of the Hunter: The Story of an African Safari.* 2nd printing. illus. lacking dj.
$150.00–$200.00

Ruark, R. *Use Enough Gun.* 1st ed. dj. $65.00–$75.00

Rubin, Jerry. *We Are Everywhere.* 1971. 1st ed. dj. $20.00–$25.00

Rundell, Maria E. *A New System of Domestic Cookery.* Bos. 1807. $150.00–$200.00

Russell, Bertrand. *ABC of Atoms.* NY. Dutton. 1923. $25.00–$35.00

Rush, Benjamin. *An Account of the Bilious Remitting Yellow Fever.* Phil. Dobson. 1794. 2nd ed. leather.
$200.00–$350.00

Rush, Benjamin. *Medical Inquiries and Observations upon the Diseases of the Mind.* Phil. Kimber & Richardson. 1812. 1st ed. 2nd issue. ads. rebacked. $1,000.00–$1,500.00

Rush, Benjamin. *Medical Letters of the American Philosophical Society.* Princeton. 1951. 1st ed. 2 vols. red cloth. $50.00–$60.00

Rushdie, Salman. *Ground Beneath Her Feet, The.* Lon. Cape. (1999). ltd 150 cc. sgn. slipcase. $450.00–$600.00

Rushdie, Salman. *Moor's Last Sigh, The.* Pantheon. (1995). wraps. ltd 1000 advanced readers cc. numbered. sgn. $60.00–$75.00

Rushdie, Salman. *Satanic Verses.* Lon. Viking. 1989. 1st ed. $150.00–$300.00

Ruskin, John. *King of the Golden River, The.* Lon. Harrap. (1932). illus. by Rackham. ltd 570 cc. sgn by Arthur Rackham. slipcase. $700.00–$800.00

Russell, Dr. Nicholas. *Fog Signal, The.* China. North China Star. 1924. 1st ed. wraps. saddle stitched. 15 pp. $70.00–$90.00

Russell, Dr. Nicholas. *Reprehensible Aspirations of an Underdog....* China. 1924. 1st ed. wraps. saddle stitched. 22 pp. $70.00–$90.00

Russo, J. *Desert Bighorn Sheep in Arizona, The.* AZ. 1965. 3rd printing. wraps. $35.00–$45.00

Ruth, Babe. *Babe Ruth Story, The.* NY. Dutton. 1948. 1st ed. dj. as told to Bob Considine. sgn by Ruth. $5,000.00–$9,000.00

Ruth, Babe. *Babe Ruth's Big Book of Baseball.* n.p. Quaker Oats Co. 1935. 1st ed. wraps. illus. colorful cover of the Babe . $75.00–$150.00

Ryan, J. M. *Rat Factory, The.* Englewood Cliffs, NJ. Prentice-Hall. (1971). 1st ed. dj. $50.00–$75.00

Ryan, Lynkall. *Aboriginal Tasmanians.* S. Lucia. Univ Queensland Press. 1981. 1st ed. dj. $20.00–$25.00

Sackville-West, Edward. *Piano Quintet.* Lon. Heinemann. 1925. 1st ed. author's first book. cloth. $50.00–$75.00

Sackville-West, Vita. *Country Notes.* Lon. Joseph. (1939). 1st ed. dj. $30.00–$40.00

Sackville-West, Vita. *Nursery Rhymes.* Lon. Joseph. (1950). 1st trade ed. tan cloth. $30.00–$50.00

Sackville-West, Vita. *Passenger to Teheran.* NY. Doran. (1927). 1s US ed. 500 cc. $150.00–$200.00

Sackville-West, Vita. *Women's Land Army, The.* Lon. Joseph. (1944). dj. $75.00–$90.00

Sadleir, Michael. *Authors and Publishers.* Lon. Dent. (1932). 1st ed. dj. $15.00–$20.00

Sadleir, Michael. *Desolate Splendour.* Lon. Constable. 1923. 1st trade ed. dj. $40.00–$50.00

Saint Exupery, Antoine de. *Wind, Sand and Stars.* NY. Reynal & Hitchcock. (1939). 1st US ed. ltd 500 cc. sgn. slipcase. $1,500.00–$2,200.00

Salinger, J. D. *Catcher in the Rye.* 1951. 1st ed. black cloth. pictorial dj with photograph on back. $5,000.00–$15,000.00

Salinger, J. D. *Catcher in the Rye.* 1951. 1st ed. black cloth. pictorial dj with photograph on back. sgn. $25,000.00–$30,000.00

Salinger, J. D. *Franny and Zooey.* Bos. Little Brown. (1961). 1st ed. dj $500.00–$1,000.00

Salinger, J. D. *Kitbook for Soldiers, Sailors & Marines.* 1943. 1st ed. $60.00–$150.00

Salinger, J. D. *Nine Stories.* Bos. (1953). 1st ed. dj. $1,200.00–$7,000.00

Salinger, J. D. *Twenty-two Stories.* np. Train Bridge Recluse. (1998). blue wrappers. pirated ed of uncollected stories from periodicals. $500.00–$575.00

Salk, Jonas. *Man Unfolding.* NY. Harper & Row. 1972. 1st ed. first book by Salk. inscrb. dj. $200.00–$300.00

Samelius, W. and Charles Purdom. *It's Timing that Counts.* Denver. Roberts Pub. 1944. 1st ed. wraps. illus. green cloth, lettering on cover. 59 pp. ads, scarce. $30.00–$40.00

Sandburg, Carl. *Abraham Lincoln: The Prairie Years.* NY. (1926). 1st trade ed. 2 vols. illus. inscrb. sgn. $575.00–$600.00

Sandburg, Carl. *Lincoln and Whitman Miscellany, A.* Chi. 1938. 1st ed. 250 cc. illus. plates. inscrb. $750.00–$800.00

Sandburg, Carl and Paul Angle. *Mary Lincoln: Wife and Widow.* NY. (1932). ltd 260 cc. numbered. sgn. plates. folding chart. teg. slipcase. $1,800.00–$2,000.00

Sandoz, Mari. *Battle of the Little Bighorn.* Phil. Lippincott. (1966). uncorrected proof. wraps. $25.00–$40.00

Sansom, William. *Bed of Roses, A.* NY. Harcourt Brace. (1954). 1st US ed. dj. $35.00–$50.00

Sargent, Lucious Manlius. *Well Enough for the Vulgar.* Bos. Damrell. 1836. 1st ed. #12 in Temperance Tales. printed wraps. $35.00–$50.00

Saroyan, William. *My Name is Aram.* NY. Armed Services. nd. wraps. published for military distribution. $15.00–$25.00

Sarton, May. *Education of Harriet Hatfield, The.* NY. Norton. 1989. 1st ed. sgn. dj. $75.00–$90.00

Sartre, Jean-Paul. *Age of Reason, The.* NY. Knopf. 1947. 1st US ed. red cloth. dj. $30.00–$40.00

Saukie Indians and Their Great Chiefs Black Hawk and Keokuk, The. Vaile Co. Rock Island. Il. 1926. 1st edition. $25.00–$65.00

Saunders, J. C. *Anatomy of the Human Ear, The.* Phila. Warner. 1821. illus. 1st Amer ed. lea. plates. $550.00–$700.00

Savoy Cocktail Book, The. NY. Richard R. Smith. 1930. illus. gold/black decorated cover. front and rear hinges cracked. $150.00–$395.00

Scarpa, Antonio. *Treatise on the Principal Diseases of the Eyes, A.* Lon. Cadell & Davies. 1818. illus. 2nd UK ed. plates. $600.00–$750.00

Scarpa, Antonio. *Practical Observations on the Diseases of the Eye.* Lon. Cadell & Davies. 1805. 1st ed. lea. $700.00–$900.00

Schaldach, William J. *Currents & Eddies: Chips from the Log of an Artist-Angler.* New York. Barnes and Co. 1944. 1st ed. illus. cloth. lettering on cover. 1/5000 cc. $15.00–$30.00

Schaller, G. *Mountain Monarchs: Wild Sheep and Goats in the Himalayas.* 1977. 1st ed. illus. dj. $50.00–$90.00

Schmeil, Lotte. *Children and Animals.* Racine, Wis. Whitman. 1935. 1st ed. wraps. illus. School of Emmy Zweybruck, Vienna, oblong wrps. $45.00–$75.00

Schmoe, F. W. *Our Greatest Mountain.* NY. Putnam. 1925. 1st ed. illus. green cloth with gold lettering on cover and spine, fold-out map. $15.00–$65.00

Schuchert, Charles and Clara M. LeVene. *Earth and Its Rhythms, The.* New York. D. Appleton. 1927. 1st ed. illus. red decorated cloth with gold lettering on cover and spine. $12.00–$20.00

Schwarze, Rev. Edmund. *History of the Moravian Missions Among the Southern Tribes.* Bethlehem. Times. 1923. 1st ed. illus. dark blue cloth, near fine. $100.00–$150.00

Scidmore, E. R. *China The Long-Lived Empire.* NY. Century. 1900. illus. yellow dec. cloth. profusely illus. $6.00–$30.00

Scott, George Ryley. *History of Cockfighting.* Lon. Skilton. 1st ed. 205 pp. frontis. ltd cc. $150.00–$175.00

Scott, Mrs. O. W. *Prove It.* Chi. Woman's Temperance Publishing. (1889). green cloth. $70.00–$80.00

Scott, Thomas. *Holy Bible.* Phil. Woodward. 1811–13. 3rd American ed. 5 vols. $500.00–$900.00

Scudder, Horace E. *Dream Children.* Cambridge. Sever and Francis. 1864. illus. plates. $75.00–$100.00

Sears, Herbert Mason. *Journal of a Canteen Worker.* Bos. Privately printed. 1919. 1st ed. illus. small red cloth with leather spine. $20.00–$50.00

Seger, John H. *Tradition of the Cheyenne Indians.* Oklahoma. Arapaho Bee. (1905). 1st ed. wraps. illus. photos. $350.00–$450.00

Seller, Charles Coleman. *Lorenzo Dow, the Bearer of the Word.* Minton, Balch. 1928. 1st ed. illus. sgn. dj. $25.00–$50.00

Selous, F. C. *Hunter's Wanderings in Africa, A.* Lon. 1895. early edition. 3 gold animals on cover. green cloth. $900.00–$1,100.00

Sendak, Maurice. *In the Night Kitchen.* NY. Harper & Row. 1970. 1st ed. illus. Caldecott Honor winner. $200.00–$400.00

Sendak, Maurice. *Outside Over There.* NY. Harper & Row. (1981). 1st ed. illus. color. dj.
$50.00–$125.00

Sendak, Maurice. *Posters by.* Harmony, NY. 1986. 1st ed. dj.　　　　$28.00–$35.00

Sendak, Maurice. *Where the Wild Things Are.* NY. Harper & Row. 1963. 1st ed. 1st issue.
$8,500.00—$15,000.00

Seton, Ernest Thompson. *The Ten Commandments in the Animal World.* New York. Doubleday Page & Co. 1925. small green cl. frontis port.　　　　$10.00–$35.00

Seuss, Dr. *Happy Birthday to You!* NY. Random House. (1959). 1st ed. illus. first edition of Seuss book in full color. dj.　　　　$850.00–$1,000.00

Seuss, Dr. *The Lorax.* NY. Random House, 1971.　　　　$400.00–$1,000.00

Seventh Annual Round the World Cruise. *Canadian Pacific.* 1929. 1st ed. illus. black boards illus. paste-down on cover. very good.　　　　$10.00–$25.00

Sewell, Anna. *Black Beauty.* Boston. 1890. 1st US ed. boards.　　$1,000.00–$1,500.00

Sewell, Anna. *Black Beauty: His Grooms and Companions.* Bos. American Humane Society. (1890). wraps. early printing in US.　　　　$350.00–$375.00

Sexton, R. W. *American Apartment Houses, Hotels, and Apartment Hotels of Today.* NY. (1929). illus. photo plates.　　　　$500.00–$600.00

Shakespeare, William. *Works in 10 Volumes.* Lon. Bickers. 1880–81. illus. 4th ed.
$200.00–$300.00

Shakespeare, William. *Works of. . . .* Lon/NY. Nonesuch/Random House. 1929–33. 7 vols.
$1,200.00–$1,500.00

Shakespears, Capt. H. *Wild Sports of India, The.* Lon. 1860. 307 pp. cloth.　$400.00–$500.00

Shastid, Thomas Hall, M. D. *Duke of Duluth, The.* Ann Arbor. Wahr. 1926. 1st ed. 2 vols. pictorial paper labels.　　　　$25.00–$40.00

Shaw, Albert, ed. *American Monthly Review of Reviews, The.* NY. 1901. 3/4 lea. and bds. bnd vol. #1, Vol. XXIV.　　　　$25.00–$40.00

Shaw, Fred G. *Science of Fly Fishing for Trout, The.* NY. Scribner's. 1925. 1st ed. illus. photos, diagrams. boards.　　　　$75.00–$100.00

Shaw, George Bernard. *Are We Heading for War?* Lon. (1934). wraps. 12 pp.
$30.00–$40.00

Shaw, George Bernard. *From the Savoy.* Bos. Luce. 1905. 1st ed.　　　$25.00–$50.00

Shaw, George Bernard. *Misalliance, the Dark Lady of the Sonnets, and Fanny's First Play.* New York. Brentano. 1914. 1st ed. black cloth, lettering on spine.　　　$50.00–$90.00

Shaw, George Bernard. *Misalliance, The Dark Lady of the Sonnets . . .* Constable and Co. Lon. 1914.　　　　$30.00–$50.00

Shaw, George Bernard. *Short Stories, Scraps and Shavings.* Dodd Mead & Co. 1934. Wood engravings. dust jacket. 1st. edition.　　　　$50.00–$90.00

Shaw, George Bernard. *Three Plays.* Franklin Library. 1979. ltd ed. illus by Hogarth. lea. aeg. $30.00–$35.00

Shaw, George Bernard (ed.). *Fabian Essays in Socialism.* Lon. Scott. (1890). 2nd ed. green cloth. $40.00–$65.00

Shaw, George Bernard. *The Apple Cart.* Lon. Constable & Co. 1930. $6.00–$15.00

Sheckley, Robert. *Alchemical Marriage of Alistair Crompton, The.* Lon. Joseph. 1978. 1st ed. sgn. dj. $50.00–$75.00

Sheckley, Robert. *Crompton Divided.* NY. Holt Rinehart Winston. 1978. 1st US ed of The Alchemical Marriage of Alistair Crompton. sgn. dj. $25.00–$40.00

Sheldon, C. *Wilderness of the Upper Yukon.* 1913. 1st ed. 2nd printing. frontis. gilt pictorial cover. $500.00–$600.00

Shelley, Mary. *Frankenstein, or The Modern Prometheus.* Pennyroyal Press. 1983. ltd 350 cc. sgn by Moser, publisher and illustrator. half morocco and red cloth. teg. extra plates. slipcase. $1,500.00–$2,000.00

Shepard, Lucius. *Golden, The.* Shingletown, CA. Zeising. 1993. 1st ed. sgn. #11/500 cc. dj.
$80.00–$100.00

Shepard, Lucius. *Jaguar Hunter, The.* UK. Kerosina. 1988. 1st UK ed. sgn. dj.
$40.00–$50.00

Shepard, Lucius. *Jaguar Hunter, The.* UK. Kerosina. 1988. 1st UK hardcover ed. #220/250 cc. numbered and sgn. World Fantasy Award winner. dj. $100.00–$150.00

Shepard, Sam. *Lie of the Mind, A.* SF. Arion Press. 1993. 1st illustrated ed. ltd 300 cc. numbered. sgn. $350.00–$500.00

Sheppard, W. Crispin. *Knight of the West Side, A.* Phil. Penn. 1909. 1st ed. dj. frontis. plates.
$100.00–$130.00

Sherwood, Mary Martha. *Lady of the Manor, The: Being a Series of Conversations on the Subject of Confirmation.* NY. Phil/Balt. 1825–1829. 7 vols. frontis. $500.00–$600.00

Shiel, M. P. *Lord of the Sea, The.* Lon. Grant Richards. 1901. 1st ed. 1st issue. cloth.
$600.00–$700.00

Shields, Walter C. *Ancient Ground, The.* Nome, Alaska. Keenok Club. 1918. 1st ed. green buckram. 47 pp. $80.00–$90.00

Silverberg, Robert. *Lord Valentine's Castle.* Harper & Row. (1980). 1st ed. sgn. dj.
$20.00–$25.00

Silverberg, Robert. *Shadrach in the Furnace.* Ind. Bobbs Merrill. (1976). 1st ed. dj.
$15.00–$25.00

Silverberg, Robert. *Starborne.* Norwalk. Easton Press. (1996). 1st ed. ltd 1500 cc. numbered. sgn. bound in maroon bookmark. not issued in dj. $75.00–$85.00

Silverberg, Robert. *Tower of Glass.* NY. Scribners. 1970. 1st ed. sgn. dj. $80.00–$90.00

Silverberg, Robert. *Unfamiliar Territory.* NY. Scribners. 197. 1st ed. sgn. dj. $50.00–$75.00

Simak, Clifford D. *Cosmic Engineers.* NY. Gnome. 1950. 1st ed. author's first full-length novel. dj. $75.00–$100.00

Simak, Clifford D. *Fellowship of the Talisman, The.* NY. Del Rey. 1978. 1st ed. dj.
$20.00–$30.00

Simmons, Dan. *Phases of Gravity.* Lon. Headline. 1990. 1st hardcover ed. ltd 250 cc numbered and sgn. lea. slipcase. $175.00–$225.00

Simmons, Dan. *Prayers to Broken Stones.* IL. Dark Harvest. 1990. 1st ed. sgn. ltd 550 cc. numbered. dj. slipcase. $100.00–$150.00

Simpkins, Cuthbert Ormone, M.D. *Coltrane: A Biography.* NY. Herndon House. 1975. 1st ed. illus. purple cloth with lettering on spine, dj. $35.00–$100.00

Simpson, George. *Narrative of a Journey Round the World. . . .* Lon. Colburn. 1847. 1st ed. 2 vols. frontis. folding map. 438 pp. 469 pp. $750.00–$1,000.00

Simpson, James. *Homeopathy: Its Tenets and Tendencies. . . .* Phil. Lindsay & Blakiston. 1854. 1st US ed. brown cloth. $150.00–$200.00

Sinclair, Emil (Herman Hesse). *Demian.* Berlin. 1919. 1st ed. in German.
$4,000.00–$5,000.00

Sinclair, Upton. *Jungle, The.* NY. Doubleday. 1906. 1st ed. 2nd state. brown cloth.
$75.00–$100.00

Sinclair, Upton. *Jungle, The.* NY. Jungle Pub. 1906. 1st ed. published by Sinclair.
$1,200.00–$1,500.00

Sinclair, Upton. *Jungle, The.* NY. Doubleday. 1906. 1st ed. inscrb. sgn.
$2,000.00–$2,500.00

Sinclair, Upton. *King Coal.* NY. Mac-millan. 1917. 1st ed. $125.00–$150.00

Singer, Isaac Bashevis. *Gentleman from Cracow, The, and The Mirror.* NY. Limited Editions Club. 1979. illus. by Soyer. ltd 2000 cc. sgn by editor and illustrator. $300.00–$350.00

Singer, Isaac Bashevis. *Lost in America.* Garden City. Doubleday. 1981. 1st ed. illus. by Soyer. ltd 500 cc. sgn by Singer with Soyer print laid in. slipcase. $200.00–$250.00

Siringo, Charles A. *History of Billy the Kid.* Austin. 1967. pictorial cloth. $30.00–$75.00

Siringo, Charles A. *Lone Star Cowboy.* Santa Fe. 1919. 1st ed. pictorial cloth.
$100.00–$400.00

Siringo, Charles A. *Riata & Spurs.* Bos/NY. Houghton Mifflin. 1927. 1st ed. illus. pictorial cover. $200.00–$300.00

Skinner, H. M. D. *American Book of Cookery, Containing More than Five Hundred Receipts, The.* Bos. J.B. Hall. 1851. 1st ed. wraps. small illustrated cover 110 pages worn, browned pages. $300.00–$500.00

Skoman, Larry. *Reefer Madness: the History of Marijuana in America.* Indianapolis. Bobbs Merrill. 1979. 1st ed. dj. $25.00–$30.00

Slane, O. B. *Reminiscences of Early Peoria.* Peoria. Privately Printed. 1933. 1st ed. gray boards. #28/500 cc. presentation copy. signed by author. $25.00–$40.00

Slavery in the West Indies. NY. Negro Univ Press. 1969. reprint. $30.00–$40.00

Sloan, Richard E. *Memories of an Arizona Judge.* Stanford. Stanford Univ Press. 1932. 1st ed. dj. $125.00–$160.00

Sloan, W. B. *Complete Farrier, The.* Chi. Sloan. 1848. 32 pp. $800.00–$1,000.00

Smedley, Agnes. *Daughter of the Earth.* 1929. 1st ed. $50.00–$75.00

Smiles, P. *Land of the Black Buffalo.* Lon. 1961. illus. dj. $150.00–$200.00

Smith, Adam. *Inquiry into the Nature and Causes of the Wealth of Nations....* Phil. Dobson. 1796. 2nd American edition. 3 vols. $1,000.00–$2,000.00

Smith, Adam. *Inquiry into the Nature and Causes of the Wealth of Nations.* Lon. 1811.
                                                                        $300.00–$800.00

Smith, Adam. *Inquiry into the Nature and Causes of the Wealth of Nations, A.* Lon. 1799. 3 vols. $600.00–$800.00

Smith, Adam. *An Inquiry into the Nature and Causes of the Wealth of Nations.* Lon. 1830. 2 vols. djs. $80.00–$100.00

Smith, Adam. *An Inquiry into the Nature and Causes of the Wealth of Nations.* Edinburgh. Silvester Doig and Andrew Stirling etc. 1817. 3 volume set, decorated leather, raised bands on spine, gold lettering on spine, marbleized endpaper. $200.00–$450.00

Smith, Albert. *Wassail Bowl, The.* Lon. Bentley. 1843. 1st ed. 2 vols. $150.00–$225.00

Smith, Clarence R. (ed.). *American Legion in New York State, The . . . for the years 1919–1939.* American Legion, Dept of New York. 1942. illus. photos. 543 pp. dj. $25.00–$35.00

Smith, Cordwainer. *Norstrilla.* Lon. Gollancz. 1988. 1st hardcover ed. dj. $30.00–$50.00

Smith, Cordwainer. *Quest of the Three Worlds.* Lon. Gollancz. 1989. 1st hardcover ed. dj.
                                                                        $15.00–$30.00

Smith, Cordwainer. *Rediscovery of Man, The.* Lon. Gollancz. 1988. 1st trade ed. dj.
                                                                        $20.00–$30.00

Smith, J. H. *Guide to Health; Being a Compendium of Medical Instruction, upon Botanic Principles....* Ann Arbor. Sullivan. 1842. $200.00–$250.00

Smith, Jessie Wilcox. *In the Closed Room.* McClure. 1904. 1st ed. illus. by Jessie Wilcox Smith. $30.00–$80.00

Smith, John. *Book of Mormon.* Palmyra, NY. Grandin. 1830. 1st ed. original calf. 5000 cc.
                                                                    $60,000.00–$75,000.00

Smith, Martin Cruz. *Gorky Park.* NY. Random House. (1981). 1st ed. dj. $20.00–$40.00

Smith, Martin Cruz. *Gypsy in Amber.* NY. (1971). 1st ed. dj. $60.00–$75.00

Smith, Martin Cruz. *Indians Won, The.* NY. Belmont. (1970). 1st ed. wraps.
$100.00–$125.00

Smyth, Rev. Thomas. *Rule and Measure of Christian Charity, The.* Charleston. Jenkins. 1847. 1st ed. 24 pp. disbound. $85.00–$100.00

Snyder, Fairmont. *Rhymes for Kindly Children.* Volland. (1916). 1st ed. illus. by Johnny Gruelle. $100.00–$200.00

Soddy, Frederick. *Radio-Activity: An Elementary Treatise. . . .* Lon. Electrician. 1904. 1st ed. author's first book. brown cloth. $600.00–$900.00

Soiland, Albert. *Viking Goes to Sea, The.* Los Angeles. Times Mirror. 1924. 1st ed. illus. inscrb. sgn. log of racing schooner. $35.00–$45.00

Solzhenitsyn, Aleksandr. *Gulag Archipelago.* NY. Harper & Row. 1973. 1st ed. 3 vols.
$35.00–$75.00

Solzhenitsyn, Aleksandr. *One Day in the Life of Ivan Denisovich.* NY. Dutton. 1963. 1st ed. dj.
$40.00–$50.00

Some Queer Americans and Other Stories. NY. Werner. 1899. illus. $25.00–$40.00

Sommer, F. *Man and Beast in Africa.* Lon. 1953. illus. foreword by Ernest Hemingway.
$90.00–$110.00

Sontag, Susan. *In America.* NY. Farrar Straus & Giroux. (2000). sgn. dj. $50.00–$90.00

Speck, Frank and George Herzog. *The Tutelo Spirit Adoption Ceremony.* Harrisburg. Penn Historical Commission. 1942. 1st ed. illus. black cloth. logo on cover. $12.00–$30.00

Spence, Lewis. *Encyclopaedia of Occultism.* NY. University Books. (1960). 1st ed. illus.
$15.00–$25.00

Spillane, Mickey. *Deep, The.* NY. Dutton. 1961. 1st ed. dj. $50.00–$75.00

Spillane, Mickey. *Kiss Me Deadly.* NY. 1952. 1st ed. dj. $100.00–$225.00

Sprague, George F. *Soldiers' Record Town of Craftsbury, Vermont 1861–1865.* Craftsbury. 1914. 1st ed. wraps. wrps. frontis. $25.00–$35.00

Spyri, Johanna. *Heidi.* Phil. McKay. 1922. illus. by Jessie Wilcox Smith. $25.00–$45.00

Stanhope, Philip Dormer. *Letters Written by the Late Honourable Philip Dormer Stanhope . . . To His Son. . . .* Lon. Dodsley. 1775. 6th ed. rebound. frontis. $100.00–$150.00

Stanley, H. *Congo and the Founding of the Free State.* NY. 1885. illus. 2 vols. 528 pp and 483 pp. folding maps in pockets. gilt. $600.00–$700.00

Stanley, Henry M. *Through the Dark Continent.* NY. Harper & Bros. 1879. 2 vols. maps. plates. $100.00–$200.00

Stanton, Elizabeth Brandon. *Fata Morgana: A Vision of Empire _ the Burr Conspiracy in Mississippi Territory. . . .* Louisiana. Signal. 1917. 1st ed. black cloth. 348 pp. presentation copy. sgn.
$60.00–$75.00

Stanton, G. Smith. *When the Wildwood Was in Flower*. NY. Ogilvie Pub. Co. 1909. 1st ed. illus. red cloth with illustrated. paste-down on front cover. presentation copy. signed by author. $85.00–$200.00

Stanton, Henry Brewster. *Random Recollections*. NY. Macgowan & Slipper. 1886. 2nd enlarged ed. original wrappers. inscrb to Chief Justice Morrison R. Waite. $200.00–$300.00

Star Trek. Random House. 1977. 4 fan-folded pop-ups. $65.00–$100.00

Star Trek Technical Manual. 1975. 1st ed. $35.00–$50.00

Steele, Matthew Forney. *American Campaigns*. DC. Adams. 1909. 1st ed. illus. 2 vols. maps. plates. $800.00–$900.00

Stegner, Wallace. *Big Rock Candy Mountain, The*. NY. Duell, Sloan and Pearce. (1943). 1st ed. dj. $1,000.00–$1,500.00

Stegner, Wallace. *Crossing to Safety*. PA. Franklin Library. 1987. 1st ed. sgn. lea. $100.00–$125.00

Stegner, Wallace. *Preacher and the Slave, The*. Bos. Houghton Mifflin. 1950. 1st ed. about union activist Joe Hill. sgn. dj. $900.00–$1,250.00

Stegner, Wallace. *Preacher and the Slave, The*. Bos. Houghton Mifflin. 1950. 1st ed. dj. $500.00–$900.00

Stegner, Wallace. *Sound of Mountain Water, The*. NY. Doubleday. 1969. 1st ed. 1st issue. dj. $200.00–$250.00

Stein, Gertrude. *Autobiography of Alice B. Toklas*. NY. Harcourt Brace. 1933. 1st ed. dj. $900.00–$1,000.00

Stein, Gertrude. *How to Write*. Paris. Plain. (1931). 1st ed. ltd 1000 cc. gray boards. $200.00–$250.00

Stein, Gertrude. *World is Round, The*. NY. Scott. (1939). 1st ed. illus. by Clement Hurd. dj. $200.00–$250.00

Stein, Joseph. *Zorba*. NY. Random House. (1969). review copy. review slip laid in. dj. $100.00–$175.00

Steinbeck, John. *East of Eden*. NY. Viking. 1952. 1st ed. ltd 1500 cc. sgn. $4,000.00–$5,000.00

Steinbeck, John. *East of Eden*. NY. Viking. 1952. 1st ed. dj. $275.00–$450.00

Steinbeck, John. *East of Eden*. NY. Viking. 1952. 1st trade ed. dj. $600.00–$750.00

Steinbeck, John. *The Grapes of Wrath*. NY. Viking. 1939. illustrated cover. no dj. soiled. $150.00–$200.00

Steinbeck, John. *Grapes of Wrath, The*. NY. 1939. 1st ed. dj. $7,000.00–$7,500.00

Steinbeck, John. *Of Mice and Men*. NY. 1937. 1st ed. points. sgn. dj. $8,000.00–$9,000.00

Steinbeck, John. *Of Mice and Men*. NY. Covici Friede. 1937. 1st ed. 1st issue. inscrb. sgn. dj. $9,000.00–$11,000.00

Steinbeck, John. *Of Mice and Men*. NY. Covici Friede. 1937. 1st ed. 2nd issue. dj.
$225.00–$500.00

Steinbeck, John. *Of Mice and Men*. NY. Covici Friede. 1937. 1st ed. 1st issue. dot between 8s
on pg 88. dj. $1,200.00–$2,500.00

Steinbeck, John. *Of Mice and Men*. NY. Covici Friede. 1937. 1st ed. good condition. soiled
and damaged dj. $2,000.00–$2,500.00

Steinbeck, John. *Pastures of Heaven, The*. NY. Brewer, Warren & Putnam. 1932. 1st ed. 650
cc. bottom edges rough. dj. $10,000.00–$15,000.00

Steinbeck, John. *Red Pony, The*. NY. Covici Freide. 1937. 1st ed. 699 cc. numbered. sgn. slipcase. $2,250.00–$2,500.00

Steinbeck, John. *Tortilla Flat*. NY. 1935. 1st ed. wraps. pictorial dj. ltd 500 cc in this state.
$4,000.00–$5,000.00

Steinbeck, John. *To a God Unknown*. 1st ed. fine condition. dj. $3,000.00–$4,000.00.

Steinbeck, John. *Travels with Charley*. NY. Viking. 1962. 1st ed. dj. $350.00–$600.00

Steinbeck, John. *Travels with Charley*. NY. Viking. 1962. 1st ed. inscrb. dj.
$4,000.00–$6,500.00

Steinbeck, John. *In Dubious Battle*. Covici.Friede. NY. 1936. 1st ed. no dust jacket.
$200.00–$500.00

Steinbeck, John. *In Dubious Battle*. Covici.Friede. NY 1936. 1st ed. dust jacket.
$500.00–$3,500.00

Steinmetz, Charlies Proteus. *Four Lectures on Relativity and Space*. NY. McGraw-Hill. 1923.
1st ed. stereo cards in rear pocket. 126 pp. $75.00–$100.00

Stephenson, Gilbert Thomas. *Race Distinctions in American Law*. NY/Lon. 1910. 1st ed.
cloth. 388 pp. $175.00–$250.00

Stevenson, Robert Louis. *Black Arrow, The*. NY. Saalfeld. 1926. illus. by Francis Brundage.
$150.00–$200.00

Stevenson, Robert Louis. *Black Arrow, The*. NY. Scribner's. 1888. 1st ed. yellow wrappers.
$350.00–$400.00

Stevenson, Robert Louis. *Child's Garden of Verse, A*. Lon. 1886. 1st ed. ltd 1000 cc. cloth.
$4,000.00–$5,000.00

Stevenson, Robert Louis. *Merry Men, The*. Lon. Chatto & Windus. 1887. 1st ed. 32 pp ads.
blue cloth. $300.00–$500.00

Stevenson, Robert Louis. *Strange Case of Dr. Jekyll and Mr. Hyde*. The. NY. Scribner's. 1886.
1st ed. 14 pp ads. 1/3000 published in original yellow wrappers. $6,000.00–$7,000.00

Stevenson-Hamilton, J. *Animal Life in Africa*. Lon. 1912. 1st ed. illus. foreword by Theodore
Roosevelt. cloth. recaased. $90.00–$110.00

Stewart, Dugald. *Elements of the Philosophy of the Human Mind.* Brattleboro, VT. Fessenden. 1813. $100.00–$175.00

Stiefel, H.C. *Slices From a Long Loaf.* Pittsburgh. Bissell Block. 1905. illus. brown cloth. lettering on cover. decorated endpapers. $10.00–$15.00

(Stieglitz) *Alfred Stieglitz: Photographs & Writings.* DC. National Gallery of Art. (1983). 1st ed. photo plates. folio. dj. $40.00–$140.00

Stieglitz, Alfred. *Georgia O' Keefe: a Portrait.* NY. MOMA. 1st ed. illus. dj. slipcase.
                                                                              $80.00–$110.00

Stille, Charles. *Life and Times of John Dickinson, The.* Phil. Phil. Historical Soc. 1891. cloth. paper spine label. $95.00–$130.00

Stille, Charles. *Major General Anthony Wayne and the Pennsylvania Line in the Continental Army.* Phil. Lippincott. 1893. 1st ed. ltd 150 cc. steel engraved frontis portrait.
                                                                              $100.00–$135.00

Stille, Charles. *Reminiscences of a Provost.* Privately Printed. 1866. wraps. in org. wrps.
                                                                               $25.00–$40.00

Stocking, Amer Mills. *Saukie Indians and Their Chiefs Black Hawk and Keokuk, The.* Rock Island. The Vaile Company. 1926. 1st ed. illus. red cloth, gilt lettering on cover and spine.
                                                                               $25.00–$35.00

Stone, Rev. Collins. *Address Upon the History and Methods of Deaf Mute Instruction.* OH. 1869. 1st ed. wraps. disbound. 23 pp. $200.00–$300.00

Stoppard, Tom. *Arcadia.* Lon/Bos. Faber and Faber. (1993). 1st ed. $40.00–$50.00

Story of John Smeaton and the Eddystone Lighthouse, The. Lon. Nelson and Sons. 1884. 1st ed. small green dec cloth, col frontis. $40.00–$60.00

Stout, Rex. *And Four to Go.* NY. Viking. 1958. 1st ed. dj. $100.00–$250.00

Stout, Rex. *Before Midnight.* NY. Viking. 1955. 1st ed. dj. $100.00–$175.00

Stout, Rex. *Black Orchids.* NY. Collier. 1941. 1st ed. dj. $200.00–$1,000.00

Stout, Rex. *Death of a Doxy.* NY. Viking. 1966. 1st ed. dj. $75.00–$100.00

Stout, Rex. *Death of a Dude.* NY. Viking. 1969. 1st ed. dj. $50.00–$90.00

Stout, Rex. *Family Affair.* Lon. 1975. 1st UK ed. dj. $35.00–$45.00

Stout, Rex. *Might As Well Be Dead.* Collins. 1957. 1st UK ed. dj. $40.00–$55.00

Stout, Rex. *Mother Hunt.* NY. Viking. 1963. 1st ed. dj. $30.00–$35.00

Stowe, Harriet Beecher. *Key to Uncle Tom's Cabin, The.* Bos. 1853. 1st ed. $500.00–$1,000.00

Stowe, Harriet Beecher. *Men of Our Times.* Hartford. 1868. 1st ed. $65.00–$100.00

Stowe, Lyman. *Stowe's Bible Astrology.* Detroit. Lyman Stowe. 1907. 1st ed. illus. small dec. cloth. $95.00–$150.00

Stowell, Jay S. *Methodist Adventures in Negro Education*. New York. The Methodist Book Concern. 1922. 1st ed. illus. yellow cloth, black lettering on cover and spine.
$15.00–$40.00

Stratton Porter, Gene. *A Girl of the Limberlost*. NY. Doubleday Page. 1909. 1st ed. dj.
$250.00–$450.00

Stratton Porter, Gene. *A Girl of the Limberlost*. NY. Doubleday Page. 1909. 1st ed. dj. inscribed.
$800.00–$1,000.00

Straub, Peter. *Mystery*. NY. Dutton. 1990. uncorrected proof. stiff blue wrappers.
$45.00–$60.00

Strieber, Whitley. *Black Magic*. NY. Morrow. 1982. 1st ed. dj. $35.00–$45.00

Strode, Hudson. *Jefferson Davis: American Patriot; Confederate President; Tragic Hero; Private Letters*. NY. 1955–56. 1st ed. 4 vols. $200.00–$300.00

Stuart, Ruth McEnery. *River's Children: An Idyl of the Mississippi*. NY. Century. 1904. 1st ed. illus. frontis. plates. pictorial green cloth. dj. $100.00–$125.00

Stuart, Ruth McEnery. *River's Children: An Idyl of the Mississippi*. NY. Century. 1904. 1st ed. illus. frontis. plates. pictorial green cloth. $40.00–$50.00

Stump, Rev. Adam. *Secret of the Canon, The*. Phil. Lutheran Publication. 1898. red and green cloth, gilt lettering on cover and spine. $25.00–$45.00

Sturgeon, Theodore. *Caviar*. Lon. Sidgwick & Jackson. 1968. 1st ed. dj. $200.00–$250.00

Sturgeon, Theodore. *More Than Human*. NY. 1953. 1st ed. dj. $100.00–$150.00

Sturgeon, Theodore. *Sturgeon in Orbit*. Lon. 1970. 1st UK ed. dj. $150.00–$200.00

Sturgeon, Theodore. *Touch of Strange, A*. Garden City. Doubleday. 1958. 1st ed. dj.
$100.00–$300.00

Styron, William. *Admiral Robert Penn Warren & The Snows of Winter: A Tribute*. Winston-Salem. Palaemon Press. 1978. ltd 250 cc. blue wrappers. tipped in frontis photo. sgn.
$100.00–$125.00

Styron, William. *Confessions of Nat Turner*. NY. Random House. (1967). 1st ed. sgn. dj.
$75.00–$150.00

Styron, William. *Confessions of Nat Turner*. NY. Random House. (1967). 1st ed. dj.
$25.00–$50.00

Styron, William. *Lie Down in Darkness*. IN. Bobbs Merrill. 1951. 1st ed. author's first book. dj.
$120.00–$150.00

Styron, William. *Sophie's Choice*. NY. Random House. (1979). National Book Award winner. sgn. dj. $300.00–$500.00

Sulston, John and Georgina Ferry. *Common Thread, The*. DC. Joseph Henry Press. 2002. 1st ed. inscrb. dj. $500.00–$650.00

Sutter, Johann August. *Diary of Johann August Sutter.* SF. Grabhorn. 1932. illus. color litho.
$70.00–$80.00

Sutton, Margaret. *Haunted Attic, The.* Grosset & Dunlap. 1932. 1st ed. Judy Bolton series. dj.
$10.00–$25.00

Sutton, Margaret. *Mark on the Mirror.* Grosset & Dunlap. 1942. 1st ed. Judy Bolton series. dj.
$15.00–$30.00

Sutton, Margaret. *Secret of the Barred Window.* Grosset & Dunlap. 1943. 1st ed. Judy Bolton series. dj.
$20.00–$50.00

Swayne, H. *Seventeen Trips to Somaliland and a Visit to Abyssinia.* Lon. Ward. 1893. 1st ed. illus. cloth.
$800.00–$1,000.00

Swedenborg, Emanuel. *Doctrine of the New Jerusalem Concerning the Sacred Scripture.* Bos. Folsom. 1795. blue paper over boards.
$350.00–$425.00

Swift, Jonathan. *Gulliver's Travels.* Lon. Motte. 1726. 1st ed. illus. later printing. 2 vols. frontis. plates. teg.
$5,000.00–$8,000.00

Swiggett, Howard. *Rebel Raider, The: A Life of John Hunt Morgan.* Indianapolis. (1934). 1st ed. illus. map.
$100.00–$125.00

T. A. B. *Trials and Trust: A Story of the French Revolution.* Phil. Presbyterian Bd. of Pub. 1872. illus. small green blindstamped cloth. frontis.
$25.00–$50.00

Tarkington, Booth. *Claire Ambler.* NY. Doubleday. 1928. 1st ed. dj. dark blue cloth. decorated endpapers.
$25.00–$100.00

Tarkington, Booth. *Gentleman From Indiana, The.* NY. Doubleday, McClure. 1899. 2nd issue binding.
$200.00–$250.00

Tarkington, Booth. *Harlequin and Columbine.* Garden City. Doubleday Page. 1921. 1st ed. inscrb. dj.
$175.00–$200.00

Tarkington, Booth. *Women.* Garden City. Doubleday Page. 1925. 1st ed. inscrb. dj.
$150.00–$190.00

Tarkington, Booth. *World Does Move, The; An Autobiographical Narrative.* Lon. Heinemann. 1929. 1st UK ed. inscrb. dj.
$800.00–$900.00

Taylor, Ann and Jane. *Correspondence Between a Mother and a Daughter at School.* NY. Gilley. 1818. 1st US ed.
$40.00–$50.00

Taylor, J. *African Rifles and Cartridges.* 1948. 1st ed. 430 pp.
$150.00–$225.00

Taylor, John. *History of Ten Baptist Churches, of Which the Author has been Alternately a Member. . . .* KY. Holeman. 1823. 1st ed. lea. 300 pp.
$1,000.00–$1,250.00

Taylor, Rev. Ernest. *History of Brome County Quebec, Vol II.* Montreal. John Lovell & Son. 1937. 1st ed. illus. green cloth, gilt lettering on cover and spine.
$40.00–$50.00

Teller, Walter. *Joshua Slocum.* New Brunswick. Rutgers Univ Press. 1971. 2nd ed. ilus.
$30.00–$40.00

Ten Little Niggers. NY. McLoughlin. wraps. illus. Bo-Peep Series. colorful plates. tape on spine, some soil to cover, tears on rear page. plates vgd. $450.00–$1,200.00

Tennyson, Alfred Lord. *Harold: A Drama.* Lon. Henry S King. 1877. 1st ed. $50.00–$75.00

Tennyson, Alfred Lord. *Passing of Arthur.* Lon. Macmillan. 1884. 1st ed. printed wraps.
$200.00–$300.00

Tenzing, Norgay. *After Everest.* Lon. Allen & Unwin. (1977). 1st English ed. sgn by Tenzing and Edmund Hillary. dj. $500.00–$1,000.00

Terkel, Studs. *Working.* Pantheon. 1974. 1st ed. dj. $40.00–$65.00

Thackeray, William M. *Mahogany Tree, The.* Bos. Cassino. 1887. $25.00–$140.00

Thayer, Bert Clark. *Steeplechasing.* NY. The Artful Press. 1949. 1st ed. illus. green cloth. paste-down on cover. $20.00–$40.00

Thayer, Emma Homan. *Wild Flowers of the Rocky Mountains.* NY. Cassell. (1889). illus. revised. $250.00–$325.00

Thayer, Ernest Lawrence. *Casey at the Bat (in A Treasury of Humorous Poetry).* Bos. Estes and Company. 1902. 1st appearance in hardbound book. $1,000.00–$2,000.00

Thayer, Frank S. (ed.). *Colorado in Color and Song.* Denver. Thayer. 1899. 1st ed. illus. 23 color photos. tan cloth. gilt photo on cover. $300.00–$400.00

Theory and Art of Penmanship a Manual for Teachers. Bos. Crosby and Nichols. 1864. illus. brown cloth decorated cover very good cond. $15.00–$40.00

Theroux, Alexander. *Darconville's Cat.* Garden City. Doubleday. 1981. 1st ed. 1st issue. sgn. dj. $100.00–$150.00

Theroux, Paul. *London Embassy.* Bos. Houghton Mifflin. 1974. 1st ed. dj. $25.00–$40.00

Theroux, Paul. *Mosquito Coast.* Bos. Houghton Mifflin. 1982. 1st ed. dj. $15.00–$20.00

Theroux, Paul. *Waldo.* Bos. Houghton Mifflin. 1967. 1st ed. author's first book. sgn. dj.
$250.00–$350.00

Thomas, Benjamin P. *Abraham Lincoln, A Biography.* NY. 1952. ltd 500 cc. sgn. illus. maps. lea. $600.00–$700.00

Thomas, Dylan. *Adventures in the Skin Trade.* Lon. Putnam. (1955). 1st ed. dj.
$70.00–$200.00

Thomas, Dylan. *Child's Christmas in Wales, A.* CT. New Directions. 1954. 1st ed. dj.
$40.00–$300.00

Thomas, Dylan. *Under Milk Wood.* New Directions. 1954. 1st ed. dj. $60.00–$135.00

Thompson, C. *Mildred. Reconstruction in Georgia: Economic, Social, Political, 1865–1872.* Goucester, MA. 1964. reprint of 1915 ed. $22.00–$65.00

Thompson, Hunter. *Great Shark Hunt.* NY. Summit/Rolling Stone. (1979). 1st ed.
$45.00–$100.00

Thompson, Hunter S. *Fear and Loathing in Las Vegas*. NY. Random House. (1971). illus. by Steadman. dj. $325.00–$800.00

Thompson, Hunter S. *Fear and Loathing Letters, The*. 1st ed. 1997/2000 2 vols. black lea. ltd 50 cc. slipcase. sgn. dj. $900.00—$4,000.00

Thompson, Ruth Plumly. *Handy Mandy in Oz*. Chi. (1927). 1st ed. 16-page signatures. $150.00–$800.00

Thompson, Ruth Plumly. *Hungry Tiger of Oz*. Chi. Reilly & Lee. 1926. illus. by J. R. Neill. pictorial green cover. $60.00–$500.00

Thompson, Ruth Plumly. *Lost King of Oz*. Chi. Reilly & Lee. (1925). illus. by J. R. Neill. 12 color plates. $60.00–$400.00

Thompson, Ruth Plumly. *Pirates of Oz*. Chicago. (1931). 1st ed. $125.00–$300.00

Thompson, Ruth Plumly. *Yellow Knight of Oz*. Chi. Reilly & Lee. 1930. no dj. illus. b/w illustration. cloth. $90.00–$200.00

Thompson, Ruth Plumly. *Yellow Knight of Oz*. Chi. Reilly & Lee. 1930. dj. illus. $375.00–$1,500.00

Three Bears, The. Racine. Whitman. 1927. 1st ed. wraps. illus. tall colorful linen-like finish cover. $25.00–$35.00

Three Little Kittens. Ohio. Saalfield. 1943. 1st ed. wraps. illus. oversized cloth-like. $10.00–$15.00

Tissot, Samuel. *Advice to the People in General, with Regard to Their Health*. Lon. 1768. 3rd revised ed. $400.00–$600.00

Tocqueville, Alexis de. *Democracy in America*. Lon. 1836. 1st English Language ed. 2 vols. frontis. lea. $1,500.00–$2,500.00

Tocqueville, Alexis de. *Democracy in America*. NY. 1838. 1st American ed. $3,000.00–$4,000.00

Tolkien, J. R. R. *Father Christmas Letters*. Bos. Houghton Mifflin. 1976. 1st ed. $25.00–$75.00

Tolkien, J. R. R. *Hobbit, The*. Bos. 1966. dj. $100.00–$300.00

Tolkien, J. R. R. *Hobbit, The*. Bos. Houghton Mifflin. 1938. 1st US ed. 1st issue with bowing Hobbit on title page. dj. $2,000.00–$12,000.00

Tolkien, J. R. R. *Lord of the Rings*. Lon. Allen & Unwin. 1954–55. 1st ed. 3 vols. djs. $12,000.00–$45,000.00

Tolkien, J. R. R. *Lord of the Rings*. NY. Houghton Mifflin. 1967. 3 vols. $2,000.00–$4,000.00

Tolkien, J. R. R. *Lord of the Rings*. Lon. Allen & Unwin. 1955. later impressions. 3 vols. $2,000.00–$3,500.00

Tolkien, J. R. R. *Silmarillion*. 1977. 1st ed. dj. $100.00–$200.00

Tolkien, J. R. R. and Donald Swann. *Road Goes Ever On, The: A Song Cycle*. Bos. Houghton Mifflin. 1967. 1st ed. dj. $75.00–$150.00

Tormé, Mel. *It Wasn't All Velvet*. NY. Viking. 1988. 1st ed. illus. photos.dj. $75.00–$100.00

Tormé, Mel. *Traps, the Drum Wonder: the Life of Buddy Rich*. NY. Oxford Univ Press. 1991. 1st ed. illus. photos. sgn dj. $100.00–$150.00

Tower Report. *Report of the President's Special Review Board*. DC. President's Special Review Board. (1987). sgn by Tower, Edmund Muskie and Brent Scowcroft. wrappers.
$450.00–$600.00

Tract Primer, The. NY. American Tract Society. illus. blue blindstamped and dec binding, woodcuts, fair cond. $15.00–$50.00

Trapper's Companion, The. Columbus. Fur-Fish-Game. 1946. 1st ed. wraps. illus. small illus. cover wrps. very good cond. $5.00–$15.00

Traver, Robert. *Anatomy of a Fisherman*. NY. (1964). 1st ed. $125.00–$175.00

Traver, Robert. *Anatomy of a Murder*. NY. St. Martin's. 1958. 1st ed. dj. $800.00–$1,000.00

Traver, Robert. *Trout Madness*. NY. St. Martin's Press. 1960. 1st ed. green boards. dj.
$50.00–$90.00

Traver, Robert. *Trout Magic*. NY. Simon & Schuster. 1989. 1st ed. maroon cloth. dj.
$16.00–$30.00

Traver, Robert. *Trout Magic*. NY. McGraw. 1964. 1st ed. illus. color photos. dj.
$75.00–$200.00

Trial of Andrew Johnson, President of the United States, Before the Senate of the United States. . . . DC. GPO. 1868. 1st ed. 498 pp. black cloth. 2 vols. $100.00–$125.00

Trial of the Assassins and Conspirators at Washington City, D. C., May and June, 1865 for the Murder of President Abraham Lincoln. Phil. (1865). wraps. illus. $500.00–$550.00

Trillin, Calvin. *Education in Georgia, An*. NY. Viking. 1964. 1st ed. errata slip laid in. sgn. dj.
$100.00–$150.00

Trollope, Anthony. *Duke's Children, The*. Lon. Chapman and Hall. 1880. 3 vols.
$200.00–$300.00

Trollope, Anthony. *Letter from Anthony Trollope Describing a Visit to California in 1875*. San Francisco. Colt Press. 1946. 1st ed. ltd 500 cc. wood engravings. green cloth spine, orange paper boards. $50.00–$75.00

Trollope, Anthony. *Phineas Finn*. NY. Harper. 1869. 1st US ed. $150.00–$200.00

Trollope, Mrs. *Domestic Manners of the Americans*. Lon. Whittaker, Treacher. 1832. 2nd ed. 2 vols. ads. plates. $500.00–$750.00

Trowbridge, Bertha Chadwick. *Old Houses of Connecticut*. New Haven. Yale Univ Press. 1923. 1st ed. ltd. sgn. $130.00–$150.00

Trumbo, Dalton. *Johnny Got His Gun*. Phil. Lippincott. 1939. 1st ed. dj. $300.00–$1,000.00

Trumbo, Dalton. *Johnny Got His Gun.* Phil. Lippincott. 1939. 1st ed. sgn. dj.
$2,000.00–$3,000.00

Trumbo, Dalton. *Washington Jitters.* Bos. Knopf. 1936. 1st ed. dj. $100.00–$200.00

Tudor, Tasha. *Amanda and the Bear.* NY. Oxford Univ Press. 1951. 1st ed. illus. inscrb.
$300.00–$400.00

Tudor, Tasha. *And It Was So.* Phil. Westminster. 1958. 1st ed. illus. $90.00–$100.00

Tudor, Tasha. *First Graces.* NY. Oxford Univ Press. 1955. 1st ed. illus. dj. $75.00–$150.00

Tudor, Tasha. *First Prayers.* NY. Oxford Univ Press. 1952. 1st ed. illus. sgn. dj.
$200.00–$300.00

Tudor, Tasha. *First Prayers.* NY. Oxford Univ Press. 1952. 1st ed. illus. dj. $75.00–$100.00

Tudor, Tasha. *Tale for Easter, A.* NY. Oxford Univ Press. 1941. 1st ed. illus. by Tudor. pictorial dj. $375.00–$400.00

Tudor, Tasha. *Tasha Tudor's Bedtime Book.* NY. Platt & Munk. (1977). 1st ed. illus. plates.
$9.50-$20.00

Turrou, Leon G. *Where My Shadow Falls: Two Decades of Crime Detection.* D. Doubleday. 1949. dj. $50.00–$80.00

Turrou, Leon G. *Where My Shadow Falls: Two Decades of Crime Detection.* Doubleday. 1949. 224 pp. worn. $30.00–$50.00

Twain, Mark (Samuel Clemens). *Adventures of Huckleberry Finn, The.* NY. Charles L. Webster & Co. 1885. 1st ed. illus. rebound. points for later issue. original cloth spine bound in.
$6,000.00–$7,000.00

Twain, Mark (Samuel Clemens). *Adventures of Huckleberry Finn, The.* NY. Charles L. Webster & Co. 1885. 1st ed. illus. points for later issue. pictorial blue cloth. $2,300.00–$5,000.00

Twain, Mark (Samuel Clemens). *Adventures of Huckleberry Finn, The.* NY. Charles L. Webster & Co. 1885. 1st ed. illus. 1st state. morocco. marbled boards. points.
$12,000.00–$20,000.00

Twain, Mark (Samuel Clemens). *Autobiography and First Romance.* New York. Sheldon & Co. 1871. illus. terra cotta cloth lettering on cover. 2nd issue. $150.00–$250.00

Twain, Mark (Samuel Clemens). *Innocents Abroad, The.* Lon. Ward, Lock. nd. early edition, unauthorized. pictorial wrappers. $300.00–$400.00

Twain, Mark (Samuel Clemens). *Sketches New and Old.* Chi. American Publishing Co. 1875. 1st ed. 1st issue. blue cloth. points. $1,500.00–$2,000.00

Twain, Mark (Samuel Clemens). *Tramp Abroad, A.* Leipzig. Tauchnitz. 1880. 2 vols. 1st Continental ed. green cloth. gilt. $100.00–$150.00

Tydeman, William (ed.). *Medieval European State, 500–1550.* Cambridge Univ Press. 2001. 1st ed. illus. dj. $100.00–$150.00

Tyler, Anne. *Accidental Tourist, The*. NY. Knopf. (1985). 1st ed. National Book Critics Circle Award winner. dj. $40.00–$55.00

Tyler, Anne. *Celestial Navigation*. NY. Knopf. 1974. 1st ed. sgn. dj. $400.00–$500.00

Tyler, Anne. *Clock Winder, The*. NY. Knopf. 1972. 1st ed. sgn. dj. $2,750.00–$3,500.00

Tyler, Anne. *Clock Winder, The*. NY. Knopf. 1972. 1st ed. uncorrected proof.
$1,500.00–$2,500.00

Tyler, Anne. *Saint Maybe*. NY. Knopf. 1991. 1st ed. dj. $50.00–$85.00

Tyndall, John. *Forms of Water in Clouds and Rivers Ice and Glaciers, The*. Ohio. The Werner Co. n.d. illus. small green cl. dec. spine. $5.00–$15.00

U.S. Camera. NY. 1953. $12.00–$20.00

U.S. Camera. NY. 1945. $30.00–$50.00

United States Sanitary Commission. *Narrative of Privations and Sufferings of United States Officers and Soldiers while Prisoners of War*. . . . Bos. Little's. 1864. 1st ed. illus. woodcut plates.
$750.00–$950.00

University-High School of Milwaukee. *Milwaukee*. Boardman. 1886. 1st ed. blue cloth, gold lettering on cvr. $25.00–$35.00

Updike, John. *Centaur, The*. NY. Knopf. 1963. later printing. dj. $40.00–$60.00

Updike, John. *Centaur, The*. NY. Knopf. 1963. 1st ed. dj. $75.00–$100.00

Updike, John. *Midpoint and Other Poems*. NY. Knopf. 1969. 1st ed. dj. $50.00–$75.00

Updike, John. *Pigeon Feathers*. NY. 1962. 1st ed. dj. $40.00–$60.00

Updike, John. *Poorhouse Fair, The*. NY. Knopf. 1959. 1st ed. dj. $300.00–$400.00

Updike, John. *Rabbit at Rest*. NY. Knopf. 1990. 1st ed. dj. $30.00–$50.00

Updike, John. *Rabbit Redux*. NY. Knopf. 1971. 1st ed. sgn. dj. $100.00–$250.00

Updike, John. *Rabbit Redux*. NY. Knopf. 1971. 1st ed. dj. $30.00–$60.00

Updike, John. *Rabbit, Run*. NY. Knopf. 1960. 1st ed. dj. $800.00–$900.00

Updike, John. *Rabbit, Run*. NY. Knopf. (1960). 1st ed. sgn. dj. $1,400.00–$2,000.00

Updike, John. *Witches of Eastwick*. NY. Knopf. 1984. 1st ed. ltd 350 cc. slipcase. unopened.
$175.00–$250.00

Updike, John. *Witches of Eastwick*. NY. Knopf. 1984. 1st ed. dj. $75.00–$90.00

Uris, Leon. *Exodus*. NY. Doubleday. 1st ed. dj. $50.00–$90.00

Uris, Leon. *Mila 18*. Doubleday. 1961. 1st ed. dj. $50.00–$120.00

Utah. *Hastings House*. 1941. black cloth. $45.00–$50.00

Van Buren, Martin. *Piracy and Murder. A Message From*. . . . DC. 1840. 1st ed. 76 pp.
$45.00–$60.00

Van Deusen, John G. *Economic Bases of Disunion in South Carolina.* NY. 1928. 1st ed. folding map. $125.00–$150.00

Van Vogt, A. E. *Mind Cage, The.* NY. Simon & Schuster. 1957. 1st ed. dj. $50.00–$90.00

Vanderbilt, Gertrude Lefferts. *The Social History of Flatbush and Manners and Customs of the Dutch Settlers in Kings County.* New York. D. Appleton. 1881. 1st ed. grey-blue cloth lettering on spine, pull-out map of Flatbush, 1842. $100.00–$150.00

Varney, Harold Lord. *Revolt.* 1919. 1st ed. $45.00–$65.00

Varney, Philip. *Arizona's Best Ghost Towns.* Flagstaff. Northland Press. (1980). 1st ed. illus. cloth. maps. photos. $40.00–$50.00

Vermont in the Civil War. Burlington. Free Press. 1886. 1st ed. 2 vols. $150.00–$200.00

Verne, Jules. *American Gun Club.* NY. Scribner, Armstrong. 1874. early US ed. trans by Louis Mercier. illus. $900.00–$2,000.00

Verne, Jules. *Archipelago on Fire, The.* Lon. Sampson Low Marston Searle and Rivington. 1886. 1st English ed. 32 pp ads. green cloth decorated in black. $4,000.00–$5,000.00

Verne, Jules. *Around the World in Eighty Days.* NY. Osgood. 1874. illus. engr. cloth. $700.00–$900.00

Verne, Jules. *Around the World in Eighty Days.* Bos. Osgood. 1873. 1st illustrated US ed. terra-cotta cloth. $3,000.00–$4,500.00

Verne, Jules. *Around the World in Eighty Days.* Lon. Sampson, Low, Marston, Searle & Rivington. illus. 1879. rebound. $800.00–$1,000.00

Verne, Jules. *Castle of the Carpathians, The.* OH. Saalfield. 1900. 2nd US ed. illus. terra cotta cloth. black and blue pictorial decoration 7. $700.00–$800.00

Verne, Jules. *Doctor Ox.* Bos. Osgood. 1874. 1st US ed. blindstamped green cloth. gilt decoration. $600.00–$800.00

Verne, Jules. *Facing The Flag.* NY. F. Tennyson Neely. 1897. blue cloth. decorated. spine. $50.00–$135.00

Verne, Jules. *Mysterious Island, The.* Lon. 1875. 1st English ed. 3 vols. cloth. aeg. $5,000.00–$7,000.00

Verne, Jules. *Their Island Home.* NY. 1924. 1st US ed. $40.00–$50.00

Verne, Jules. *Twenty Thousand Leagues Under the Sea.* Lon. Wark Lock. nd. early UK ed. green cloth. aeg. $500.00–$600.00

Verne, Jules. *Twenty Thousand Leagues Under the Sea.* Bos. Smith. 1875. 3rd ed. green cloth. $1,500.00–$1,750.00

Verne, Jules. *Twenty Thousand Leagues Under the Sea.* NY. Heritage Press. (1956). slipcase. $25.00–$40.00

Verne, Jules. *Twenty Thousand Leagues Under the Sea.* NY. Grosset & Dunlap. (1917). Photo-Play ed. copyright Universal Film Company. pictorial dj. $1,500.00–$2,000.00

Verne, Jules. *Twenty Thousand Leagues Under the Sea*. Bos. Smith. 1873. 1st US ed. 2nd issue. sold only by subscription. green cloth. aeg.　　　　　　　　$4,500.00–$5,500.00

Verne, Jules. *Wreck of the Chancellor*. Bos. 1875. 1st ed.　　　　$20.00–$30.00

Vidal, Gore. *Lincoln*. NY. Random House. 1984. 1st trade ed. dj.　　$40.00–$55.00

Vidal, Gore. *Lincoln*. Franklin Center. Franklin Library. 1984. 1st ed. illus. sgn. lea. deluxe.
　　　　　　　　$80.00–$100.00

Vidor, King. *A Tree is a Tree*. NY. Harcourt Brace. 1953. 1st ed. inscrb to Merle Oberon. dj.
　　　　　　　　$300.00–$350.00

Vonnegut, Kurt. *Breakfast of Champions*. NY. Delacorte Press. (1973). 1st ed. orange cloth. sgn. dj.　　　　　　　　$375.00–$500.00

Vonnegut, Kurt. *God Bless You, Mr. Rosewater*. Holt Rinehart Winston. 1965. 1st ed. dj.
　　　　　　　　$150.00–$400.00

Vonnegut, Kurt. *God Bless You, Mr. Rosewater*. Holt Rinehart Winston. 1965. 1st ed. sgn. dj.
　　　　　　　　$750.00–$1,000.00

Vonnegut, Kurt. *Jailbird*. np. 1979. 1st ed. dj.　　　　　　$25.00–$30.00

Vonnegut, Kurt. *Slapstick*. NY. Delacorte. 1979. 1st ed. dj.　　　$30.00–$40.00

Vonnegut, Kurt. *Slaughterhouse Five*. NY. 1969. sgn. dj.　　$1,000.00–$1,800.00

Wade, Wyn Craig. *Fiery Cross, The; the Ku Klux Klan in America*. NY. Simon & Schuster. 1987. 1st ed. illus. dj.　　　　　　　　$18.00–$20.00

Wadsworth, Wallace C. *The Real Story Book*. New York. Rand McNally. 1927. 1st ed. illus. by Margaret Evans Price, tall green illus. cloth with paste-down on front cover.
　　　　　　　　$25.00–$250.00

Wagner, Henry Raup. *Juan Rodriguez Cabrillo, Discoverer of the Coast of California*. San Francisco. California Historical Society. 1941. 1st ed. 94 pp. color frontis. cloth-backed boards. printed paper spine label. ltd 750 cc.　　　　$100.00–$150.00

Wagner, Henry Raup. *Sir Francis Drake's Voyage Around the World*. San Francisco. Howell. 1926. 1st ed. frontis portrait. illus. maps. charts. navy cloth.　　$150.00–$200.00

Walford, Lionel A. *Marine Game Fishes of the Pacific Coast From Alaska to the Equator*. Berkeley. Univ of California Press. 1937. 1st ed. illus. by Link Malmquist. sgn by Malmquist. maps.　　　　　　　　$225.00–$250.00

Walker, Alice. *Color Purple, The*. NY. Harcourt Brace. (1982). 1st ed. dj.　$500.00–$600.00

Walker, Alice. *Good Night, Willie Lee, I'll See You in the Morning*. NY. Dial. (1979). 1st ed. yellow wraps. uncorrected proof.　　　　　　$700.00–$800.00

Walker, Alice. *Good Night, Willie Lee, I'll See You in the Morning*. NY. Dial. (1979). 1st ed. dj.
　　　　　　　　$700.00–$800.00

Walker, Alice. *Horses Make a Landscape Look More Beautiful*. NY. Harcourt Brace. 1981. 1st ed. dj.　　　　　　　　$30.00–$40.00

Walker, Alice. *Langston Hughes, American Poet.* NY. Crowell. (1974). 1st ed. dj.
$750.00–$900.00

Walker, Alice. *Temple of My Familiar, The.* San Diego. Harcourt Brace Jovanovich. 1989. 1st ed. sgn. dated. dj. $90.00–$100.00

Walker, Alice. *You Can't Keep a Good Woman Down.* NY. Harcourt Brace Jovanovich. (1981). 1st ed. dj. $200.00–$300.00

Wallace, Lew. *Ben-Hur: A Tale of the Christ.* New York. Harper & Bros. 1903. 2 vols. inscrb and sgn. $300.00–$800.00

Wallace, Lew. *Ben-Hur: A Tale of the Christ.* NY. 1960 Ltd Editions Club. $100.00–$125.00

Wallace, Lew. *Ben Hur: A Tale of the Christ.* New York. Harper & Bros. 1880. 1st ed. brown decorate cloth. six word dedication. $250.00–$1,000.00

Wallace, Lew. *Ben Hur.* New York. Harper & Bros. 1880. 1st ed. 1st issue. blue cloth. 2 line dedication. $1,200.00–$1,500.00

Waller, Robert James. *Love in Black and White.* Lon. Sinclair-Stevenson. 1992. 1st UK ed. British version of The Bridges of Madison County. dj. $30.00–$50.00

Wallis, Allan D. *Wheel Estate. The Rise and Decline of Mobile Homes.* NY. Oxford Univ Press. 1991. 1st ed. illus. photos. dj. $15.00–$20.00

Walt Disney Studios. *Three Little Pigs.* NY. Blue Ribbon Books. 1933. 1st ed. illus. by Disney Studios. $100.00–$125.00

Walton, H. Haynes. *Treatise on Operative Ophthalmic Surgery.* Phila. Lindsay & Blakiston. 1853. illus. 1st Amer ed. lea. $275.00–$375.00

Walton, Izaak. *Compleat Angler or the Contemplative Man's Recreation, The.* Lon. Freemantle Co. 1902. illus. 2 vol. ltd 150/55 cc. lea. gold emblem on cover. gold lettering on spine.
$1,400.00–$1,750.00

Walton, Izaak. *The Compleat Angler.* Phil. David McKay. illus. 12 color plates by Arthur Rackham. green decorated cloth. $65.00–$200.00

Wandering Pilgrim, The; or the Way to be Happy. With a Warning to the Old and Young. NY. Gould. 1840. wraps. 16 pp. sewn. $200.00–$400.00

Ward, Lynd. *God's Man.* NY. Jonathan Cape. 1929. 1st ed. illus. by Lynd Ward. blue decorated boards. $115.00–$300.00

Ward, Lynd. *God's Man.* NY. Jonathan Cape. 1930. illus. by Lynd Ward. 1st ed. 2nd issue.
$90.00–$200.00

Ward, Rowland. *Records of Big Game.* Lon. Ward. 1896. 2nd ed. illus. $500.00–$900.00

Warhol, Andy. *From A to B & Back Again.* Lon. Dempsey. 1975. 1st UK ed. inscrb. dj.
$250.00–$300.00

Warren, Hon. J. Leicester. *A Guide to The Study of Book-Plates.* Lon. John Pearson. 1880. illus. rust color cloth, frontis, paste-down on spine. $30.00–$100.00

Warren, Lillie E. *Defective Speech and Deafness.* NY. Werner. 1895. 116 pp. $50.00–$70.00

Warren, Robert Penn. *All the King's Men.* NY. Harcourt Brace. (1946). 1st ed. dj. Pulitzer Prize winner. $3,000.00–$5,500.00

Warren, Robert Penn. *All the King's Men.* NY. Harcourt Brace. (1946). 1st ed. inscrb. dj. Pulitzer Prize winner. $10,000.00–$12,000.00

Warren, Robert Penn. *Chief Joseph of the Nez Perce.* NY. Random House. 1983. 1st ed. ltd 250 cc. sgn. numbered. burgundy cloth. slipcase. $175.00–$250.00

Warren, Robert Penn. *John Brown, the Making of a Martyr.* NY. Payon & Clarke. 1929. 1st ed. dj. $2,000.00–$2,500.00

Warren, Robert Penn. *Meet Me in the Green Glen.* NY. 1971. 1st ed. presentation copy. sgn.
                                                                                            $100.00–$200.00

Warren, Robert Penn. *Place to Come to, A.* NY. Random House. 1977. 1st trade ed. sgn. dj.
                                                                                             $60.00–$90.00

Warren, Robert Penn. *Wilderness.* NY. 1961. 1st ed. $30.00–$50.00

Warren, Robert Penn. *World Enough and Time.* NY. Random House. 1950. 1st ed. dj.
                                                                                             $60.00–$90.00

Washington, Booker T. *Up From Slavery.* NY. Doubleday Page. 1901. 1st ed. photos. inscrb. sgn. $1,700.00–$3,500.00

Washington, Booker T. *Working With the Hands.* NY. Doubleday Page. 1904. 1st ed. cloth.
                                                                                            $75.00–$150.00

Washington, Booker T. *Working With the Hands.* NY. Doubleday Page. 1904. 1st ed. incrb. sgn. $2,500.00–$3,000.00

Washington, Booker T. (ed.). *Negro in Business.* Bos. Hertel, Jenkins. 1907. 1st ed. illus. photos. $250.00–$300.00

Washington, George. *Legacy of the Father of His Country. . . .* Bos. John Russell. 1796. wraps. stitched. $1,200.00–$1,300.00

Watanna, Onoto. *Heart of Hyacinth.* Harper. 1903. 1st ed. illus. teg. $15.00–$50.00

Watanna, Onoto. *Japanese Blossom.* NY. Harper. 1906. 1st ed. illus. color plates.
                                                                                            $10.00–$65.00

Waters, Ethel. *His Eye is on the Sparrow.* Garden City. Doubleday. 1951. 1st ed. inscrb. dj.
                                                                                            $75.00–$100.00

Waters, Ethel. *His Eye is on the Sparrow.* NY. 1951. 1st ed. autobiography. dj.
                                                                                            $15.00–$30.00

Waters, John. *Pecker.* 1st ed. original shooting script. 107 pp. with rewrite pp.
                                                                                            $90.00–$150.00

Waterton, Charles. *Essays on Natural History, Chiefly Ornithology.* Lon. Longmans. 1838. 2nd ed. $40.00–$50.00

THIS EDITION, limited
to five hundred copies, has
been printed by The Grab-
horn Press of San Francisco in May,
1930. The type used is Weiss Anti-
qua, hand-set. Each copy is signed
by the author,

Virginia Woolf

Copy No. 393

Virginia Woolf, *Street Hauntings.* San Francisco. Grabhorn Press. 1930. limited and signed. With stained cover and cocked spine, it sold in 2007 for $750.00.

Signature page, Virginia Woolf, *Street Hauntings,* limited edition from Grabhorn Press, 1930.

Waterton, Charles. *Wanderings in South America.* Lon. Fellowes. 1828. illus. 2nd edition. frontis. woodcuts. $300.00–$400.00

Watson, Francis Sedgwick. *Operative Treatment of the Hypertrophied Prostate.* Cupples & Hurd. 1888. 167 pp. photogravures. $50.00–$75.00

Watson, Hildegarde Lasell. *Edge of the Woods, The.* Lunenberg, VT. Stinehour. 1979. 1st ed. ltd 1000 cc. cloth. $20.00–$25.00

Watson, Idelle Beaufort. *The True Story of a Real Garden.* New York. Moffat Yard & Co. 1922. 1st ed. illus. small green cloth gold lettering on cover and spine color frontis. $15.00–$20.00

Watson, James D. *Double Helix, The.* NY. Atheneum. 1968. 1st ed. Nobel Prize winning author. dj. $400.00–$500.00

Watson, Wilbur J. *Bridge Architecture.* NY. 1927. illus. $50.00–$60.00

Watson, William. *Adventures of a Blockade Runner.* Lon. 1892. 1st ed. $40.00–$60.00

Watts, Isaac. *Arrangement of Psalms, Hymns and Spiritual Songs of. . . .* Bos. Loring. 1818. $75.00–$90.00

Watts, Isaac. *Improvement of the Mind.* Bennington, VT. Haswell. 1807. 382 pp. $80.00–$100.00

Waugh, Evelyn. *Brideshead Revisited.* Bos. Little Brown. 1946. dj. $20.00–$50.00

Waugh, Evelyn. *Brideshead Revisited*. Lon. Chapman and Hall. 1945. 1st ed. inscrb. sgn.
$2,500.00–$9,000.00

Waugh, Evelyn. *Edmund Campion*. NY. Sheed & Ward. (1935). 1st ed. dj. $25.00–$40.00

Waugh, Evelyn. *Love Among the Ruins*. Lon. Chapman and Hall. 1953. 1st ed. ltd 350. sgn.
$400.00–$500.00

Waugh, Evelyn. *Love Among the Ruins*. Lon. Chapman and Hall. 1953. $25.00–$50.00

Waugh, Evelyn. *Mr. Loveday's Little Outing and Other Sad Stories*. Bos. Little Brown. 1936.
1st ed. ltd 750 cc. dj. $500.00–$700.00

Waugh, Evelyn. *Mr. Loveday's Little Outing and Other Sad Stories*. Lon. Chapman & Hall.
(1936). 1st ed. ltd 750 cc. no dj. $150.00–$350.00

Waugh, F. A. *Landscape Gardening*. NY. 1899. 1st ed. $25.00–$50.00

Waugh, Frank A. *Textbook of Landscape Gardening*. NY. Wiley. 1922. 1st ed. illus.
$30.00–$45.00

Weaver, Clarence E. *Sketches of Richmond Virginia*. Central. illus. b/w photos.
$65.00–$100.00

Weaver, Lawrence. *Small Country Houses*. Lon. Country Life. 1914. 1st ed. illus.
$115.00–$500.00

Weaver, Warren A. *Lithographs of N. Currier and Currier & Ives*. NY. Holport. (1925).
$40.00–$50.00

Webb, Edith Buckland. *Indian Life in the Old Missions*. Los Angeles. Lewis. 1952. 1st ed.
illus. photos. dj. $125.00–$150.00

Webb, Frank J. *Garies and Their Friends, The*. Lon. Routledge. 1857. 1st ed. 2nd issue. blue
cloth. African American author. Introduction by Harriet Beecher Stowe.
$15,000.00–$19,500.00

Webb, Walter Prescott. *Texas Rangers, The*. NY. Houghton Mifflin. 1935. 1st ed. illus.
$90.00–$150.00

Webb, Walter Prescott. *Texas Rangers, The*. NY. Houghton Mifflin. 1935. 1st ed. illus. sgn.
$200.00–$350.00

Weber, Carl J. *Fore-Edge Painting*. Irvington-on-Hudson. Harvey House. 1966. illus. dj.
$200.00–$400.00

Webster, Noah. *American Dictionary of the English Language, An*. Springfield, MA. Merriam. 1859. rev. $200.00–$270.00

Webster, Noah. *Collection of Essays and Fugitive Writings*. Bos. Andrews. 1790. 1st ed. lea. rebacked. 414 pp. $750.00–$800.00

Webster, Noah. *Dissertations on the English Language*. Bos. Isaiah Thomas. 1789. 1st ed. illus.
$1,500.00–$1,800.00

Webster, Thomas. *Encyclopedia of Domestic Economy.* Lon. Longmans. 1844. 1st ed. lea.
$450.00–$700.00

Webster, Thomas. *Encyclopedia of Domestic Economy.* NY. 1845. rev. $75.00–$90.00

Weeden Toy Steam Engines. New Bedford, MA. Weeden Manufacturing Corp. 1939. pictorial wraps. illus. 19 pp. $70.00–$90.00

Weeden, Howard. *Songs of the Old South.* NY. 1900. 1st ed. illus. color plates.
$100.00–$150.00

Weegee (Arthur Fellig). *Naked City.* Cinn. Zebra. 1945. wraps. $40.00–$50.00

Weegee (Arthur Fellig). *Naked City.* NY. Essential. 1945. 1st ed. tan cloth. inscrb. sgn.
$950.00–$2,000.00

Weegee (Arthur Fellig). *Naked City.* NY. Essential. 1945. 1st ed. tan cloth.
$300.00–$400.00

Weegee (Arthur Fellig). *Weegee's People.* NY. 1946. $200.00–$300.00

Weeks, John. *History of Salisbury, VT.* Middlebury. 1860. 1st ed. frontis. b/w illus.
$150.00–$300.00

Weems, John Edward. *If You Don't Like the Weather. . . .* Austin. Texas Monthly. (1986). 1st ed. dj. $15.00–$20.00

Weight, Harold and Lucile Weight (eds.). *Calico Print.* 1950–1952. 1st ed. illus. early tabloid publications. pulp paper. illustrations. original issues. $350.00–$500.00

Weiner, Charles. *Perou Et Bolivie Recit De Voyage.* Paris. Librairie Hachette. 1880. illus. red 3/4 lea and bds. $250.00–$350.00

Weissl, August. *Mystery of the Green Car, The.* Lon. Nelson. 1913. 1st ed. $50.00–$140.00

Weld, Isaac. *Travels through the States of North America and the Provinces of Upper and Lower Canada during the years 1795, 1796, and 1797.* Lon. 1799. 1st ed. 464 pp. plates. maps laid in. small folio. $400.00–$500.00

Well, Samuel R. *New Physiognomy of Signs of Character, A.* Fowler & Wells. 1883. illus. brown decorated cloth. $550.00–$650.00

Wellman, Manly Wade. *After Dark.* Garden City. Doubleday. 1980. 1st ed. inscrb. sgn. dj.
$75.00–$150.00

Wellman, Manly Wade. *After Dark.* Garden City. Doubleday. 1980. 1st ed. dj.
$25.00–$50.00

Wellman, Manly Wade. *Lost and the Lurking, The.* Garden City. Doubleday. (1981). 1st ed. sgn. fine in fine dj. $100.00–$200.00

Wellman, Manly Wade. *Old Gods Awaken.* Garden City. Doubleday. 1979. 1st ed. first Silver John novel. $20.00–$35.00

Wells, Carolyn. *Folly for the Wise.* Bobbs Merrill. 1904. 170 pp. illus. $15.00–$30.00

Wells, Carolyn. *Marjorie in Command*. NY. Dodd Mead. 1910. 1st ed. 15. $15.00–$25.00

Wells, Carolyn. *Merry-Go-Round*. Russell. 1901. 1st ed. 152 pp. illus by Peter Newell.
$125.00–$150.00

Wells, Carolyn. *Murder in the Bookshop*. Phil. 1936. 1st ed. dj. $250.00–$350.00

Wells, Carolyn. *Story of Betty, The*. NY. 1899. 1st ed. author's first book. $150.00–$200.00

Wells, Emma M. *History of Roane County, Tennessee, 1801–1870*. Chattanooga. 1927. 1st ed. illus. $50.00–$100.00

Wells, H. G. *Country of the Blind, The*. Lon. Nelson. nd. 1st ed. blindstamped blue cloth.
$300.00–$400.00

Wells, H. G. *History of Mr. Polly*. Lon. Nelson. (1910). 1st ed. 10 pp ads. green cloth.
$250.00–$325.00

Wells, H. G. *Invisible Man*. NY. 1897. 1st ed. 1st printing. orange cloth. $1,500.00–$2,500.00

Wells, H. G. *Invisible Man*. Lon. 1897. Pearson. 1st UK ed. red cloth. sgn.
$20,000.00–$27,000.00

Wells, H. G. *Invisible Man, The*. NY. Limited Editions Club. 1967. 1500 cc. sgn by illustrator Mozley. $60.00–$75.00

Wells, H. G. *Time Machine, The*. Lon. Heinemann. 1895. 1st ed. 1st issue. tan cloth.
$4,000.00–$6,000.00

Wells, H. G. *Time Machine, The*. NY. Random House. 1931. ltd 1200 cc. illus by Dwiggins.
$150.00–$350.00

Wells, H. G. *Tono Bungay*. Lon. Macmillan. 1909. 1st ed. 8 pp ads. $150.00–$250.00

Wells, H. G. *Tono Bungay*. NY. 1908. 1st US ed. $100.00–$150.00

Wells, H. G. *War of the Worlds*. Lon. 1898. 1st ed. gray cloth. $1,800.00–$2,000.00

Wells, H. G. *War of the Worlds, The*. Lon. Heinemann. 1898. 1st ed. gray cloth. ad catalogues. $2,500.00–$3,000.00

Wells, H. G. *When the Sleeper Wakes*. Lon/NY. Harper & Bros. 1899. 1st ed. illus. red cloth.
$700.00–$800.00

Wells, Helen. *Cherry Ames, Jungle Nurse*. Manchester. World Pub. 1965. 1 UK ed.
$100.00–$150.00

Wells, Helen. *Cherry Ames, Jungle Nurse*. NY. Grosset & Dunlap. 1965. 1st Amer ed. #25. pictorial cover. $60.00–$85.00

Wells, Helen. *Cherry Ames, Visiting Nurse*. Lon. World Books. (1947). 1st ed.
$20.00–$25.00

Wells, Helen. *Cherry Ames, Visiting Nurse*. NY. Grosset & Dunlap. 1947. #21. list to #23 on cover. $10.00–$15.00

Wells, Henry. *City Boys in the Woods*. NY. Harper. (1889). 1st ed. illus. $30.00–$75.00

Wells, Richard A. *Manners, Culture and Dress.* Mass & Iowa. King Richardson & Co. 1890. illus. green dec cloth with gilt lettering on cover and spine. $45.00–$90.00

Welo, Samuel. *Practical Lettering.* Chi. Drake. (1930). 1st ed. illus. $45.00–$55.00

Welsh, Herbert. *Report of a Visit to the Navajo Pueblo, and Hualpais Indians of New Mexico and Arizona.* Phil. Indian Right Association. 1885. 1st ed. wraps. 48 pp. $100.00–$125.00

Welty, Eudora. *Curtain of Green, A.* Garden City. Doubleday, Doran. 1941. 1st ed. author's first book. dj. $1,500.00–$2,500.00

Welty, Eudora. *Delta Wedding.* NY. (1946). 1st ed. dj. $300.00–$600.00

Welty, Eudora. *Golden Apples, The.* NY. Harcourt Brace. (1949). 1st ed. dj. $55.00–$90.00

Welty, Eudora. *Golden Apples, The.* NY. Harcourt Brace. (1949). 1st ed. inscrb. dj. $300.00–$500.00

Welty, Eudora. *Place in Fiction.* NY. House of Books. 1957. 1st ed. 300 cc. sgn. dj. $400.00–$500.00

Welty, Eudora. *Robber Bridegroom, The.* Garden City. Doubleday Doran. 1942. 1st ed. dj. $500.00–$800.00

Welty, Eudora. *Robber Bridegroom, The.* Garden City. Doubleday Doran. 1942. 1st ed. inscrb. sgn. $4,500.00–$5,500.00

Wentworth, Patricia. *Gazebo, The.* Phil. Lippincott. 1955. 1st ed. dj. $50.00–$60.00

Wentz, Robert W., Jr. *Portsmouth, A Political History.* Donning. illus. b/w photos. sgn.dj. $55.00–$100.00

Wentz, Roby. *Grabhorn Press, The.* San Francisco. Book Club of California. 1980. 1st ed. ltd 750 cc. plain paper dj. $75.00–$100.00

Wesley, John. *Calm Address to Our American Colonies, A.* Bristol. Bonner and Middleton. 1775. wraps. 2nd printing. $800.00–$900.00

West, James E. *Lone Scout of the Sky.* NY. Boy Scouts of America. 1927. true 1st ed. illus. green cloth. $50.00–$80.00

Westell, Percival. *Book of the Animal Kingdom, The.* Lon. Dent & Sons. 1910. 1st ed. illus. green illus. cover, color plates. $12.00–$150.00

Westerners Brand Book. *Hollywood.* Boelter. 1961. illus. 550 cc. cloth. $50.00–$65.00

Westerners Brand Book. *LA.* Corral. 1963. 525 cc. $75.00–$90.00

Westerners Brand Book. *Los Angeles Westerners.* 1956. 1st ed. 400 cc. $90.00–$110.00

Westmarck, Edward. *Marriage Ceremonies in Morocco.* Lon. Macmillan. 1914. 1st ed. brown cloth. $90.00–$100.00

Westwood, T. and T. Satchell. *Biblioteca Piscatoria: A Catalogue of Books on Angling....* Lon. 1883–1901. ¼ blue morocco and blue cloth. teg. complete with 1901 supplement. original supplement wraps preserve. $75.00–$300.00

Wetmore, Helen Cody. *Last of the Great Scouts: The Life Story of Buffalo Bill.* Chicago. Duluth. 1899. 1st ed. wraps. illus. plates. $250.00–$800.00

Wetmore, Mrs. Helen C. *Last of the Great Scouts: The Life Story of Buffalo Bill.* Chicago. Duluth. 1899. 1st ed. wraps. illus. 2nd issue. plates. $75.00–$200.00

Whalen, Will. *Priest Who Vanished or Murderer at Large.* Ozone Park. Catholic Literary Guild. 1942. 1st ed. dj. $75.00–$100.00

Whall, W. B. *Sea Songs & Shanties.* Glasgow. 1910. illus. 4th ed. $60.00–$80.00

Wharton, Edith. *Age of Innocence, The.* NY. Appleton. 1920. 1st ed. Pulitzer Prize winner. sgn. dj. $19,000.00–$25,000.00

Wharton, Edith. *Book of the Homeless, The.* NY. Scribner's. 1916. Merry-mount Press deluxe. folio. ltd 125 cc. numbered. $2,500.00–$3,500.00

Wharton, Edith. *Book of the Homeless, The.* NY. Scribner's. 1916. 1st ed. illus. buckram and paper covered boards. fine condition. $350.00–$550.00

Wharton, Edith. *Children, The.* NY. Appleton. (1928). 1st ed. 4th issue. points. dj.
                                                                             $60.00–$80.00

Wharton, Edith. *Crucial Instances.* NY. Scribner's. 1901. 1st ed. gray boards.
                                                                           $200.00–$500.00

Wharton, Edith. *Crucial Instances.* Lon. Murray. 1901. 1st UK ed. $75.00–$125.00

Wharton, Edith. *Custom of the Country.* NY. Scribner's. 1913. 1st ed. $75.00–$100.00

Wharton, Edith. *Ethan Frome.* NY. Scribners. 1911. 1st ed. 1st issue. dj missing.
                                                                        $1,500.00–$2,500.00

Wharton, Edith. *Ethan Frome.* NY. Scribner's. 1911. 1st ed. 1st issue. teg. points. rare dj.
                                                                        $4,000.00–$5,000.00

Wharton, Edith. *Ethan Frome.* NY. Scribner's. 1922. ltd 2000 cc. intro by Wharton. dj.
                                                                           $300.00–$600.00

Wharton, Edith. *House of Mirth.* NY. Scribner's. 1905. 1st ed. $100.00–$175.00

Wharton, Edith. *Italian Villas and Their Gardens.* NY. Century. 1904. 1st ed. illus. by Maxfield Parrish. green cloth. sgn by Parrish. $800.00–$2,000.00

Wharton, Edith. *Italian Villas and Their Gardens.* Lon. Bodley Head. 1904. illus. by Maxfield Parrish. 1st UK ed. teg. $1,000.00–$1,300.00

Wharton, Edith. *Sanctuary.* NY. Scribner's. 1903. 1st ed. illus. by Appleton. green cloth.
                                                                            $90.00–$300.00

Wharton, James George. *What the White Race May Learn from the Indian.* Chi. Forbes. 1908. 1st ed. illus. photos. inscrb. $175.00–$225.00

Wharton, James George. *What the White Race May Learn from the Indian.* Chi. Forbes. 1908. 1st ed. illus. photos. vg condition. $150.00–$200.00

Wheeler, F. G. *Billy Whiskers at the Fair.* Akron. 1909. 1st ed. illus. plates. $30.00–$60.00

Whelen, Townsend. *American Big Game Shooting*. Illinois. Western Cartridge Co. 1931. wraps. illus. small gray decorated wrps. 48 pp. $15.00–$30.00

Whelen, Townsend. *American Big Game Shooting*. East Alton. Western Cartridge. 1931. 1st ed. wraps. illus. green wrps. illustrated cover. 48 pp. $20.00–$90.00

Where To Hunt American Game. Mass. United States Cartridge Co. 1898. 1st ed. illus. green decorated cloth. $125.00–$150.00

Whilt, James W. *Mountain Memories*. Chi. Conkey. 1925. 1st ed. illus. sgn. $30.00–$75.00

Whipple, Maurine. *Giant Joshua, The*. Bos. Riverside. 1941. 1st ed. author's first book. dj.
$40.00–$50.00

White, Alma. *Ku Klux Klan in Prophecy*. NY. Zarepath. 1925. 1st ed. $45.00–$100.00

White, Charles E. Jr. *Successful Houses and How to Build Them*. NY. Macmillan. 1916. reprint. $100.00–$125.00

White, E. B. *Charlotte's Web*. NY. Harper & Bros. 1952. 1st ed. illus. by Garth Williams. 184 pp. good dj. $500.00–$1,200.00

White, E. B. *Charlotte's Web*. NY. Harper & Bros. 1952. 1st ed. illus. worn.
$250.00–$500.00

White, E. B. *Stuart Little*. NY. Harper & Bros. 1945. 1st ed. illus. dj. fine cond.
$850.00–$1,200.00

White, E. B. *Stuart Little*. NY. 1945. 1st ed. illus. dj. good condition. $250.00–$500.00

White, Edmund. *Farewell Symphony, The*. NY. Knopf. 1997. 1st US ed. sgn. dj.
$20.00–$30.00

White, Edmund. *Married Man, The*. Lon. Chatto & Windus. 2000. 1st ed. dj. $70.00–$80.00

White, James. *Early Life and Later Experiences of Elder Joseph Bates*. Battle Creek. 1878. purple cloth. $60.00–$95.00

White, Leslie. *Pioneers in American Anthropology*. NM. Univ of New Mexico Press. 1940. 1st ed. illus. 2 vols. ltd 400 sets. photos. map. dj. $200.00–$225.00

White, Mrs. Alma. *Titanic Tragedy*. Bound Brook. Pentecostal Union. 1913. 1st ed.
$50.00–$500.00

White, Paul Dudley. *My Life and Medicine*. Bos. Gambit. 1971. 1st ed. presentation. dj.
$300.00–$400.00

White, Paul Dudley and Helen Donovan. *Hearts. Their Long Follow-up*. Phil/Lon. 1967. 1st ed. inscrb by White. $700.00–$900.00

White, Randy Wayne. *Heat Islands, The*. NY. St. Martin's. 1992. 1st ed. dj. $135.00–$250.00

White, Randy Wayne. *North of Havana*. NY. Putnam's. 1997. 1st ed. wraps. sgn. dj.
$30.00–$50.00

White, Stewart Edward. *Sign at Six, The*. Indianapolis. Bobbs Merrill. (1912). 1st ed. Percy Darrow mystery. green cloth. $100.00–$150.00

White, Stewart Edward. *Cabin, The*. Doubleday Page. 1911. 1st ed. $30.00–$50.00

Whitehead, George. *Bernard Shaw Explained*. Watts & Co. Lon. 1925. 1st. edition. dust jacket. $50.00–$95.00

Whitehead, George. *Bernard Shaw Explained*. Watts & Co. Lon. 1925. 1st edition. no jacket. $30.00–$45.00

Whitely, Isaac H. *Rural Life in Texas*. By Ike Whitely. Atlanta. Harrison. 1891. 1st ed. errata slip. illus. wraps. 82 pp. $200.00 $250.00

Whitman, Walt. *Franklin Evans; or The Inebriate*. NY. Random House. 1929. 2nd ed. ltd. Whitman's first pub. $100.00–$200.00

Whitman, Walt. *Franklin Evans; or The Inebriate*. NY. Winchester. 1842. 1st ed. 32 pp. disbound. Whitman's first pub. $4,000.00–$4,500.00

Whitman, Walt. *Leaves of Grass*. Brooklyn, NY. private. 1856. green cloth. 2nd ed. ltd 1000 cc. frontis. $9,000.00–$11,000.00

Whitman, Walt. *Leaves of Grass*. Phil. McKay. 1891. Deathbed edition. presentation copy. sgn. $25,000.00–$40,000.00

Whitman, Walt. *Leaves of Grass*. Brooklyn, NY. 1855. 1st ed. ltd 795 cc. $45,000.00–$60,000.00

Wiesel, Elie. *Dawn*. Lon. MacGibbon and Kee. 1961. 1st ed. dj. $40.00–$50.00

Wiesel, Elie. *Night*. Paris. 1958. 1st ed. author's first book. $250.00–$350.00

Wiesel, Elie. *Night*. Lon. MacGibbon and Kee. 1960. 1st UK ed. dj. $275.00–$400.00

Wiesel, Elie. *Night*. NY. 1960. 1st Amer ed. author's first book. dj. $100.00–$200.00

Wiggin, Kate Douglas. *Bird's Christmas Carol, The*. Boston. Houghton Mifflin. 1912. reprint. $30.00–$45.00

Wiggin, Kate Douglas. *A Cathedral Courtship*. Bos. Houghton & Mifflin. 1901. 1st ed. illus. by Charles Brock. red decorated cloth. teg. $5.00–$100.00

Wiggin, Kate Douglas. *The Diary of a Goose Girl*. Bos. Houghton Mifflin. 1902. illus. by Claude A. Shepperson. decorated cover. $20.00–$50.00

Wiggin, Kate Douglas. *Kindergarten Chimes, A Collection of Songs and Games. . . .* Bos. Ditson. 1885. 1st ed. cloth. $400.00–$500.00

Wiggin, Kate Douglas. *Rebecca of Sunnybrook Farm*. Cambridge. Houghton Mifflin. 1903. 1st ed. $125.00–$200.00

Wiggin, Kate Douglas. *The Romance of a Christmas Card*. New York. Burt. 1916. illus. by Alice Hunt. dj. $12.00–$40.00

Wiggin, Kate Douglas. *Story of Patsy, The*. Boston. Houghton Mifflin. 1889. 1st ed. $50.00–$150.00

Wiggin, Kate Douglas. *Susanna and Sue*. Boston. Houghton Mifflin. 1909. 1st ed. illus. by N. C. Wyeth. pictorial cloth cover. $45.00–$50.00

Wiggin, Kate Douglas and Nora A. Smith. *Arabian Nights, The*. NY. Scribner's. 1935. reprint. illus. by Maxfield Parrish. $130.00–$160.00

Wilbur, Richard. *Ceremony*. NY. Harcourt Brace. (1950). 1st ed. dj. $200.00–$250.00

Wilde, Oscar. *Ballad of Reading Gaol, The*. New York. Dutton & Co. 1928. 1st ed. illus. by John Vassos, blue cloth, leather spine, dust jacket. $30.00–$45.00

Wilde, Oscar. *Ballad of Reading Gaol*. NY. Limited Editions Club. 1937. illus. ltd 1500 cc. numbered. sgn. slipcase. $200.00–$300.00

Wilde, Oscar. *Poems of Oscar Wilde*. NY. Boni & Liveright. 1927. ltd 2000 cc. $100.00–$120.00

Wilder, Laura Ingalls. *Little House in the Big Woods*. NY. Harper Bros., 1932. First edition in very good condition. Illustrated by Sewell. $3,000. Typical later editions sell for $15.00–$50.00

Wilder, Laura Ingalls. *Little House on the Prairie*. NY. HarperCollins. 1953. Illustrated by Garth Williams. $20.00–$25.00

Wilder, Thornton. *Bridge of San Luis Rey, The*. NY. Albert & Charles Boni. 1929. illus. by Rockwell Kent. ltd 100 cc. sgn by author and illustrator. slipcase. $300.00–$400.00

Wilder, Thornton. *Cabala, The*. NY. Boni. 1926. 1st ed. author's first book. sgn. $200.00–$225.00

Wilder, Thornton. *Long Christmas Dinner and Other Plays in One Act, The*. NY. Coward, McCann. 1931. 1st ed. inscrb. dated. dj. $175.00–$250.00

Wilder, Thornton. *Our Town*. NY. Coward-McCann. (1938). 1st ed. Pulitzer Prize–winning drama. cloth. dj. $1,900.00–$2,200.00

Wildwood, Will. *Fishcraft: A Treatise on Fresh Water Fish and Fishing*. Ohio. Sportsman's Digest. 1924. illus. small gold color decorated cloth, 146pp. $10.00–$20.00

Wilkinson, Nevile. *The Guards' Chapel 1838–1938*. Lon. The Chiswick Press. illus. Centenary edition. blue buckram covers with gilt lettering. $18.00–$30.00

Willert, James. *March of the Columns*. CA. Upton. 1994. 1st ed. illus. photos. maps. drawings. sgn and dated. $75.00–$85.00

Williams, Egerton. *Plain-Towns of Italy*. NY. Houghton Mifflin. 1911. 1st ed. illus. green decorated cloth, foldout frontis. $7.00–$50.00

Williams, John H. *Guardians of the Columbia, The*. Tacoma. John Williams. 1912. 1st ed. wraps. illus. illus. wrps. $15.00–$50.00

Williams, John H. *Mountain That Was "God," The*. Tacoma. G.P. Putnam's Sons. 1911. wraps. illus. green pictorial cover. maps in rear. color plates. $15.00–$25.00

Williams, Tennessee. *In the Winter of Cities*. NY. New Directions. (1956). 1st trade ed. dj. $40.00–$50.00

Williams, Tennessee. *Moise and the World of Reason*. NY. Simon & Schuster. 1975. 1st ed. ltd 350 cc. numbered. sgn. teg. blue lea. no jacket issued. $375.00–$500.00

Williams, William Carlos. *Autobiography*. NY. Random House. 1951. 1st ed. cloth. dj.
$100.00–$125.00

Williams, William Carlos. *White Mule*. Norfolk. New Directions. (1937). 1st ed. dj.
$200.00–$350.00

Williamson, Mary L. *Life of J. E. B. Stuart, The*. Richmond. (1914). 1st ed. illus.
$40.00–$50.00

Wilson, Francis. *John Wilkes Booth: Fact and Fiction of Lincoln's Assassination*. Cambridge, MA. 1929. ltd 300 cc. illus. teg.
$350.00–$450.00

Wilson, Lois. *Lois Remembers*. NY. Al-Anon. 1979. 1st ed. illus. inscrb. cloth. dj.
$650.00–$1,000.00

Wilson, Rufus R. *Lincoln Among His Friends: A Sheaf of Intimate Memories*. Idaho. Caxton. 1942. 1st ed. illus.
$200.00–$300.00

Winslow, Lyttleton S. *Manual on Lunacy: A Handbook Relation to the Legal Care and Treatment of the Insane*. Lon. Smith, Elder. 1874. 1st ed. brown cloth.
$700.00–$800.00

Winsor, Kathleen. *Forever Amber*. NY. Macmillan. 1944. 1st ed. dj.
$275.00–$350.00

Winters, Yvor. *Proof, The*. NY. Coward-McCann. 1930. 1st ed. dj.
$40.00–$50.00

Wirt, Mildred A. *Brownie Scout at Silver Beach*. N.Y. Cupples and Leon. 1952. illus. orange cloth, illustrated dust jacket.
$5.00–$34.00

Wister, Owen. *When West Was West*. Lon. Macmillan. 1928. 1st UK ed.
$40.00–$50.00

Withers, Alexander S. *Chronicles of Border Warfare, or a History of the Settlement by Whites of Northwestern Virginia.* . . . Clarksburg. Israel. 1831. 1st ed.
$500.00–$900.00

Wodehouse, P. G. *Few Quick Ones, A*. NY. Simon & Schuster. (1959). 1st ed. dj.
$90.00–$125.00

Wodehouse, P. G. *Golf Without Tears*. NY. A. L .Burt. 1924. dark blue cloth.
$7.00–$15.00

Wodehouse, P .G. *Laughing Gas*. NY. Sun Dial Press. 1936. orange dec. cover, illus. dj.
$10.00–$20.00

Wodehouse, P. G. *No Nudes is Good Nudes*. NY. Simon & Schuster. 1970. 1st US ed. dj.
$60.00–$90.00

Wodehouse, P. G. *Printer's Error*. Half Moon Bay. Paper Crane Press. 1990. 1st ed. ltd 250 cc. wraps. issued by the Wodehouse Society.
$40.00–$60.00

Wolf, Simon. *American Jew as Patriot, Soldier, and Citizen, The*. Phil. 1895. 1st ed.
$375.00–$400.00

Wolfe, Thomas. *From Death to Morning*. NY. Scriber's. 1935. 1st ed. dj. $200.00–$300.00

Wolfe, Tom. *Mauve Gloves & Madmen, Clutter & Vine*. NY. Farrar Straus & Giroux. (1976). 1st ed. dj.
$100.00–$150.00

Wolfe, Thomas. *Of Time and the River*. NY. Scribner's. 1935. 1st ed. dj. $175.00–$200.00

Wolfe, Tom. *Radical Chic and Mau-Mauing the Flak Catchers.* NY. Farrar Straus & Giroux. 1970. 1st ed. dj. $50.00–$90.00

Wolfe, Tom. *Right Stuff, The.* NY. Farrar Straus & Giroux. 1979. 1st ed. $50.00–$100.00

Wolfe, Tom. *Right Stuff, The.* NY. Farrar Straus & Giroux. 1979. 1st ed. $300.00–$400.00

Wolff, Tobias. *Back in the World.* Houghton Mifflin. 1st ed. sgn. sj. $150.00–$200.00

Wolff, Tobias. *Barracks Thief.* NY. Ecco Press. 1984. 1st ed. sgn. dj. $150.00–$200.00

Wolff, Tobias. *This Boy's Life—A Memoir.* NY. Grove/Atlantic. 1989. 1st ed. dj. $70.00–$90.00

Woodruff, Hiram. *Trotting Horse of America, The.* NY. Ford. 1868. 1st ed. frontis. $30.00–$50.00

Woodson, Carter G. (ed.) *The Works of Francis J. Grimke.* Wash. The Associated Publishers. 1942. 1st ed. brown cloth, lettering on spine, 4 volumes. $800.00–$1,000.00

Woodson, Carter G. (ed.) *The Works of Francis J. Grimke.* Wash. The Associated Publishers. 1942. 1st ed. brown cloth, lettering on spine, 4 volumes, ex-lib. 300.00–$500.00

Woolf, Virginia. *Kew Gardens.* Hogarth Press. 1927. First ed. thus (first illustrated ed.), ltd 500 cc. signed by Woolf and her sister, artist Vanessa Bell. $4,000.00

Woolf, Virginia. *A Room of One's Own.* 1st ed. sgn. $3,589.00

Woolf, Virginia. *Monday or Tuesday.* 1st ed. no dj. $788.00

Woolf, Virginia. *On Being Ill.* Hogarth Press. limited. sgn. dj. slipcase. $1,500.00

Woolf, Virginia. *Street Haunting.* San Francisco. Grabhorn Press. 1930. limited. sgn. stained cover. cocked spine. $750.00

Woolf, Virginia. *Three Guineas.* Harcourt, 1938. dj. $75.00

Woolf, Virginia. *To The Lighthouse.* Hogarth Press. London. limited. sgn. dust jacket soiled and damaged. $4,500.00

Woolf, Virginia. *A Haunted House and other stories.* The Hogarth Press. London. 1943. 1st ed. $200.00–$900.00

Woolf, Virginia. *Flush A Biography.* The Hogarth Press. London. 1933. Large Paper Edition. dj. $80.00–$300.00

Woolf, Virginia. *London Scene, The.* Lon. Hogarth. (1982). 1 UK ed. dj. $35.00–$70.00

Woolf, Virginia. *Monday or Tuesday.* Richmond. Hogarth. 1921. 1st ed. illus. first book of stories. cloth. woodcuts. decorated boards. no dj issued. $900.00–$3,500.00

Woolf, Virginia. *Mrs. Dalloway.* Harcourt, Brace and Co. (1925). orange cloth. paste-down on spine with lettering. no dj. $10.00–$500.00

Woolf, Virginia. *Orlando A Biography.* NY, Crosby Gaige. 1928. 1st ed. 565/861 numbered copies. signed by Woolf. no dj. $2,500.00–$5,000.00

Woolf, Virginia. *Roger Fry A Biography.* The Hogarth Press. Lon. 1940. $75.00–$200.00

David P. Todd, ***Stars and Telescopes,*** Boston: 1901.
Decorated cloth with gilt illumination on cover.
$80.00–$100.00

Woolf, Virginia. *The Common Reader.* The Hogarth Press. Lon. 1933. New Edition.
$15.00-$30.00

Woolf, Virginia. *The Death of The Moth.* The Hogarth Press. Lon. 1942. dj. $90.00-$350.00

Woolf, Virginia. *On Being Ill.* Hogarth Press. 1930. 1st ed. Limited Edition 49/250 copies. signed by Woolf. dust jacket. $6,000.00–$12,000.00

Woolf, Virginia. *To the Lighthouse.* NY. 1927. 1st ed. 4000 cc. $4,000.00–$21,000.00

Woolf, Virginia. *Writer's Diary, A.* Lon. Hogarth. 1953. 1st ed. dj. $35.00–$225.00

Woollcott, Alexander. *Shouts and Murmurs.* NY. Century. 1922. $20.00–$30.00

Wouk, Herman. *War and Remembrance.* Bos. Little Brown. 1978. 1st trade ed. dj.
$30.00–$50.00

Wouk, Herman. *Youngblood Hawke.* Garden City. Doubleday. (1962). 1st ed. dj.
$100.00–$150.00

Wright, Frank Lloyd. *An Autobiography.* NY. Duell, Sloan and Pearce. 1943. 1st ed. later printing. $125.00–$145.00

Wright, Frank Lloyd. *Modern Architecture.* Princeton. 1931. illus. plates. cloth.
$150.00–$200.00

Wright, Frank Lloyd. *Story of the Tower, The.* NY. 1956. 1st ed. illus. dj. $150.00–$200.00

Wright, John Kirtland. *Geographical Lore of the Time of the Crusades.* NY. Dover. 1965. wraps. reprint of 1925 ed. $10.00–$15.00

Wright, Richard. *Jeunnesse Noire (Black Boy).* Paris. Gallimard. (1947). 1st French ed. wraps. inscrb. dj. $10,000.00–$12,000.00

Wright, Richard. *Native Son.* NY. 1941. 1st ed. play. dj. $400.00–$500.00

Wright, Richard. *Native Son.* NY. 1940. 1st ed. 1st state binding. blue cloth. red and gray stamp. dj. $1,200.00–$2,000.00

Wright, Richard. *Native Son.* NY. Harper. 1940. 1st ed. 1st state. inscribed. dj.
$1,000.00–$3,000.00

Wright, Richard. *Native Son.* NY. Harper. 1940. 1st ed. 2nd state. gray cloth. dj.
$60.00–$120.00

Wright, Richard. *Uncle Tom's Children.* NY. 1938. 1st ed. dj. $250.00–$700.00

Wright, Richard. *Uncle Tom's Children.* NY. Harper. 1938. 1st ed. sgn and inscrb. dj.
$2,500.00–$8,000.00

Wright, William H. *Grizzly Bear, The.* New York. Scribner's Sons. 1909. 1st ed. illus. green decorated cloth with gold lettering on cover and spine. $40.00–$90.00

Wylie, Elinor. *Black Armour.* NY. George Doran. 1923. 1st ed. black cloth with pictorial cover. $20.00–$45.00

Wynn, Marcia Rittenhouse. *Desert Bonanza: The Story of Early Randsburg, Mojave Desert Mining Camp.* CA. Clark. 1963. 2nd ed. illus. frontis. photos. folding map. $90.00–$125.00

Wynn, Marcia Rittenhouse. *Pioneer Family of Whiskey Flat*. Los Angeles. Haynes. 1945. 1st ed. frontis. plates. photos. red cloth. pictorial dm. sgn. $150.00–$200.00

Yaggy, L. W. and T. L. Haines. *Museum of Antiquity*. NY. Standard Pub. 1882. illus. ¾ lea and decorated cloth. raised bands. marblized edges and end papers. $20.00–$80.00

Yaggy, L. W. and T. L. Haines. *Museum of Antiquity*. Chi. Western Pub. 1880. 1st ed. illus. 944 pp. ¾ lea and cloth. steel plates. $200.00–$500.00

Yarbro, Chelsea Quinn. *Music When Sweet Voices Die*. NY. Putnam. 1979. 1st ed. dj.
$18.00–$22.00

Yarbro, Chelsea Quinn. *Ogilvie, Tallant & Moon*. NY. Putnam. 1976. 1st ed. inscrb. dj.
$50.00–$75.00

Yarbro, Chelsea Quinn. *Signs and Portents*. CA. Dream Press. 1987. 1st ed. review slip laid in. dj. $35.00–$60.00

Yarrell, Wiliam. *History of British Birds*. Lon. 1843. 1st ed. in book form. 3 vols. illus. engravings. $500.00–$700.00

Yates, Richard. *Cold Spring Harbor*. Ny. Delacorte. (1986). inscrb. dated. dj.
$400.00–$550.00

Yau, John. *Hawaiian Cowboys*. Santa Barbara. Black Sparrow. 1995. 1st ed. 100 cc sgn. pictorial boards. dj. $30.00–$50.00

Yeats, William Butler. *Celtic Twilight, The*. Lon. Lawrence and Bullen. 1893. 1st ed. green cloth. $350.00–$500.00

Yeats, William Butler. *Collected Works in Verse and Prose*. Lon. Chapman & Hall. 1908. ltd 250 cc 8 vols. teg. $3,000.00–$4,000.00

Yerby, Frank. *Devil's Laughter, The*. NY. Dial. 1953. 1st ed. dj. $50.00–$80.00

Yerby, Frank. *Floodtide*. NY. Dial. 1950. 1st ed. dj. $50.00–$80.00

Yoder, Joseph W. *Rosanna's Boys*. PA. Yoder Publishing. 1948. 1st ed. illus. sgn. dj.
$35.00–$45.00

Yonge, Charlotte M. *The History of Sir Thomas Thumb*. Edinburgh, Thomas Constable and Co. 1855. 1st. edition. $200.00–$325.00

Young, Andrew. *Songs of Night*. Lon. 1910. Author's first book. $200.00–$400.00

Young, Jesse Bowman. *Battle of Gettysburg*. NY. 1913. $85.00–$125.00

Younger, Helen, Marc Younger and Dan Hirsch. *First Editions of Dr. Seuss Books: A Guide to Identification*. Saco, Me. Custom Communications, 2002. ltd 1000 cc. sgn.
$150.00–$200.00

Zaccarelli, John. *Zaccarelli's Pictorial Souvenir Book of the Golden Northland*. Dawson. (1908). $75.00–$150.00

Zangwill, Israel. *Blind Children*. Heinemann. Lon. 1903. $18.00–$20.00

Zeitlin, Jacob. *What Kind of Business Is This? Reminiscences of the Book Trade and Book Collectors.* Lawrence. Univ of Kansas Libraries. 1959. 1st ed. wraps. 19 pp. $15.00–$25.00

Zeitlin, Jake. *For Whispers and Chants.* San Francisco. 1927. Author's First Book.
$50.00–$150.00

Zelazny, Roger. *Blood of Amber.* Seventh in Amber series.1986. ltd 400 cc. sign and numbered. dj. slipcase
$60.00–$90.00

Zelazny, Roger. *Lord of Light.* NY. Arbor House. 1987. 1st ed. review slip laid in. dj.
$35.00–$60.00

GLOSSARY

ADDENDA (OR ADDENDUM). Supplemental material inserted at the end of a book.

ADVANCE COPY. Copies of a book issued ahead of schedule to gain final approval from the author or to send to reviewers before the edition is released. Sometimes the advance copies will be identical to the regular edition, but often they are not, at least to the extent that they are labeled advance copies. If the only difference is in style or color of binding, it may be difficult to determine if the copies are an advance issue or simply a binding variant, which could be part of a normal trade run.

Collectors often value advance copies since they represent an early state of the text and, however rare the case, they may contain notations by the author.

ALL EDGES GILT (A.E.G.). Indicates that all three edges of the leaves (top, bottom, and fore-edge) have been gilded. If only the top edge is gilded, t.e.g.

AMERICANA. In the strict sense, refers to material dealing with the American hemisphere. But today, the term more often refers narrowly and loosely to books, documents, pamphlets, and other period material that shows why, how, when, and by whom the United States was developed.

ANA (OR IANA). Suffix denoting items related to a particular subject, be it a person, a time or place in history, or some such. For instance, Joyceiana is material relating in some way to James Joyce, even if the connection is remote. The heading covers such things as pamphlets, books, newspaper accounts, artifacts, and letters by, about, or to the subject.

Collecting ana (or iana) is widespread among those interested in a particular author or historical time or personality. Even those who have written only one book (or none) can be the subject of an extensive collection of written and artifact items. Institutions and libraries are notable collectors of ana.

ANTIQUARIAN BOOKSELLING. Sale of used, old, and rare books, printed fare and related items; usually refers to trade in books out of print.

Until about the 12th century, most books were handcrafted in monasteries and churches and remained their property. Except to those who owned them and valued the information they contained, books had no intrinsic value unless they contained gold gilt or were inlaid with precious stones. Not until sometime around the 13th century, when craftspeople in the secular world began to make and sell books, adding topics like philosophy and literature, did books take on a broader commercial value.

Michael Olmert, author of the *Smithsonian Book of Books* (1992) remarks, "An intriguing question is when did books become valuable enough to steal?" Olmert says that thieves profited from stealing books once a commercial market for them was established. As proof that books were taking on value, he reports book owners of the 12th century began writing curses on their flyleaves to discourage theft, warning that whoever stole the books would be damned to hellfire.

Even as the first commercial markets were growing, bookmaking was done slowly by hand, comparatively few books were produced, and those were often custom made for specific buyers. Bookselling was primarily a second-hand business but was not yet antiquarian bookselling. Since bound books were still in their infancy, you wouldn't term their trade antiquarian.

By the 17th century, enough time had elapsed; printing had become mechanized, and enough books were in circulation for true antiquarian bookselling to arise in England, France, and elsewhere.

Few catalogues were issued at first. Most early shops gathered in clusters, such as those that sprang up in St. Paul's Churchyard, London. Most shopkeepers were located in large cities, primarily in stalls with much of their material displayed on the sidewalk and very little within. The PENNY BOXES that became such a favorite of the bargain hunters in later years were probably not present early on. Prints, engravings, maps and such were sold by at least some of the dealers.

The emergence of the scholar-dealer—the collector at heart who studied his merchandise with interest—did not occur until the early part of the 19th century. By this time, bookselling was big business. The Bohn brothers of London are generally credited with giving birth to modern rare-book dealing. By 1900, at least a half dozen English dealers boasted inventories in excess of half a million volumes. Several German dealers by this time had stocks even larger.

APPRAISAL. Estimation of the value of a book or collection. An appraisal should be made by a qualified professional in the antiquarian book trade with the tools and the experience to do the job right. Some appraisers will offer an opinion based on a mere list and description of volumes, but that is not recommended. The value of a book depends on many factors, not the least of which is its condition. The best appraisals are done by experts who can hold the books in their hands and examine them in fine detail. This can't be done with a list.

Appraisals are often sought by individuals planning to insure a collection. They are also used to determine the value of books being left to benefactors or being donated to libraries or other charitable institutions to establish tax benefits or liabilities. In such cases, care must be taken that the appraiser meets all requirements set by the Internal Revenue Service for the appraisal to be recognized as accurate.

AQUATINT. A method of etching that stresses soft tones and shades, resembling wash paintings. The French artist LePrince is generally credited with perfecting the process during the late 18th century. The technique became popular in Britain during the 18th and 19th centuries.

Sometimes aquatint printing was done in color, and sometimes the coloring was added by hand later. When printing in colored aquatint, a separate plate for each color is necessary. A few famous artists such as Goya and Picasso experimented with the process.

ART PAPER. Shiny, coated stock on which most art books (or at least the illustrations) are printed. The paper ages badly and is easily damaged by moisture. Also, dirt stains cannot be removed without damaging the surface of the paper.

AS NEW. Showing no signs of wear; the book so described doesn't look used. Basically a British expression. Americans have preferred MINT, which carries the same meaning.

ASSOCIATION COPY. A book that was part of the author's own library or was associated in one way or another with a famous person. It may be that the author inscribed the book to a friend, or the book may contain an inscription by another famous owner, perhaps a dedication or a presentation, or the book was merely included—without inscription—in a famous person's library. But the point is, there must be proof that the book has been in the possession of someone famous.

The value of association copies to the collector derives from the book's connection to history, or in modern times, to people who are perceived as larger than life. If we were to learn that Abraham Lincoln had a favorite book of sonnets that he daily carried with him, we would love to have that book. It would be an association copy.

Association copies should be distinguished from signed copies, which proliferate these days with the popularity of book tours and autograph signings. And beware the forgeries, which have become easier to create with modern printing and copying technology! Experts in the trade can help you weed them out.

AUTHORIZED EDITION. Usually refers to biographies written with the approval or even help of the subject. The term is intended to draw attention and interest, but a drawback to authorized editions is the public perception that if the subject of a biography authorized the work, it wouldn't tell tales of the subject's secret life.

B.A.L. The *Bibliography of American Literature,* authored by Jacob Nathaniel Blanck and published in 1955 by the Yale University Press for the Bibliographical Society of America. Virginia Smyers and Michael Winshop edited the work and later added a final volume. The seven-volume work is a detailed bibliography of important American literature through much of the 20th century, and an indispensable research tool for the serious book person.

BASTARD TITLE. Another name for the HALF-TITLE PAGE, the leaf preceding the title page that carries the title in small print but no other information. Use of this page is a holdover from the incunabula days when the title page consisted of only this. It has no other real purpose and is retained in many volumes merely because old habits die hard. With a nod to decorum, many bibliographers refer to this as the "bas. title."

BAY PSALM BOOK. The first full-length American-printed book. Issued in Cambridge, Massachusetts, in 1640 by Stephen Daye, the name derives from the Massachusetts Bay Colony. Only 11 volumes are known to remain, all but one in public institutional collections. The total number of copies printed isn't known, but is guessed to be from 100 to 300. Though the usual press run at the time was considerably more, experts theorize that Daye would not have had a large market for books printed locally and would have printed less than the usual number. The book was collected as a rarity as early as the mid-1700s. The actual title of Daye's volume is *The Whole Booke of Psalmes Faithfully Translated into English Metre,* but printers in Europe had produced works with similar titles and therefore Bay Psalm Book more clearly distinguishes Daye's work from the others.

BEVELED EDGES. Angle-cut edges on wooden boards once used in bookbindings. They're of little consequence when judging the value of an antiquarian book.

BIBLIOGRAPHY. Commonly, a list of books organized by subject or author. For instance, libraries consider an author bibliography to be a list, as complete as possible, of all specimens of an author's work that have appeared in print.

The term has taken on an alternate meaning coming into its own as the study of books themselves, including their origins, history, development, physical appearance, construction, and value.

BIBLIOMANIA. A preoccupation with books; a compulsion to be around them, learn about them, and own them. Booksellers and collectors are prone to this disease. The malady can be observed at library sales, auctions, and estate sales.

BIBLIOPHILE. An ardent and avid book collector. One who loves books. A person having a mild, benign form of bibliomania.

BIBLIOTHECA AMERICANA. A comprehensive directory of books on Americana, 29 volumes in all, dating from the coming of the Europeans to the 20th century. Begun by Joseph Sabin, who completed the first thirteen volumes, the work was continued by Wilberforce Eames and completed by R. W. G. Vail.

BINDING COPY. A book in need of a new binding. A British term.

BINDINGS. The permanent cover of a book, not to be confused with a removable dust jacket. As soon as books were made of folded leaves instead of scrolls, they needed a proper covering. The earliest bindings were probably uncovered wooden boards with a hide spine—what we call today HALF LEATHER binding. This evolved into a full leather binding. Early ornamentation on books consisted of painting and encrusting with jewels and bone carvings. In time, these gave way to BLINDSTAMPING and finally gold-stamping and gilding.

Materials used over the centuries for binding books are numerous and even macabre. Most common are vellum, pigskin, calf, morocco, and various types of cloth or muslin. A practice arose during the Middle Ages of stripping the skin of slain enemy soldiers. One use of the leather made out of these skins: book bindings. (In some cathedrals in Europe are seen doors covered in these human hides. Tour guides often hesitate to mention this.)

Collecting fine bindings is a major area of book collecting.

BLINDSTAMPING. Recessed or raised impressions on the bindings of books which are not inked or colored. Blindstamping did not originate with bookbinding but was long a popular means of hand-decorating leather. As a decoration for bindings, the process did not begin until the 12th century.

BOARDS. Uncovered hard cardboard or wooden boards, or boards covered with thin paper, linen, buckram, etc., used as front and back covers in bindings. The term is a holdover from the early days of printing when books were bound with actual wooden boards held together by leather or buckram at the spine. In the bookselling trade today, "boards" refers to stiff bindings covered in paper instead of cloth or leather.

BOOK OF HOURS. Illuminated medieval prayer books. During the Middle Ages, wealthy patrons commissioned these stunning books for their personal use. They were prized for their calendars, which frequently featured pictures of month-by-month activities—planting in spring, harvesting in fall, etc. providing historians with valuable insights into medieval society and habits. Small in size, handy to carry to church services, the books included psalms, litanies, and various offices of the church. The organization of these books was based on the church's prescribed daily schedule for devotions, hence the name Book of Hours.

BOOK OF KELLS. An Irish manuscript of Christian scripture from the 8th century. The opening page of each Gospel is lavishly illustrated with brightly colored designs and images of saints and religious persons and events. Depictions of nature, such as animals, fish, and trees abound throughout. The art of the monks and their use of color and whimsy shows the attainment of the Irish artists of the early Middle Ages. By the way figures are depicted in the hand illuminations, it is obvious artists of the day had not perfected the study of anatomy, but that deficiency was made up for in their exquisite concepts of color and design. The folio manuscript is housed in the Library of Trinity College, Dublin, Ireland.

BOOKPLATES. A label identifying ownership usually pasted on the inside of a book cover. Older, intricately designed and executed bookplates are collector's items in their own right. Some are delightful examples of art. Their use dates from the 15th century.

If a modern bookplate is inserted by a person of no particular renown, the plate does not detract from the book; when properly applied, they do no harm, but they should not be affixed over existing plates or in such a way that they obscure important inscriptions or writings.

Plates of antiquity, either engraved by some famous craftsman or showing possession by some notable person, are highly sought after by collectors, but they really should not be removed from the books. Contrary to common belief, this practice damages the books and destroys evidence of a book's PROVENANCE, or history, an important phase of bibliography.

BOOK SCOUT. A person who beats the bushes looking for saleable books, and who then markets these finds to booksellers. Since a bookseller is often occupied with a shop, scheduling time for a buying trip can be a problem. Enter the book scout. With no overhead and unfettered by the minutiae of a bookseller's store, scouts have time to ferret out books sitting on somebody's shelf, in an attic, or at the eternal Friends of the Library book sale.

A bookseller might have several scouts scattered in different parts of the country haunting flea markets, Salvation Army stores, and estate sales. But for the most part, scouts work independently, seeking out the bookseller with the strongest interest in their finds.

Often a person starting out as a scout develops into a fulltime bookseller. Scouts of the seedy, unsavory character described by John Dunning in his mystery novel, *Booked to Die* (1992), may exist somewhere, but our experience of scouts in New England (Marie started out as a scout more than 25 years ago) reveals a type of person who loves books to begin with and is delighted to chase them for booksellers.

Book scouting is not as common as it once was, but with the Internet as an outlet for amateurs to market books, a good scout who can find quality stock for a store still provides a valuable service.

BOOK SIZES. Industry terms loosely describing the size of volumes. The terms describe books according to their FORMAT (the way they are printed and bound, based on traditional sheet printing on a press) rather than by their actual measurement, giving only an indication of how big the books really are.

The common book size formats are folio, quarto, octavo, and duodecimo, indicating the manner in which the printer folds the printed paper sheets, which come off the printing press, to form leaves (pages). Regardless of the planned format, all sheets are fed through a press in full size and folded later into "quires" or "signatures." These are collected and bound together, the closed edges of the folded sheets are slit, and—presto—you have a book.

If each printed sheet is folded once to create two leaves, the book becomes a folio, the largest format. If folded twice, we get four leaves, or a quarto, often written "4to." Fold again and there are eight leaves, an octavo, or "8vo." Twelve leaves are duodecimo, "12mo." Keep going and you have progressively smaller sizes and larger numbers: 16mo, 24mo, 32mo, and 64mo. A 128mo format exists but it's only seen in the very tiniest of miniature volumes.

You can't divine the actual measure of a book from the format—the unfolded sheets can vary in size—but the designations aren't a useless convention. What you can reliably ascertain from a statement of format is something about the shape of a volume. Octavos tend to be sleek, at least 1½ times as tall as they are wide. Quartos tend to be squarish and dumpy. Folios are

tall and well proportioned. The Gutenberg Bible is a folio. Most modern novels are 8vos. Coffee table art books are folios and large quartos.

BOOKWORMS. The larval stage of a beetle that likes to eat books, a pesky little worm that feeds upon the bindings and the leaves. They've been preying on libraries since the very earliest times. These maggots were the scourge of monastic libraries in the Middle Ages. No area of Europe was free of the bookworm, and contrary to some beliefs, they did not seek out only filthy habitations but ate books in fine homes and libraries as well. Modern chemicals have virtually eliminated them.

BREAKER. Someone who takes books apart and then sells the parts separately, especially the illustrations. Breaking a book may bring a higher price for the parts than the book would fetch as a whole. When a book is so badly damaged that it cannot be repaired or recovered as a book, breaking is a way of preserving the plates and leaves and putting them into circulation, even at times rebinding them with new material relevant to the original work.

Breaking books that are not otherwise damaged is looked down on by serious antiquarian booksellers and collectors as a horrendous practice.

BROADSIDE. A poster, announcement, or proclamation, usually printed on one side of a sheet and meant to be posted on a wall. Many a political statement was brought to the people's attention in this manner even after the advent of newspapers. Old auction posters, especially horse auction, might be adorned with an illustrated display of wares adding to the value and desirability of the artifact.

Broadsides are popular with collectors today.

BUCKRAM. A modern binding material very much like cloth but tougher and somewhat more attractive. Libraries almost always have their books rebound in buckram. Inexpensive, buckram can be dyed all the colors of the rainbow, as well as goldstamped. The natural shade, which is rather like a cross between straw and wheat, is preferred by many.

Buckram bindings are often described in catalogues as cloth and vice versa, a fact of life that collectors must endure.

CALF. Leather used for bookbinding.

CALLED FOR. Elements of a book—POINTS—mentioned in bibliographies that determine the edition of a book. For instance, if a handbook on first editions written by Smith says that a blank leaf follows the title page in a certain edition of a certain book, then the blank leaf is "called for" to establish that edition and must be there for the book to be complete.

CAXTON, WILLIAM. First English printer. Born at Kent, Caxton started his business life as a mercer, or dealer in yarn goods, a trade he followed for most of his life, showing no particular mechanical skill or flair for literature. Around 1441, Caxton went to Burgundy. He spent most of his adult life on the continent. In 1471, he entered the service of the Duchess of Burgundy and, under her influence, he performed his first effort with books, translating the *Recuyell of the Historyes of Troye*.

On a visit to Cologne that year, he was apparently introduced to the art of printing, which he brought back to Bruges, setting about to give the city a printing press. Together with a Flemish calligrapher, Colard

Mansion, Caxton issued the first printed English-language book, the same *Recuyell*. After printing two more books with Mansion, Caxton returned alone to England and founded a printing office in the parish of Westminster.

Compared to the best French and Italian printing of the time, Caxton's books come off a sorry second. His fame has led many to assume that his talent as a craftsman and type designer must have been extraordinary, but this was not the case. He did however exert much influence upon his contemporaries and followers. He began with types modeled on German gothic and stuck with them to the end. This set the trend for English printers and it was not until a century after his death that the types were replaced by the more graceful Roman.

A craze for Caxtons among collectors began in the early part of the 19th century and has gathered steam ever since The finest collections are at the British Museum and John Rylands Library. In the U.S., the Morgan and Huntington libraries have been notable for their Caxtons.

CHAPBOOKS. A small pamphlet or booklet usually associated with children's stories or rhymes. Most are diminutive in size and illustrated with woodcuts. In the 18th century, itinerant peddlers, or "chapmen," hawked the booklets door to door. Because they were cheaply made, many of the books have not survived in very good condition, but those that have are highly prized by collectors of classical antiquarian books.

CHEAP COPY. A defective copy which is being offered at a discount. The dealer wants the prospective buyer to be aware of the poor condition.

CLOTH BINDING. The ideal binding substance, cheap, durable, easy to apply, comes in a variety of colors. For modern books, cloth has replaced leather as the binding of choice. True, the disappearance of leather is lamentable, but the cost of leather binding would prohibit ownership of books to all but a limited class of collectors.

In the very first years of cloth binding, publishers let their imaginations run wild. Every effort was made to ornament bindings lavishly. The books were gilded and blindstamped using patterns copied from notable bindings of earlier ages. But unlike the books of old, gilding was done with large panel stamps impressed by machine rather than with tools worked by hand. The purpose was to make the public forget leather. It succeeded: out of sight, out of mind. In time, only connoisseurs who kept fine libraries retained any affection for leather. That is not to say, however, that we have become so undiscriminating that we cannot still appreciate a book bound in fine, soft leather.

CODEX. Applies to leaves bound in book form—this book you are holding, for example—as opposed to scrolls or tablets. The invention is generally credited to Roman legal clerics who grew weary of cumbersome scrolls and cut them down to convenient size. The practice made sense at a time when the whole process of managing information was time-consuming and laborious.

COLLATED. Inspected from cover to cover to be sure all pages, plates, maps and the like are present, intact, and in their proper place. In the case of earlier books, a perfect copy—or comprehensive knowledge of one—is necessary to make a comparison when collating.

A good practice when purchasing a book is to check out the list of illustrations in the table of contents and confirm that they are all there. If maps should be present, check them out. Nothing is more frustrating when you get home than to discover pages missing from a book you were all excited about purchasing.

And never, never send out a book to a dealer or customer before collating it. Selling a book with missing pages could be cause for harsh repercussions, or at least it would label you as unprofessional.

COLOPHON. The "finishing touch." The tradition of medieval scribes when completing their manuscripts was to record, on the very last page, their name and place of residence and, sometimes, the day on which the book was finished.

At times, the addition of a colophon was done out of vanity but, more often than not, such information was necessary. Without it, a printer or publisher could not identify an edition as his own, which might result in legal difficulties if the book were printed or stolen by another printer.

The average colophon was a model of simplicity, one sentence or so, giving the essential facts. Colophons were replaced after the 16th century by information included on the title page. However, some modern books, usually limited editions, still add a colophon, perhaps out of respect for tradition. You might find one that starts out: "This book was set on monotype in Fournier . . ."

CONDITION. The general state of a book. This singularly most important point cannot be overemphasized when considering whether to buy or sell a collectible book.

Like people, books are either in fine shape, very good shape, bad shape, or various states in between these. As no hard and fast definitions exist, the terms used to designate a book's condition are subject to personal opinion. Having said that, we hasten to add that there is some agreement in the book trade as to what the terms mean.

Mint. As new. Right off the press.

Fine. Nearly new. Sometimes a dealer might overlap this with Mint.

Very Good. Definitely shows wear, but not damaged. Usually a clean, tight copy. Most collectible books fit this category.

Good. Obviously read. Perhaps the covers show moderate wear, a hinge is cracked in front or back, some minor spine fading might be present, the binding scuffed. Perhaps the book is even a little shaken, not quite as tight as it used to be. All in all, the condition shows the book has been around for a while and was used. No really major defects.

Fair. Worn and used. Cover soiled, scuffed, evidence of repairs, shaken, perhaps a page torn here or there. The book had definitely been around the block.

Reading Copy. About all it is good for. Or, it may interest collectors of modern first editions who keep their pristine copies on a shelf, safe from prying hands, but who may still want to read Hemingway or Faulkner. Reading copies come in handy for research.

Now when all is said and done, should a disheveled rare book come up at auction, you can bet your bottom dollar—and you might have to—that book will not lack for spirited bidding. Rebinding or restoration can often resurrect a measure of its origi-

nal value. So extenuating circumstances call for common sense. If a book is being purchased for investment, then by all means, abide by the most rigid rules of condition and rarity.

COPPERPLATE ENGRAVING. A process for producing prints and book illustrations. Plates were prepared by a battery-hammer method, then smoothed by rubbing with pumice and oilstone. Thought costly and time consuming, this method gave the best possible surface for engraving. The majority of English illustrated books of the 18th century used copper plates.

COPYRIGHT. The equivalent of a patent on a work of literature. A copyright prohibits anyone from reproducing the work, either in whole or in part, without consent of the copyright holder. Books and their various editions are often identified in part by their copyright date, which is the year in which they were copyrighted.

CURIOSA. In today's market, books that deal with off-beat subjects like a monograph on foot fetishes or the psychology of wearing hats. During the Victorian age, anything of a sexual nature was hidden under the heading of curiosa. Today's bookseller has no problem with such subjects and classifies erotic material where it belongs, under erotica.

C.W.O. Cash With Order. Most booksellers append this notation to their ads, safeguarding their interests, choosing not to send a book out to a customer before they have payment in hand. Payment under C.W.O. may be in the form of cash, checks, money orders or credit cards.

During our long experience over many years, we have not yet encountered a deadbeat customer or bookseller and do not expect to. We have occasionally sent out a book before the check arrived, in particular, one $5,000 book went many years ago to an established dealer with a fine reputation. We believe it is important to maintain some confidence in our fellow human beings, though in this case it was easy as we knew the man's reputation.

Still, with changes brought on by the influx of large numbers of people marketing books on the Internet, we are now more cautious dealing with the casual buyer or seller and do not ship a book until payment has cleared our accounts.

DAMP STAINS. Damage caused by excessive humidity but not water, as is sometimes thought. Books damaged by dampness are ragged and musty rather than crisp.

Improper ventilation can cause as much damage as water. Humidity constantly above 70 percent can damage a book as it stands untouched in a bookcase. In a book with lovely plates, dampness can cause the pages to stick together. Pulling them apart scuffs or strips the images on the plates, thus greatly altering the esthetics and value of the book.

DAYE, STEPHEN. An important individual, the first man to print mechanically in America. Daye, a British locksmith, came to the Massachusetts Bay Colony in 1633. He and his son, Matthew, a printer's apprentice, set up a printing shop in Cambridge at Harvard College. The earliest surviving book of the Daye's press is commonly known as the Bay Psalm Book, after the colony where it was printed.

DELUXE EDITION. Meant to imply extraordinary production qualities; those books which, by superior design, type, paper, binding, or other factors, are set above the pale.

DISBOUND. Refers to a pamphlet or other brief work that once was part of a larger work and has been separated. Purists look down on this practice of removing the piece from the larger collection, much as they look down on breaking a book.

DISCARD STAMP. A mark used by libraries when they are culling their collections to show that the books have been released for sale or distribution. This is a matter of procedure to guard against theft and to show the book is legitimately no longer part of a library collection.

How nice it is when a librarian thinks like a book collector and carefully selects an unobtrusive place for the discard stamp.

DOG-EARED. Originally referred to the corners of pages that have become ragged or creased. Now, it applies to any pages that have the appearance of heavy use. One of the causes of dog-earing is the regrettable habit many readers have of turning down the corner of a page to mark their place when reading. Thank goodness not all readers are guilty of this barbaric practice, choosing instead to use bookmarks.

DÜRER, ALBRECHT. A German artist, painter, and book illustrator at the turn of the 16th century. He was famous and in great demand for quality woodcuts used in book illustrations. Among his early works are the woodcuts for Sebastian Brant's famous *Ship of Fools*.

Most of Dürer's fame came after 1500 when he was prolific in his output not only in book illustration but working in oils, watercolors, silverpoint, and other artistic media.

DUST JACKET (OR DUSTWRAPPER, DJ). The decorative paper cover that protects the binding from soil and wear. Jackets were sometimes used during the 19th century, and if you find a volume with a jacket of such antiquity, hooray for you. Jackets for books dating back to the early part of the 20th century, too, are like icing on the cake. They're desirable, but hard to come by. For newer books, however—the MODERN FIRST EDITIONS—jackets are a must.

If a book such as William Faulkner's *Light in August* has no dust jacket, it can lose half or more of its collectible value. Even reprints of Zane Grey or Edgar Rice Burroughs command higher prices when accompanied by their dust jackets. A modern book with a jacket missing can be likened to an antique table without its legs.

EDGES. Refers to the three outer edges of the book's leaves. Style of edges is a very important part of a book's makeup, especially in fine or rare editions. New books are delivered to the binder in folded but uncut sheets, or gatherings, and the binder must separate the leaves by cutting the folds. The edges are usually trimmed to make them perfectly even. Books bound without trimming the edges, showing the original state of the paper with all its irregularities, are valued by some collectors. But then, there's a collector for just about anything.

ELSE FINE. A term used after a recitation of a book's faults indicating that, otherwise, something is right with the book. The phrase "o/w very good" (indicating "otherwise very good") is more common.

ENGRAVING. Illustrations printed from a metal plate or wood block. Engravings on steel were developed in the 15th century, an improvement over wood that permitted more fine detail and delicate shading.

Collectors of engravings seek the early impressions in a print run, those among the first taken from a plate, as the fine lines of the engraved image sometimes wear down with repeated use.

EPHEMERA. Items that were meant to last a short time. Some booksellers abhor the myriad postcards, sheet music, and advertising paper that appear at book shows under this heading. But many of these items are extensions of book collecting that we accept as not only legitimate but desirable. As the Internet continues to affect the availability of books and the way they are sought and sold, these have risen in stature and interest in the book trade.

Say you are putting together a collection of P. G. Wodehouse. Why would you reject the sheet music that he wrote? (Wodehouse did not write the music, he wrote the lyrics for music.) Or the Christmas cards by Robert Frost to round out a collection of his books and poetry? Or the screen scripts written by now famous authors when they were down on their luck and needed to eat?

Ephemera is fun and exciting, and some very famous artists like Maxfield Parrish produced beautiful ads as well as book illustrations for some of the most sought-after children's books. Tucked into old volumes, many ephemera treasures have come to light. A Stevensgraph, or a hollow-cut silhouette, even a letter with historical information, are some of the bonuses possible when turning the pages of an old book.

A Burlington, Vermont, bookseller was a little chagrined when she learned she'd sold a book on Calvin Coolidge with a holograph letter tucked unnoticed among the leaves. The next day, the customer returned and asked did she have any more of those books with the letters of the presidents inside?

ERASURES. Removal of underlining or notations with an eraser, discussed further under "Notations and Underlining" in the section on Care and Repair of Books.

A bookseller may resort to erasing pencil or pen markings made by former owners of a book, generally by use of a wad of art gum or pencil eraser. Collectors have mixed feelings about notations and whether or not they should be removed. The value and rarity of a book will influence whether a book is rejected due to the presence of notations or purchased and lived with as is. For the bibliophile, a notation might suggest some continuity with the former owner and be cherished. The erasures themselves should be clean and not leave unsightly blotches or destroy the print.

ERRATA. Mistakes in printing. The "errata leaf" is still used in cases where a blooper was spotted too late to correct the print run but early enough to bind a note into the book stating the error and correction. More frequently seen is the "errata slip," a small strip of paper containing the correction which may be pasted in the book, or laid-in loosely, after the book has been bound.

EX-LIBRARY, EX-LIB. Indicates a book belonged to a library or bears evidence of having been in a library collection, e.g., the library stamp, card pockets, or identifying marks on the spine. These books, unless they are exceedingly rare, are not often sought by collectors as they usually show considerable wear and damage due to use and library mutilation.

Ex-lib books are almost as difficult to sell as Book of the Month Club or Reader's Digest editions, although many catalogues feature ex-lib books.

FINE PRINTING. Any book in which the quality of type and layout are a main consideration. Books printed by individuals or presses which design their own type may rate as fine printing if the type is well designed. Such books do not necessarily have to be limited editions or kept from public sale. All the products of early typographers were sold on the general market, yet some represent excellent presswork. Had these men bought their types from foundries rather than having a hand in their design, their books might not be so respected.

FIRST EDITION. The first appearance of a book in print. Collectors refer to the first impression (print run), or first printing of the book as the "true first edition." Identification of true first editions can be an art and even the most experienced booksellers and collectors run the risk of making an error.

The way printers specify the edition somewhere inside the book—or fail to give any indication at all of which edition it is—varies widely from printer to printer, era to era, and country to country. Best to go prepared with a pocket guide on the subject when browsing for books, for you could not possibly keep in mind the vast number of codes that publishers have used or the legions of points that identify specific titles.

Unfortunately, if a book does not readily admit in print to being a second or a third or a 15-thousandth edition, the uninformed public automatically assumes the book is a first. The collector or bookseller cannot afford the casual assumption as most collectors acquire first editions for many reasons, not the least among them as an investment.

FIRST IMPRESSION. The first time a set of plates has been used to print a book. Also called a PRINTING.

All impressions using the same set of plates constitute one edition, thus each edition can include more than one impression, or print run. Most sellers and collectors are speaking of the first impression of the first edition when discussing collectible first editions.

FIRST STATE. The FIRST IMPRESSION before any corrections or changes are made in the middle of a print run or edition. In decades and ages past, pages coming off a press were occasionally seen to contain mistakes, which caused printers to stop the press and make corrections before a print run was completed. The pages that came off first, without the changes, are the first state of the print run.

FIRST THUS. Not the first edition, but you may see this used to describe an altered edition of a book. Since the revised book is an edition unlike the original, perhaps issued by a different publishing house or illustrated by some other artist, the book can be presented as first thus. It's like a distant cousin to a first edition.

FLYLEAF. Blank leaf after the front endpaper, not always present. The term misapplied to the front endpaper.

FOLDING PLATES. Plates that fold out to a larger size than the book's leaves. Volumes published by the Government Printing Office during the 19th century have many folding maps and color illustrations bound into them. Guide books are designed with folding illustrations and maps, too.

Through the years, unfortunately, folding plates begin to show wear and tear from handling.

FOLIO. A standard book size, measuring from about 12" tall on up. An atlas folio is 24", and an elephant folio is 20" or more. Audubon's *Birds of America* is a most valued natural history book measuring 37" tall.

FORE-EDGE. The outer edge of a book, opposite the spine.

FORE-EDGE PAINTING. Painting the edges of a book's leaves with a scene or other picture. The book must be held in a special press and, while the leaves are slightly fanned out, the artist paints or decorates the exposed fore-edges of the leaves. When the book is fully closed, the edge is gilded to conceal traces of the painting. But lightly fan out the edges, and the fore-edge painting can be a lovely surprise. Because the painting is hidden, a book with a fore-edge painting can go undetected even by a knowledgeable bookseller until the book is opened.

FORMAT. The size of a book determined by the specific number of times the original printed sheet of paper has been folded to form the leaves. For standard format sizes used in the book trade, see BOOK SIZE.

FOXED. Discoloration with brown spots and blotches caused by microorganisms that find the paper in certain books appetizing. Dampness can encourage the problem. The spots are often dark and, when the foxing is heavy, can seriously detract from the value of an otherwise good book.

FRAKTUR. A German style of gothic or black-letter type. Fraktur was most prevalent at Augsburg and Nuremburg in the post-incunabula period when gothic had been almost totally dropped by French and Italian printers. Popular with the Pennsylvania Dutch, early birth certificates decorated and embellished with fraktur are becoming harder to find and more expensive to buy.

FRONTISPIECE (FRONTIS). An illustration appearing opposite the title page. More often than not, the frontis (most often referred to in abbreviated form) is a portrait of the author, but in many books, the frontis is a lovely color plate or a steel engraving.

GILT EDGES. Gold applied to all three edges of a book's leaves. In book parlance, t.e.g. means "top edge gilt," and a.e.g. means "all edges gilt."

HALF-LEATHER (HALF-BOUND). A book with (usually) leather extending over the spine and about two inches or so along the front and back covers. The rest of the binding is either cloth or paper-covered boards. If the spine and part of the boards are leather and the four corners of the book are covered in large leather triangles, you have a book which is described as THREE QUARTER LEATHER. Thought to be an English custom, the practice goes back to the 17th century, but did not become popular until the 18th century.

HALF-TITLE. Usually the first appearance of print in a volume, the title printed on an otherwise blank sheet before the title page. This is a holdover from the days of early printing when the title was the only information given on the title page.

The half-title is also known as BASTARD TITLE. Grant Uden, in his book *Understanding Book Collecting*, puts this appellation down to the insensitivity of Americans who he says often adopt their own bibliographical terminology. But whosoever puts these terms together, all you have to remember is that the half-title

is most often the first appearance of print in a volume.

In the past, when restoring a book, binders often discarded the half-title page. They may have considered it superfluous, and well it might be, unless you are a collector, and then, if it was in the original, that half-title page had better be in the restored copy.

HEADBAND. A (usually) colorful band on the inside of the spine, sewn across the top of the leaves. In modern bindery, it has no function and is primarily decorative, if it is present at all. Headbands are more often seen in older books. The term is used to include the tailband (sewn across the bottom inside of the spine) as well.

HIGH SPOTS. Notable and important books in a genre. For instance, high spots include the first edition of the first book written by a giant of literature and the first books written by founders of scientific and mathematic disciplines (e.g., Newton on gravity, Einstein on relativity).

HINGE. The ridge where the front or back cover meets the spine. Occasionally, the ridge on the outside of the book is referred to as the JOINT, distinct from the inside hinge covered by endpapers, which provide stability to the binding. When a book has a hinge crack, the cover is intact but loosely held when the endpapers tear. It definitely needs attention before worse can happen, which is separation of the covers from the book.

HOLOGRAPH. A document written wholly in the hand of the author. Although autograph collectors use the term more frequently, booksellers often find it helpful to indicate more than mere inscription or presentation material on the flyleaf of a book; specifically, a laid-in letter or a MANUSCRIPT.

HORNBOOK. A sheet of paper, printed on one side with the alphabet or some other rudiments of school work, pasted onto a handled piece of wood then covered with transparent horn. In colonial America, these were a child's first school books. Used from the 16th to the 18th century, genuine hornbooks are rare, but imitation copies turn up now and then, no doubt prompted by the high price an original would command.

ILLUMINATED MANUSCRIPT. A work containing dazzling letters, initials, and sentence openings, hand decorated in bold colors and finished off with gold and silver. Spectacular and colorful, the artwork did, in essence, brilliantly shed light upon the text. Manuscript illumination is known to have been practiced as early as the 5th century. Monks in the 7th and 8th centuries produced specimens of great artistry in Ireland, including the awe-inspiring Book of Kells.

Illuminating manuscripts remained the province of monastic scribes until the end of the 14th century when the commercial manuscript industry came into its own and the secular world took a serious interest in book ownership.

Unfortunately, the invention of printing, which literally set the book business on its head, also contributed to the demise of the manuscript trade. By 1470, the German manuscript industry had virtually ceased to function; those of Italy and Spain gave way soon after. France was the last stronghold of illuminated manuscripts, turning out specimens of quality even after the age of INCUNABULA (INCUNABLES). But in the end, the writing was on the wall

and manuscripts were only hand-illuminated by special request.

IMPRESSION. In the strictest sense, a run of copies, large or small, ordered by a publisher from the printer at one time. Traditionally, after the first impression of a book has come off a press, other runs may be printed from the same setting of type. These are usually so noted.

Collectors of first editions are looking for the first impression of the first edition of a volume, as all impressions taken from one setting of type constitute an edition.

In days past, when type was set in metal and was ungainly and difficult to store for long periods, a book that remained in demand after its first edition was sold out was likely to need resetting before it could be reissued.

IMPRINT. The information at the foot of the title page that refers to the publisher or the place of publication. The book industry includes collectors who specialize in imprints. Those of the Revolutionary period and the Confederacy are especially prized.

INCUNABULA (INCUNABLES). Books printed on presses in the 15th century. The word is derived from the Latin root meaning "in the cradle," and indicates printing in its infancy. Incunabula (often referred to as "incunables" today) are automatically valuable and collectible.

INDIAN BIBLE. The name commonly given to an edition of the Bible in a Native American language, an Algonquin dialect, translated and compiled by the Rev. John Eliot and published at Cambridge, Massachusetts in 1663. The Bible is also known as the "Natick Bible" and the "Eliot Bible."

INSCRIBED COPY. A book carrying a signed inscription, usually saying something like "with regards to" or "for a special friend," written by the author or a person of note. Should the author of the inscription be famous, the book's value is enhanced. However, simply an inscription by the former owner, who may be a nice person, does not constitute an inscribed copy.

ISSUE. A term applied to a second printing (impression) of an edition that includes some changes or corrections—but not a complete resetting of type—made after the first impression was printed. Adding to the confusion are "state," or printings in which changes have been made during the actual print run. The terms are technical but important to the identification of older first edition. Many booksellers use "issue" and "state" interchangeably.

JOINT. See HINGE.

LAID IN. Refers to a piece of paper, such as a letter or photo, placed in the book but not attached.

LEAF. A single sheet of paper with a RECTO (front) page and a VERSO (back) page. Many people confuse pages and leaves. Pages are one side of a leaf.

LIBRARY OF CONGRESS. America's largest library, located in Washington, D.C. Founded as a working library for members of Congress, the library now holds not only government documents, but is one of the largest collections of incunabula in the U.S.

LIMITED EDITION. Special printing of a limited number of books. Printing and binding is often a higher quality than the usual trade books or may be the product of a PRIVATE PRESS. The books are often numbered and signed by the author and illustrator, if there is one.

LIMP. Refers to bookbindings made of material that is not supported by boards. The cover is literally hanging limp. Limp vellum was used as a trade binding for printed books almost since the beginning of typography and remained popular in Italian, Spanish, and Portuguese binderies during the 15th to 17th centuries. Limp bindings were often fitted with leather thong ties in place of clasps, which were often used to hold the volume closed.

In the 19th century, limp leather was often used as a binding for Bibles, giving way to imitation leather in later years.

LITHOGRAPHY. A principal method of printing developed in the 19th and 20th centuries, especially suited to reproducing drawings and illustrations. The process consists of printing from an impression drawn on smooth lithographic limestone using chemical inks. Many artists came to use the process to replace engraving, including the renowned Currier and Ives. Lithography is now a prominent art form.

LOOSE. A book that is in danger of separating from its binding. No longer held tightly at the spine, the hinges cannot support the weight of the book.

MADE-UP COPY. A volume created by assembling parts from books of the same title that may have been damaged.

MANUSCRIPT. In the book world, refers to a handwritten document. Technically, it is a work written by hand, but in the modern world a manuscript can be typewritten and still be considered a manuscript. The distinction is that it was not typeset or printed on a press. If the writing is in the author's hand, it is termed a HOLO-GRAPH manuscript. In the Middle Ages, monks copying sacred texts created ILLU-MINATED (illustrated) manuscripts of great beauty, but with the invention and proliferation of mechanical printing, the practice died out.

MARBLED. A technique of decorating paper to create the effect of marble, mostly used for endpapers. Some examples have intriguing patterns that craftspeople today are duplicating to frame or to function as bookcovers.

MARRIED. A first edition volume in good condition but without a dust jacket may occasionally be paired with a first edition dust jacket taken from a damaged volume. This is termed "marrying" the volume with the dust jacket.

MEZZOTINT. The process of engraving on copper plates.

MINIATURE. Actually, not what you'd think: derived from "miniate," which means to paint with vermilion. The ancient artists who used this red paint were called miniators. Originally, miniatures referred to the colored drawings in early manuscripts.

MINT CONDITION. Like new. Right off the press.

MISPRINT. An error in printing, very important when identifying first editions. For instance, in the first American edition of Mark Twain's *Adventures of Huckleberry Finn,* the word "saw" was printed incorrectly as "was" on line 23, page 57. Misprints are often among the important POINTS which must be present if a book is to be identified as a true first edition.

MODERN FIRST EDITIONS. Includes books published since the turn of the 20th century. Here again in book parlance, phrases are evolving with time, and most people use the term in reference to books from the 1920s onward.

MOROCCO. Leather made from goatskin.

ND. No date of publication is given.

NP. No place of publication is given.

OCTAVO. The most common size/format of books. Usually seen expressed as "8vo," the most common octavos measure approximately 8" high.

OUT OF PRINT. No longer obtainable from the publisher.

PAMPHLET. A small work, issued unbound or in wraps, and usually sewn or stapled together.

PAPERBACK. Softcover books, primarily books bound in heavy paper, published from the 1930s on. Today, early paperbacks are collectible and sought after, especially the horror, science fiction, and some mystery genres.

PARTS. Books released in serial form or installments. Many books started out this way and were only later published in book form. The works of Dickens followed this pattern—his *Dombey and Son* was printed in parts, 19 of the 20 parts in green pictorial wrappers, as were several other works. Amassing all the parts can be a daunting task since unprotected paper is fragile, and many did not survive.

PENNY BOXES. Trays or boxes outside antiquarian bookshops where the bookseller puts cheap, miscellaneous stock to attract browsers.

PLATE. A full page devoted to an illustration separate from the text pages of a book. The verso is blank.

POINTS. Characteristics that determine whether or not a book is a first edition. For instance, the first edition of a book may contain a specific spelling or other publishing mistake on a certain page that was corrected in later editions. The presence of this mistake is a point.

PRESENTATION COPY. Inscribed by the author as a gift. Not to be confused with a signature acquired by a total stranger who asked for an author's autograph in the book.

PRESS BOOK. A finely produced book, published by a private press, an individual, or established publisher for the sake of excellence in printing and binding and not necessarily for the book's literary value. Prices run high on these specialties—from the outset, not just as collectibles—again for the high manufacturing standard, not because the book is wonderful literature, though it might be.

PRINT RUN. The number of volumes of a book run off the press at one time.

PRIVATELY PRINTED. Not produced by a publisher. The author pays for the publication out of his own pocket. Some very collectible books have been privately published, not the least of which was Edgar Allen Poe's *Tamerlane*, a copy of which sold at auction for a quarter of a million dollars in the late 20th century.

Quite often in the past, privately printed books were produced for the author's friends and family. This remains true today, but in response to changes in the publishing industry, private printings are much more common for trade sales, as well. These are alternatively termed SELF-PUBLISHED.

PRIVATE PRESS. Publishers of limited editions or, simply, a single person producing (publishing) books.

PROVENANCE. The history of a book's ownership. Provenance may add to a book's value if it shows prized associations. Many bibliophiles like information on the provenance of a book for its own sake. A love of old books and their history seems to go hand in hand.

QUARTER BOUND. Only the spine of a book is of a sturdier material, probably leather. The rest is boards or cloth.

QUOTES. Historically, the backbone of the bookseller's trade, a written description of a book with the asking price of a book stated. This can be communicated to the prospective buyer in paper form or over the Internet.

When quoting, include all pertinent information about the book: the title, author, publisher, date, edition, number of pages, whether or not illustrations or maps are present, and the type of binding. Then carefully describe the condition. It is here that a book professional appreciates full disclosure of the defects. Even if you are as accurate as you know how to be, sometimes a buyer will envision something different and find the quote wanting. Include your name, address, and sale requirements and state whether the transaction is C.W.O. (Cash With Order) or future billing.

READING COPY. A book that has seen better days, worn from use and in less than good condition. They're appreciated by scholars for research, but not by collectors unless the volume is exceedingly rare.

REBACKED. Fitted with a new spine and hinges. When considering such repairs, be prepared to pay well for a competent job. Unless you have a personal affinity for a book, have your volume appraised to see if it is worth the preservation cost before ordering any restoration by a professional bookbinder. And be sure not to replace something on a volume only to find out that you have devalued a rare find.

REBOUND. Fitted with a new binding. Here again, as with the rebacked book, we are talking restoration and expensive repairs. Whenever this route is undertaken, opt for reattaching the original covers, if that is possible. Again, if you are selling the book, value should be there to justify the expense.

RECTO. The right-hand page of a book; the front of the leaf.

REPRINT. A reissue of a book previously published. A. L. Burt and Grosset & Dunlap reissued and made available many famous works to those who otherwise could not afford the first editions. In an elderly farm woman's house we visited in Vermont, the shelves in an upstairs bedroom were lined with books, reprints of Zane Grey, E. R. Burroughs, Dixon, Henty, Horatio Alger, and more. And she was proud that she had read them all.

REVIEW COPY. Complimentary copies of books sent to editors, journalists, and institutions, in the hope of gaining a review or at least a mention in their publications or programs.

RUBBED. Scratches or wear spots on bindings.

SABIN, JOSEPH. An English bookseller who emigrated to the United States and became one of the foremost authorities on Americana, setting about to publish a comprehensive bibliography of the genre.

Unfortunately, Sabin lived to see only the first thirteen volumes realized. Wilberforce Eames and R. W. G. Vail completed the monumental task, finishing with a total of twenty-nine volumes.

SCUFFED. Worn, scratched, nicked.

SEARCH SERVICE. Precisely what the term implies, initiating a search for a title through dealership and trade channels. In the recent past, if you wanted a particular book and you could not find it in a used bookstore, a bookseller would print an inquiry in the trade journals welcoming quotes from other dealers. Since the advent of the Internet, most of these trade journals are no longer available.

Now, dealers and collectors go directly to book-finding Web sites on the Internet where they can almost instantaneously collect information on the myriad of books available worldwide.

Booksellers continue to offer professional search services for a fee that is charged whether or not a book is found. Many today prefer to search for themselves on the Internet, but good booksellers often have channels for finding special items that are not yet listed in cyberspace.

Back in the good old days, Wright Howes noted in his Fall 1993 catalogue, "out of print and scarce books sought for and reported free of charge." The times they have a-changed.

Among those excellent catalogues and publications that have gone the way of the horse and buggy is the publication, *AB Bookman,* which was the Bible of the collectible book industry for half a century. The magazine has ceased publication.

SPINE. The backstrip of a book.

STATE. A number of books in a print run showing changes or corrections made during that print run or impression. Sometimes the word is used interchangeably (but incorrectly) with ISSUE, which technically indicates changes or corrections—but not a full resetting of type—made between print runs or impressions.

SUNNED. Faded. The original color of the book loses brightness and freshness when exposed to direct bright light, especially sunlight.

THREE-QUARTER LEATHER. Leather on the spine extending several inches across the front and rear boards, along with large triangles of leather at the corners of the book. The rest of the binding could be cloth or boards.

TIPPED-IN. Glued into the book, as when illustrations are not bound into a book but glued in after binding is completed. The technique is most often used to add glossy pictures or maps, with glue applied to the back of the illustration at the top only. Tipping-in was used to incorporate illustrations that would have been too expensive to print and bind into a book in ages past.

TISSUE GUARDS. Tissue paper bound into the book to protect the plates.

TITLE PAGE. The page at the front of each book that gives the title, author, publisher and, sometimes the printing date. In most books, this information is on a recto page. Always consult the title page for pertinent information about a book; never depend upon what is printed on the spine or cover.

TOOLING. Impressing a design by hand into leather.

UNCUT. Untrimmed leaves. When sheets are printed, folded and bound, the trimming process to open the leaves can miss some folds, leaving pages both uncut and unopened.

UNOPENED. Uncut leaves with the fold remaining closed. Tearing can open them, but they remain uncut.

VELLUM. Calfskin binding, also sometimes called parchment. Vellum and other leather bindings should be carefully cared for to keep them from drying and cracking (see Care and Repair of Books).

VERSO. Left-hand page of a book; the back side of a leaf.

W.A.F. With All Faults. As is. Indicates faults or deficiencies probably exist. Does not guarantee collating or condition.

WANT LIST. A listing of books needed either to fill a dealer's bookshelves or to accommodate customers looking for particular works. There was a time when booksellers regularly sent out want lists to other dealers and many still do. Often the bookseller includes a "permanent want list" in which case there is no cut-off date for acquiring these books, and duplicates may even be welcome.

In today's computer environment, both collectors and dealers look to the Internet to fill their want lists. However, a collector who is not knowledgeable would do better to consult a book dealer to search his wants. Established dealers have additional resources for finding collectible books.

WESTERN AMERICANA. The genre covering the settling of the American West and American western culture, including indigenous peoples. Everyone seems to want this category, and the prices are high for the really good stuff. The collector, of course, is looking for pioneer imprints, broadsides, handbills, documents, handwritten journey narratives, or ledgers. Books on Indians, explorations, outlaws, mining, and whatever else attested to the westward path are collectible.

WRAPPERS. Paper binding. This does not refer to modern paperbacks, which are bound in stiff paper with illustrations. The term actually refers to simple paper covering, sometimes plain paper, serving also as a title page. Before modern bindings, books were often published with plain paper covers. Customers brought the works to their own binderies to have custom leather or cloth covers put on. Older pamphlets were often published with thin paper covers, or wrappers.

WRAPS. Same as wrappers.

REFERENCES AND RESOURCES

American Book Prices Current. Box 1236. Washington, CT 06793. This is the annual compilation of realized prices for books sold at auction. It lists sales of $50 or more. It is available on CD-ROM. While an excellent investment, it is expensive in print or CD and your best bet is to find a good library that carries it in the reference department.

Firsts, the Book Collector's Magazine. Robin H. Smiley, publisher. Katherine Smiley, editor. Tucson, Arizona. A full-color publication offering extensively researched and documented features and columns on all aspects of first editions, modern and antiquarian. A booklover's treasure trove.

Identification of First Editions—A Pocket Guide. Bill McBride, Hartford, CT 06105. Provides pointers for identifying first editions from varying publishers down through the years. A staple in the industry for decoding the indicators publishers have used to indicate a first printing. Available used and new. The 6th edition was published in 2001 by McBride Publishing.

Book Prices Used and Rare. E. Zempel and L. A. Verkler (eds.). Spoon River Press, Peoria, IL 61064. Includes more than 30,000 entries of bibliographic data and prices. The 1999 edition is available.

Book Collecting as a Hobby and *Minding My Own Business*. By Percy Muir. This writer is well worth searching out, as are all his titles on book collecting.

USiana. Wright Howes. R. R. Bowker, Co. New York. A comprehensive bibliography of books on the United States, compiled in the 20th century.

Understanding Book Collecting. Grant Uden, Antique Collectors' Club, Woodbridge, Suffolk, England. 1982. Contains invaluable information, education, and discourse for the serious bibliophile.

Price Guide and Bibliographic Checklist for Children's Illustrated Books 1880–1970. E. Lee Baumgarten. Baumgarten Books, West Virginia. 2004 edition. A voluminous compendium of bibliographic information for the collector and dealer.

Book Collecting 2000: A Comprehensive Guide. Allen and Patricia Ahearn. A guide to first books by collectible authors. The Ahearns' guides have long been staples in the industry for identifying first editions and books in hand. Extensive bibliographic and descriptive information can be gleaned. Various titles by these authors, recent and older, contain a wealth of information for the collector.

A Primer of Book Collecting. John T. Winerich, Greenberg, New York, 1926.

ABC For Book Collectors. John Carter and Nicholas Barker. 8th edition, Oak Knoll Press, 2004. Another favorite of book lovers, dealers and collectors alike, the book is an extensively researched glossary of book terms and abbreviations, many of which are referenced to actual elements of the book itself, appearing on the pages as the reader progresses through the book.

Printing and the Mind of Man: A Descriptive Catalogue Illustrating the Impact of Print on the Evolution of Western Civilization. John Carter and Percy Muir. NY, 1967. An edited catalogue with expanded information about a museum exhibit on the history and influence of printing at the British Museum and at Earl's Court, 1963. (Second, revised edition, 1983.)

National Union Catalogue (NUC). Contains listing of pre-1956 imprints in Library of Congress holdings plus the holdings of reporting libraries in the United States.

Additional print references are included in the discussions of Genre Collecting in the text of this volume.

Great Books and Book Collectors. Alan G. Thomas. New York: Putnam. (1975). Well illustrated, it follows book development down through the ages, and discusses major collections.

A Gentle Madness, Nicholas Basbanes. New York: Henry Holt & Co. 1996. An examination of bibliomania, benign and otherwise, from ancient Alexandria to modern times.

The Smithsonian Book of Books. Michael Olmert. D.C. Smithsonian. 1992. Beautifully illustrated volume tracing the history of books and printing with special emphasis on technologies down through the ages.

Colorado Antiquarian Book Seminar, Colorado College, Colorado Springs, CO. Held annually in the summer, the seminar is billed as "boot camp for book dealers," and includes five days of intense training and workshops in antiquarian and rare book scholarship and sales.

Taught by accomplished booksellers and specialists. Contact by phone at 719–473–6634, or e-mail kathy@bookseminars.com.

Additional Resources

Below, we have listed associations, dealers, and auction houses from which we have gleaned information and advice.

Abracadabra Booksearch International
7030 East 46th Avenue Drive, Unit E
Denver, Colorado 80216
orders@abrabks.com
www.abrabks.com

Antiquarian Booksellers' Association of American (ABAA)
20 West 44th Street
New York, NY 10036

Antiqbook
www.antiqbook.com

Barry R. Levin
Science Fiction & Fantasy Literature
720 Santa Monica Blvd.
Santa Monica, CA 90401
310–458–6111
www.raresf.com

Bauman Rare Books
1608 Walnut Street, 19th Floor
Philadelphia, PA 19103
215–546–9064
and
535 Madison Avenue
New York, NY 10022
212–751–0011
brb@baumanrarebooks.com
www.baumanrarebooks.com

Beasley Books
Paul and Beth Garon, proprietors
1533 W. Oakdale
Chicago, IL 60657
773–472–4528
Showroom at

703 Washington Street
Evanston, Illinois 60202
847–328–2132
Beasley@beasleybooks.com
www.beasleybooks.com

Biblio.com (listings)
www.biblio.com

Bookfinder Search Engine
www.bookfinder.com

Bolerium Books
Social Movements
2141 Mission, Suite 300
San Francisco, CA 94110
1–800–326–6353
info@bolerium.com
www.bolerium.com

Brick House Bookshop
632 Morristown Corners Rd.
Morrisville, VT 05661
802–888–4300
brickhouse@vtlink.net

Bulwagga Books and Gallery
3 South Main Street
Whiting, VT 05778
802–623–6800
bulwagga@shoreham.net
http://middlebury.net/bulwagga

Bygone Books
P.O. Box 5034
Burlington, VT 05402
Inventory at Champlain Valley Antique
Center, Route 7, Shelburne, VT
802–862–4397
bygone.books@verizon.net

Cattermole
20th Century Children's Books
9880 Fairmont Rd.
Newberry, OH 44065
440–338–3253
www.cattermole.com

Center for Western Studies
Box 727, Augustana College
2001 S. Summit Avenue
Sioux Falls, SD 57197
1–800–727–2844 or 605–274–4007
cws@augie.edu
www.augie.edu/CWS/

Dan Wyman, Books
47 Dartmouth St.
Springfield, MA 01109
413–846–6357
dan@danwymanbooks.com
www.danwymanbooks.com

David M. Lesser
Fine Antiquarian Books
One Bradley Rd., #302
Woodbridge, CT 06525
203–389–8111
dmlesser@lesserbooks.com
www.lesserbooks.com

DeWolfe & Wood
P.O. Box 425
2 Waterboro Road (RT 202)
Alfred, ME 04002
207–490–5572
dewofeandwood@adelphia.net
www.dwbooks.com

Edwin V. Glaser, Rare Books
Edwin Glaser
P.O. Box 755
Napa, CA 94559
707–258–6281
mail@glaserrarebooks.com
www.glaserrarebooks.com

Raymond Giordano
The Antiquarian Scientist
P.O. Box 448
Southampton, MA 01073
423–539–2731
antiqsci@comcast.net

Foundations Antiques
Stephen Smith
148 North Main St.
Fair Haven, VT 05743
802–265–4544

Frances L. Robinson
US Rt. 2, 81 South St.
South Hero, VT 05486
802–372–6622

George F. Kolbe
Fine Numismatic Books
P.O. Drawer 3100
Crestline, CA 92325–3100
909–338–6527
GFK@numslit.com
www.numislit.com

The Great Site
Collectible Bibles
John Lawton Jeffcoat, III
407–996–4400
800–42-ANCIENT
director@greatsite.com
www.greatsite.com

Hurley Books
1752 Rt. 12
Westmoreland, NH 03467
603–399–4342
info@hurleybooks.com
www.hurleybooks.com

James Cummins, Bookseller
699 Madison Ave.
New York, NY 10021
212–688–6441
cummins@panix.com
www.jamescumminsbookseller.com

Kenneth Andersen
Kenneth Andersen Books.
Middlebury, VT
802–388–8412

Ken Lopez—Bookseller
51 Huntington Rd.
Hadley, MA 01035
413–584–4827
mail@lopezbooks.com
www.lopezbooks.com

Knollwood Books
P.O. Box 2206
Waukesha, WI 53187
262–751–8350
books@wi.rr.com

K. Rogers Fine Books
Kathleen V. Roberts
203 South Cove Road
Burlington, VT 05401
802–863–2144

L. W. Currey, Inc.
P.O. Box 187
203 Water St.
Elizabethtown, NY 12932
518–873–6477
lloyd@lwcurrey.com
www.lwcurrey.com

Michael Ginsberg Books
P.O. Box 402
Sharon, MA 02067
781–784–8181
info@ginsbook.com
www.ginsbook.com

Monroe Street Books
Dick & Flanzy Chodkowski
70 Monroe St.
Middlebury, VT 05753
802–388–1622
books@monroestreebooks.com
www.monroestreetbooks.com

Mountain Reverie Books
Marie Tedford, proprietor
P.O. Box 26
Underhill Center, VT 05490
reverie@surfglobal.net
www.abebooks.com/home/mountainreverie/

New England Book Auctions
Leif Laudamus, proprietor
P.O. Box 470
Sunderland, MA 01375
413–665–3253
www.nebookauctions.com

PBA Galleries
133 Kearny St., 4th Floor
San Francisco, CA 94108
415–989–2665
pba@pacificbook.com
www.pbagalleries.com

**Philadelphia Rare Books and
Manuscripts Company**
2375 Bridge Street, Box 314
Philadelphia, PA 19137
215–744–6734
rarebks@prbm.com
www.prbm.com

Richard Adelson Antiquarian
Bookseller
Jane & Richard Adelson
1162 Galaxy Hill Road
North Pomfret, VT 05053
802–457–2608
booksjra@sover.net

Roy C. Kulp
Handwritten Americana
Box 264
Hatfield, PA 19440
215–362–0732

Second Life Books, Inc.
P.O. Box 242, 55 Quarry Rd.
Lanesborough, MA 01237
413–447–8010
info@secondlifebooks.com
www.secondlifebooks.com

Swann Auction Galleries
104 East 25th Street
New York, NY 10010
212–254–4710
swann@swanngalleries.com
www.swanngalleries.com

The Eloquent Page
Donna Howard
21 Catherine St.
St. Albans, VT 05478
802–527–7243
eloquent.page@verizon.net
*www.abebooks.com/home/
theeloquentpage/*

The Unique Antique
Johnathan Flaccus
71 Main Street, P.O. Box 485
Putney, VT 05346
802–387–4488
flaccus@sover.net

TomFolio (bookseller listing site)
www.tomfolio.com

**Waverly Auctions at Quinn's Auction
Galleries**
431 North Maple Avenue
Falls Church, VA 22046
info@waverlyauctions.com
www.waverlyauctions.com

William L. Parkinson, Books
William & Anne Parkinson
P.O. Box 40
Hinesburg, VT 05461
802–482–3113

John T. Zubal, Inc.
2969 West 25th Street
Cleveland, Ohio 44113
www.zubalbooks.com

Rulon-Miller Books
Robert Rulon-Miller, Jr.
400 Summit Avenue
St. Paul, Minnesota 55102
651–290–0700
rulon@rulon.com
www.rulon.com

Tom Twetten
Craftsbury Antiquarian Books
P.O. Box 111
Craftsbury Common, VT 05827
802–586–2483
craftbry@pshift.com
www.biblio.com/bookstores/Craftsbury.html

**Vermont Antiquarian Booksellers
Association (VABA)**
www.vermontisbookcountry.com
William Reese Company
409 Temple Street
New Haven, CT 06511
203–789–8081
coreese@resseco.com
www.reeseco.com

SELECTED INDEX BY COLLECTIBLE AUTHOR AND GENRE

Pages in italics indicate illustrations.

M

N